SPIRIT SERVICE

SPIRIT SERVICE

Vodún and Vodou in the African Atlantic World

ERIC J. MONTGOMERY,
TIMOTHY R. LANDRY,
CHRISTIAN N. VANNIER,
EDITORS

INDIANA UNIVERSITY PRESS

This book is a publication of

Indiana University Press
Office of Scholarly Publishing
Herman B Wells Library 350
1320 East 10th Street
Bloomington, Indiana 47405 USA

iupress.org

© 2022 by Indiana University Press

All rights reserved
No part of this book may be reproduced or utilized in any form or by any means, electronic or mechanical, including photocopying and recording, or by any information storage and retrieval system, without permission in writing from the publisher. The paper used in this publication meets the minimum requirements of the American National Standard for Information Sciences—Permanence of Paper for Printed Library Materials, ANSI Z39.48-1992.

Manufactured in the United States of America

First printing 2022

Library of Congress Cataloging-in-Publication Data

Names: Montgomery, Eric James, editor. | Vannier, Christian, editor. | Landry, Timothy R., editor.
Title: Spirit service : Vodún and Vodou in the African Atlantic world / Eric J. Montgomery, Timothy R. Landry, Christian N. Vannier, editors.
Description: Bloomington, Indiana : Indiana University Press, 2022. | "This book began as a double panel at the American Anthropological Association annual meetings in Washington, DC, in November 2017 ("Vodun/Vodou Matters")"—Page 379. | Includes bibliographical references and index.
Identifiers: LCCN 2021058446 (print) | LCCN 2021058447 (ebook) | ISBN 9780253061904 (hardback) | ISBN 9780253061911 (paperback) | ISBN 9780253061935 (ebook)
Subjects: LCSH: Vodou—Caribbean Area. | Vodou—Africa, West.
Classification: LCC BL2490 .S65 2022 (print) | LCC BL2490 (ebook) | DDC 299.675—dc23/eng/20211202
LC record available at https://lccn.loc.gov/2021058446
LC ebook record available at https://lccn.loc.gov/2021058447

CONTENTS

Introduction / *Christian Vannier and Timothy R. Landry*   1

PART I. ENCOUNTER

1. Vodou Genesis: Africans and the Making of a National Religion in Saint-Domingue / *Terry Rey*   17
2. Universalism and Syncretism in Beninese Vodún / *Douglas J. Falen*   40
3. Crossing Currents: Gorovodu and Yewevodu in Contemporary Togo / *Eric J. Montgomery*   70
4. A Prayer for a Muslim Spirit: Islam in Gorovodu / *Christian Vannier*   97
5. Where Have All the *Ounsi* Gone? / *Karen Richman*   118
6. Sailing between Local and Global: Vodou in the Modern and Contemporary Arts of Haiti / *Natacha Giafferi-Dombre*   139

PART II. ENGAGEMENT

7. Taking Hold of a Faith / *Jeffrey Anderson*   169
8. The Physic(s)ality of Vodún and the (Mis)behavior of Matter / *Venise N. Adjibodou*   189
9. Vodou Skins: Making Bodily Surfaces Social in Haitian Vodou Infant Care / *Alissa Jordan*   208
10. Spirited Forests and the West African Forest Complex / *Timothy R. Landry*   230
11. Vodou, an Inclusive Epistemology: Toward a Queer Ecotheology of Liberation / *Nixon S. Cleophat*   259

12. Necroscape and Diaspora: Making Ancestors in Haitian Vodou / *Elizabeth McAlister*   283

Conclusion: Global Vodún and Vodou—Encounter and Engagement / *Eric J. Montgomery and Timothy R. Landry*   307

Contributor Biographies   319

Index   321

Spirit Service

INTRODUCTION

Christian Vannier and Timothy R. Landry

THIS VOLUME begins in eighteenth-century Dahomey, a small but determined kingdom centered in the forested Abomey plateau of what is known today as the Republic of Benin. In Dahomey, ancestor veneration dominated the religious lives of most families. Individuals and communities served divinities that were informed deeply by local histories, politics, and needs. Assimilation and integration between communities and lineages often produced powerful regional spirits (*vodún*[1]) who attracted sizable followings. Vodún service was widely practiced by 1658 (Sweet 2011, 19),[2] and those practices that surrounded these spirits were generally similar throughout the region even though spirits and shrines dedicated to them held no formal or centralized recognition (Law 2004, 88–89).

In the early eighteenth century, sociospiritual exchange began to intensify. Under the rulership of Agaja (r. 1718–1740), warfare and enslavement facilitated Dahomey's rise in military power. This resulted in refugees, slaves, and other forced migrations that accelerated the introduction and exchange of spirits and ritual practices around the region. At the beginning of his rule, Agaja propitiated his royal ancestors, who were known to repay their descendants with military success against their neighbors. Beginning in 1727, after a string of defeats to other regional powers, the Dahomean state began to appropriate and import deities—along with their shrines and priests—from vanquished communities. Once in Abomey these new deities were integrated into the local pantheon. Spirits such as Hevioso, the sky vodún of thunder; Sakpata, the earth vodún of smallpox; and Dan, the serpent vodún of Ouidah, were all subsumed under royal Dahomean control. Dahomey's repertoire of spirits also expanded when immigrants and war captives were obliged to install shrines in Abomey and when the state sent individuals to neighboring groups to become priests of spirits that Dahomey perceived as powerful and important to their political agendas (see Falen, this volume). Over time, Vodún priests grew increasingly more powerful and became political threats to the legitimacy of the divine king. This did not escape royal attention. Unable to execute such priests for fear of reprisals from the deities whom they served, Agaja instead neutralized spiritual-political threats by selling the priests into slavery (Bay 1998, 156; Sweet 2011, 19–22). Slaves exported from Dahomean controlled territories, such as Ouidah, were subsequently taken against their will to such afar places as the Caribbean, Brazil, and other parts of Africa.

Healers, diviners, and ritual specialists of all types and from numerous cultures were forced aboard slave ships and withstood the brutal Middle Passage and chattel slavery of US, Brazilian, and Caribbean colonies. Because of the tremendous cultural flow among groups in West Africa, many of these individuals likely shared worldviews and ritual practices in addition to strong similarities in language, as many came from regions united in larger language families such as Gbe[3] (Sweet 2011; Pares 2005, 2013). Those religious systems that migrated forcibly alongside enslaved Africans underwent intense processes of restructuring and redefinition. This led to the formation of new religious meanings and new forms emerged that suited their different cultural contexts. In Haiti, and indeed throughout the Caribbean, spiritual worldviews and practices that were flexible, assimilative, and integrative became valuable assets as Africans engaged spiritually with other Africans, Caribbean natives, and Europeans. Homologies between African systems and between African and European systems (specifically Catholicism) were constructed and elaborated. Beliefs were altered, united, or pushed creatively aside to produce a new symbolic multiverse and innovative ritual practices. Processes of bricolage (Lévi-Strauss 1966) imbued Haitian Vodou with a creativity, adaptability, and resilience—especially among the rural poor, for whom Vodou reached a sort of "achieved indigeneity" (Sheller 2003, 182).

Vodou holds an important, yet politically contentious, place in Haiti. The legendary Vodou ceremony of 1791 in Bwa Kayiman launched the Haitian Revolution, yet through much of modern Haitian history (1835–1987) popular Vodou rituals were banned by the Haitian government (Ramsey 2011), and cosmopolitan Haitian elites considered Vodou to be a religion fit only for the uneducated peasant masses. For practitioners, Vodou is a ritual complex closely aligned with family and land; Haitian Vodou represented a ritual economy of debt and reciprocation with the spirits (*lwa*) and the dead. Ritual specialists manage the relationships between people, the spirits, and each other. During the Duvalier regime (1957–1971), Vodou symbolism and many ritual specialists were deployed by the government to exert ideological control over the masses and against the mulatto elite. Yet, following the demise of the Duvaliers, Vodou took on a new mantle as an authentic manifestation of Haitian culture— symbolic of a true Haiti and a form of resistance against political and social encroachments to Haiti's cultural sovereignty. The 1987 Constitution explicitly abrogated anti-Vodou laws, and Vodou was recognized as an official religion of Haiti in 2003. Emerging from the shadows of marginality, Vodou has been undergoing sustained changes as it becomes more popularized and mainstream (Hurbon 2008).

SPIRITS AND SPIRIT SERVICE: HAITIAN, WEST AFRICAN, OR GLOBAL?

The title of this volume reflects the distinctive yet related nature of spirit service on both sides of the African Atlantic world. *Vodún* is an Adja-Fon word that today refers to ritual complexes found in West Africa, and *Vodou* is the same for Haiti. Each term is thus a particular religious, geographical, and cultural referent. As Jeffrey Anderson argues in this volume, using one term exclusively is to lay claim to a particular region and history and assert the authority of this claim over others. We deploy both appellations in our title to problematize the geographical and cultural bounding of truly globalized spiritualities and philosophies while simultaneously recognizing their interrelated histories, spirits, and ritual practices. We seek to move beyond highlighting the specific African roots of Haitian and North American religious phenomena and focus instead upon the complex relationships between and among practitioners, scholars, and spirits across the African Atlantic.

While many Haitian lwa exhibit homologous relationships with West African vodún, we suggest framing them as Haitian spirits that aid the practical and spiritual ends of their devotees. Emphasizing the specific African roots of particular spirits or practices of Caribbean religions has become passé in Caribbean studies (see Apter 2018) even as these studies spark debates about "authenticity" and "supremacy" between ritual specialists (e.g., *bokɔ́nɔ̀*, oungan, and *babaláwos*) on both sides of the Atlantic (Olupona and Rey 2008). Mintz and Price (1978) argue that African cultural elements could not survive unchanged the creolizing institutions of the slave ship and plantation. Initiation rites in Vodou, to take one of their examples, are a "truly Haitian innovation, constructed in particular ways and under particular circumstances by particularly enslaved Africans" (Mintz and Price 1978, 17). Arguing for a direct continuity or a cultural survival from eighteenth-century Dahomean practices leaves too many caveats, incompletions, and guesses. Other critiques quickly followed, culminating in Stephan Palmié's (2006) position that the perceived African cultural heritage of Caribbean cultural phenomena is really a historical process of ethnogenesis carried out by the cumulative efforts of anthropologists, governments, missionaries, ritual specialists, and so on (see Apter 2018, 8; Rey, this volume; Wirtz 2008). These arguments are not without their critics. Werner-Lewis (2003) presents a linguistic analysis to detail Central African presence in contemporary Caribbean culture and memory. Apter (2018, 97) argues for scholars to shift their attention "from roots to routes," to avoid embarking on misguided searches for survivals and retentions rather than the more productive deep analyses of cultural extensions, innovations, and inventions. This volume follows this argument. We are not looking to identify specific histories related to ritual elements in Caribbean Vodou or to locate Vodou's origins in the contemporary Vodún of West Africa. Rather, we seek to put Vodún and Vodou into the same conversation, recognizing the "implicit grammatical principles" (Mintz and Price 1992, 53), "semantical heritage" (Montilus 1989, 25), and "continuity of perspective" (Raboteau 1978, 16; Smith 1994, 35) through which we may better understand the complexities of the globalizing Atlantic and the ritual systems that now pervade it.

Olupona and Rey (2008) argue that West African religions should be counted among so-called "World Religions." This volume builds on this notion by exploring the aspects of Vodou and Vodún that make this possible from a global vantage. Though this volume exhibits scholars from history, the arts, and religious studies, a greater number come from anthropology. Through observant participation, ethnography is positioned uniquely to highlight the ways in which Vodún and Vodou transcend ethnicity, race, and territory to be panethnic, transnational, and always emergent (Landry 2019; McCarthy Brown 1991; Rush 2013). Examining the influences and encounters brought on by global interconnectivity is fundamental to understanding histories of slavery, colonialism, and lived realities of migrant subjectivity and socioeconomic marginality. Serving the spirits has never been limited by region, race, or time but instead acculturates and molds itself to external religions and peoples, including Christianity and Islam (Landry 2019; McCarthy Brown 1991). This protean nature of spirit service allows it to move, adapt, and assimilate into new geographies and cultural contexts. We now recognize that what Vodún and Vodou share across vast physical and social geographies is not so much a collective, recognizable "Africanness" but rather an open heterogeneity that permits creativity, experimentation, and integration. This allows us to move past tired debates surrounding "authenticity and invention," "African continuities," or "legacies" that stand in ontological opposition to "European influences" and examine how confluences of political economies, histories, ritual practices, ways of being, modern symbolisms, and material migrations continue to produce and reproduce and modify the spirits, values, and practices that surround them. It is through transcultural and transnational encounters that these religions have developed. Indeed, these encounters—past and present—manifest themselves endlessly in ritual, material culture, and ethnography. Understanding these dynamic religions and their place in the modern, globalizing Atlantic world is the subject of this book.

TRANSATLANTIC: UNIFYING THEMES ACROSS THE AFRICAN ATLANTIC WORLD

Despite variation in history, symbolism, and local practice, underlying themes unite spirit service in the African Atlantic world. First, serving the spirits is political. Spirits are deployed and regulated by the elite to control and intimidate and by subalterns to obtain their own power and prosperity. They also protect and defend the marginalized and others in contexts of racism, penury, and oppression and so serve as powerful sources of resistance and identity construction.

Secondly, the meanings and forms of spirit service in West Africa and in the Caribbean were elaborated upon during the same historical moments as were the transatlantic slave trade and European colonial conquest. Hence serving the spirits is an act of resistance—to slavery and colonialism, racism, and dehumanization. Practitioners mobilize alongside their spirits and ancestors to empower themselves and their communities through resiliency, adaption, and assimilation. Whether practitioners are adopting new spirits from Yorùbá or Akan peoples—or even from Islam and Christianity—spirits and those who serve them are constantly and consistently learning, adapting, and reconfiguring themselves in an open-ended way, meaning they are always, as Rush (2013) notes, unfinished.

Altogether, Vodún and Vodou are coherent philosophies built upon a cosmological foundation rooted in the ubiquitous notion that the spirit world runs parallel to our own. Nature spirits, forest dwellers, divine presences, and ancestors—even internationally recognized beings, such as Legba—can all be encountered and engaged with through dreams, visions, revelatory illnesses, trance possession, and divination. Communication, travel, and affect between these two worlds are not only possible but also routine. Simply put, one can affect the spirits, but the spirits can also affect humanity. Each spirit possesses different qualities, dispositions, and domains of influence that result in them possessing different sorts of powers to help or hinder those with the means and knowledge to engage with them. One may build and maintain relationships with these spirits in the hopes of the spirits affecting the lives of their devotees positively. These relationships are accomplished through ritual, divination, and spirit service and confirmed in ceremonies. Without such rituals as spirit possession, divination, and sacrifice, the relationships and possibly even the spirits themselves would not seem present in one's daily life.

Vodún and Vodou recognize a Supreme Creator who fashioned the world and its domains, natural and supernatural, but maintains little involvement in human affairs. Rather, hosts of spirits created by the Supreme Creator did their own creating and engage and work with people, affecting and being affected by human action. These vodún (Vodún) and lwa (Haitian Vodou) are recognized across communities and regionally (though in different ways) and exist alongside other, more personal spirits, such as lineage ancestors. The spirit and natural worlds form a single community in which spirits and people serve as the source of life and empowerment for each other. This mutual interdependence leads to spiritual power: the power to make things happen; a power that is pluralistic, confederative, and horizontal leading adepts not toward adoration but to service (Montilus 1989, 16–17).

Spirits are not abstractions. They are defined, limited, and circumscribed beings. They have personalities and are conscious of themselves. To engage in such a relationship is known as serving the spirits (*sevi lwa*, in Haitian Kreyòl; *vodúnsínsén*, in Fon). Serving the spirits means appeasing them through obeisance and veneration, in such material gifts as animal blood, food, and drink; by obeying taboos or moral codes and proscriptions; and by being initiated into the spirit's cult. The result is often long-standing relationships, based upon reciprocity, in which the adept serves the spirits and the sprits empower individuals and communities to seek health, fortune, protection, and success. Without such reciprocation, a spirit can certainly take vengeance but more likely will simply withdraw protection and responsibility, leaving the adept at the mercy of fate, disease, enemies, witchcraft, and all other sorts of misfortunes.

Despite the need for spirits to provide protection, health, and fortune, practitioners of these religious systems do not conceive of humans as beings in need of salvation from sin or deliverance into heaven. The vodún resemble the God of the Torah more than the New Testament, for they can be forgiving or unrelenting. They understand the human experience as being susceptible to chaos, misfortune, disease, and conflict, so religious practices are oriented toward identifying and overcoming specific problems that impede well-being, vitality, and success (Stewart 2005, 166). Accomplishing this is done with aid from the spirits, and the focus of much ritual practice is upon healing and the use of medicine, making ritual specialists first and foremost healers and herbalists. The terms "medicine" and "healing" possess much wider and deeper meanings than in Eurocentric Christianity for they contend with "illness," a multidimensional concept itself. Illness may be disease, a mental condition, misfortune or bad luck, the persistent lack of success, or many other forms of spiritual suffering. Illness may stem from a biological pathogen, but the initial task of any healer is to determine *why* that individual is suffering from that pathogen at that time. An individual may be suffering because of the actions of another. Individuals motivated by jealousy, envy, greed, and other antisocial emotions and transgressions may perform witchcraft or sorcery upon an individual or entire community and cause suffering (Falen 2018). The immoral behavior, taboo violation, abandonment of ritual responsibility, or prescription may cause suffering as spirits wreck vengeance or one's own misdeeds invoke guilt, pain, envy, and illness (*move san*, in Haiti; *dolele* or *n'bia*, in Ewe). Finally, spirits themselves may deploy illness to call individuals to them (revelatory illness) or punish individuals for immoral or wayward behavior. Once the cause of suffering is known, the healer may use accumulated knowledge and experience in addition to divination to organize the appropriate rituals and medicines to evoke healing. We paraphrase Blier (1995, 215) to define medicines as materials and ritual practices that, when combined, produce dynamic power that can be deployed to offset, counterbalance, or oppose other powers at play upon an individual or community. Emphasis is placed upon protection and defensive measures against the deployed power of others that often emerge through rifts, hypocrisies, tensions, and social conflicts that produce immorality, jealousy, and abandonment and so break down harmony and peace (Sweet 2011). Identifying these root causes to physical ailment makes healing inherently political as well as spiritual and so often makes healers at odds or collaborating with dominant power regimes.

STUDYING SPIRIT SERVICE

For centuries, African religious systems have crossed oceans and been adopted by diverse and disparate ethnic and sociocultural groups. Despite this global scope, so-called African traditional religions have been popularly understood as systems found in only a few scattered corners of the world and imagined problematically as exotic and primitive. Such interpretations have also viewed practices surrounding spirit service as static and unchanging, thus undermining their meaning and potential and engendering stereotypical conclusions about what spirit service is (Rush 2013). No matter its appellation, spirit service in the Afro-Atlantic world is perceived by governments, missionaries, pastors, and members of other religious systems as a superstitious anachronism from a bygone era. In some cases, governments like those of Benin and Haiti have tried to market Vodún and Vodou to tourists (e.g., Landry 2019). Eurocentrism, Christianization, neoliberalism, capitalism, secularization, and modernity itself all seem to conspire against the spirits and all but assure their demise. Yet despite periods of legal repression and demonization, these religions have adapted, assimilated, and flourished (Meyer 1999). Instead of receding in the face of Christianity, Islam, and global capitalism or being relegated to apolitical realms of "local folklore," African religious systems continue to act as repositories of sacred knowledge by reproducing themselves according to the flows of human experience. Today, scholars of these systems recognize their dynamism and influence, and this is changing our approach to them.

A key feature of African Vodún and Haitian Vodou is—and has always been—mobility. Maupoil (1943; see also Brivio 2016, 3) argues that Vodún spirit cults are best understood outside of geographical perspectives and rather through movements and migrations. The so-called modern world, especially the Atlantic, was made by the circulation of people, goods, information, and ideas that began in earnest in the sixteenth century. Vodún was an early component in these movements. Early Vodún, as a particular assemblage of ritual practices and spirits, was deterritorialized as soon as it was established. On board ships, in plantation estates, in the streets of emerging urban centers, in conquered spaces, the spirits permeated the social fabric of life in the early modern Atlantic world (see Gomez 2017). Hence, serving the spirits is not some anachronistic holdover from slavery or memory of Africa. Rather, it is built into modernity itself. Today, forces of globalization, migration, and socioeconomic growth in West Africa propel imagined "local" religions onto the world stage. Interest in Haitian Vodou has intensified since the 2010 earthquake. Members of the diaspora in Brazil, Haiti, and elsewhere throughout the African Atlantic world are crossing borders and seas in search of knowledge, training, and materials to become better practitioners and ritual specialists. Cosmopolitan outsiders from the United States, Europe, Asia, and many other places are learning, becoming initiated, and carrying shrines and liturgy back to their homes. Understanding these contemporary processes compels us to recognize that Vodou and Vodún are, and perhaps always have been, global. The spirits' ability to endure was not made possible by a rigid fixing of law or deepening of dogma but rather through the power of fluidity and flexibility. Today, the practices, forms, and symbols of spirit service are never fixed or static but are dynamic, diverse, and better experienced than defined.

DEFINING SPIRIT SERVICE THROUGH ENCOUNTER AND ENGAGEMENT

Rather than deploying generic geopolitical demarcations of "Haiti" and "West Africa" to organize the chapters in this volume, we instead divide it into two sections through which we may draw similarities as well as highlight differences between Vodún and Vodou. The first section, "Encounter," is based on how spirit service across the African Atlantic world is characterized by continuous contact with Others. Here, contributors deploy analyses of spirits' and adepts' ability to cross borders, a polyvalent concept that includes the political, cultural, and secular/sacred. Spirits and rituals across the Atlantic periphery are products and producers of exchange and culture. Migrations and exchange among Africans and Creoles were prevalent in the early modern Caribbean up to today, and spirits, ritual, medicinal knowledge, and other cultural experiences traveled extensively across the Atlantic world (Gomez 2017). Indeed, scholars in this volume outline how forms of spirit service in both Haiti and West Africa were born in and through these migrations and exchanges with and between other religions and spiritualties, such as Catholicism (Rey, Falen), Protestantism (Richman), and Islam (Vannier); other African spiritual systems (Montgomery); and other aesthetics (Giafferi-Dombre). Spirits cross geographical and cultural boundaries, healing and divination practices are adopted and modified, and philosophies quickly adjust to new realities. Throughout the African Atlantic, shrines are adorned with foreign material culture: cowry shells, medicines of all sorts from other countries, copies of the Qur'an, rosaries, and other ritual paraphernalia display deep historical and geographical reproduction. As the authors in this section demonstrate, encounters between cultures often find common ground through such concepts as divination, healing, witchcraft, ritual practice, and shared symbolism. Through these shared concepts, religious elements are adopted, assimilated, and even pirated. Through analyses of *encounter*, authors in this section lay bare how serving the spirits is dynamic and pragmatic as practitioners use engagements with other religious systems to evolve, gain power, and build a spiritual tool kit. Such agency is often a means of survival for those caught in slavery, revolution, colonialism, and penury.

The second section, "Engagement," explores new directions in the study of spirit service through insights of the lived experience of Vodou and Vodún.

A key reason to serve the spirits is to maintain personal and social health by diminishing or enhancing powers or forces within the personal body and community. Such forces have agencies of their own, and ritually appealing to these agencies is often done through a mediator or specialist. Through intense participant observation, many scholars engage these mediators and even the spirits to better understand how personhood and identity are forged and enhanced through the knowledge and experience that accompanies spirit service. It is precisely in the scholars' intense, personal engagement with the spirits, drumming, sacrifice, divination, and other aspects of spirit service that the religious systems reveal themselves in their full depth and complexity. Participating in initiations and ceremonies, the contributors of this volume have endeavored to unpack sites of religious practice as portals for understanding broader histories and social processes, but we have also tried to document direct, sensorial engagements with communities of spirits and practitioners as they share experiences steeped in global engagements with resilience and resistance. Anderson shows that in the United States, what he calls "Mississippi Valley Voodoo" has always been engaged globally, and while the religion itself died out in the 1940s, its dynamic memory is still present on the global stage.

Authors of this volume then move to examine multisensorial engagements. Venise N. Adjibodou and Alissa Jordan highlight the attention to our and others' bodily senses that gives us insight into the lived physical and intellectual experience of serving the spirits. The second source of engagement is the natural environment. Timothy Landry highlights the centrality of the forest in Vodún cosmology. He helps to make clear the unifying symbolic and ontological force of the sacred forest, which, according to Landry, exists across the African Atlantic world, across borders and beyond space. Nixon S. Cleophat too explores cosmology through the natural environment but highlights the dynamism of gender identities through spirit possession. The final source of engagement is the practitioners with whom scholars share the research experience. Elizabeth McAlister deploys the event of a funeral for a friend and fellow friend to explore how practitioners and spirits cross borders of all sorts. Altogether, chapters in this part explore new methodologies and new ways of conceptualizing ritual experience through reliance on reflexivity and attention to the sensorial experience of spirit service. Gender and sexuality, ecology and environment, even reality itself—all are interrogated through experiential attention to the senses, the body, and personal action.

Altogether, the chapters in this volume present a macroscopic view of spirit service across the African Atlantic world rather than individualized, localized, and isolated communities of practitioners. Individually, scholars here deploy an extensive conceptual tool kit that includes materialism, sensing, political economy, postcolonial studies, embodiment, and queer studies to address new questions and open new avenues for exploring Vodún and Vodou in a twenty-first-century, cosmopolitan Atlantic world.

NOTES

1. Note that in this volume, lowercase *vodún* refers to the deities, while the capitalized *Vodún* refers to the religion.
2. Blier (1995) provides an extensive speculation upon the etymology of the word *vodún* (38–40).
3. Gbe is a West African linguistic family that includes Ewe, Mina, Adja, and Fòn.

REFERENCES

Allman, Jean, and John Parker. 2005. *Tongnaab: The History of a West African God*. Bloomington: Indiana University Press.
Apter, Andrew. 2018. *Oduduwa's Chain: Locations of Culture in the Yoruba-Atlantic*. Chicago: University of Chicago Press.
Bay, Edna G. 1998. *Wives of the Leopard: Gender, Politics, and Culture in the Kingdom of Dahomey*. Charlottesville: University of Virginia Press.
Blier, Suzanne Preston. 1995. *African Vodun: Art, Psychology, and Power*. Chicago: University of Chicago Press.
Brivio, Alessandra. 2016. "Gorovodu: The Genesis of a 'Hausa Vodun.'" *Journal of West African History* 2 (1): 1–26.
Falen, Douglas. 2018. *African Science: Witchcraft, Vodun, and Healing in Southern Benin*. Madison: University of Wisconsin Press.
Friedson, Steven M. 2009. *Remains of Ritual: Northern Gods in Southern Lands*. Chicago: University of Chicago Press.
Gomez, Pablo. 2017. *The Experiential Caribbean: Creating Knowledge and Healing in the Early Modern Atlantic*. Chapel Hill: University of North Carolina Press.
Hurbon, Laennec. 2008. "Globalization and the Evolution of Haitian Vodou." In *Orisa Devotion as World Religion: The Globalization of Yoruba Religious Culture*, edited by Jacob K. Olupona and Terry Rey, 263–277. Madison: University of Wisconsin Press.
Landry, Timothy R. 2019. *Vodun: Secrecy and the Search for Divine Power*. Philadelphia: University of Pennsylvania Press.
Law, Robin. 2004. *Ouidah: The Social History of a West African Slaving 'Port,' 1727–1892*. Athens: Ohio University Press.

Lévi-Strauss, Claude. 1966. *The Savage Mind*. Chicago: University of Chicago Press.
Maupoil, Bernard. 1943. *La Géomancie à l'ancienne Côte des Esclaves (Travaux et Mémoires de l'Institut d'Ethnologie)*. Vol. 42. Paris: Université de Paris.
McCarthy Brown, Karen. 1991. *Mama Lola: A Vodou Priestess in Brooklyn*. Berkeley: University of California Press.
Meyer, Birgit. 2000. *Translating the Devil: Religion and Modernity among the Ewe in Ghana*. Trenton, NJ: Africa World.
Mintz, Sidney W., and Richard Price. (1978) 1992. *The Birth of African-American Culture: An Anthropological Perspective*. Boston: Beacon.
Montilus, Guerin. 1989. *Dompim: The Spirituality of African Peoples*. Nashville: Winston-Derek.
Montgomery, Eric, and Christian Vannier. 2017. *An Ethnography of a Vodu Shrine in Southern Togo*. Leiden, Netherlands: Brill.
Olupona, Jacob K., and Terry Ret, eds. 2008. *Orisa Devotion as World Religion: The Globalization of Yoruba Religious Culture*. Madison: University of Wisconsin Press.
Palmie, Stephen. 2006. "Creolization and Its Discontents." *Annual Review of Anthropology* 35:433–456.
Parés, Luis Nicolau. 2005. "Transformations of the Sea and Thunder Voduns in the Gbe-Speaking Area and in the Bahian Jeje Candomblé." In *Africa and the Americas: Interconnections during the Slave Trade*, edited by Jose C. Curto and Renee Soulodre-La France, 69–93. New York: Africa World.
———. 2013. *The Formation of Candomblé: Vodun History and Ritual in Brazil*. Chapel Hill: University of North Carolina Press Books.
Raboteau, Albert J. 1978. *Slave Religion: The "Invisible Institution" in the Antebellum South*. New York: Oxford University Press.
Rosenthal, Judy. 1998. *Possession, Ecstacy, and Law in Ewe Voodoo*. Charlottesville: University Press of Virginia.
Rush, Dana. 2013. *Vodun in Coastal Benin: Unfinished, Open-Ended, Global*. Nashville: Vanderbilt University Press.
Sheller, Mimi. 2003. *Consuming the Caribbean: From Arawaks to Zombies*. New York: Routledge.
Smith, Theophus H. 1994. *Conjuring Culture: Biblical Formations in Black America*. New York: Oxford University Press.
Stewart, Dianne M. 2005. *Three Eyes for the Journey: African Dimensions of the Jamaican Religious Experience*. Oxford: Oxford University Press.
Sweet, James H. 2011. *Domingo Alvares, African Healing, and the Intellectual History of the Atlantic World*. Chapel Hill: University of North Carolina Press.
Venkatachalam, Meera. 2015. *Slavery, Memory and Religion in Southeastern Ghana, c. 1850–Present*. Cambridge: Cambridge University Press.

Warner-Lewis, Maureen. 2003. *Central Africa in the Caribbean: Transcending Time, Transforming Cultures*. Kingston: University of West Indies Press.
Wirtz, Kristina. 2008. "Divining the Past: The Linguistic Reconstruction of 'African' Roots in Diasporic Ritual Registers and Songs." In *Africas of the Americas: Beyond the Search for Origins in the Study of Afro-Atlantic Religions*, edited by Stephen Palmie, 141–177. Leiden, Netherlands: Brill.

CHRISTIAN VANNIER is a lecturer in the Department of Behavioral Science at the University of Michigan, Flint. He is coauthor of *An Ethnography of a Vodu Shrine in Southern Togo* and coeditor of *Cultures of Doing Good: Anthropologists and NGOs*.

TIMOTHY R. LANDRY is Associate Professor of Anthropology and Religious Studies at Trinity College, Hartford, Connecticut. He is the author of *Vodún: Secrecy and the Search for Divine Power*, the winner of the 2019 Clifford Geertz Prize in the Anthropology of Religion.

PART ONE

Encounter

ONE

VODOU GENESIS

Africans and the Making of a National Religion in Saint-Domingue

Terry Rey

OVERVIEW

Our knowledge of the emergence of Haitian Vodou as a religion relies almost entirely on the writings of white observers in the French colonial Caribbean, most of them Frenchmen, of course. Their perceptions of the ritual practices of Africans were clouded by the privileged, sanctimonious, and imperialist biases of their own station in the world. Once a postcolonial optic is employed to dull such biases, however, and relatedly once we consider the power disequilibrium that shaped their encounters with Africans in Saint-Domingue (colonial Haiti), polish is given to their observations. Subsequently, a careful, contextualized reading thereof fosters a clearer understanding of Vodou's origins and the various spiritual resources that the nascent religion drew upon in cementing its foundation. Based on a close and generally chronological reading of five of the most important primary source accounts of Africana religious culture in Saint-Domingue (by Jean-Baptiste Labat, Médéric Louis Elie Moreau de Saint-Méry, Colonel Malenfant, Louis Narcisse Baudry des Lozières, and Félix Pascalis Ouvière), this chapter provides a critical analysis of Vodou genesis that aims to contribute to our understanding of the religion's colonial history and to map out a general model for the periodization thereof.

JEAN-BAPTISTE LABAT

A Dominican priest, explorer, botanist, planter, slave owner, mathematician, and soldier, Père Jean-Baptiste Labat first arrived in the French Caribbean colonies in 1694, spending a total of twelve years there. Published in 1722, his six-volume tome *Nouveau voyage aux iles françoises d'Amérique*, "a veritable 18th-century best seller" (Toczyski 2007, 485), is one of the earliest published accounts of religion in the French Caribbean, including of course Saint-Domingue, though Labat spent most of his time in Martinique. Once in the colonies, it quickly became evident to Labat that to gain knowledge about African culture, he would need to study what seemed to him, and rightly so, the most important African language at the time in the French Caribbean, a creolizing variant of Fongbe, called by the French (and likely, too, by many Africans) "Arada."

Labat was especially interested in dance and healing among Africans in the colonies. In fact, his first mention of Africana spirituality concerns healing, where, in volume 1, he details the case of a "19- or 20-year-old" Black man who had been bitten on the foot by a massive snake, "some seven feet long ... as thick as the leg of a man." While covered in blankets, holding the priest's hand, and lying infirm between two fires, the victim felt that he was dying, and his massively swollen leg gave Labat that very impression, thus he heard his confession. When an African herbalist was summoned to treat the man, the priest, as a botanist, took keen interest and asked about the herbs he employed. The healer declined to answer, "because these secrets allowed him to make a living, thus he did not want to publicize them." He did promise, though, that if ever a snake bit the priest himself, he would treat him, too, with the utmost care. "I thanked him for the offer," notes Labat (1742a, 163), "hoping to never have to take him up on it." Notably, the snake-bite victim survived, leaving Labat quite impressed.

This case reflects the pivotal role that individual clerical knowledge played in sustaining African spirituality in the Americas. With the communal dimensions of African religions disrupted in serious ways that would require generations to restore in the so-called New World, early in colonial history it was especially the individual healer—his or her knowledge left largely intact and adapted to the local flora and fauna—that laid the first structural cornerstone for Africana religion across the Atlantic,[1] as well as a cornerstone for its remarkable resilience that has helped sustain it ever since.[2] Although Labat's observations in this instance were of Martinique, the entire French Caribbean was, for all intents and purposes, the same cultural contact zone. It is also important to note here that most slaves who fell under Labat's gaze (or his whip) were West Africans, primarily from Senegambia and the Bight of Benin, as was then the case throughout the French Caribbean colonies. This would change in the second half of the eighteenth century in Saint-Domingue, however, with the massive influx of enslaved Africans from Kongo and environs (West Central Africa) then rapidly surpassing the West African influx, which of course would have a significant influence on Vodou genesis, as is further explained later in this section.[3]

Part of chapter 20 of Labat's (1742a, 445) first volume focuses on "Maladies of Blacks and Creoles." It opens with a discussion of a Mina slave who had taken ill after repeatedly eating dirt, followed by Labat's observation that Minas in general believed that upon dying they would be reincarnated in Africa, hence their putative proclivity to committing suicide (446). As such, we also have in Labat's text an early colonial Caribbean commentary about African notions of death, dying, and rebirth, notions that continue to animate Haitian Vodouist belief to this day. Labat's slave ate dirt to die and return to see his father in Africa, even though he loved his master, who had, after all, baptized him and instructed him in the "true" faith. But Père Labat simply "could not shake him from this fantasy" (447).

Because "almost all Blacks who leave their homeland as adults are 'sorcerers', or they at least have some tainting of magic, sorcery, and poison," Labat (1742b, 137) was surrounded by these things and thus devotes an entire chapter to the subject, entitled "The History of Some Black Sorcerers," which contains four case studies. Labat first speaks here about a slave whose master had taken from him "a sack" and who was supposedly adept at divining when ships would arrive in Martinique, but Labat (1742a, 137) dismissed him as "a charlatan who duped simple folks in order to earn their money."[4] Though the "sorcerer" in question would seek to mend his ways and become Catholic to the satisfaction of the missionary, eventually he would confide in Labat that he was quite miserable without his pagan wares and that he missed making all of the money that he once did in his former trade. Incensed by such illusory persistence, Labat (1742a, 491) threatened to have him burned alive, and the Catholic priest torched the sack, the secrets of which went up in smoke with its contents.

Though lumping them together as "sorcery," rather than categorically denouncing the African healing practices he observed in the colonial French Caribbean, Labat seemingly admired some of them and found therein certain benefits to the colonial enterprise. For instance, when a young male slave from Guinea overheard missionaries lamenting the lack of rain and how their gardens would thus be unfruitful, "he asked them if they would prefer a downpour or a drizzle, assuring them that he could make it happen at once." With "curiosity prevailing over reason," the missionaries took him up on the offer, after which the boy performed a ritual employing three peeled oranges, three branches, and supplicant prayers. Then, scanning the horizon attentively, he noticed a distant thin cloud, which he summoned with the sticks to hover over the garden and produce a light rainfall for an hour. The boy next buried the oranges and the sticks in the garden, which, much to the missionary's stupefaction, was now "perfectly watered"; what's more, not a single drop of rain fell outside of the garden. Interestingly, he had been taught this art of rainmaking by elders from his homeland whom he had encountered during the Middle Passage (Labat 1742a, 494).

The third case discussed by Labat is that of a female African slave who had been infirm for some time with a mysterious condition. French doctors could not cure her, prompting Labat to take her to African healers, who also failed to do so, leaving the missionary to suspect that she had been poisoned. One night the priest went out for a walk to find the woman sprawled out on a mat in a coffee field, with a "fake Black doctor" kneeling over her with a calabash, a candle, and an "idol," and "he appeared to be praying with a great deal of attention." The healer asked the woman if she was now cured, at which point she started to scream and cry, alarming Labat (1742a, 497), who broke up the ritual and "had the sorcerer arrested." The missionary in turn asked the woman what had made her cry, "and she responded that the devil told her that she would die in four days," with the icon having served as Satan's mouthpiece. Labat then denounced "the sorcerer" as a charlatan who only served as the devil's ventriloquist, thus subjecting him to three hundred lashes of the whip "between the shoulders and knees." Labat then spit on, stomped on, and burned the ritual paraphernalia that had been employed in the ceremony. This iconoclastic act horrified the priest's slaves, who warned him that the devil would kill him because of it. But Labat (498) had no fear and proceeded to have the lashed "sorcerer" shackled and bathed in "crushed peppers and lemon juice," a concoction that was intended both to cause him "horrible pain" (even though Labat believed that African "sorcerers can never feel pain" [498]) and to combat gangrene. As for the woman, she indeed passed away four days later, but Labat (499) got to hear her confession in time so that "she died a good Christian."

Labat's fourth case study is of an African slave who had been sentenced to death for allegedly practicing sorcery in St. Thomas. The sorcerer was said to have made an earthen icon talk, a crime for which he was sentenced to be burned at the stake. Present at the execution was a Dane named Vanbel, who saw fit to mock the shackled sorcerer by pontificating: "Hey, you will no longer make your little icon talk; it is now shattered." This provoked the following reply: "If you want, Sir, I can make that cane that you are holding in your hand talk." Intrigued, Vanbel had the judge delay the execution to see if the sorcerer could indeed do so. The Dane's cane was passed to the slave, who "planted it in the earth and performed some ceremonies around it" and then invited its owner to ask the cane to, in effect, prophesy. Vanbel "replied that he wanted to know if a ship that he had been waiting for had disembarked, when it would arrive, what it carried, and what it might have encountered along the way" (Labat 1742a, 500). The slave performed some more rituals around the cane and then invited its owner to approach and listen. The cane spoke and offered details that turned out to be entirely accurate, with the ship arriving three days later, and thus was the convicted sorcerer exonerated (141).[5]

To Labat, equally striking as their healing modalities were the funerary customs among Africans in the Caribbean, for even when a slave who had no relatives on a given plantation died, "everyone cried," while the bereaved often brought the priest "money or fowls in order to have Mass said for them." His efforts to refuse such offerings were futile, meanwhile, because those bringing them were of the staunch belief that the masses would only be effective if paid for; so the priest resigned himself "to accept the fowls in order to keep the peace" (Labat 1742a, 162–163).[6] Labat goes on to describe what was an offertory ritual that today in Haitian Vodou is called *manje lemò* (food for the dead), which was observed on the anniversary of the death of a relative, especially an elder. At this communal ritual in Martinique in the late seventeenth century, the participants "prayed to God that the deceased's soul rest in peace. Afterwards, they all fall to their knees and recite every prayer that they know; then, they eat everything that has been brought and drink to the health of the dead" (164).[7]

Despite the enchantment that some of these events might have inspired—and seemingly sometimes did inspire among French missionaries—Labat ultimately took them to be proof "that there really are people who work with the devil and use him for a variety of purposes." For our purposes, Labat's observations illuminate the following nine key features of African religious culture in the early colonial French Caribbean: (1) healing, (2) prophecy, (3) divination, (4) sorcery and the negotiation thereof, (5) the manufacture and use of amulets and icons, (6) charismatic religious leadership, (7) drumming and dance, (8) the veneration of the dead, and (9) rainmaking. Significantly, all nine features were of West African origin. To be sure, there were central Africans among the slaves in the colonies at the time, but they were a distinct minority then, such that Labat only mentions them in passing.

In sum, Labat leaves us with an image of vibrant forms of "traditional" African religion in the early colonial history of the French Caribbean, where the Catholic church then struggled to gain a foothold. Things would markedly change in the latter regard with the expansion of the Jesuit mission (1704–1763), which soon found itself ministering to about half of a rapidly expanding African population, especially in Saint-Domingue. It may be suggested, therefore, that the first phase of Vodou's development, from 1669 to roughly 1750, was largely devoid of any extensive Catholic or Kongolese influences, which would later intertwine in a developmental phase and transform the religion quite dramatically. In fact, Labat's descriptions of Africana religion in the French Caribbean colonies cannot really be said to be of Vodou per se, as the crucial second phase had not really begun, a phase during which the religion truly crystallized and took on much of the identity that marks Haitian Vodou to this day. As such, Labat offers insight into several West African religious forms in early Caribbean history, though Vodou, as a Creole religion, was still aborning. With that said, West African cornerstones to Vodou were certainly laid during the period in question, such as healing modalities, divination, ancestor veneration, and the cult of Danbala, the serpent lwa (spirit) who remains one of the most important in Haitian Vodou today.

MÉDÉRIC LOUIS ELIE MOREAU DE SAINT-MÉRY

Of the four authors under consideration in this chapter, Médéric Louis Moreau de Saint-Méry has received by far the most scholarly attention, chiefly because his two-volume tome *Description topographique, physique, civile, politique, et historique de la partie française de l'isle Saint-Domingue* is the single most important source of information about Saint-Domingue that we have. Published in 1797–1799, though completed ten years earlier, *Description* is based on Moreau's sustained analyses of a wide range of cultural forms in Saint-Domingue. To execute the project, the Martinican-born French attorney and colonial administrator collected a great deal of textual material, much of which has been preserved in the Archives Nationales de France, including folders dedicated specifically to Catholic feast days, Jews, Jesuits, minerals, and poison, each of which offers additional insights into Dominguan religious culture that are not included in *Description*.[8]

For the purposes of the present inquiry, *Description* is especially of interest because it contains the first-ever use in print of the word *Vaudoux*, in reference here to an ensemble of ritual practices that were "accompanied by such circumstances that placed it on the level of those institutions made up in large part by superstition and bizarre practices." There is no irrefutable evidence that Moreau ever personally encountered any Vodou rituals in Saint-Domingue— the one that he famously described was esoteric, after all, so one wonders how a white man would have been permitted to be even remotely present. That said, Moreau was knowledgeable enough to correctly ascribe the religion's origins in Saint-Domingue to "Arada blacks, who are the true sectarians of *le Vaudoux* in the colony, and who oversee its principles and rules." Furthermore, by 1788 Vodou had "been known for a long time, especially in the Western part" of Saint-Domingue. The cultic focus of "the Vaudoux sect" was a serpent, one situated in a box on an altar, which served in effect as an oracle and "signified an all-powerful, supernatural being upon whom depended all the events in the entire world." It is noteworthy that Moreau does not infer deific status to the "non-venomous" serpent itself, as God is not present in the rituals that he describes but is only channeled through the mediumistic reptile, which nonetheless possessed an impressive divinatory range: "Knowledge of the past, science of the present, prophecy of the future—all belonged to this snake." A priest and a priestess, who carried the titles of king and queen and "claimed to be inspired by God," conducted the rituals and served as the gatekeepers for what was essentially a secret society (Moreau 1958, 64). It was also clearly a recreation of the royal divinatory ritual in Allada that Labat had described some sixty years earlier, suggesting that for the first half century of Vodou's genesis, West African—and especially Arada—religious forms predominated, as recognized by Moreau (1958, 68) himself (see also Labat 1742b, 121–124). Such is in keeping with the data now available about the ethnicity of enslaved Africans brought to the French Caribbean up until the 1780s.[9]

With the devotees assembled in secrecy, dressed appropriately in sandals with "a more or less considerable number of red kerchiefs draped over their bodies," the ritual starts: "Once confirming that no curious onlookers are there, the ceremony begins with the worship of the snake, with calls to remain faithful to its cult and to follow all that it demands. The pact of secrecy between the king and the queen, which is the foundation of the cult, is renewed, accompanied by the most horrible delirium imaginable, in order to make it even more imposing."

Following this overture, the king and queen "assume the affectionate air of a sensitive father and mother," thereby fortifying the faith of the congregation. Then "the crowd explodes, and each, according to his or her needs, in an order based on one's seniority in the sect, approaches to implore the Vaudoux," with the term here being used to refer to the snake itself: "Most ask it for the power to influence their masters; but that is not all, as one asks for more money, another the gift of appeasement towards those one has miffed, another for the return of an unfaithful lover, another for swift healing or a longer life," and so on (Moreau 1958, 66–67).

Spirit possession ensues, as the king places the snake box on the ground and guides the queen to stand thereupon, whereafter "she is penetrated by the God, agitated, her entire body in a convulsive state, and the oracle speaks through her mouth." The convulsing queen shouts messages about "faithfulness" and "reproaches" the "imbecilic group, who never harbor the slightest doubt about even the most monstrous absurdity, and who blindly obey everything that is despotically commanded." A series of additional questions are answered by the oracle, and then the snake box is returned to the altar, around which the congregation forms a circle. The sectarians renew their vows of secrecy and smear warm goat's blood on their lips to seal the pact, to which they swear allegiance on the pain of death (Moreau 1958, 66–67).

"After that begins the Vaudoux dance," which opens with the king initiating new members into the sect. The initiates each receive "a packet composed of herbs, horse hairs, pieces of horn and other likewise disgusting objects." Next the king taps an initiate lightly on the head with a wooden board and sings "an African song," which the congregants repeat in epiphanic cadence—the kind of call and response that remains common today in all the main forms of Haitian religion, Vodou, Protestant, and Catholic. The initiate begins to tremble and dance and evidently is possessed by the serpent, an experience that Moreau reports as carrying the title *"monter Vaudoux."* This literally translates as "to mount the Vodou," but it surely signified "mounted by the Vodou," which is consistent with the expression used widely in Haitian Vodou for spirit possession to this day. The king brings the dance to a close by lightly striking the possessed dancer/initiate once again on the head with the board and then escorts him to the altar "to swear him in, at which moment he belongs to the sect." Charms and bells are then introduced from the altar by the queen, which sparks renewed frenzy among the faithful, who tear their clothes and bite themselves, while some, "who have lost all use of their senses and who have fallen to the ground, are taken, while still dancing, to an adjacent space" to participate in what was, for all intents and purposes— and, reading through Moreau's excoriating rhetoric—a kind of tantric orgy (Moreau 1958, 67–68).

The lyrics to "the African song" are recorded by Moreau (1958, 67) as follows:

Eh! eh! Bomba, hen! hen!
Canga bafio té
Canga moune dé lé
Canga do ki la
Canga li.

Generations of scholars have debated the meaning of this chant, which Moreau himself did not attempt to translate. There is disagreement about the correct translation of this verse and even about what language it is. However, most agree that the term "canga" means to tie or to bind (Kikongo, *kanga*), that "do ki" means sorcerer (Kikongo, *ndoki*), and that "moune dé lé" means white person (Kikongo, *mundele*). As for "bafio," meanwhile, the term is widely thought to mean "Black person" or perhaps a group of Africans who trafficked in slaves or uninitiated onlookers who had no business being at the Vaudoux ceremony. "Bomba," the first word in the chant and seemingly its addressee, is of crucial importance but is also disputed among two camps of scholars. The first follows a lineage begun in 1934 by the Cuban ethnographer Fernando Ortiz (1975) that translates the term as "secret" or "mystery," while the second follows a scholarly lineage begun by the Belgian Catholic missionary to the Congo Jean Cuvelier (1947) that understands the term to refer to a Central African serpent divinity named Mbumba.[10] Christina Mobley's (2015, 222) recent impressive research convinces me that Cuvelier's, and not Ortiz's, interpretation is correct, for "Mbumba is the central mythic figure in Yombe [a Central African ethnic group] cosmology who presides over the society's two main initiatory rites Bakhimba and Lemba."

Alasdair Pettinger astutely reviews the long history of interpretations, translations, and appropriations of the chant and offers the following additional persuasive conclusions: that the chant is in Kikongo; that it invokes a snake deity named Mbumba from Central Africa who is associated with rainbows; and that it bespeaks a merger of African religious forms, those of the Arada and those of the Bakongo. Pettinger's additional suggestion about what the chant reflects about religious change in Saint-Domingue/Haiti is irrefutable: that Vodou has undergone significant adaptations since Moreau's observations in the late eighteenth century, and that "it was only during the course of the nineteenth century that vaudoux became the dominant Afro-Haitian religion—embracing other forms under its ecumenical umbrella—a process that seems to have been accompanied by a diminution of the role of the snake" (Pettinger 2012, 93–94).[11] Danbala is, however, one of many lwa in the Vodou pantheon today, and among the most prominent, as reflected in the chapter by Karen Richman in this volume.

The word *boumba* remains part of the lexicon of Haitian Vodou today, as Benjamin Hebblethwaite (2012, 222) explains in his expansive "Dictionary of Vodou Terms": "Boumba—The name of a lwa and a people from the Kongo region and hence a part of the Petwo rite. Boumba is located near Mondong and Lenba, other toponyms that became lwa in Vodou. A rhythm and dance in the Petwo rite. The Kikongo etymology *búmba* refers to a medicine bag." Hebblethwaite (223) also refers to an entire Vodou rite called "Boumba Mazwa," and yet neither the lwa nor the rite have ever seemingly been considered by, or perhaps even known to, partakers in the age-old and sometimes politicized debate over the meaning of the chant.

"But perhaps we should question such an exclusive focus on the *meaning* of the chant," adds Pettinger, "for it tends to reduce it to a text removed from its ritual context, thereby obscuring much of its evocative power." If, for example, most participants in the ritual under consideration were, as Moreau suggests, Arada, whereas the chant was in Kikongo, then they likely would not have understood it anyway, while "the power of ritual invocations such as prayers or curses are [sic] often enhanced by their unintelligibility" (Pettinger 2012, 94). It simply does not matter, then, whether Bomba meant mystery or was the name of a snake deity. To this suggestion, I would add that in Haitian Vodou today all spirits, as well as saints, angels, and the living dead, are called "mysteries" (*mystè*), and this has likely been the case since the colonial era.

COLONEL MALENFANT

Colonel Malenfant served the French empire well in its crown-jewel colony of Saint-Domingue, whether in combat or on his slave plantation. He also lived to write about it, offering his 1824 memoir *Des colonies et particulièrement de celle de Saint-Domingue* as "an impartial exposé of the causes and a historical sketch of the civil wars that rendered this colony independent." In the imperialist France of his day, titles were of great importance, and Malenfant was not lacking thereof, being the "Sub-Inspector of Reviews, Knight of the Legion of Honor ... and Ex-Delegate of the French Government in Suriname." The intrepid colonel intended his memoir as an "eye-witness" account of what he clearly realized was race and class warfare exploding in the colony as of 1791, an epic struggle that would leave him wounded and exiled (Malenfant 1814, v).

Numerous observers of the Haitian Revolution attest that Black combatants, Africans and Creoles alike, believed that French bullets and cannonballs were made of water and thus not to be feared, and Malenfant offers his first glimpse into African magic when discussing this belief. Writing of the insurgent leader Hyacinthe, who led uprisings in March 1792 in the mountains and surrounding plains near Cul-de-Sac, the French knight scoffed that "their blindness was so strong that they stuck their arms into canons," declaring that they were harmless. Championing the cause, Hyacinthe himself strode boldly into the face of gunfire, holding and shaking a "small whip made of horsehair," imploring his charges, "Charge! Charge! It's only water. It's only water that comes out of their canons. Have no fear" (Malenfant 1814, 232). It did not go well, however, as five hundred Black fighters were killed and fewer than one hundred French troops, driving Hyacinthe to the local Catholic church to seek absolution and blessings for his troops, a reflection of how Africans and Creoles generally viewed the Catholic ritual paraphernalia and sacraments that they encountered in the colony as potent weapons in their struggle against white supremacy and brutal oppression.

To Malenfant (1814, 232), Africans like Hyacinthe seemed to be the most religious people in the colonies: "Wander about the Americas, and you will see what it means to worship God, where the Blacks are as observant of religious law as you, French, Italians, English, are wanting." Though he probably did not consider "the Vodou sect" to be a religion per se, Malenfant, like Labat and Moreau before him, associated Vodou with snake veneration of Arada origins: "There exists among the Vodou priests a large adder snake, hidden under the earth in a wooden case, which is placed upon a kind of altar for ceremonial occasions. Oaths are taken under the gaze of the great priestess. Dancing ensues, which causes people to convulse, that only ends when oil is drunk, which I am told derives from the snake. It is rubbed on the temples, hocks, and armpits" (216).

Esoterica initially shrouded Vodou from Malenfant's gaze, and he was threatened with death by poisoning were he ever to delve too deeply into the sect's mysteries, thus the above description is likely a secondhand account. But the colonel didn't have to go out of his way to find Vodou himself—he stumbled upon it in dramatic fashion one day in February 1792. Leading a sizable battalion in a raid on an insurgent camp near Fonds-Parisien, just east of Port-au-Prince, Malenfant discovered the following: "along the pathway, large, steep mounds of dirt on which were placed an assortment of dead birds, each arranged in a different manner. On some were herons [*oiseaux crabiers—Ardeolla ralloides*] and on others black chickens. In the path itself bird parts had been cut up and tossed here and there, encircled by carefully arranged rocks; finally, there were about eight broken eggs scattered near the large circles in zigzags."

With their dancing and singing suddenly disrupted by the raid, members of the Fonds-Parisien camp, including some two hundred women and led by a "high priestess" who was "a very beautiful, well dressed black woman" were shocked that the French colonel and his troops "were able to pass beyond the obstacles that the great female Vodou master had spread beneath our steps. That is the assurance that the *Negresse* had given them, which gave them confidence and made them dance" (Malenfant 1814, 217–218).

Notably, details about the ritual paraphernalia at the Fonds-Parisien camp reaffirm the long-standing scholarly impression that Africans in Saint-Domingue placed much faith in protective amulets. Malenfant's description also suggests an ascendant Kongolese influence on Haitian Vodou during the latter half of the eighteenth century, for the "zig-zag" circles portend the *vèvè* of contemporary Vodou, pictographic symbols that represent the lwa, as well as the *firma* symbols of the Afro-Cuban tradition of Palo, which are decidedly Kongolese in origin (Martínez-Ruiz 2013). Malenfant notes that there were almost no Creole slaves (those born in the Caribbean) involved in the Vodou sect at the time, and though he does not mention any chanting, the presence of Kongolese symbolism in the form of the vèvès and in the boumba chant recorded by Moreau clearly indicate a rise in West Central African religious forms in the nascent religion, not to mention a merger of West African and Central African snake cults. This is especially noteworthy in light of the virtual absence of Kongolese religious forms in Labat's observations from much earlier in the eighteenth century and late seventeenth century. One may thus establish that religious syncretism during the genesis of Haitian Vodou occurred first between diverse African forms, which preceded any major developments of Creolization or of any extensive fusion of European Catholic and African indigenous forms in Vodou genesis.

LOUIS NARCISSE BAUDRY DES LOZIÈRES

Given the dramatic rise in the percentage of slaves brought from Central Africa during the second half of the eighteenth century, who would then outnumber West African slaves in Saint-Domingue, it is to be expected that a proportionate rise in Kongolese influences on the genesis of Haitian Vodou would ensue. By the time that he himself arrived in Saint-Domingue, in 1789, Louis Narcisse Baudry des Lozières, Moreau's brother-in-law and the possessor of several honorific titles and a slave plantation, Kongolese slaves had become so numerous in the colony—the African ethnic majority, in fact—that Baudry learned Kikongo and saw the need for a Kikongo-French dictionary (Depréaux 1924). And so, he wrote one.

Baudry was an attorney cum military officer who was forced to flee Saint-Domingue in 1792 because of the outbreak of the Haitian Revolution, but not before having done some fighting against insurgents and having himself been wounded in battle there. The dictionary in question is a thirty-nine-page section of his 1802 *Second voyage à la Louisiane*, which talks a great deal more about Saint-Domingue than Louisiana. It is largely a compilation of wide-ranging observations about the colony that was intended to be of service to France in the eventual reconquest of its lost and lucrative colonial paradise (which never happened, of course). A good deal of *Second voyage* discusses African slaves based on Baudry's extensive experience with them while on his Dominguan plantation, which had been sacked more than ten years prior to his writing the text. Overall, the book provides much advice for masters on how to best deal with *bosal* (African-born) slaves, and this is where the Kikongo dictionary comes in.[12]

Just prior to the outbreak of the Haitian Revolution, more than half a million slaves toiled on plantations like Baudry's in Saint-Domingue, and fully three-quarters of them were Central African, and fully half had been brought to the colony during the five years immediately preceding the initial slave uprisings of August 1791 (Sweet 2017, 85). This alone, along with the very existence of Baudry's dictionary, clearly suggests that by the end of the eighteenth century the impact of Central African religious forms must have been great on the development of Haitian Vodou, perhaps supplanting certain West African forms or surpassing them in influence. Such is evinced, at any rate, in the chant recorded by Moreau in the Vaudoux ceremony that he famously described. For the purposes of the present chapter, I have carefully analyzed Baudry's entire dictionary and list below its entries that are "religious" in nature to shed some additional light on that development and ultimately contribute, as much as possible, to a periodization of colonial and revolutionary-era Vodou.

Before considering the list, it should be noted that Baudry was not exactly fluent in Kikongo, having "only made the effort to learn enough to understand my slaves, and enough for them to understand me" (Baudry 1802, 72). He was especially interested in creating a dictionary that would help to engender African slaves' trust in their masters and would improve their health care (74). This interest combines with Baudry's portrayal of life in "Angola" to provide us with an interesting glimpse into herbalism in Central Africa and a passing allusion to a local taboo against eating shellfish, as dictated by "the Fetish, the God that they adore," as well as dietary restrictions among Central African slaves against consuming "chickens, partridges, turtles, does, duck, beef, and the ubiquitous pigeons there" (92, 101). As if a harbinger to Émile Durkheim's (1912) early twentieth-century theory that such is an "elementary form" of "religious life," in effect, Baudry interprets this as a form of totemism: "It is from the religion of these men that they adopt certain animals or many animals and worship them as divinities" (101). Also noted in passing are Africans' passions for dancing and for strong alcohol, which both remain ubiquitous components of Haitian Vodou even now, indulged in by humans and spirits alike in communal rituals.

From Baudry's dictionary, the following terms are the most relevant to the question of Vodou genesis and our effort to elucidate the Kongolese influence on the religion's colonial history, one that intensified on the eve of the Haitian Revolution:

linba—to soothe
zanbiam; pongoé; zabiam pongou; zabi—good god; God

motonzambe—good person
ndoki—brigand, rascal, poisoner
gangan kizi—surgeon
ilou—the sky/heaven
m'singa—cord
zabiam pongou; zambi—God
fouili—to be dead
melongo—medicine
mountou; fiote iagala—a Black man
fiote—Black
m'kisis/mlongo—cure
tili—revere
zaba—knowledge
kanga—tie (as in the tying up of sacks and human bodies for religious purposes)
dongou/dougou—drum

Three of the key terms in the Bomba chant recorded by Moreau appear in Baudry's dictionary, indicative of how Kongolese religious forms were then being so deeply imbued in Vodou's preexistent West African baseline: *kanga*, *ndoki*, *bafiote*. Also reflected here are emergent influences of Kongolese Catholicism on Dominguan religious culture and African intellectual history in the Americas, as "a good person" is here literally "a person of God," while the sky is also called "heaven." The prevalence of health-related nomenclature in Baudry's dictionary might be interpreted as underscoring the centrality of healing in early Haitian Vodou, but it is more clearly the result of one of Baudry's intentions in producing it in the first place, which was to help doctors in Saint-Domingue to better diagnose and treat sick slaves. All the same, Kongolese slaves perceived of French surgeons in the colony as priests and of Catholic priests as healers, for even today in Haitian Vodou a priest is a *gangan*—in effect a descendent of the Kongolese *gangan kizi* (*nganga nkisi*) who made his way into Baudry's dictionary two and a quarter centuries ago.[13]

FÉLIX PASCALIS OUVIÈRE

A secular Catholic priest, physician, and political agitator, Abbé Ouvière was a mercurial opportunist who, like the commentators already discussed above, was awash in the raging seas of the revolutionary Atlantic world. Ouvière's case was somewhat different, though. Like both Baudry and Moreau, after the outbreak of the Haitian Revolution, he fled to Philadelphia, but unlike them, who were each only in the city for a few years, the abbé would spend the rest of his storied life in the United States. He did so not as a Catholic priest, however, but as a pioneering figure in early American science and medicine known as Dr. Pascalis (Rey 2017, 179–183).

During his roughly two-year stay in Saint-Domingue, Pascalis had ingratiated himself to the leaders of the free colored population, who were then clamoring and taking up arms for their full rights as French citizens, largely in reaction to the 1789 promulgation of the *Declaration of the Rights of Man and the Citizen*. A thorn in their sides was the mystical free colored warlord Romaine-la-Prophétesse (né Romaine Rivière), a free colored who was born on the Spanish side of the island around 1750 but was residing in Saint-Domingue by the late 1770s. As a religiously inspired insurgent leader, the prophetess conquered the cities of Jacmel and Léogâne by 1792, yet he was decried by other free coloreds for his excessive violence and putative fanaticism. Thus, the more "civilized"—and French—free colored elites sent Pascalis to negotiate with Romaine in his mountain redoubt high above those coastal cities, a remote place called Trou Coffy, which is the context of the memoir that the priest/scientist would pen some thirty years later in New York, "Anecdote historique" (Pascalis 1821). Unknown until recently to any scholar of Haitian history, this document contains some remarkable observations about the religious culture of the quasi-cult that sprung up around Romaine, the self-proclaimed godson of the Virgin Mary, and his volatile brood of free coloreds and liberated slaves.

Until I discovered Pascalis's "Anecdote" and cited it profitably in my 2017 book on Romaine and Ouvière, *The Priest and the Prophetess*, the most important source of information about the religion of the prophetess was a far less sympathetic, denunciatory report written by Father J. P. M. Blouët, who was the curé of Jacmel when the city was conquered by Romaine-la-Prophétesse. Though there is no evidence that the curé ever visited Trou Coffy himself, his report offers the following intriguing details about Romaine's religious practice there: The prophetess had constructed a chapel on his small coffee plantation, where he would say Mass before his followers and retrieve written messages left for him in the tabernacle by his godmother, the Virgin Mary, and preach with a sword in his hand. Most notably, Blouët adds that Romaine "composed remedies," an obvious reference to herbalism.[14] Other contemporary sources have Romaine manufacturing amulets and prophesying that he would one day be king of the entire island of Hispaniola, while he himself expressed profound loyalty to the doomed king of France (Rey 2017, 60, 68–70).

Besides the references to herbalism and amulets, the details about Romaine's religious practice provided by Blouët and other contemporary observers do not amount to any evidence that the prophetess was a Vodou priest per se, contrary to widespread assumptions both in Haiti and among scholars today. For his part, Pascalis also describes Romaine and the religious culture at Trou Coffy as being altogether Catholic, albeit this was a form of Catholicism that heavily teetered on heresy, even though Romaine held Catholic priests in high esteem. It was that esteem that afforded Pascalis, as Abbé Ouvière, access to the prophetess, for he was brought to the notoriously inaccessible mountaintop insurgent camp at Trou Coffy after having promised Romaine that he would say Christmas Mass there, in 1791 (Rey 2017, 142).

Trou Coffy was similar in certain respects to the camp that Malenfant had raided at Fonds-Parisien: It was steeped in religion, led by a charismatic figure, and enough feared by local white and Creole elites for them to send an armed battalion to crush it. One might thus have expected to find similar protective forms of ritual paraphernalia surrounding Romaine's insurgent camp as those that Malenfant had encountered near Fonds-Parisien before driving out "the great female Vodou master" and her acolytes. However, save for the severed head of a Frenchman who had been killed in one of Romaine's raids and fixed atop a fence surrounding his commune at Trou Coffy, none are mentioned in the archival material. In effect, the Fonds-Parisien Vodou priestess and Romaine-la-Prophétesse each presided over respective forms of what Michel Laguerre (1989, 33–34) calls "Voodoo cells," distinct congregations in Saint-Domingue that were mostly unrelated to one another and quite diverse in their religious practice, and this "diversity was related to the slaves' past religious experiences," whether in Africa or among bosals and Creoles in the colony.[15] Although Romaine-la-Prophétesse thus cannot be said to have been a Vodou priest, he did reign supreme over one of the most important "Voodoo cells" in Saint-Domingue at the outbreak of the Haitian Revolution, one that was predominately Catholic in orientation and practice.

Pascalis is one of only two authors of any archival documents pertaining to the Trou Coffy insurgency who actually knew Romaine-la-Prophétesse and visited him at his chapel in Trou Coffy, and he details the religious practice that he witnessed while there, although flamboyant and heterodox, as being Catholic and, technically speaking, not Vodouist.[16] In a 1792 letter, for instance, Pascalis notes that Romaine "was passionately devoted to the cult," an observation that he would echo in the description of the prophetess and

Trou Coffy that he wrote in New York thirty years later.[17] Upon his dramatic arrival at the insurgent camp on Christmas Eve of 1791, Pascalis, as Abbé Ouvière, was taken to meet Romaine, where he found the prophetess and a small group of his devotees "at prayer in the chapel . . . in commemoration of the birth of the savior," vigilantly guarded by about eight armed men and women. It was around one o'clock on Christmas morning as Pascalis entered Romaine's sanctuary, "a superbly illuminated long room full of rather crudely formed images, adorned with flowers and relics all about and a grotesque crest of the nativity scene or the birth of Jesus." Much like his chapel, Romaine himself was splendidly adorned, wearing "ribbons, rosaries, and a cross on his chest" and "a turban topped with a plume on his head." To Pascalis, the prophetess "had the appearance of a priest of the Roman religion" dressed in "the clothing of a Turk." Even Romaine's parting gesture to the priest as Pascalis was about to leave Trou Coffy was steeped in religious meaning: "He touched my hand, tracing with his finger the cross of salutation in the manner of the Spanish."[18]

The relative lack of "traditional" African religious forms in Romaine's chapel, appearance, and practice, when compared to the African ritual contexts described above by Labat, Moreau, and Malenfant, should thus not be surprising; for, by the time the prophetess stormed to political prominence in Saint-Domingue in late 1791, the colony's religious field had been flooded with newish African Catholic forms by way of the rapid growth of the population of Central African and especially Kongolese slaves. In its royalism and mariocentrism, as well as in his gender-bending religious leadership, Romaine's form of Catholicism was clearly influenced by Kongolese religion, and it is quite possible that his own parents had been Kongolese slaves—they had him baptized Catholic at birth. Furthermore, he was as devout a religious figure in Saint-Domingue as any other that historians have ever described.

As Dominguan and Haitian religious history unfolded, the distinctive kinds of religious forms that one would have encountered among Romaine's congregation increasingly merged with those found among "the great Vodou master" of Fonds-Parisien and earlier forms like that of the Arada/Kongo serpent cult. With independence about to dawn, Vodou was going through a process of Catholicization, which was itself largely a process of Kongoization and part of the process that Alfred Métraux (1972, 331) refers to as "a veritable seizure of Catholicism by Vodou." Given the centrality of the Virgin Mary in Kongolese Catholicism and in the Trou Coffy commune, these processes surely led to the growth in stature in Vodou of the Ezili lwa, the predominant female divinities in Haitian Vodou who are widely conflated with the

Virgin Mary. No Ezili, after all, is mentioned anywhere or even intimated in any primary source material on religion in Saint-Domingue (as far as I know), plausibly suggesting that the cult of Danbala predates the cult of Ezili in Dominguan/Haitian Vodou. In time, though, they would each become predominant spirits in Haitian Vodou.

CONCLUSION: TOWARD A PERIODIZATION OF COLONIAL VODOU IN THE CARIBBEAN

Although the word *Vodou* is clearly of West African, not Kongolese, origin (Hebblethwaite 2012, 299), it does not appear in print until the late eighteenth century, well more than one hundred years after the first enslaved Africans were brought to Saint-Domingue, at a moment in the colony's history when Kongolese slaves outnumbered West African slaves. It is interesting to observe that the word *zombie*—perhaps the most famous idea associated, however superficially or sensationally, with Haitian Vodou—appeared in print one hundred years before Moreau published *Description*. In the last decade of the seventeenth century, a French indentured servant and libertine named Pierre-Corneille Blessebois wrote the first novel in Caribbean history, *Le zonbi de Grand-Perrou*, in Guadeloupe. The erotic thriller does not shed much light on African religious practices in the Caribbean, as it focuses on French characters, but it is most noteworthy for bespeaking that the idea of the zombie already gripped people then and there.

When Blessebois arrived in Guadeloupe, somewhat earlier than Father Labat's initial landing in Martinique, the African population there was almost entirely West African, and thus Kongolese religious forms were yet to make much of an impact on Afro-Creole religion in the French Caribbean. Inventories of slave ships flying the French flag in the seventeenth century report that 29,042 African slaves had by then been transported to the colonies, with their regions of embarkation broken down as follows:

1. Senegambia   11,075   38%
2. Bight of Benin   9,033   31%
3. Bight of Biafra   3,607   13%
4. West Central Africa 3,070   11%
5. Gold Coast   1,106   4%
6. Sierra Leone   406   1%[19]

It is thus unsurprising that Labat's observations about Africana religion in the colonial Caribbean are entirely about West African religious forms, whereas

Central Africans are only mentioned in passing throughout his six-volume magnum opus. By the second half of the eighteenth century, things would change dramatically, however, with Central African slaves rapidly becoming the majority, especially in Saint-Domingue, where Moreau then observed "the Vaudoux sect" and heard chanting in a Kongolese dialect among initiates in a putatively West African serpent cult, one centering on divination.

The first French slave ship left Africa for the Caribbean in 1669, and more than four thousand horrific journeys under *le tricolore* would follow, until 1864 (Geggus 2001, 119).[20] By the mid-eighteenth century, the focus of the French slave trade had shifted to Central Africa, which would have a marked influence on the early development of Haitian Vodou. The evidence about Africana religion in the texts under consideration in this chapter reflects as much, suggesting a general periodization of Vodou genesis: From 1669 until 1750, a West African, especially an Arada, baseline was established. This included such ritual forms as divination, rainmaking, amulets, healing, drumming and dance, ancestor veneration, and spirit possession, with the cult of Danbala likely predominating in certain "voodoo cells," like those connected to the serpent ritual in West Africa described by Labat in the early eighteenth century. Later that century, by the time that Moreau described a strikingly similar ceremony in Saint-Domingue, French slave trading efforts had largely shifted from West Africa to Central Africa. It is thus to be expected that Kongolese religious forms, like the famous chant that the vaudoux sectarians sang, were grafted onto the West African religious baseline in the genesis of Haitian Vodou. The French slave trade also intensified in the 1750s and the ensuing decades up until the Haitian Revolution, with the peak year for its entire history being 1790, when over forty thousand enslaved Africans, most of them Kongolese, were forcibly brought in chains to Saint-Domingue. The resultant Kongoization of Haitian Vodou is the key feature of the second period of Vodou genesis, with Central African divinities like the *simbi* populating local waterways and with Catholic saints accompanying Central Africans in their encounters with French Catholicism and with West African "traditional" religion. Thus, following the *Arada baseline* period of 1669 to 1750, the second historical period of Vodou genesis was that of *Kongoization*, from 1750 to 1791. The rise of Romaine-la-Prophétesse as a religious leader at the end of this second period illuminates how the Kongoization of Vodou entailed considerable Catholicization.

Though beyond the scope of this chapter, it is worth suggesting, by way of conclusion, that a subsequent period of Vodouist history should be that of *revolution*, from 1791 to 1804, when African slaves, Creole slaves, and free coloreds turned to religion to empower them in their struggle against oppression. In addition to featuring the largely legendary 1791 ceremony led by Boukman Dutty at Bois Caïman, paradoxically this period also witnessed, especially in 1795, the persecution of Vodouists at the hands of Jean-Jacques Dessalines, who would ten years later become the first ruler of independent Haiti. This likely meant the end of the likes of Romaine-la-Prophétesse and the great Vodou master of Fonds-Parisien (Rey 2017, 218–219). But, by then, the "Voodoo cells" over which they presided had already been cemented as cornerstones for Haiti's remarkable religious culture, underscoring the key role that charismatic religious leaders played in preserving African religious forms in Saint-Domingue, as they continue to play in Haiti today.

NOTES

1. Observations about similar developments in colonial Brazil have been quite effectively articulated by Luis Nicolau Parés (2013) in his work on the early history of Candomblé, a sibling religion to Haitian Vodou.

2. For further glimpses of Haitian Vodou's adaptability and resilience, see the chapters in this volume by Nixon Cleophat, Alissa Jordan, Elizabeth McAlister, and Karen Richman.

3. More than three-fourths of all slaves imported by the French into the Caribbean up until the Haitian Revolution (nearly 1.2 million) arrived during the four decades prior to 1791. On the ethnicity of slaves imported to various regions of the Americas, see especially the remarkable database produced by a team of scholars under the direction of David Eltis (Trans-Atlantic Slave Trade—Database n.d.).

4. The "sack" to which Labat refers here is clearly a colonial-era version of what is called in Vodou today a *pakèt* (lit., "packet"). On this form of ritual paraphernalia, see Hebblethwaite 2012, 277; Thompson 1984, 125–127; and Pressley-Sanon 2017, 54–86.

5. Though these four case studies in the French colonial Caribbean concern male sorcerers, Labat does discuss another case at sea that implicated several women who had caused a slave ship to stall, forcing its return to Gorée Island and winning for them freedom.

6. According to a Dominican priest who preceded Labat in the Caribbean, Jean-Baptiste Du Tertre (1667, 528), West African slaves also took keen interest in the Catholic sacrament of baptism: "Their greatest rejoicing occurs upon the baptism of their children, on which occasions they invite all of the Blacks from their respective homelands, as well as those on their plantations, and they sell everything they own in order to have alcohol to solemnize their births." Du

Tertre served as a missionary in the Antilles, primarily in Guadeloupe, from 1640 to 1658.

7. On contemporary funerary rites in Haitian Vodou, see the chapter by McAlister in this volume. More generally, on manje rituals in Haiti, see Hebblethwaite 2012, 262–263.

8. Collection Moreau de Saint-Méry, Archives Nationales de France, Section Outre-Mer, COL F/3.

9. For figures, see the conclusion to this chapter.

10. I owe my awareness of these sources and scholarly lineages to Pettinger (2012). Maureen Warner-Lewis (2018, 325) offers an alternative interpretation of this term from the Anglophone and the Danish and Dutch colonial Caribbean, where the word identified "an African in a supervisory position," one who negotiated with Europeans in the sale of slaves.

11. It is also possible that in West Africa "devotees of the snake, Dangbe, have drawn the inordinate attention of European observers since the seventeenth century," as James Sweet (2011, 17) suggests. Such an obsession likely carried over into the Americas, meaning that other forms of African religion may well have been more prevalent in Saint-Domingue and elsewhere, but they were simply not as captivating to people like Labat and Moreau.

12. For a fuller treatment of Baudry's biography and literary effort, see Sweet 2017; on his military career, see Depréaux 1924. For further insight into the form of Kikongo used in the dictionary and its origins, see Mobley 2015.

13. On this term, see Hebblethwaite 2012, 237.

14. Rapport fait a l'assemblee coloniale le 14 fev 1792, signé J. P. M. Bloüet, Curé de Jacmel D. S., Archives Nationales de France, DXXV 61 615.

15. Diversity in the religion today is clearly reflected in all of the other excellent chapters on Haitian Vodou in this volume.

16. One other contemporary observer, meanwhile, the Léogâne native Bonnet (1864, 12), did recall that Romaine-la-Prophétesse combined "religious ideas with superstitions from Africa," though unfortunately providing no details on what these "superstitions" might have looked, sounded, felt, or smelled like.

17. Lettre de M. Abbé Ouvière aux membres réunis les commissaires de la paroisse et de l'armée combinée de l'Ouest séante à la Croix de bouquets, Léogâne, 29 decembre 1792, Archives Nationales de France, DXXV 110 868.

18. It is worth adding here that the two men conversed in Spanish during the short time they spent together, although their written correspondence was in French (Rey 2017, 145). Romaine-la-Prophétesse was illiterate, meanwhile; thus, his letters were surely dictated to a scribe.

19. See Pritchard, Eltis, and Richardson 2008, 222.

20. It should be noted that not all these ships were destined for the Caribbean, as some sailed instead to Indian Ocean ports, as Geggus (2001) informs here.

REFERENCES

Baudry des Lozières, Louis Narcisse. 1802. *Second Voyage à la Louisiane.* Paris: Charles.

Bonnet, Edmond. 1864. *Souvenirs historiques de Guy-Joseph Bonnet, Premier partie.* Paris: Durand.

Cuvelier, Jean. 1947. *Ancien royaume du Congo.* Bruges: Desclée de Brouwer.

Dépréaux, Albert. 1924. "Le commandant Baudry des Lozières et la Phalange de Crête Dragons (Saint-Domingue, 1789–1792)." *Revue de l'histoire des colonies françaises* 17:1–42.

Durkheim, Émile. 1912. *Les Formes élémentaires de la vie religieuse: Le système totémique en Australie.* Paris: Alcan.

Du Tertre, Jean-Baptiste. 1667. *Histoire générale des Antilles habitées par les français, Tome II.* Paris: Thomas Ilolly.

Geggus, David. 2001. "The French Slave Trade: An Overview." *William and Mary Quarterly* 58 (1): 119–138.

Hebblethwaite, Benjamin. 2012. *Vodou Songs in Haitian Creole and English.* Philadelphia: Temple University Press.

Labat, Jean-Baptiste. 1742a. *Nouveau voyage aux îles de l'Amérique, Tome I.* Paris: Delespine.

———. 1742b. *Nouveau voyage aux îles de l'Amérique, Tome IV.* Paris: Delespine.

Laguerre, Michel. 1989. *Voodoo and Politics in Haiti.* New York: St. Martin's.

Malenfant, Colonel. 1814. *Des colonies et particulairèment de celle de Saint-Domingue.* Paris: Audibert.

Martínez-Ruiz, Bárbaro. 2013. *Kongo Graphic Writing and Other Narratives of the Sign.* Philadelphia: Temple University Press.

Métraux, Alfred. (1959) 1972. *Voodoo in Haiti.* Translated by Hugo Charteris. New York: Schocken Books.

Mobley, Christina Frances. 2015. "The Kongolese Atlantic: Central African Slavery and Culture from Mayombe to Haiti." PhD diss., Duke University.

Moreau de Saint-Méry, Médéric Louis Elie. (1797–1798) 1958. *Description topographique, physique, civile, politique, et historique de la partie française de l'isle Saint-Domingue, Tome Premier.* Paris: Société de l'Histoire des Colonies Françaises.

Ortiz, Fernando. (1934) 1975. *De la Música Afrocubana: Un Estímulo para su estudio.* Madrid: Ediciones Júcar.

Parés, Luis Nicolau. (2006) 2013. *The Formation of Candomblé: Vodun History and Ritual in Brazil.* Translated by Richard Vernon. Chapel Hill: University of North Carolina Press.

Pascalis, Felix. "Anecdote historique." New York, 1821. New York Academy of Medicine, MS Folio Pascails Ouviere, 1819–1823.

Pettinger, Alasdair. 2012. "'Eh! Eh! Bomba, Hen! Hen!': Making Sense of a Vodou Chant." In *Obeah and Other Powers: The Politics of Caribbean Religion and Healing*, edited by Diana Paton and Maarit Forde, 80–102. Durham, NC: Duke University Press.

Pressley-Sanon, Susan. 2017. *Istwa across the Waters: Haitian History, Memory, and Cultural Imagination*. Gainesville: University Press of Florida.

Pritchard, James, David Eltis, and David Richardson. 2008. "The Significance of the French Slave Trade to the Evolution of the French Atlantic World before 1760." In *Extending the Frontier: Essays on the New Transatlantic Slave Trade Database*, edited by David Eltis and David Richardson, 205–227. New Haven, CT: Yale University Press.

Rey, Terry. 2017. *The Priest and the Prophetess: Abbé Ouvière, Romaine Rivière, and the Revolutionary Atlantic World*. New York: Oxford University Press.

Sweet, James H. 2011. *Domingos Álvarez: African Healing and the Intellectual History of the Atlantic World*. Chapel Hill: University of North Carolina Press.

———. 2017. "New Perspectives on Kongo in Haiti." *The Americas* 74 (1): 83–97.

Thompson, Robert Farris. 1984. *Flash of the Spirit: African and Afro-American Art and Philosophy*. New York: Vintage.

Toczyski, Suzanne C. 2007. "Navigating the Sea of Alterity: Jean-Baptiste Labat's *Nouveau voyage aux îles*." *Papers on French Seventeenth Century Literature* 67:485–509.

Trans-Atlantic Slave Trade—Database. n.d. SlaveVoyages (website). Accessed March 13, 2018. https://www.slavevoyages.org/voyage/database.

Warner-Lewis, Maureen. 2018. "The African Diaspora and Language: Movement, Borrowing, and Return." In *Tracing Language Movement in Africa*, edited by Ericka A. Albaugh and Kathryn M. de Luna, 321–341. New York: Oxford University Press.

TERRY REY is Professor of Religion at Temple University. He is author of several books, including *Our Lady of Class Struggle: The Cult of the Virgin Mary in Haiti*; *The Priest and the Prophetess: Abbé Ouvière, Romaine Rivière, and the Revolutionary Atlantic World*; and coeditor of *Orisa Devotion as World Religion: The Globalization of Yoruba Religious Culture*.

TWO

UNIVERSALISM AND SYNCRETISM IN BENINESE VODÚN

Douglas J. Falen

"THE CRADLE OF VOODOO"

Aside from scholars of African religions, and other individuals with more than a mild curiosity for African-derived spiritual traditions, most Euro-Americans have only a vague sense of West African Vodún.[1] People are more likely to know something about its North American cousin "Voodoo," with which the West African religion is commonly conflated.[2] Thanks to Hollywood and other popular culture productions, the images that people come to know are almost universally negative depictions of Voodoo as a form of black magic. Western exotic curiosity about Voodoo may explain why tourist materials and online media about indigenous West African religion rarely fail to reference Vodún's relationship to related diasporic religions. Benin's government publicized the country as the "cradle of Vodún" in its push to attract tourists and diasporic practitioners for the 1993 UNESCO-sponsored Festival of Vodún Arts and Cultures (see Forte 2009; Landry 2011; Law 2004; Rush 2001).[3] Vodún remains a key feature of tourism marketing in Benin, and websites targeting Americans portray Benin as the source of Voodoo (e.g., Explore! n.d.; News24 2016; Wanderlust n.d.). This association is likely to color the vague ideas that people possess about the West African religion, resulting in Vodún being appreciated only as the parent of New World Voodoo and Vodou. Predictably, this reduces Vodún to an ancient and timeless tradition, an idea that is reinforced by amateur scholars, religious buffs, and online aficionados of the paranormal and occult, who essentialize Africanness and declare unproblematically that the religion is at least six thousand years old (e.g., Ann n.d.; George 2009, 44; Painter n.d.).

It is true that Vodún likely arose in the Bight of Benin, in the forest belt of today's Ghana, Togo, Benin, and Nigeria. But as a rich body of scholarship suggests, there is little reason to think that the religion is a static, monolithic tradition that has remained intact over the centuries (Bay 2008; Falen 2016; Landry 2015; Norman 2009; Rush 2013; Tall 1995). I join these scholars in challenging popular culture's facile and one-dimensional image of West African religion. Vodún is anything but timeless, unchanging, and ancient; it is instead a flexible, dynamic, and contemporary manifestation of both local and global spiritual elements. Although the general point about the continual reworking of religion is well established in anthropology, this chapter argues that contemporary syncretism involving Beninese Vodún is notable for the way that it reflects a universalizing philosophy that blends the domains of "religion" and "the occult." Beninese Vodún survives in part through its articulation with foreign spiritualities and local ideas about "witchcraft" (àzĕ in the Fon language, called Fongbe). That is, Vodún and other spiritual traditions are syncretically absorbed into the category of àzĕ, fusing both local and foreign religions with the occult. This is because, for many people, the spiritual power that animates Vodún and imported spiritualities is àzĕ itself. Through an exotic gaze on the power of the Other, Beninese have created a supercategory of "witchcraft" that draws up the domains of magic, Vodún, Christianity, and foreign esoteric traditions like Hinduism, Freemasonry, and Chinese healing (Falen 2018). In this process, syncretism defies a simplistic model of acculturation that would result from the hegemony of colonization and globalization. Instead, Vodún's contemporary manifestations show that Beninese people today, as in the past, are intentionally seeking out exotic foreign spiritual traditions.

Although Vodún is an omnipresent cultural feature of southern Benin, I did not initially set out to study it. In 2006, I was investigating Christian marriage and polygyny (Falen 2008), but in the course of my discussions about different religions, I quickly came to understand that the primary reason for joining a Christian church or for participating in Vodún rituals was for spiritual protection against what Fongbe speakers call àzĕ (witchcraft) and bŏ (sorcery).[4] This led to a prolonged research project focusing on the significance and understandings of occult forces in the lives of Beninese people, revealing the ways that syncretism has blended ideas about witchcraft, Vodún, and Christianity (Falen 2018). This chapter draws on that ethnographic fieldwork spanning more than a decade, primarily in the Fon ethnic group's heartland of Abomey and Bohicon, but I also conducted research in Ouidah and the metropolitan center of Cotonou. The material I present derives from five field seasons between

2006 and 2017, including numerous interviews with pastors, Vodún priests, traditional healers, and ordinary women and men practicing various religions. During my research on occult ideas and practices, I grew to appreciate the ways that Vodún, Christianity, and the occult overlapped and interconnected and the role that exoticism regarding alterity—that is, otherness—plays in the religious outlook of the people with whom I interacted. This analysis is an attempt to capture the dynamic qualities of both historical and contemporary religion in southern Benin. I will show how the blending of elements from multiple cultures, commonly called syncretism, is driven largely by local people's belief that all religious and supernatural entities and forces collapse into a single universal power, known as àzĕ.

VODÚN'S RECEPTIVITY TO FOREIGN GODS

In August 2017, my Beninese friend Gaston drove me on the back of his motorcycle along the dusty four-mile road joining the regional capital of Abomey to the village of Mougnon.[5] We were attending a reception at a funeral ceremony held for the mother-in-law of our mutual friend Joël. I did not know the deceased, but I had first met Joël's family nearly twenty years before, and over time, I had become friendly with Joël and his elderly father, Paul, who was the head priest in the Kutito (ghost masquerade) society.[6] On this occasion, the old man was quite sick and was suffering from a fall and swollen legs that prevented him from walking. I assumed Paul was over eighty years old, but Gaston reconstructed his age through stories from his father and by comparison to other elderly people who said Paul was much older than they were. The verdict was that Paul must be at least one hundred. Whatever his age, he was extremely frail and was also starting to lose his mental faculties. On previous visits over the years, I would sit with Paul and drink *sodabì* (palm liquor) while talking about the recent ceremonies in which he called down the Kutito ghosts to perform their vigorous and menacing masquerade dance. But Paul's condition prevented him from anything more than a brief greeting, so we sat outside Joël's house and chatted with his other guests. The women in the family served us plates of corn *wo* with chicken and spicy sauce, accompanied by Coke, beer, and sod.abì. I made a customary financial gift to help Joël, though Gaston had secretly bankrolled a significant portion of the ceremonial expenses, since Joël was a poor farmer with little more than an occasional Kutito ceremony or ritual service to put some extra cash into his pocket.

As Gaston and I enjoyed our food and drink, a young man named Fidèle greeted us and sat down on a chair to our left. Gaston, a middle school social

Figure 2.1. Paul seated at home in front of a mural depicting him. Photograph by the author.

studies teacher, recognized Fidèle as one of his former students. In the few years since Gaston had lost contact with the young man, Fidèle had become a bokɔ́nɔ̀ (diviner). Gaston was always looking to generate conversations that might help me in my research, and he suggested that we take the opportunity of meeting Fidèle to conduct an impromptu interview with the diviner. During this field season, I had come to Benin to investigate the rise of a new Christian religious movement led by a young woman named Parfaite, who split from the Catholic church amid her claims that she was the incarnation of God, sent to earth to rid the world of witchcraft and "false religions," including Vodún.[7] Parfaite had gained prominence not only for claiming to be God but for her pointed criticism and provocation of Vodún religious leaders, culminating in a violent clash between her followers and residents of Abomey in January 2017. This clash struck me as an unusual occurrence in a country known for tolerance and religious pluralism. I asked Fidèle what he thought about Parfaite and her movement and how a bokɔ́nɔ̀ like him reacted to her teachings.

Figure 2.2. A mural on the wall of Paul's house, depicting the Kutito spirits. Photo by the author.

At this funeral ceremony among rural mud-walled homes where the old patriarch was a respected leader in the Vodún religion, the setting might inspire one to regard this as a cliché scene of "traditional" Africa. Consistent with this view, I expected Fidèle, a Vodún practitioner, to condemn Parfaite's movement and her attacks on his religion. In previous discussions, Gaston and a few other intellectuals who practiced Vodún had rejected Parfaite's religion, and they sometimes referred to Christianity as a foreign religion brought by Europeans. Since Fidèle was an official representative of Vodún, I imagined he would also consider Parfaite to be a threat to his heritage and religious identity. Instead, he said that he does not recognize a sharp divide between religions and does not feel threatened by Parfaite. He confided that many Christians visit bokɔ́nɔ̌ for spiritual insight and to gain control over their lives. He admitted that Parfaite is arrogant, but he did not judge her religion as good or bad, and he held no grudge against her. He went on to say that all religions work together toward common goals.

In hindsight, I realize that his answer should not have surprised me. Notwithstanding the antagonism between Parfaite and her detractors, and a few intellectual voices like Gaston's, objecting to Christianity's social and political dominance, Fidèle's comments illustrate the widespread tolerance, overlap, and fluidity that characterize Vodún spirituality and the general religious philosophy in Benin. In fact, during an interview in Abomey that morning, a pastor in the Celestial Church of Christ told me that his church's visionaries are available to people of all faiths, and he emphasized that this is consistent with the way bokɔ́nɔ̌ are a source of knowledge for people of any religion. A few days earlier, a xunɔ̌ (Vodún priest of the deity Tron) told me that Tron celebrates Christmas. These examples highlight Vodún's constant state of flux and fusion, allowing its practitioners to accept the legitimacy of Christianity and other foreign religions without necessarily abandoning Vodún. I argue that this spiritual philosophy of inclusion and universalism accounts for the historical and contemporary religious syncretism and dynamism in Benin. The fact that Fidèle's receptiveness to multiple religions is neither unusual nor especially new undermines Western folk notions of a presumed "traditional" or "ancient" Vodún religion. What is novel is that global commerce, travel, and communication have accelerated, making far-flung and previously unknown spiritual ideas available to Beninese people. Moreover, foreign spiritual beliefs are finding their way into the local category of witchcraft (àzě).

As I show in this chapter, this phenomenon raises important theoretical questions about the process of syncretism and the degree to which the incorporation of foreign spirituality into local practices is a sign of cultural imperialism from abroad or of local agency from within. In Benin, I contend that these borrowings are not merely examples of assimilation, a wholesale adoption of foreign religious beliefs, but in keeping with the blending process of syncretism, it is a piecemeal and opportunistic sampling of foreign ideas (see Peel 2016). It is now axiomatic in anthropology that religions, including "indigenous" religions, are the result of the blending and reinterpretation of different cultural elements, and among West African religions, syncretism has probably always been the norm (Peel 2016). Beninese Vodún is an outstanding example of syncretism, as it adapted to new religious and social conditions, often through the accumulation of whatever foreign and local powers were deemed useful. Syncretism could be termed "creolization" or "hybridization," but Natacha Giafferi-Dombre's (this volume) use of "assemblage" or "bricolage" captures the agency implicit in the idea of a tradition built from different components.

Although the capitalized form *Vodún* has become the academic term for the indigenous religion, the word *vodún* simply means "deity" or "spirit" in Fongbe and several related languages. Perhaps the first recorded mention of the term *vodún* was in the 1658 Spanish missionaries' translation of the *Doctrina Christiana* into the language of Allada (Labouret and Rivet 1929; Law 1991; Yai 1993, 2013). Although we cannot be sure what Vodún was like prior to European contact or how long the term has existed, the archaeological and historical records confirm that religion in this part of West Africa has been dynamic for a long time. This dynamic quality is evidenced by Neil Norman's (2009) archaeological analysis of shrines in Savi, dating from the seventeenth and eighteenth centuries. His excavations reveal the cosmopolitan character of Savi's religious life, which included ritual offerings comprising foreign trade items, such as beads, gin bottles, and pipes. Although the general purpose of offerings—to bring health, wealth, and protection—probably has not changed significantly, the exposure to new political and economic relationships that accompanied contact with Europeans and other ethnic groups during the seventeenth and eighteenth centuries must have had a profound impact on all aspects of people's lives, including Vodún.

In precolonial times, there was rich cultural mixing among neighboring West African peoples as they traded, waged war, and migrated across ethnic, geographic, and political boundaries. During his visit to Ouidah at the end of the seventeenth century, the Dutch trader Willem Bosman (1705, 369) referred to a "new batch of gods." It is not clear who these gods were or where they were from, but his comment alludes to a Vodún religion that was already acquiring foreign deities in the seventeenth century. Burton (1864) likewise refers to the deities of Dangbwe (serpent spirit), Loko (tree god), and Hu (god of the sea) as having spread from Ouidah into the rest of Dahomey. In the precolonial kingdoms of Dahomey and Ouidah, some of the early deities probably included the royal ancestor cult of Nesuxwe and Dan the snake god,[8] but peoples subsequently borrowed many gods from the Ewe and Aja peoples to the west and the Yoruba to the east. Fon people's oral history tells of many Vodún deities, including Mawu the creator, Sakpata the earth god, the Kutito ghost cult, and even the Fá divination system, being imported from neighboring peoples. Fá divination was introduced from the Yoruba in the early eighteenth century, under the reign of Dahomey's King Agaja (Bay 1998, 94; Bertho 1951; Herskovits and Herskovits 1933; Maupoil 1943).[9] It is illustrative of Vodún's incorporative potential that a practice so central to the religion today was a transplant. Legends talk of King Tegbesu's mother, Hwanjile, who, in the middle of the eighteenth century, brought the divine male-female couple of Mawu and Lisá to Dahomey from the Aja region (Bay 1998, 92; Herskovits [1938] 1967, vol. 2; Le Herissé 1911; Maupoil 1943).[10] The introduction of these two deities was so successful that they came to reside at the top of the entire Vodún pantheon as the creators of the world and the parents of the lesser deities. Other gods that originated with neighboring groups include Gu, the god of war and iron; Legba, the trickster messenger spirit; and Hevioso, the god of thunder (Bay 1998, 22).[11] Divinities were easily transported by immigrants, but the king of Dahomey also invited war captives to install their gods on Dahomean soil in order to appropriate their power, and in some cases, Dahomey sent people to live among neighboring groups to become priests of their deities (Bay 1998, 22; Sweet 2011, 19). The Kutito ancestor masquerade cult came to Dahomey from the Yoruba as recently as the nineteenth or early twentieth century (Bay 1998, 24; Herskovits [1938] 1967, vol. 1; Noret 2008), but like so many of these religious imports, it is now fully indigenized. Nevertheless, in the case of Sakpata and Kutito, the spirits' foreign origins have been retained through the initiates' use of Yoruba (Nago) as the sacred language. As part of initiates' training, they learn Yoruba to serve as interpreters between spirits and audience members during possession ceremonies. In fact, initiates of Sakpata are addressed by the title Anagonu, meaning a Nago (Yoruba) person.

Despite frequent cultural borrowings, the adoption of foreign deities should not be regarded as automatic, particularly when deities threatened local political authority. For example, Dahomey's monarchy initially perceived the Kutito ancestor society as a threat to their own royal divinities (Herskovits [1938] 1967, 1:245; Noret 2010). Likewise, Sakpata the god of the earth and smallpox spread into Dahomey from the north, but Dahomey's rulers were at first wary about this foreign god and the competition from its increasingly powerful priests (Sweet 2011, 20). The rulers reluctantly accepted the deity because of its popularity and in an effort to co-opt its power and to control smallpox (Falen 2016; Herskovits [1938] 1967; Sweet 2011, 20; Verger 1954).[12] Therefore, despite some royal sponsorship of deities, as in the case of Mawu and Lisá, and in the example of inviting the spirits of foreign war captives, deities spread through the grassroots efforts of ordinary people to seek control of their lives and solutions to their problems. Vodún, like other African religions, did not necessarily exhibit a top-down orthodoxy given by priests but rather has always been a more democratic religion that allows individuals to interpret deities and supernatural events (see Thornton 1998). This suggests that, rather than a purely hegemonic religious order, Vodún contained an element of individual agency in the choice of deities to worship. Agency is indicated by the testimony provided early on to Bosman (1705, 367–368) by a man in Ouidah who explained that divinities were constantly being invented and discarded by individuals, depending on their effectiveness. Although this resident of Ouidah was apparently a Christian convert who could have been attempting to undermine the legitimacy of Vodún in the eyes of a European, his assessment is consistent with Karin Barber's (1981) claim that Yoruba people are conscious of the "made" quality of their gods. She argues that people are cognizant of their right to worship or abandon their deities depending on their success in satisfying people's needs. Among Fongbe-speakers, there is a long tradition of "purchasing" gods from other priests (Le Herissé 1911, 102), and the practice continues today, with religious leaders regularly installing new shrines for deities that they commission from other Vodún priests.

Receptiveness to foreign gods is an abiding characteristic of the spiritual worldview in West Africa (see Mercier 1954). Edna Bay (1998, 24) notes that precolonial Dahomey had a marked openness to foreign ideas in many domains: "Eclecticism and pragmatism were characteristic of Dahomean approaches to religion. They also characterized Dahomean attitudes to other cultures. Dahomean leaders eagerly looked to friends as well as enemies for innovations that they considered efficacious or simply interesting; not only new gods, but technology, dress, art forms, foods, offices, and titles were tried, adopted, and sometimes discarded."

Emmanuelle Tall (1995, 818) writes, "One of the constants in the history of African religions is their foreign origins," and Dana Rush (2013, 12) argues that Vodún is "unfinished," in a constant state of creation and flux by incorporating new "peoples, spirits, histories, ideas, and faiths." These observers all point to a tolerance and receptiveness with respect to foreign beliefs that I witnessed in my discussion with Fidèle and on numerous other occasions. Over the past ten years, my fieldwork with priests, healers, and laypeople revealed that the exotic origin of religions and their deities is an appealing feature rather than a source of fear. People sometimes distinguished between the ancient, inherited family deities, such as Gu, Sakpata, Legba, Dan, and Kutito (even though they were originally imports), and those deities that arrived more recently. Some gods are acknowledged as new, imported, or having foreign associations. For example, Mami Wata, the female spirit of water and beauty, is well established in Benin but is still regarded as a relatively recent addition to the religious landscape. Scholars demonstrate that Mami Wata is a syncretistic fusion of African snake and water spirits with European mermaids, whom local people saw on the prows of trading vessels (Drewal 1988, 2008a, 2008b, 2008c; Rush 2008, 2013). She was further syncretized with the image of a Hindu "snake charmer" that circulated in Africa at the end of the nineteenth century; even today, shrines are decorated with paintings of mermaids, the snake charmer, and other Hindu iconography (Drewal 1988; Falen 2016; Rush 2008, 2013).[13] As a sign of Mami Wata's connection to foreign wealth and luxury, adepts decorate themselves

Figure 2.3. A Mami Wata devotee stands in her shrine. Photograph by the author.

with extravagant makeup, hairstyles, and jewelry. Some informants claim an equivalence between Mami Wata and the snake spirit Dan, who also brings wealth and success to adherents (see Montgomery, this volume).

The newest vodún on the scene include the antiwitchcraft deities Atingale and Tron, which spread from Ghana throughout West Africa in the midtwentieth century (Apter 1993; Bay 2008; Montgomery and Vannier 2017; Rosenthal 1998; Tall 1995). These deities are significant for their ability to identify and combat witches, making them popular spiritual weapons during a time of rampant fear of witchcraft. Atingale (Atchigale, Tingare, etc.) is not as widespread in Benin today, but a number of related deities like Kunde, Banguele, and Gambada have coalesced into the Tron pantheon. People say this collection of gods comes from the Muslim regions of northern Ghana, and Tron's symbolic associations bear many connections to Islam, such as white clothes and taboos on the consumption of pork. Tron and the related spirits are all classified as *gorovodún* (kola nut vodún), because the ritual kola nut is cultivated in the Muslim Sahel of northern Ghana, from which the spirits hail.[14] The fact that informants explicitly identify Tron's origins in the foreign religion of Islam and in foreign countries renders this a quintessential and overt example of both exoticism and syncretism. As Christian Vannier (this volume) notes, there is a romantic fascination with the Muslim north that permeates Tron's identity. Furthermore, Tron demonstrates the eclectic way that Vodún incorporates and articulates with foreign religious traditions through an inclusive, universalist principle. As Bay (2008) reports, Tron expects adherents to follow the rules of Christianity, Islam, and the older vodún, in addition to employing Hindu imagery. Such historical trajectories and local developments demonstrate that Vodún is far from monolithic or static, either across space or through time. The Vodún religion, even if it existed six thousand years ago, was surely an entirely different religion. Ironically, the one thing that might have been preserved over time is the religion's malleable, heterogeneous, and receptive nature. But new vodún are not the only foreign influences that are a part of religious syncretism in Benin. Christianity and foreign esoteric traditions are also popular for their role in combatting witchcraft, but as I describe in the final section, they inevitably merge with the occult.

SYNCRETISM OF CHRISTIANITY AND VODÚN IN BENIN

The introduction of Christianity was a profound event for this region of West Africa, though it was a long time in the making. The first Christian mission in what was known as the Slave Coast (present-day Benin) was established by Spanish Capuchins, who translated a catechism text, the *Doctrina Christiana*, into a local language in 1658 (Labouret and Rivet 1929).[15] The translation bears witness to an early example of syncretism between Vodún and Christianity. In the text, Jesus was equated with the vodún named Lisá. The Capuchin mission failed, due to the missionaries' illness and their eventual expulsion by local rulers, who uncharacteristically must have found little value in the foreign religion at that time (Labouret and Rivet 1929). Perhaps Europeans were still too unfamiliar to Africans, and their god's powers were unknown, making local people indifferent to Christianity. It was not until the mid-nineteenth century that Europeans established their first permanent missions in Dahomey, beginning with Ouidah's Catholic mission in 1861 (Alladaye 2003; Clement 1996; François 1906; Henry 2008b).

Throughout Africa, European missionaries condemned traditional religion as Satanic, and generations of devout Christians after them have maintained this negative appraisal (Claffey 2007; Rousse-Grosseau 1992, 237–238). John Thornton (1998) suggests that Europeans acknowledged some African supernatural experiences as a kind of "revelation," a means of communicating with supernatural entities, but to claim the upper hand in their religious contests, missionaries labeled most African revelations as the work of the devil, as compared to biblical revelations as acts of God. In Dahomey, missionaries translated the deity Legba as Satan, a moniker that people still use today (see Ekoué and Rosenthal 2015).[16] These missionary critiques were fueled by European travelers who decried Dahomey's annual royal "customs," consisting of human sacrifices to the ancestors (Burton 1864; Forbes 1851; Skertchly 1874). Eighteenth- and nineteenth-century travelers also judged the indigenous religion as disgusting and inferior to Christianity (Dalzel 1793; Duncan 1847; Forbes 1851; M'Leod 1820; Snelgrave 1971). Despite travelers' and missionaries' attacks on Vodún, the reception of Christianity in the nineteenth century was noticeably better than in the seventeenth century. Christianity's appeal may have been facilitated by African returnees from Brazil who claimed membership in the Catholic church, though mainly for pragmatic reasons, since Christianity afforded them a higher status than Vodún (Yai 2001, 76). Predictably, accounts of the time portrayed the returnees' religious practices as mixtures of Christianity and Vodún.[17] The foreign religion's social capital inaugurated an enduring trend whereby Christianity, and especially Catholicism, provided people with prestige and a claim to modernity (de Surgy 2001; Henry 2001; Mayrargue 2001, 2003; Sargent 1989; Strandsbjerg 2005; Tall 1995, 2005). Under French rule following the 1894 conquest, the Catholics were responsible for introducing education, and a Catholic upbringing became a path to employment in the colonial administration (Claffey 2007). Today Christians often possess a mentality of superiority over practitioners of Vodún, which they disparage as backward and Satanic.

Given the condemnation of Vodún by missionaries and their converts, it is telling that non-Christians like Fidèle do not necessarily perceive Christianity as a threat. This is not to say there is no ideological conflict between Vodún and Christianity, but when it occurs, it tends to serve as an exception to prove the rule. For example, at a funeral I attended in 2006 for Gaston's father, a high-ranking member of Abomey's royal family, a debate arose among family members over the religious nature of the ceremony. Catholic family members insisted that the deceased be honored in a Christian ceremony, since he had converted shortly before his death. Among the deceased's twenty children, some like Gaston followed Vodún and felt that their father had spent his life dedicated to their traditional deities, arguing that he deserved a Vodún ceremony. Gaston was unusually militant in expressing disgust that people would forsake their traditions and religious heritage for an imported religion. For their part, Christian family members were incensed that people would violate

Christian principles by holding a Vodún ceremony. In the end, and in keeping with the pragmatic and cumulative approach that has long characterized West African religious culture, the opposing family members compromised, holding a Catholic mass, followed by traditional sacrifices, drumming, and dancing.

Although some Vodún adherents like Gaston resent and resist Christianity, I maintain that the supposed battle between the religions is largely one-sided. Those Vodún practitioners who oppose Christianity are generally reacting to a hundred years of Christian attacks. Their response is a necessary attempt to protect Vodún rather than an outright rejection of Christianity. This means that those Christians who revile Vodún and its practitioners may be speaking into a void when it comes to Vodún. In reality, the attacks on Vodún are not directed at Vodún practitioners as much as they are a way for Christian denominations to compete with one another for converts and for the honor of being the most "authentic" form of Christianity. As Christine Henry (2008a) points out, people change religions easily and often, so the number of people in Christian congregations is never assured (see also Barnes 1997, 11). In addition, the critiques of Vodún reflect a concern among church leaders that converts are insincere backsliders and that they secretly maintain a foothold in Vodún. Such individuals are characterized as hypocrites and are accused of practicing syncretism. The French word *syncrétisme* is used as a negative label in Christian congregations because it implies contamination and impurity. The perception that converts dabble in Vodún is justified in many cases, as I know Christians who continue to perform the annual ancestral offerings and who visit diviners and traditional healers. This is acknowledged in a popular expression in Benin that states that people practice Christianity by day but Vodún by night.

In keeping with the additive religious philosophy, many Beninese feel that adhering exclusively to one religion does not satisfy all of one's spiritual needs, particularly when faced with the dangers of witchcraft. As one Beninese quoted by Michel Croce-Spinelli (1982, 37) stated, "I prefer to be Christian because that seems clearer to me. I remain a fetishist out of fear." Despite churches' official stances, such people see no contradiction in their behavior. A Catholic school principal offered me the following Fon adage to explain how Christians think of their reliance on Vodún practices: "Mi na kpà gláglá nu Aklúnɔ́ de" (We'll lend the Lord a hand). One respondent in Abomey told me that he knew a Catholic woman who approached the spirit Legba asking for his assistance in passing her catechism exam. After succeeding, the woman gratefully provided offerings to Legba. Catholic priests and other Christian pastors are accused of hypocrisy, as many are suspected of secretly consulting diviners, possessing Vodún paraphernalia, or initiating in Vodún societies (Landry 2015). This evidence shows that Christians may occasionally hedge their bets and perform Vodún rituals, reinforcing the image of hybridity in their religious practices.

Despite the compromises and overlaps between Vodún and Christianity, missionaries and church leaders have been relatively successful in constructing a theological boundary between the two faiths. People alternately practice both religions, but despite accusations of syncretism, they generally do not conceive of them as fused into a single new religion. As noted, the first Spanish missionaries translated Jesus as the vodún Lisá, but this association was subsequently abandoned. Today the Christian God is known by the name of the Vodún god Mawu, but the Christian understanding of a supreme male creator has overtaken Mawu's original identity as the female half of a divine couple, and even Voduisants today refer to their creator God as Mawu, with Lisá remaining one among many other vodún (Claffey 2007). The result of the distinction between Christianity and Vodún is that Beninese Vodún does not usually contain the symbolic convergence found in Caribbean Vodou's one-to-one correspondence between African gods and Catholic saints. Therefore, rather than practicing a religion that blends elements from Vodún and Christianity, people typically perform rituals from both religions alternately at different times. This ideological separation promulgated by religious leaders, and the accusations of inauthenticity to which it gives rise, assumes an insurmountable divide between Christianity and Vodún. This may be a legacy of missionary debates over the presumed incompatibility between African culture and Christianity (Falen 2008). However, in recognizing this dilemma, the early twentieth-century Catholic missionary to Dahomey Francis Aupiais argued for the respect of local culture within Catholicism, an idea that has since been elaborated in the Mewi Hwendo (African custom) policy that incorporates local culture into Catholic liturgy (Adoukonou 1993; Bay 2008). But for evangelicals and many others, the two cultures should be kept apart, and this policy only fuels their claims of Catholicism's compromises with traditional religion.

HEGEMONY AND APPROPRIATION IN BENINESE SYNCRETISM

Benin's religious landscape sheds light on syncretism and on the theoretical questions about the role of power in the religious encounter between peoples. There are different ways that we might explain the process by which people adopt foreign religious elements. For example, syncretism like that found in Haitian Vodou resulted in part from the unequal power between peoples. In colonial Haiti, after passage of the 1685 Code Noir, African slaves were required to convert to Catholicism, and this coercive relationship may have shaped

Vodou's well-known merging of Catholic saints and African spirits (Desmangles 1992, 23; Murrell 2010, 62).[18] Despite similar laws throughout the New World, colonial planters varied in the level of religious indoctrination they gave to slaves, and the number of conversions to an exclusive Catholicism were limited (Peabody 2002; Raboteau 2004; Sweet 2011, 47). As Terry Rey (this volume) argues, during the early years of Saint Domingue (Haiti), slaves may have practiced a predominantly West African religion, without substantive mixing with European Catholicism. But even without forced conversion, at the least, power and subjugation played a role in introducing Africans to European religion and eventually helped shape the syncretism that came to characterize Vodou. While religious imposition was unknown in Benin, the legacy of missionaries and colonialism still shapes the meanings and manifestations of contemporary religion in such postcolonial settings. The workings of hegemony help explain how Christian missionaries, with the backing of colonial authorities, encouraged the conversion of colonized peoples, and the missionary views of African spirituality did influence the way Dahomean (Beninese) subjects viewed their religion. For example, I have already mentioned the hegemonic relationship by which Christian ideas of God and Satan crept into Beninese understandings of Mawu and Legba. Today, some devout Christians in Benin still parrot missionary discourse about the inherent evil in Vodún and animal sacrifice, often declaring that Vodún is diabolical black magic (see Landry 2015). This is evidence that the implantation of Christianity can be read as a product of unequal power relations.

On the other hand, religious contact can also reflect a more complicated set of cultural relations that challenge the simple equation of hegemony with the sociopolitical control of others. For example, in the emergence of Haitian Vodou, we can detect an element of agency in the blending of African spirits with Catholic saints. Vodou's syncretism has been described as a form of resistance insofar as the slaves disguised and maintained their gods behind a veneer of Catholic religion (Cosentino 2005; Desmangles 1992; Herskovits 1937). However, we can also perceive a more nuanced articulation of power and culture, such that Vodou was the result of a more cooperative rather than a confrontational fusion between the religions of slaves and masters. Andrew Apter (1991, 178) writes: "The Catholicism of Vodoun, Candomblé and Santeria was not an ecumenical screen, hiding the worship of African deities from official persecution. It was the religion of the masters, revised, transformed, and appropriated by slaves to harness its power within the universes of discourse."[19]

Similarly, Sue Peabody (2002) contends that slaves were attracted to Catholicism for the social respectability it provided, and Michel Laguerre (1977) claims that slaves interpreted Catholicism as a new type of European magic they could exploit. As noted for Benin, the acceptance of Catholicism could have taken place through an additive process rather than as a replacement of African religion. Thus, the enslaved or colonized group need not perceive the dominant group's religion as a threat. In that case, syncretism is not merely a product of subjugation or resistance to a superior power but rather an appreciation of the value of the other group's religion and a conscious strategy to co-opt it. Seen in this light, it is both a sign of the insidiousness of the dominant culture, as well as a sign of the subordinate group's agency in mimetically appropriating the Other (Taussig 1993).

West African syncretism can be compared to New Guinea cargo movements, which show signs of local agency in the face of hegemonic influence. In Papua New Guinea, despite the marked discrepancy between Europeans and natives in terms of power and wealth, scholars have found that formerly colonized people's appreciation of Christianity and Western consumer goods is not simply a form of self-hatred. Instead, local people use foreign products and religious symbols to comment on their lives and even to critique Westerners (Bashkow 2006; Kempf 1994). As Ira Bashkow (2006) explains, the Orokaiva people may adopt elements from the colonizer's culture, such as Christianity and Western trade goods, but people use these foreign elements to express indigenous morality about social harmony, jealousy, and sharing. Christianity and "whiteman foods" (145) can reflect both positive and negative qualities. Being a sincere Christian represents an ideal of spirituality and faith that can provide the Orokaiva access to the material wealth that is a blessing from the ancestors. Similarly, whitemen's foods like rice and tinned fish are valued for their exotic qualities, but they are also associated with white people's antisocial selfishness. Even though New Guineans may have had little say in white colonizers introducing their religion and goods, Bashkow argues that the enduring interest in these foreign elements should be explained by reference to the local meanings that people attribute to them.

Likewise, in Benin, the implantation of Christianity may lend itself to a reading of hegemony, but as I have shown, the discourses about Christianity reflect a range of views—positive, negative, and indifferent—rather than a blind acceptance of foreign religion. Discourses about Western science and technology also reveal ambivalent views of the West, such as nuclear technology that can be harnessed for both productive and destructive purposes (Falen 2018). Culture does not simply flow predictably along the lines of power. Less powerful people can initiate cultural borrowings and perhaps achieve a degree of ownership or control over the Other. In other cases, the dominant group may value the culture of subordinate peoples. For example, in Togolese Gorovodún, the spirits passed from subordinate to dominant groups rather than the other way around (Montgomery, this volume; Vannier, this volume). Southern Ewe people who historically enslaved northern ethnicities co-opted their former slaves' spirits because they admired them as different and powerful (Montgomery and Vannier 2017; Rosenthal 1998). This resembles the attitude of precolonial Fon monarchs who deliberately invited slaves captured from neighboring Yoruba regions to transport their deities to Dahomey in order to reinforce the kingdom's strength.

Recent transformations in Beninese Vodún illustrate how the process of cultural appropriation is driven from within rather than an imposition from without. Interviewees demonstrated a strong interest in acquiring new deities and new spiritual powers from abroad. Overwhelmingly, my informants value the power of the Other. Henry Drewal (1988, 160) has stated that, with respect to the spirit Mami Wata, Africans' exoticism inspired them to incorporate alien gods: "African peoples ... take exotic images and ideas, interpret them according to indigenous precepts, invest them with new meanings, and then re-create and re-present them in new and dynamic ways to serve their own aesthetic, devotional, and social needs."

This same exoticism has animated Beninese interest in foreign religions like Christianity and Tron. Today, and for similar reasons, new religious and spiritual ideas from distant lands are finding fertile ground in Benin and being incorporated into the local category of witchcraft. Beninese are exploiting the power of foreign traditions like Freemasonry, Rosicrucianism, Eckankar, Hinduism, and Chinese healing. As a result, the syncretistic blending of religions in Benin today is not merely a result of colonial or missionary imposition but rather is a sign of the conscious efforts to appropriate the spirituality of others in order to combat witchcraft. For many Beninese residents, religion is valued more for its utility than as an abstract expression of faith. As I have noted, inequality is apparent in the relationship between Africans and Europeans, so we cannot dismiss the role of power and hegemony in the spread of European religions and spirituality. However, it is significant that Asian spiritualities have no colonial or missionary history in Benin, and therefore we should acknowledge agency in people's quest for foreign ideas.

OCCULT UNIVERSALISM

A key feature of Beninese people's cultural appropriation is the fact that many of the foreign spiritual traditions taking root in Benin are interpreted as occult forces, particularly as foreign examples of witchcraft (Falen 2018).[20] Beninese people frequently told me that they were attracted to foreign religions, mystical traditions, and esoteric societies for their ability to provide spiritual power and protection similar to àzĕ. For example, informants told me that esoteric belief systems like Freemasonry, Rosicrucianism, and Eckankar are foreign forms of witchcraft (àzĕ).[21] I first learned about these secret societies when a friend in Abomey told me that he was involved in mail-order correspondence with a French organization that was inducting him into Rosicrucianism. At the time, he told me that he was interested in Rosicrucianism because it promised to provide him with the ability to concentrate and realize his desires, but I later discovered that people equate Rosicrucianism with àzĕ. This realization occurred when I informed an Abomey friend that I was interested in conducting research on àzĕ. He grew angry with me and argued that I should begin by studying witchcraft in my own country before attempting to understand other societies. I was confused, and after I made a few awkward and apparently irrelevant remarks about Wicca, he eventually blurted out that he was referring to Freemasonry, Rosicrucianism, and Eckankar.[22] Like the secret society of àzètɔ̃ (witches), these esoteric traditions require initiation and specialized training, after which one acquires a heightened consciousness and achieves worldly success. One Abomey member of Eckankar explained that in chanting their sacred word "hu," he fortified himself against witches in his family and achieved professional success. In the past, he said, money would practically fall through his hands, and he spent it without realizing where it went, but since joining the Eckankar society, his life had improved dramatically. The ability to generate and retain money is closely linked to supernatural powers, and witchcraft is one asset that people believe can ensure financial stability.[23] Many people compared Eckankar members' nocturnal meditative travels to the nighttime soul journeys that witches take to consume the souls of their victims. My friend denied that Eckankar was witchcraft, but he admitted that he understood why people would believe that.

Benin, like many African countries, has been experiencing an intensification of witchcraft fears and accusations (Ashforth 2005; Comaroff and Comaroff 1993; de Boeck 2000; 2005; Geschiere 1997; 2008; 2013; Henry 2008b; Smith 2008; West 2007). This "spiritual insecurity," as Adam Ashforth (2005) calls it, is rooted in witchcraft, which is responsible for death and financial ruin. Every Beninese person can relate a story about a witch's attack or the supernatural feats made possible by witchcraft. In Benin, the search for security and protection from witchcraft is the primary reason to practice religion (Tall 1995). However, witchcraft is the strongest force in existence, so people say that the only way to protect themselves is to acquire another form of witchcraft. Thus, in pursuing ever more powerful witchcraft, Beninese employ their long-standing practice of seeking exotic spiritual forces to add to their supernatural arsenals.

Figure 2.4. A patient submits to an Asian-inspired healing ritual. Photograph by the author.

In his comprehensive review of global historical and contemporary occult beliefs, Peter Geschiere (2013) posits that exoticism may be a universal feature of witchcraft, and Benin is a perfect example of the way exoticism contributes to the accumulation of new religious ideas.

Hindu mysticism and Chinese healing are also treated as new forms of witchcraft.[24] One healer I know boasted about his travels in India and China, where he acquired new spiritual knowledge. He said that he returned to Benin after many years of research to apply these Eastern traditions in the battle against witchcraft. He openly acknowledged that he was himself employing witchcraft in his healing rituals. Many people claim that Hindu mysticism is the most powerful form of witchcraft, and several stated that the Indian national soccer team is banned from international tournaments because their opponents fear their magical interference in the match. Hindu mystics offer televised instruction and traveling seminars on healing and spirituality. A friend of mine said that he participated in a training seminar with Indians who taught the Pranic healing techniques, but eventually he and others abandoned it out of fear that it was a form of witchcraft and that he might attract the attention of dangerous witches (Falen 2018).

Tron, Mami Wata, and Christianity are also foreign spiritual traditions that are sometimes equated with witchcraft. Because all religious movements in contemporary Benin claim the ability to overcome witchcraft, many people conclude that these religions are themselves a form of witchcraft (Falen 2018). Numerous informants confided that they suspected Tron's effectiveness against witches was due to the fact that Tron uses witchcraft. Others told of Christian pastors who secretly bury a magical charm on the grounds of their churches, to attract converts and to combat witchcraft. Parfaite, the woman who preaches against the proliferation of witches in Catholicism and Vodún, is famous for performing miraculous healing of witchcraft victims. But critics told me that they attribute her success to her own witchcraft. A number of interviewees suggested that Parfaite must be an adept of Mami Wata, whom they say is animated by another variety of àzě. While people typically described Vodún as distinct from àzě, there are two spirits known as *azevodún* (witchcraft vodún), who are described as patrons of witchcraft or protectors from witchcraft (Falen 2018).[25] Furthermore, a few people quietly told me that the recipe used to install a new Vodún shrine is the same kind of magical concoction that witches use as the source of their supernatural power. I have argued elsewhere (Falen 2018) that the idea of recipes, nearly always involving magical leaves and other products of nature, is one of the features that unifies vodún, àzě (witchcraft), bŏ (sorcery), and herbal healing, thereby merging categories of religion, magic, and medicine. This argument is consistent with Timothy Landry's (this volume) suggestion that the underlying reliance on nature and the forest may be common to West African and diasporic religions, paving the way for the universalizing tendencies that I have described. Furthermore, because Beninese believe magic and healing are ultimately means of harnessing nature's powers, they consider these forms of knowledge to be an "African science" (Falen 2018)—an argument similar to that made by Venise Adjibodou (this volume).

The message conveyed by the testimony about recipes for deities and religious power is that, whatever the religion—Christianity, Tron, Vodún, or Hinduism—the underlying source of all spiritual power is witchcraft. Thus, in incorporating multiple religions into a single category of the occult, witchcraft is a poignant example of the exotic syncretism in West African religious philosophy. A cosmopolitan healer whom I interviewed in Cotonou drew on a wide array of spiritual ideas in sharing his perspectives on occult research. Departing from the more common ideological separation between Vodún and Christianity, he listed a series of spiritual equivalencies, linking ancient Egyptian and Hebrew gods and the Virgin Mary to the Vodún spirits. At the conclusion of our "lesson," which included sweeping generalizations spanning Vodún, Christianity, and Asian mysticism, he simply said, "It's all witchcraft!"

CONCLUSION

Contrary to popular stereotypes, Beninese Vodún has always been dynamic, innovative, and receptive to foreign religions, including European Christianity and the numerous vodún borrowed from neighboring West African peoples. However, today witchcraft preoccupations and exoticism inspire people to acquire new spiritual ideas from as far away as North America, Europe, India, and China. Some of the exoticism can be attributed to hegemonic relations, but I have shown that Beninese also initiate religious borrowings from people without a colonial history in Benin. Rather than regarding Beninese people as victims without agency, I see them employing a long-standing custom of appropriating the power of the Other. A novel feature of recent religious appropriation is the universalizing discourse that unites religions, esoteric practices, and the occult into the single supercategory of witchcraft (àzě). In some ways, this is a logical extension of the exoticism that has always characterized Vodún. However, this universalism produces a new kind of syncretism that no longer involves solely Vodún but rather one that signals a profound and far-reaching disruption of the distinctions between magic and religion. Beyond the well-known syncretism within and between individual religions, this suggests a broader cultural blending that unites all religions and spiritual traditions, both foreign and local, into a single universal force. Vodún's long-standing receptive, exotic stance toward other religions has been assumed by witchcraft, which is now the primary mover in the creation of spiritual syncretism in Benin. This phenomenon is a dramatic illustration of the impact of globalization on contemporary cultures, even those cultures casually and misleadingly labeled as "traditional." What do these developments mean for the future of Vodún? Given its proven malleability and adaptability, it would be difficult to predict the long-term outcome. However, in the short term, it seems evident that Vodún adherents and other Beninese who are preoccupied with the dangers and opportunities of witchcraft will continue to incorporate foreign elements into their spiritual tool kit, allowing their religious repertoire to grow and adapt to an ever-changing cultural landscape.

I am grateful to Agnes Scott College for supporting several seasons of fieldwork on which this chapter is based.

NOTES

1. The term *Vodún* refers to the indigenous religion practiced in southern Benin. The similar Ewe religion is called Vodu, while the Haitian version is Vodou, and the North American variety is Voodoo. For more detailed descriptions of Beninese Vodún deities and rituals, see Falen 2016; Herskovits 1938; Herskovits and Herskovits 1933; Maupoil 1943; Rush 2013.
2. Voodoo has origins in the West African and Caribbean religions, but it has been transformed by racist policies, essentialist popular culture, and commercialism (see Long 2002 for a brief history).
3. The festival was known in Benin as Ouidah 92: Retrouvailles Amérique-Afrique, though it actually took place in 1993 (Forte 2009).
4. Although the English terms *witchcraft* and *sorcery* carry connotations of malevolence, the Fongbe terms are more ambivalent (Falen 2018).
5. The names used here are pseudonyms, with the exception of Paul, who passed away a few months after the events described here.
6. Kutito is the Fon equivalent for the Yoruba Egungun ghost masquerade society that was imported by Fon people in the nineteenth century. I have transcribed proper nouns such as spirit names using the English alphabet to conform to conventional spellings in the literature. For other words in Fongbe, I have used international phonetic characters to capture the proper pronunciation.
7. Parfaite's original name is Vicentia Tchranvoukinni. She claims that she descended to earth as a baby and was discovered by a Fulani shepherd in the north of Benin, but her critics argue that her birth certificate contains her given name and proof of her mortal birth.
8. The kingdoms along the Slave Coast (present-day Benin) consisted of different groups of related peoples. According to oral history, the royal

families of Allada, Dahomey, and Hogbonou (Porto-Novo) all claimed a common sixteenth-century origin in the town of Tado, in present-day Togo (Herskovits [1938] 1967, 1:167–169).

9. Bay (1998, 94) reports that Fá divination may have arrived in Allada and Whydah even earlier.

10. As Yai (1993) points out, the *Doctrina Christiana*'s 1658 translation of Jesus as the deity Lisá indicates that perhaps the Mawu-Lisá couple had already spread eastward toward Ouidah and Allada one hundred years before Hwanjile is credited with introducing the creator couple to Dahomey.

11. Bay (1998, 22) suggests that these gods were originally Yoruba, but Sweet (2011, 18) claims that they were imported from Aja.

12. Sweet (2011, 21) also claims that Dahomey's rulers sold off Sakpata priests into the slave trade in a bid to defuse their ability to rival the monarchy.

13. According to Drewal (1988), the "snake charmer" print was likely based on the photo of a Somoan woman who performed during the 1880s as a snake charmer in Germany under the name Maladamatjaute at a time when "exotic" foreign peoples were popular in Europe. The print, titled *Der Schlangenbandiger* (Snake charmer), was produced in Germany but reprinted in India and England for distribution in Europe and Africa.

14. Kola nuts figure prominently in Tron ritual, and shrines in Benin often have kola trees growing through an open space within their roofs.

15. Though the target language is clearly a Gbe language, the translation is considered a poor rendering of Allada's language, and therefore much of it cannot be deciphered (Aboh 2015, 48; Labouret and Rivet 1929). Gbe languages are a group of related languages spoken in southern Togo and Benin; they include Fongbe, Aja, Ewe, Mina (Gen), Xwla, and Gun (Ethnologue 2018).

16. Birgit Meyer (1999) also documents how indigenous religious concepts were preserved through missionaries' translations of terms like the *devil*.

17. Thornton (1998) states that Christianity was not wholly incompatible with African religion because both relied on the intervention of divine entities, which he classifies as "revelations." But Sweet (2003, 106–112) argues that claims of similarities between Christianity and African religion have been vastly overstated and that African religious revelations were rarely accepted by missionaries, who tended to condemn African religion as diabolical. As I argue here, syncretism in Dahomey (and religion in general) seemed to be more about pragmatic approaches than about theology.

18. Albert Raboteau (2004) claims that syncretism in the Americas was less of a fusion than is commonly believed, arguing that Catholicism and African religions existed as parallel systems.

19. Thornton (1988) also notes that Caribbean slaves may have been accepting of Catholicism because they were likely familiar with it before leaving Africa.

Similarly, Sweet (2011, 47–51) suggests that Brazilian slaves likely had an ambivalent view of joining the Catholic faith, respecting its access to divine power, and drawing parallels with Vodún initiation, even as their masters compelled them to undergo baptism to a foreign religion whose abstract theology was often lost on the slaves.

20. The word *occult* is a loaded term because it often implies nefarious mystical acts. However, it is commonly used in the literature to refer to African witchcraft and sorcery (Moore and Sanders 2001). I use it here in a similar way to distinguish between individualistic occult activities (magic, witchcraft, and sorcery) and the more official public aspects of "religion." Nevertheless, the occult in Benin carries ambivalent moral value and exhibits important links to "religion" (Falen 2018).

21. Eckankar is an Eastern-inspired spiritual movement based in Minnesota. It involves new-age mysticism and chanting. Beninese also regard technological innovations like computers, cell phones, and airplanes as "white people's witchcraft" (Falen 2018).

22. Wicca was irrelevant to this conversation, in the sense that he was not referring to it and probably had never heard of it. However, Ronald Hutton (1999) points out that the origins of modern Wicca were tied to Freemasonry and Rosicrucianism (my thanks to Timothy Landry for bringing this to my attention).

23. However, witchcraft is an ambivalent power, and people often say that possessing witchcraft brings health and success but can also compel one to kill (see Falen 2018).

24. Healing and the occult merge easily into one another because the Fongbe term *bŏ* (sorcery) straddles the line between medicine and magic. Furthermore, there is considerable slippage between the categories of bŏ and àzĕ (Falen 2018).

25. These two azevodún are named Minona and Kenesi.

REFERENCES

Aboh, Enoch Oladé. 2015. *The Emergence of Hybrid Grammars: Language Contact and Change*. Cambridge: Cambridge University Press.

Adoukonou, Barthélemy. 1993. "Vodún, Démocratie et Pluralisme Religieux." In *Les Publications du Sillon Noir*, no. 9, 9–93. Cotonou: Centre Q.I.C.

Alladaye, Jérôme. 2003. *Le Catholicisme au Pays du Vodún*. Cotonou: Editions Flamboyant.

Ann, Rachel. n.d. "An Introductory Explanation of the Voodoo Religion." SelfGrowth.com. Accessed October 25, 2020. http://www.selfgrowth.com/articles/an-introductory-explanation-of-the-voodoo-religion.

Apter, Andrew. 1991. "Herskovits's Heritage: Rethinking Syncretism in the African Diaspora." *Diaspora: A Journal of Transnational Studies* 1 (3): 235–260.
———. 1993. "Attinga Revisited: Yoruba Witchcraft and the Cocoa Economy, 1950–1951." In *Modernity and Its Malcontents: Ritual and Power in Postcolonial Africa*, edited by Jean Comaroff and John Comaroff, 111–128. Chicago: University of Chicago Press.
Ashforth, Adam. 2005. *Witchcraft, Violence, and Democracy in South Africa*. Chicago: University of Chicago Press.
Barber, Karin. 1981. "How Man Makes God in West Africa: Yoruba Attitudes towards the 'Orisa.'" *Africa: Journal of the International African Institute* 51 (3): 724–745.
Barnes, Sandra T. 1997. "The Many Faces of Ogun: Introduction to the First Edition." In *Africa's Ogun: Old World and New*, 2nd ed., edited by Sandra T. Barnes, 1–26. Bloomington: Indiana University Press.
Bashkow, Ira. 2006. *The Meaning of Whitemen: Race and Modernity in the Orokaiva Cultural World*. Chicago: University of Chicago Press.
Bay, Edna G. 1998. *Wives of the Leopard: Gender, Politics, and Culture in the Kingdom of Dahomey*. Charlottesville: University of Virginia Press.
———. 2008. *Asen, Ancestors, and Vodun: Tracing Change in African Art*. Urbana: University of Illinois Press.
Bertho, Jacques. 1951. "Le Gbadou Chez les Adja du Togo et du Dahomey." *Comptes Rendus: Première Conférence Internationale des Africanistes de l'Ouest*. Vol. 2. Dakar: Institut Français d'Afrique Noire.
Bosman, Willem. 1705. *A New and Accurate Description of the Coast of Guinea, Divided into the Gold, the Slave and the Ivory Coasts*. London.
Burton, Richard F. S. 1864. *A Mission to Gelele, King of Dahome*. London: Tinsley Brothers.
Claffey, Patrick. 2007. *Christian Churches in Dahomey: A Study of Their Sociopolitical Role*. Leiden, Netherlands: Brill.
Clément, Yacoubou Badorou. 1996. "Histoire de la Mission SIM et l'Eglise UEEB au Bénin." In *Nos racines racontées: Récits historiques sur l'église en Afrique de l'Ouest*, edited by James R. Krabill, 33–36. Abidjan, Côte d'Ivoire: Presses Bibliques Africaines.
Cosentino, Donald. 2005. "Vodou in the Age of Mechanical Reproduction." *RES: Anthropology and Aesthetics* 47:231–246.
Croce-Spinelli, Michel. 1982. *Les Enfants de Poto-Poto*. Paris: L'Harmattan.
Dalzel, Archibald. 1793. *The History of Dahomy*. London: self-published.
de Boeck, Filip. 2000. "Le 'Deuxième Monde' et les 'Enfants-Sorciers' en République Démocratique du Congo." *Politique Africaine* 80:32–57.
———. 2005. "Children, Gift and Witchcraft in the Democratic Republic of Congo." In *Makers and Breakers: Children and Youth in Postcolonial Africa*, edited by Filip de Boeck and Alcinda Honwana, 188–215. Oxford: James Currey.

Desmangles, Leslie G. 1992. *The Faces of the Gods: Vodou and Roman Catholicism in Haiti*. Chapel Hill: University of North Carolina Press.
de Surgy, Albert. 2001. *Le Phénomène Pentecôtiste en Afrique Noire: Le Cas Béninois*. Paris: L'Harmattan.
Drewal, Henry John. 1988. "Performing the Other: Mami Wata Worship in Africa." *TDR* 32 (2): 160–185.
———. 2008a. "Introduction: Sources and Currents." In *Mami Wata: Arts for the Water Spirits in Africa and Its Diasporas*, edited by Henry John Drewal, 23–69. Los Angeles: Fowler Museum.
———, ed. 2008b. *Mami Wata: Arts for the Water Spirits in Africa and Its Diasporas*. Los Angeles: Fowler Museum.
———, ed. 2008c. *Sacred Waters: Arts for Mami Wata and Other Water Divinities in Africa and the Diaspora*. Bloomington: Indiana University Press.
Duncan, John. 1847. *Travels in Western Africa, in 1845 & 1846, Comprising a Journey from Whydah, through the Kingdom of Dahomey, to Adofoodia, in the Interior*. London: R. Bentley.
Ekoué, Léocadie, and Judy Rosenthal. 2015. "Aze and the Incommensurable." In *Evil in Africa: Encounters with the Everyday*, edited by William C. Olsen and Walter E. A. van Beek, 128–139. Bloomington: Indiana University Press.
Ethnologue. 2018. "Languages of the World." Accessed August 26, 2021. https://www.ethnologue.com.
Explore! n.d. "The Cradle of Voodoo." Accessed October 25, 2020. https://www.exploreworldwide.com/holidays/benin-togo-culture-tour.
Falen, Douglas J. 2008. "Polygyny and Christian Marriage in Africa: The Case of Benin." *African Studies Review* 51 (2): 51–74.
———. 2016. "Vodun, Spiritual Insecurity, and Religious Importation in Bénin." *Journal of Religion in Africa* 46 (4): 453–483.
———. 2018. *African Science: Witchcraft, Vodun, and Healing in Southern Benin*. Madison: University of Wisconsin Press.
Forbes, Frederick E. 1851. *Dahomey and the Dahomans: Being the Journals of Two Missions to the King of Dahomey and Residence at His Capital in the Years 1849 and 1850*. London: Frank Cass.
Forte, Jung Ran. 2009. "Marketing Vodun: Cultural Tourism and Dreams of Success in Contemporary Benin." *Cahiers D'Études Africaines* 49 (193/194): 429–451.
François, G. 1906. *Le Dahomey*. Paris: Emile Larose.
Georges, Emily A. 2009. *The Pocket Book of Paranormal Trivia*. CreateSpace Independent Publishing Platform.
Geschiere, Peter. 1997. *The Modernity of Witchcraft*. Charlottesville: University of Virginia Press.
———. 2008. "Witchcraft and the State: Cameroon and South Africa; Ambiguities of 'Reality' and 'Superstition.'" *Past and Present* 199 (S3): 313–335.

———. 2013. *Witchcraft, Intimacy and Trust: Africa in Comparison.* Chicago: University of Chicago Press.
Henry, Christine. 2001. "Du Vin Nouveau dans de Vieilles Outres: Parcours d'un Dissident du Christianisme Céleste (Bénin)." *Social Compass* 3:353–368.
———. 2008a. *La Force des Anges: Rites, Hiérarchie et Divination dans le Christianisme Céleste, Bénin.* Turnhout, Belgium: Bibliothèque de l'Ecole des Hautes Etudes, Sciences Religieuses.
———. 2008b. "Le sorcier, le visionnaire et la guerre des églises au sud-Bénin." *Cahiers d'Etudes Africaines* 48 (1–2): 101–130.
Herskovits, Melville J. 1937. *Life in a Haitian Valley.* New York: Alfred A. Knopf.
———. (1938) 1967. *Dahomey: An Ancient West African Kingdom.* 2 vols. Evanston, IL: Northwestern University Press.
Herskovits, Melville J., and Frances S. Herskovits. 1933. *An Outline of Dahomean Religious Belief.* Menasha, WI: American Anthropological Association.
Hutton, Ronald. 1999. *Triumph of the Moon: A History of Modern Pagan Witchcraft.* Oxford: Oxford University Press.
Kempf, Wolfgang. 1994. "Ritual Power and Colonial Domination: Male Initiation among the Ngaing of Papua New Guinea." In *Syncretism/Anti-Syncretism: The Politics of Religious Synthesis,* edited by Charles Stewart and Rosalind Shaw, 108–126. London: Routledge.
Labouret, Henri, and Paul Rivet. 1929. *Le Royaume d'Arda et son évangélisation au XVIIe Siècle.* Paris: Institut d'Ethnologie.
Laguerre, Michel. 1977. "An Ecological Approach to Voodoo." *Journal of the Interdenominational Theological Center* 5 (1): 47–60.
Landry, Timothy R. 2011. "Touring the Slave Route: Inaccurate Authenticities in Bénin, West Africa." In *Contested Cultural Heritage: Religion, Nationalism, Erasure, and Exclusion in a Global World,* edited by Helaine Silverman, 205–231. New York: Springer.
———. 2015. "Vodún, Globalization, and the Creative Layering of Belief in Southern Bénin." *Journal of Religion in Africa* 45 (2): 170–199.
Law, Robin. 1991. *The Slave Coast of West Africa 1550–1750: The Impact of the Atlantic Slave Trade on an African Society.* Oxford: Clarendon.
———. 2004. *Ouidah: The Social History of a West African Slaving "Port," 1727–1892.* Athens: Ohio University Press.
Le Herissé, A. 1911. *L'ancien royaume du Dahomey: Moeurs, religion, histoire.* Paris: Larose.
Long, Carolyn Morrow. 2002. "Perceptions of New Orleans Voodoo: Sin, Fraud, Entertainment, and Religion." *Nova Religio: The Journal of Alternative and Emergent Religions* 6 (1): 86–101.
Maupoil, Bernard. 1943. *La géomancie à l'ancienne côte des esclaves.* Paris: Institut d'Ethnologie.

Mayrargue, Cédric. 2001. "The Expansion of Pentecostalism in Benin." In *Between Babel and Pentecost*, edited by André Corten and Ruth Marshall-Fratani, 274–292. Bloomington: Indiana University Press.

———. 2003. "Nouveaux Mouvements Chrétiens et Société Urbaine en Temps de Crise." In *Sécurité, Crime et Ségrégation dans les Villes d'Afrique de l'Ouest Depuis le XIXe Siècle*, edited by Laurent Fourchard and Isaac Albert, 417–434. Paris: Karthala.

Mercier, Paul. 1954. "The Fon of Dahomey." In *African Worlds: Studies in the Cosmological Ideas and Social Values of African Peoples*, edited by Daryll Forde, 210–234. London: Oxford University Press.

Meyer, Birgit. 1999. *Translating the Devil: Religion and Modernity among the Ewe in Ghana*. Trenton, NJ: Africa World.

M'Leod, John. 1820. *A Voyage to Africa with Some Account of the Manners and Customs of the Dahomian People*. London: John Murray.

Montgomery, Eric J., and Christian N. Vannier. 2017. *An Ethnography of a Vodu Shrine in Southern Togo: Of Spirit, Slave and Sea*. Leiden, Netherlands: Brill.

Moore, Henrietta L., and Todd Sanders, eds. 2001. *Magical Interpretations and Material Realities*. London: Routledge.

Murrell, Nathaniel Samuel. 2010. *Afro-Caribbean Religions: An Introduction to Their Historical, Cultural, and Sacred Traditions*. Philadelphia: Temple University Press.

News24. 2016. "Benin, Cradle of Voodoo, Democracy." Accessed October 25, 2020. https://www.news24.com/Africa/News/benin-cradle-of-voodoo-democracy-20160407.

Noret, Joël. 2008. "Memoire de l'esclavage et capital religieux." *Gradhiva* 8:48–63.

———. 2010. *Deuil et funérailles dans le Bénin méridional: Enterrer à tout prix*. Brussels: Éditions de l'Université de Bruxelles.

Norman, Neil. 2009. "Powerful Pots, Humbling Holes, and Regional Ritual Processes: Towards an Archaeology of Huedan Vodun, ca. 1650–1727." *African Archaeological Review* 26 (3): 187–218.

Painter, Sally. n.d. "Understanding Voodoo Possession." Accessed August 26, 2021. https://paranormal.lovetoknow.com/about-paranormal/understanding-voodoo-possession.

Peabody, Sue. 2002. "'A Dangerous Zeal': Catholic Missions to Slaves in the French Antilles, 1635–1800." *French Historical Studies* 25 (1): 53–90.

Peel, J. D. Y. 2016. *Christianity, Islam, and Orişa Religion: Three Traditions in Comparison and Interaction*. Oakland: University of California Press.

Raboteau, Albert J. 2004. *Slave Religion: The "Invisible Institution" in the Antebellum South*. Oxford: Oxford University Press.

Rosenthal, Judy. 1998. *Possession, Ecstasy and Law in Ewe Voodoo*. Charlottesville: University of Virginia Press.

Rush, Dana. 2001. "Contemporary Vodun Arts of Ouidah, Benin." *African Arts* 34 (4): 32–96.

———. 2008. "The Idea of 'India' in West African Vodun Art and Thought." In *India in Africa, Africa in India: Indian Ocean Cosmopolitanisms*, edited by John C. Hawley, 149–180. Bloomington: Indiana University Press.

———. 2013. *Vodún in Coastal Bénin: Unfinished, Open-Ended, Global*. Nashville: Vanderbilt University Press.

Sargent, Carolyn. 1989. *Maternity, Medicine and Power*. Berkeley: University of California Press.

Skertchly, J. A. 1874. *Dahomey as It Is: Being a Narrative of Eight Months' Residence in That Country, with a Full Account of the Notorious Annual Customs, and the Social and Religious Institutions of the Fons*. London: Chapman and Hall.

Smith, James Howard. 2008. *Bewitching Development: Witchcraft and the Reinvention of Development in Neoliberal Kenya*. Chicago: University of Chicago Press.

Snelgrave, William. 1971. *A New Account of Some Parts of Guinea and the Slave Trade*. London: Frank Cass.

Strandsbjerg, Camilla. 2005. "Les Nouveaux Réseaux Evangéliques et l'Etat: Le Cas du Bénin." In *Entreprises Religieuses Transnationales en Afrique de l'Ouest*, edited by Laurent Fourchard, André Mary, and René Otayek, 223–241. Paris: Karthala.

Sweet, James H. 2003. *Recreating Africa: Culture, Kinship, and Religion in the African-Portuguese World, 1441–1770*. Chapel Hill: University of North Carolina Press.

———. 2011. *Domingos Álvares, African Healing, and the Intellectual History of the Atlantic World*. Chapel Hill: University of North Carolina Press.

Tall, Emmanuel Kadya. 1995. "Dynamique des Cultes Voduns et du Christianisme Céleste au Sud-Bénin." *Cahiers des Sciences Humaines* 31 (4): 797–823.

———. 2005. "Stratégies Locales et Relations Internationales des Chefs de Culte au Sud-Bénin." In *Entreprises Religieuses Transnationales en Afrique de l'Ouest*, edited by Laurent Fourchard, André Mary, and René Otayek, 267–284. Paris: Karthala.

Taussig, Michael. 1993. *Mimesis and Alterity: A Particular History of the Senses*. New York: Routledge.

Thornton, John K. 1988. "On the Trail of Voodoo: African Christianity in Africa and the Americas." *The Americas* 44 (3): 261–278.

———. 1998. *Africa and Africans in the Making of the Atlantic World 1400–1800*. 2nd ed. Cambridge: Cambridge University Press.

Verger, Pierre Fatumbi. 1954. *Dieux d'Afrique: Culte des Orishas et Vodouns à l'ancienne Côte des Esclaves en Afrique et à Bahia, la Baie de Tous les Saints au Brésil*. Paris: Editions Paul Hartmann.

Wanderlust. n.d. Accessed October 25, 2020. https://www.wanderlust.co.uk/trip-finder/Explore_127/Cradle-Of%20Voodoo_7769.

West, Harry G. 2007. *Ethnographic Sorcery*. Chicago: University of Chicago Press.

Yai, Olabiyi. 1993. "From Vodun to Mawu: Monotheism and History in the Fon Cultural Area." In *L'Invention Religieuse en Afrique*, edited by Jean-Pierre Chrétien, 241–265. Paris: Editions Karthala.

———. 2001. "The Identity, Contributions, and Ideology of the Aguda (Afro-Brazilians) of the Gulf of Benin: A Reinterpretation." In *Rethinking the African Diaspora: The Making of a Black Atlantic World in the Bight of Benin and Brazil*, edited by Kristin Mann and Edna G. Bay, 72–82. London: Frank Cass.

DOUGLAS J. FALEN is Professor of Anthropology at Agnes Scott College. He is author of *Power and Paradox: Authority, Insecurity, and Creativity in Fon Gender Relations* and *African Science: Witchcraft, Vodun, and Healing in Southern Benin*.

THREE

CROSSING CURRENTS

Gorovodu and Yewevodu in Contemporary Togo

Eric J. Montgomery

INTRODUCING YEWEVODU AND GOROVODU

Vodu (Vodún, Vodou) is and always has been an adaptive and dynamic religion operating in a constantly changing world. Much like the Yorùbá Òrìsà throughout Nigeria and the African Atlantic, Vodu and its ethnic affiliates (Adja, Fòn, Ewe, Mina) have been categorized and defined by European colonial gerrymandering and are not necessarily the ethnonyms these groups themselves abide by (Matory 2015). As discussed in this volume, another key feature of Vodún is its mobility and propensity for innovation. The case study here, drawn from the community of Gbedala and neighboring villages along the Togolese coast, attests to the agility because the four gods evaluated here range from northern hinterlands (Kunde and Bangre), across diasporic oceans (Mami Wata), and from easterly forests (Sakpata). These four gods of Vodún are global entities par excellence with manifestations stretching from Senegal to Nigeria, Togo to Haiti, Congo to Brazil. Despite recent calls from other scholars to classify Òrìsà and Vodún as "world religions" (Olopuna and Rey 2008), their usage in modernity is draped in racist imagery demeaning Black people throughout the Atlantic world and the United States (McGee 2014). All the contributors in the present volume have experienced that initial conversation with others when they first hear that we research "Voodoo," and the pervasiveness of this mystification is deep and bothersome. Since Melville Herskovits (1938), anthropologists have worked hard to legitimize Vodu as a global and dynamic way of seeing and knowing contrary to the more public, negative stereotypes. This chapter adds to the anthropological narrative as to why Vodu/Vodún/Vodou matters by assessing multivocal symbols and rituals across various pantheons with "thick descriptions" of liturgical characterizations of these spirits, with an eye toward philosophy and healing. The theoretical arc exposes the holistic nature of Vodu through its many resonant appendages, including medicine, performance, symbol, ontology, and utility.

The so-called medicine cults and shrines of Gorovodu and Yewevodu continue to proliferate today surely because of their ability to cross currents and boundaries (both real and imaginary), forever mobile and resilient and successful by nature, bringing morality, healing, and social order to a world often consumed by chaos (*maso-maso*). Gorovodu is a pantheon of spirits from the northern grasslands and savannas of Ghana and greater African Sahel. The more ancient Yewe spirits originate from among Adja-Ewe and Minas along the coastal forests of southern Benin and Togo. Spirit service across both pantheons is observed and prodded for depth of meaning from within Togolese Vodu. Among Ewes in southern Togo and southeastern Ghana, the Gorovodu spirits (Tron[1]) from the north have been filtered and acculturated into the preexisting Vodún milieu, meaning that southern Vodu structure helps to mold northern spirits into a greater Vodu(n) ontology. Northern gods flourished after the abolishment of transatlantic slavery as domestic slavery increased and northern slaves were incorporated into Ewe lineages along the coast. Most of these gods stood as individual spirits with a range of followers across space and time before being assembled into a new pantheon by southern Ewes, Guin-Minas, and Akan within the past century. Elsewhere I have argued against the so-called syncretism and antisyncretism in both Vodu and Òrìsà from an anthropological analysis (Montgomery 2014), but my focus here is more on the assimilated and acculturated symbols across (at least) two distinct pantheons, so-called old or ancestral Vodu (Yewevodu[2]) and modern or foreign Tron (Gorovodu). The hunters, warriors, and market women from the north have become archetypal gods after being "bought persons" (*amefleflewo*) from northern hinterlands in slavery at the end of the nineteenth and beginning of the twentieth century. Most historians date Yewevodu to the early 1700s, with some gods and rituals going back much further. The ethnic and geographic origins of both Yewevodu and Gorovodu are diverse, attesting to the global and broad-minded nature of Adja-Fòn, Ewe, Guin-Mina, and Asante peoples while also speaking to a deep history of encounter between different African cultures.

The spirits of Yewevodu and Gorovodu are paradigmatically attached via deep symbolism. Judy Rosenthal (1998, 61) writes:

> As far as the usual human needs for gods go, the Gorovodu pantheon covers all the god bases. But other deities in other systems also keep covering the

same ground and the same concerns from one place to another. Among the gorovodus, Banguele is doing the same work as Egu (the iron god), Nana Wango is covering for Mami Wata (the coastal mermaid deity) and Yemanja (the Yorùbá water *Òrìsà*), Sacra Bode is another form of Sakpata, or Aholu (the earth deity), Kunde is *adela* (hunter spirit), and Sunia Compo is Lisa (the Adja-Fòn sun Vodu, companion twin or husband to a female Mawu, the moon god). The gorovodus address the same concerns of other gods and have similar personalities.

The synchrony and fluidity between coastal and northern gods are emblematic of the all-encompassing and open-minded religious imagination of many Ewes. Through a holistic and comparative analysis between the shrines and rituals associated with Bangre, Kunde, Sakpata, and Mami Wata, this investigation unveils understandings of what the gods mean to those who serve them. In modern-day Benin, the cradle of Vodún, many of the sacred objects—especially such ancestral objects as *asen* that once donned the marks and symbols of Vodún in Benin—have now been replaced with Christian iconography (Bay 2008, 138–168). However, this trend does not constitute "death of tradition," and since the demise of communism and the launch of "The Slave Route Project: Resistance, Liberty, Heritage" in Benin, in partnership with the UNESCO's General Conference, in 1994, Vodún is reasserting its might in many communities as the way it is represented privately and publicly evolves (Landry 2016; Rush 2013). Next door in Togo, the arts and aesthetics of Vodún continue to blossom alongside spikes in Christianity and Islam since they operate in the veins of healing and spirit possession, where ritual, myth, performance, and science create a super-Vodún culture and religion (Montgomery and Vannier 2017).

Many Ewes have appropriated and co-opted both the modern and the ancient: Gorovodu and Yewevodu and related gods like Mami Wata (water spirits) or Mama Tchamba (slave spirits) (Montgomery 2018, 2019). The sheer number and complexity of spirits in the region are innumerable, impossible to quantify. Gbedala village itself reflects the enormous scale, with what could be deemed Vodu spirits numbering in the hundreds. On one weekend in 2014, I could identify at least eighty-five different spirits, eight major shrines, and dozens of personal sanctuaries within Gbedala. Sakpata and Mami have at least three semipublic altars, and Kunde and Bangre have at least four *kpome* (altar, meaning "oven"). Other "fetishes" have been constructed by the local priest and dispersed throughout the Bight of Benin and beyond (the United States, Japan, Italy, France).[3] Even with upticks in membership across most Christian denominations from Ghana to Benin, both Gorovodu and Yewevodu continue to garner adepts, including many Christians, mostly due to high national birth rates but also due to pragmatic utility and efficacy.

The Togolese fishing village of Gbedala is the epicenter of this analysis, with Yewe spirits (i.e., Heviesso, lightning god of justice) and Mami Wata coming with the birth of Gbedala in the 1880s and Gorovodu coming in the early 1970s. For Gorovodu, there are said to be "two sticks," Gorovodu being the primary and the second called Alafia (the Hausa word for "health"). This analysis examines the first stick of Gorovodu by focusing on Kunde and his son Bangre, with comparisons to Mami Wata and Sakpata. The Yewevodu gods Sakpata and Mami Wata are housed in their own abodes nearby. Each of these gods is embodied in physical form by way of actual "fetishes," or god-objects, composed of carbonized plant and animal parts and other elements. They also manifest themselves physically by "coming on the heads" of various adepts (Tronsi or Vodusi) in trance. Each god in both Gorovodu and Yewevodu pantheons has his or her own tastes, songs, sacrifices, prayers, costumes, and ingredients (Rosenthal 1998).

RESEARCH SETTING AND BACKGROUND: THE TOGOLESE COAST

This research stems from periodic ethnographic fieldwork over the past fifteen years in the village of Gbedala along the Togolese coast. This village is not far from the Port Autonome International Shipping Port in southern Lomé and a stone's throw from the newly completed fishing port (Port du Peche). Gbedala is a village of approximately fourteen hundred Ewes, Adangbes, Guin-Minas, and closely related people of Aja-Ewe origins, nestled in southern Togo along the Atlantic coast not far from the capital city of Lomé. The Ewes migrated to modern-day southern Togo, Ghana, and Benin from the northeast along the southwestern Nigerian border with Benin several hundred years ago during the Aja-Tado migrations. They are closely related to nearby Adja-Fòn populations and greatly influenced by their western and northern Akan neighbors as well (Gayibor 1985, 1992).

This chapter is both global and local in scope: global because these gods are spread throughout western Africa and the entire Atlantic world, with Vodún/Òrìsà being the primary religion for upward of 100 million people worldwide, and local through the investigation of their existence in one specific village in coastal Togo. Participant-observation, videography with postfeedback screenings, interviews, and collaborative coding were combined to capture the meaning and makeup of Kunde, Bangre, Mami Wata, and Sakpata. At times, photo-voice was employed, with villagers photographing and recording objects and scenes of their own choice (see Montgomery 2017). The sacred objects of four primary gods (Kunde, Bangre, Mami Wata, and Sakpata) from public and private shrines of friends and associates in the village were openly discussed. Mami Wata, Sakpata, Heviesso, and Lêgba (and their corresponding shrines) came with the original village founders and were probably a part of these lineages for hundreds of years. The "ancient Vodus" precede the Tron along the coast, but comparisons within and between both orders have been scant.

Gorovodu, Yewevodu, and elements of Christianity, Islam, and even Hinduism have, to varying degrees, been integrated creatively into the worldview of many southern Ewes and others along the West African coast (see Falen on syncretism this volume). However, these ancient African gods may also be at the core of these other so-called world religions since some of these gods predate these other orthodoxies by thousands of years (Zogbe 2007). As I have written elsewhere, Vodún peoples adhere to cosmological inclusion:

> Gorovodu itself is a "mixed bag," with individual gods coming from a variety of foundations north, reassembled by the Ewes in the south to resolve their problems. The role of these gods is paradigmatic to the macro Vodus, with, for example, Bangle sitting in for Ogun, and Sunia Compo doing the work of Lêgba. The pantheon closely resembles the "syncretism" in Vodu and Òrìsà pantheons from Nigeria and Benin, and those all the way to Brazil and the Caribbean. Within Gorovodu itself are several reifications and translations of Islam and Christianity. On any given day, one can see the whole problem of "syncretism" played out through a Vodu lens that borrows symbolic components from an array of belief systems and regions. (Montgomery 2016, 5–6)

What we can never know is how much these other traditions previously borrowed from African religions; certainly, it was a great deal. I will present thick descriptions of the "ancient" gods of Yewevodu and move to more "modern" ones of the Gorovodu order. Devotees of Yewevodu and Gorovodu continue to serve their gods because performances and rituals are awe-inspiring, while local medicines save lives, and a multiplicity of personhood abounds, thus showing the world a vivacious religious culture, perhaps none more emblematic for the Black Atlantic world.

ANCIENT GODS: YEWEVODU

According to Robert Sastre (1970, 177–188), the many Vodún of Yewe provenance are mystical and cross local, regional, and global boundaries and signify on politics, identity, and social change. Suzanne Preston Blier (1996) and Sandra Barnes (1997) provide a refined understanding with serious depth of content on the efficacy and aesthetics surrounding Yewevodu to the people themselves. Others (Bay 2008; Landry 2016; Rush 2013) have delved into both the materiality and aesthetics surrounding Vodún, with Timothy Landry (this volume) focusing on how divine power is harnessed and transmitted, especially through plants. The seminal gods or Yewevodu are often considered sons and daughters of the creator god, Mawu Lisa, the sacred rainbow serpent, a hermaphrodite who bequeathed seven children onto the world: Sakpata, Heviesso, Agbe, Ogun, Adze, Dzo, and Lêgba. I have chosen to focus on two of the more prominent ancient gods: Sakpata (earth and local) and Mami Wata (water and foreign). Mami Wata is a plural pantheon of various water spirits. Often Mami Wata is conceived as "foreign" in coastal Togo and Benin, but others insist she comes from Mama Isis in ancient Egypt (Zogbe 2007). She is ancient and a much older god than the northern spirits that came about a century ago in Tron Kunde / Gorovodu. So where is she from? Sabine Jell-Bahlsen (1994) and Henry John Drewal (2009) place her origins in southwestern Nigeria among the Yorùbá, but she may have been assimilated into a preexisting Yewe matrix among the Adja-Ewes, while simultaneously replacing other water spirits throughout western Africa from Senegal to Gabon. In Nigerian Òrìsà and throughout the Atlantic world she is Mami Wata and associated with Yemaya; she is La Siren in Haiti, Oshun or Yemayá in Cuba, Oxum in Brazil, and often associated with the Virgin Mary. The macro vodus (ancient Yewevodu spirits) are considered the "sons" of Mawu, the creator god; however, most have multiple incarnations, and many are considered more "female" than "male," particularly Sakpata and Mami Wata. Dana Rush (2013) has granted Mami's provenance to India, while elsewhere I have also discussed her European and Indian roots (Montgomery 2016). For Mama Zogbe (2007), she is an original Sybil and Black prophetess stretching back to before Christ. Her exact origin is debatable, referred to early by the pidgin etymological root "Mother Water" among the Igbo and Ibibio groups of southeastern Nigeria (Bastian 1997), while Zogbe (2007) and others claim the etymology to be Sudanic in origin.

In the eastern Anlo-Ewe communities, the Mami Wata shrine is commonly near the Gorovodu shrine, but this region possessed a multitude of water spirits long before colonialism; only later was she associated with foreign metonyms, partly due to mistakes made by ethnographers, including myself (Drewal et al. 2008; Montgomery 2016). According to Jill Salmons (1997), the mermaid comes with the arrival of European sailors and is later associated with Indian Hindu iconography after the 1950s (see also Drewal et al. 2008). Crosscurrents of water-spirit worship proliferate on both sides of the Atlantic, and to this day, there are lineages in Africa, the Caribbean, and the Americas born and initiated into Mami Wata. Mami Wata is plural, and her pantheon among Igbo, Yorùbá, Fòn, and Ewe possesses an amalgamation of spirits. In Ghana and Togo, she has many cousins across the water spectrum, including Nana Wango and Densu. The pidgin term itself has become an inclusive word for probably hundreds of water-linked spirits among numerous ethnic and cultural groups. However, the words *Mami* and *Outta* have Egyptian equivalents as well. And in all of Vodún, water is essential beyond the elemental level for it is also the first offering to the spirits upon prayer. Every living thing on earth needs water to survive, our bodies are mostly made of water, the earth is majority water, so its importance is understandable.

No matter the order or orthodoxy, Vodún is more than a philosophy, religion, or way of life. Often relegated to the dustbin of the "magical and invisible," however, for most followers it has great use value. It has many applications and can be about getting things done. Rush (2013, 3) writes: "Vodún does not formulate fundamental principles by which it acts; rather, it prioritizes action. Instead of abiding by philosophical tenets and devising or following doctrine like most religions, Vodún's focus is on making things happen, and getting things done. It places high value on efficacy, which infuses Vodún and thrusts Vodún arts and aesthetics into everything from problem solving and conflict resolution to protection and healing."

These spirits and metaphysics are not easily categorized; their fluid tendencies defy conventional categorization and study. These spirits are mobile, crossing anthropological key symbols (linguistics, rituals, kinship, political economy, ethnomusicology, performance, medicine, development)—as well as the spaces of social and biological sciences, humanities and the arts.

Vodu/Vodún "functions through ongoing consultations between practitioners, spirits, and ancestors" (Rush 2013, 11). It is open to nonstop editing and multiple nonlinear flows and has always been as global as it is local. Vodu/Vodún is "unfinished" and "open-ended," in the words of Rush (2013), and no doubt ceremonial and performative, but it is also pragmatic, rational, and transformative (Montgomery 2018). Judy Rosenthal (1998), following James Boon (1983), takes an inclusive and wide-ranging approach to text, and within these confines, material culture, sacred objects, and medicine are at the practical forefront in Vodún. Rosenthal (1998) witnessed the efficacy and multiplicity of Gorovodu firsthand, as priests successfully treated her daughter for sickle-cell anemia, time and time again. The "healing scene" is deeply composite and involves singing, plant medicine, drumming, prayer, divination, offerings, and spirit possession (Vannier and Montgomery 2015).

The Ewes, Minas, and Adja-Fòn incorporate more than just foreign and local gods; they also inflict a certain multiplicity of personhood unthinkable in Western dualistic circles, making them as adaptable as they are universal. Mami Wata often visits people in dreams and sometimes abducts people and takes them under the water; she demands that they serve her alone sexually, and if they do, they can become wealthy; if they do not, they can be devasted. Edna Bay (2008, 3) writes, "The sweep of documented Fòn eclecticism is vast and includes items of material culture, technologies, deities, and principles of state organization." Mami Wata is perhaps the most intriguing of all the African spirits, in that, during my fieldwork, I received more questions, comments, and praise words for her than any other god or spirit.

SAKPATA: ANCIENT GOD OF EARTH

Sakpata, called Aholu in Ewe and Shakpana in Nigeria and much of the Caribbean, is the eldest son/daughter of Mawu and the god of stone, fertility, sickness, and earth. Like Sakra Bode in Gorovodu, Sakpata is an earth god, not just the god of disease with which people often confuse her/him (Friedson 2010, 214). For many Ewes, Sakpata/Aholu is *"de la terre"* or "Ayi Vodún," the Vodún of the soil and ground. Sakpata also possesses great humility, being of dust and soil. Her customary regalia and haunting dancing are iconic—all the way from western Africa to Brazil (Sweet 2011).[4] Sakpata has both male and female manifestations, and gender is dynamic, traversing many categories and contexts. Sakpata can be evocative. Her ties to collective health and well-being are legendary, stretching back centuries and across oceans, with devotees from Nigeria to Brazil, Togo to Haiti. Sakpata's spiritual appeal is tied to sicknesses, such as HIV/AIDS and smallpox, especially in women and children. She possesses medical instruments, scissors, and chains. Like Sacra Bode and Sunia Compo of Gorovodu, she is very close to her oldest brother, Heviesso (thunder god), and sometimes they work together in doling out punishment and rewarding adepts.

Sakpata/Aholu is also tied to agriculture and bounty, and she is invoked for all forms of work and accumulation in Togo: fishing, market, and contract work. Sakpata has many sons, including the Vodún of leprosy (Ada Tangni) and of incurable sores (Sinji Aglosumato). Sakpata is also proficient at catching witches, sorcerers, and evildoers. She is particularly useful for dealing with mental disorders and mental illness (*adava*). Sakpata's power is feared and enchanting, and when she arrives during ceremony and sometimes sporadically, she is covered in grass and thatch, carrying wooden *venaviwo* (twins) on her back, face and body covered, red and white specks on her costume. She "detected" stomach illness in me in 2014 during a divination session. I returned to the United States very ill, diagnosed with hepatitis B and many parasites. Her special black molasses medicine alleviated some of my diarrheal episodes and the bokono (priest) stated that "somebody had poisoned my food." From his perspective, feces in food is direct witchcraft (àzĕ), especially if it was intentional. For her efforts, I gifted her a black rooster, her favorite palm wine, cigarettes, and some American bourbon.

Shrines in West Africa are magnetic centers of power, sacred places for prayer, healing, adjudication, conflict resolution, memorializing history, and transformative ritual (Baum 1999; Goody 1973; Vannier and Montgomery 2015). The sheer number of ingredients that goes into making the Sakpata "fetish" and the associated sacred medicines, tools, and weapons is elaborate. The symbols are metonyms for her actions: scalpel for prodding and healing, broom and scissors for cleaning and curing, keys and bells intended for diagnosis, spears and batons for catching witches and punishing evildoers.

Sakpata is the most prominent earth deity in Vodún and Òrìsà. In Benin, Sakpata is known as King Dada Zodzi and is praised in Cuba as Asoyi. Pieces and shades of Sakpata exist across the Atlantic in Brazilian Candomblé and Umbanda, where Omolu is associated with sickness and Ossaim is the master of plants. Symbols and signs are windows into the collective conscious and memory of the creed, and once made operational through ritual, they regenerate, maintaining efficacy across borders and doctrines. These honorific titles and flexible properties of Sakpata expose the ancient nature of this god, considered benevolent by many as a producer of grain and curer of disease. Sakpata uses a scepter and broom made of palm fronds loaded with black powder medicines (*atike*), wrapped in symbolic beads and imbibed with special ingredients, used to sweep an array of diseases from the human body. (*Ha* in Fòngbe means "broom.") Morning chores involve the sweeping of dirt from homes in the village, while humming songs for Sakpata. The sacred medicines of Sakpata and the construction of the clay shrine are cumbersome and can take many months. Some of the plants come from the northern savanna, some from graveyards, and others are desert or forest horticulture. In Gbedala, there are several Sakpata shrines, and it is common for a Sakpatasi from neighboring villages and quarters to visit the village while in trance, in a costume of rainbow-colored grass and elaborate fabric, together with a guide there to translate and secure the god's path. She can disappear, play the part of an old man or woman, and often frightens children. Sakpata frequents the village, since waterborne illness and viral diseases are so common, and few have access to orthodox medicine.

Sakpata/Aholu is tied to ecology, nutrition, and the distribution of many foods; as the premiere spirit of agriculture and munificent harvest, she is universal. She is responsible for turning "raw into cooked" food, an allegory that would have pleased Levi-Strauss. In an environment where food can spoil quickly, the spices and blessings of Sakpata can extend the shelf life of foods, treat open wounds, and simply save lives. Many families who tend to small plots of land around greater Lomé often leave offerings and sacrifices to Sakpata, especially during planting and harvest cycles. Sometimes rituals are intended to honor her assistance or to make up for disrespect or neglect. For Afio Zannou et al. (2007, 140–141), Sakpata rituals become the cornerstones of yam and cowpea production in Benin, where a "diversity of rituals, food habits, technological traits and food security strategies for the two crops contributes to the maintenance of varietal diversity." For Peter De Smet (as quoted in Quiroz et al. 2016), traditional pharmacology and medicine become reliant on African rituals and "sacred objects" and utensils, made translatable in the art and visual culture of many groups. Sakpata and her priests have also been instrumental in eradicating smallpox and other diseases and pandemics throughout the coast (Rosenthal 1998, 134–14; Stocklin 1981, 405–415).

After a Fetatrotro (New Year's ceremony) held in 2013, an adept of Wango fell into trance and dragged us all to the Sakpata shrine; apparently during all the confusion of ceremony, we had forgotten to pay tribute to her, and she came to her friend Nana Wango (crocodile spirit and water spirit in Gorovodu) to demand we appease her. And appease her we did. On the spot, she was given special palm wine with black pepper (*ataku*) upon greeting; the priest then proudly displayed a handful of her "sacred tools": baton (*eha*), broom (*ekbo*), and rattle (*abaga*). All these objects are tied to the diagnosis and healing of various ailments, and Sakpata possesses her own medicines. In a context devoid of proper access and delivery for child and maternal health, Sakpata is an important innovation for health care access and delivery.

MAMI WATA: MERMAID AND WATER GODDESS

Mami Wata has been the subject of the ethnographic eye for decades (Drewal et al. 2008; Jell-Bahlsen 1995). She is the Vodún of the sea (Tovodu), and sometimes she morphs and transfigures into related orders and gods (Montgomery 2016). Mami Wata is sometimes presented as a beautiful "light-skinned" Black woman known for her beauty and market prowess. She assists with still-born births and other forms of infant mortality. She is visited by market women looking to better their lot. She helps with female and childhood illnesses. Mami Wata is associated with Vodu Da, the sacred rainbow serpent who can transverse all realms: air (climbing trees), water, and earth (tunneling beneath). Mami Wata loves perfumed powders and oils; she can sometimes be vain, and her sacred implements include mirrors, combs, makeup, dry goods, and money. One of her powerful children is Dan Toxosu, who manifests himself in the birth of "monster" babies, those with external abnormalities.

To win the favor of Mami Wata, one should enter her shrine freshly bathed and doused in sweet-smelling fragrances. It is proper to prepurchase as many fresh items as possible from the market and to have them in the shrine before entering because generalized reciprocity is necessary for ethical accumulation; in short, you reap what you sow. She normally visits people in dreams, sometimes abducts them at sea, and after divination what she requests of those she has sought out is unveiled. Worshipers bathe and submerge themselves in floral musk and perfumes and always talcum powder, before approaching her altar, neatly decorated with fruit, shells, porcelain artifacts, whitewashed sculptures, and fresh-cut flowers. Mami Wata is known for her lavish taste and durable richness, and she is associated with Europeans, Indians, and sometimes a mermaid; she is as seductive as she is dangerous. Those who pay tribute to her know her as a "capitalist" deity because she can bring good (or bad) fortune in the form of money. She demands loyalty and can make men impotent and their wives jealous, since she demands monogamy toward her and her alone. This relationship between currency and water makes sense because cowries come from the sea, and they were used to purchase slaves, which were sold across the oceans to produce even more capital. Some claim that the name *Mami Wata* is pidgin English, the language used to facilitate the slave trade and colonialism, the influence of foreign cultures on African persons, but she predates colonialism. Because of these outside influences and years of culture contact, Mami Wata takes on many forms, and in Gbedala, there are more female Mami Wata adepts and priests than men. On the Gbedala shrine, there are chromolithographs of a Samoan snake charmer, and many Hindu chromolithographs: Ganesha, Manusa Devi, and Kali, as well as a Virgin Mary, gifts I bequeathed to the priest in 2014. Mami becomes global because in the words of John Drewal et al. (2008, 22), the spiritual crossover is no problem with many Africans: "They see it as multiple insurance policies."

Mami Wata, for some, is surmised as and an amalgamation of local water spirits whose alluring attraction has turned her loose globally. There is great ubiquity and omnipresence in Mami Wata, not just in the African diaspora but throughout the world; just think of the prevalence of female water spirits cross-culturally across time. In West Africa, her colonial mimetic nature reminds us of the resistance of other regional spirit possession orders, like the Hauka, Zar, and Bori cults of other regions in Africa. These possession and healing orders reflect the empowerment and socially transformative nature of southern denominations of Vodún. Along the coast of Benin, there are many practitioners who double as Mamissi or Amengasi (Mami Wata priests or adepts). Those initiated and "married" to Mami Wata work hard to appease her. Gorovodu adepts associate her with Mama Tchamba, the slave spirit spectrum, while others insist she is of Yewe origins—Ouidah, specifically (Rosenthal 1998, 116). Some have placed her provenance to the lagoons of southwestern Nigeria, and other locals say she is from Congo or Cameroon, or even Egypt or the Middle East. In one ceremony, a drawing of a Mami Wata stool, or *mami zikpe* (throne), is made on the ground outside of the shrine, and many artisans work on making her "children," the whitewashed concrete statues that lie throughout most Mami shrines, symbolizing lost or sick babies. After a personal matter came up during divination in Ouidah in 2003, the assistant priest there took me to a local shrine, where we constructed a mimetic child of clay, cement, and stone. After a morning seaside ritual, we offered her many gifts wrapped in white cloth as the sun rose. Later we placed another offering next to a three-breasted ceramic statue and a white Christian cross in her shrine. White talcum powder, symbolic of Mami's taste for modern things, is used to make the drawing (*vèvè* in Haitian Vodou). The lines direct her spirit through the compound into her shrine and then back out to a nearby tree, which is encircled three times (Rush 2013). The shrine room contains numerous clay pots, painted white for her various reincarnation spirits, and cigarettes, placed in the mouths of ceramic statuettes for the Mami spirits.

After weeks and weeks of pestering Sofo (Priest) Amagbe about the origins of Mami Wata, he stopped me and said, "Mami Wata is not something we can explain with words; we feel her when we contemplate love, and when we need money, she comes from Nigeria and Central Africa, and before that ancient Africa; she went to India too; she means so many things to so many people" (2013). It was not until a seventy-five-year-old great-grandmother fell into trance one day in 2006 that I understood her intense power. The priestess had not fallen into trance in more than twenty years, and when she did, she shook and shimmied with enormous power along the beach. As Drewal (2009, 226) writes, "Understanding material or materiality or 'stuff' begins with the body, more specifically, the senses." Once, when I was what Steven Friedson (2010) calls being "in between," I was in a Mami Wata shrine in Ghana; the priest gifted me with a small leather talisman wrapped in white cloth with a conch shell and two cowrie shells. Mami Wata shrines and sacred objects are most often created by hand, and they are not just religious objects but also pieces of art and power. Materiality and meaning are divulged through sensory anthropology and embodiment because multiple senses (beyond the five-sense model) are on display during Vodu production, service, maintenance, and exchange with the gods (Geurts 2003; Montgomery and Vannier 2017).

Mami Wata flourishes in the New World, and "sirens and snakes" epitomize the water spirits in the arts of Haitian Vodou and Cuban Santeria (Houlberg 1996, 30). Tobias Wendl (2001, 269–292) explores Mami Wata shrines as contrary to "modernity" and "studio photography," which, like horror films in modern Ghana, seek to make modernity dangerous and scary. Mami Wata, stretching east into Nigeria (especially among Igbo and Ibibio) and Cameroon, is tied to modernity and even decides "permitted" and "prohibited" wealth, for her rituals and exchanges invoke "economic morality" by way of generalized and balanced reciprocity, through ritual purification, especially with the advent of globalization when Mami "performs the other" (Frank 1995; Drewal et al. 2008).

Analysis of possession episodes—type, quantity, duration, and message—is important because that is when body and spirit become one. Gorovodu possessions by Kunde and Bangre are commonplace and universal on the community level, but Sakpata and Mami Wata possessions are less frequent, even though they are older and more widely known spirits. During my times in Gbedala, I have only seen Mami Wata possession trance half a dozen times, all during morning oceanside rituals. And yet, her Gorovodu double, Nana Wango (Grandmother Crocodile), commonly mounts her adepts and sometimes corresponds during trance with Mami Wata of Yewe origins. Crosscurrents like resonant sound waves overlap, multimetered and multiply authored. They intersect pantheons, geographies, and symbolic domains, and sensing the spirits and their spirit wives directly opens many doors.

MODERN GOROVODU: KUNDE AND BANGRE

The Gorovodu (lit., "Vodu of kola nut") of Togo and Ghana is an amalgamation of many northern gods who were at different times singular shrines and spirits in their provincial northern lands. These medicine shrines are relatively recent, being born within the past century and disguised and shrouded in myriad of names: Kunde, Atinga, Tigare, Sakrabundi, Alafia, Bangre, Nana Tongo, Brekete,

Figure 3.1. Mami Wata Offering. Photograph of Behumbeza, by Mami Wata Priestess, 2021.

Tron, and Senya Kupo (Allman and Parker 2005; Field 1960; Friedson 2010; Goody 1972; Parker 2011; Ward 1956). There are "two sticks" to Gorovodu; one branch is "Thron Kpeto Deka Alaafia," translating from Mina as "Thron of One Stone in Peace" (Rush 2013, 78). Gorovodu is the other branch, with corresponding spirit doubles in Yewevodu. Like Yewevodu, healing and dispute resolution are paramount—even more so in Gorovodu (an *atikevodu* order meaning "tree root vodu"). The spirits overlap, connecting with their doubles across the strains of Vodún writ large. Bangre stands in for Ogun/Egu, Sunia Compo plays the role of Lêgba, while Nana Wango correlates with Mami Wata. Tron refers not only to northern spirits but also means "to turn," which is exactly what *tronsi* (adepts) do during possession-trance, referenced by adepts as "going to the other side of the street." The once singular northern gods and shrines have been reassembled through "ancient Vodún" filters by modern-day coastal southerners. The Ewes worship both Tron and Yewe together, and the gods interact in much the same manner as their devotees. Whereas most Yewe spirits are inherited and tied to kinship, clan, and lineage, Gorovodu can be purchased, although much of this is still tied to kinship. Tron, or Gorovodu, is very demanding and quite expensive, explaining why many of the colonial administrators and early ethnographers saw "Tron/Tigare" as a "sham by charlatans" (Field 1960). The Ghana and Togoland National Archives are besieged with colonial records detailing the resistance and threat that these gods had on French, British, and German colonizers, and still today Vodún is a transformative movement of peace, reconciliation, and social justice, evidenced by participation in the ongoing democratic movement "Let's Save Togo."

Whereas the Ancient Yewe gods stretch back hundreds, perhaps even thousands, of years; the Gorovodu/Tron spirits from northern Ghana are relative newcomers on the scene—at least the way they have been assembled into modern Tron or Gorovodu since the 1920s in the south (Friedson 2010; Rosenthal 1998). The common core six primary gods of Gorovodu are Kunde (Father), Ablewa (Mother) Sunia Compo (Trickster/Stone), Bangre (Warrior), Sacra Bode (Earth God), and Nana Wango (Grandmother Crocodile/Water). These six gods are just a baseline, and some, like Bangre, include countless other spirits forming a consolidation of African warrior spirits (Gueria, Mossi, Tsengue, Kanga). The actual origins of these primary Gorovodu gods are singular and stretch from Ivory Coast (as with Bangre, see Goody 1972) to Burkina Faso and northern Ghana with Kunde and Sunia Compo (Allman and Parker 2005). They were amassed into the current Gorovodu pantheon (including Alafia) sometime around a century ago by Kodzo Kuma in central Ghana (Allman and Parker 2005; Friedson 2010). It was Kodzo Kuma who taught Sofo Bisi, the head priest at Gbedala. Today, these "kola nut cults" from the north signify several ideas all at once: especially the large corpus of ritual knowledge from the northern forests and savanna where these "witch-hunting" and "morality invoking" spirits originate (Venkatachalam 2015, 53). Kunde is composed of three separate spherical fetishes. He is gestured with the left hand and a three-pulse knock, gifted three kola nuts and three chalks. Three is his life-path number and why he is tied to the trinity and Africa's "triple heritage" (Islam, Christianity, and traditional religion). "Kunde," his devotees say, "we bring kola nut to you so that you can give us a long and healthy life" (Montgomery and Vannier 2017).

PAPA KUNDE: FATHER AND HUNTER

If Sakpata is tied to the earth, and Mami Wata to water, then Kunde is the hunter (*adela*) extraordinaire. He hails from the northern bush and is armed with spears, daggers, and guns. Sharing cosmic space with cousins Ogun, Ochossi, and Egu, he is called *dzata*, meaning "rider of lions." Whereas Mami Wata is tied to a triple-breasted white sculpture and the Virgin Mary, God, and Jesus, Kunde is also associated with the trinity, and both Islamic prayer beads and Catholic rosaries are sometimes tucked behind altars. Kunde is king of the Gorovodu house, the father; his color is red, and like Bangre and Jesus, some say he died a violent death in blood (*vumeku*). Others insist he is a cool spirit, not a *zogbeku* (violent death spirit), and that is why only Bangre, not Kunde, goes to the Sacred Forest. The Kunde fetish is composed of burned black powder medicine made from hyena skin, plants from the graveyard, dog bone, monkey teeth, and about four typed pages of other materials. There is marijuana, mercury, and ground seashells in the mixture. Kunde is tied to Heviesso because he invokes justice and can strike via lightning, he is tied to Ogun with skills as hunter and master of weapons, and he is the son of Kadzanka and Allah, said to be ancient grandparent spirits from the distant desert north and even more distant past (perhaps a nod to the ancient trans-Saharan slave trade). Papa Kunde is the father of Sacra Bode, Sunia Compo, and Bangre, and he is depicted as a good Muslim, wearing a Malian kaftan and red fez cap. Sometimes he is dressed in animal skins with intricate scarifications on his arms and face. He is a good husband to Ablewa, who also finds her roots in northern witch-finding cults from the turn of the twentieth century. The way these various Tron are assembled varies from village to village, and sometimes there are as few as four spirits; other times, there are more than a dozen.

Kunde is the first in the Gorovodu medicine house and the first to be offered drink, prayer, and salutations. He is also the only Gorovodu spirit served with the left hand and offered three kola nuts, while others are served with the right hand and granted gifts in sums of four. Whereas many of the other spirits can be gender fluid, forgiving, and seek camaraderie with other spirits, Kunde is a stern cisgender patriarch, and his word is final. The left hand and odd number of kola nut blessings are indicative of his foreign/northern/slave/royal status and distinctive power. Kunde is a charismatic leader, the steady and chief-like father, and the judge and jury of the community. He is the pater, supreme judge, and keeper of the law. Dog is his totem, so Kunde "eats" dog, meaning dogs are regularly sacrificed in his honor. Kunde is the punisher and will kill those that regularly sin against Gorovodu law without remorse. As the father-provider, Kunde is regarded as a sort of jack-of-all-trades, and like any respected father, Kunde can discipline with both legitimate and coercive power; he offers carrots and sticks (blessings and beatings), but it is his unforgiving nature that makes him who he is, the prosecutor and judge, a man without depravity. When Kunde speaks, or is embodied during possession trance, dressed in blood-red garments from head to toe, wearing a fez, and a kaolin-soaked face making the adept appear ghostly and white, people listen and are on their best behavior.

The material culture and spiritual medicinal repertoire of Kunde is extensive and takes years to master. As a hunter, the many tools of the bush are his instruments, with nearly all of them becoming weaponized by way of sacred

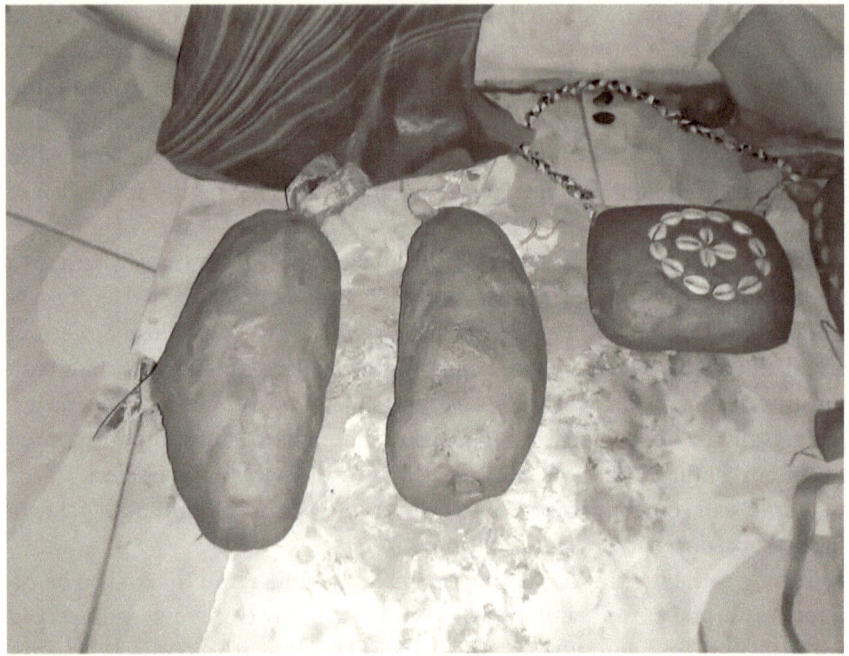

Figure 3.2. Kunde god-object in raw form. Lome, Togo. Photograph by author.

medicines and rituals. As a diviner, Kunde can see all, and his original popularity came from his skills as a hunter and witch catcher in the northern territories of Ghana during a time of exploding cocoa production, colonialism, and the social ills that come with social stratification (Allman and Parker 2005; Venkatachalam 2015). Kunde, like Bangre, is known to be a grappler and tough guy with dead-eye aim and a propensity for catching witches and transgressors, especially those violating Gorovodu laws. Behind the shrine of Kunde are special sachets of herbs, replica spears, antique arrows, model guns, and bladed items, such as knives and machetes. Instincts—such as intuition, balance, prophecy, dreams, and divinatory consultations—are every bit as important as seeing, hearing, and feeling in Brekete/Gorovodu, particularly with Kunde since the other spirits all carry his family name.

BANGRE: GOD OF WAR

Ogun or "Gu" is the Yewevodu of iron and war, and his Gorovodu equivalent is Bangre. Bangre begins with Dagari-speaking peoples of northern Ghana and into Ivory Coast and Burkina Faso, his history and mythology researched by only a few (Allman and Parker 2005; Goody 1972; Mbowura 2013, 22). He gives humanity different material technologies—namely, weapons. He is the spirit who does not accept complicity with evil; he can kill others quickly with an array of magic elements and implements. In trance, adepts aim a bow and arrow, jab with a pitchfork (*apie*), and dance to northern warrior and Brekete rhythms. Like his father, Kunde, he enjoys time in the forest. As a spirit of the bush, animals and plants are his domain, and his medicines deal with everything from sorcery upon children to HIV, schizophrenia, and sickle-cell anemia. Like Sakpata, Bangre is a medicine god, and his apothecary chest is extensive; some of the plants associated with him are also connected with Sakpata, although more of his come from northern territories. He is fond of daggers, knives, spears, guns, bullets, and arrows. This is expressed by the Adja- Fòn saying *da gu do* (cook for Ogun), a reference to empower Ogun, and for the Ewes Ogun is tied to "hot bush" (vumeku) deaths and urban deaths on the streets of Lomé and Cotonou in Togo and Benin. As a northerner and brother of Sacra Bode, Bangre is reified as Mossi, Hausa, and Fulani warriors and slave capturers (and slaves), highly skilled on horseback and as romanticized as the "tribes" of the steppe throughout the Roman and Ottoman Empires. Ogun, like Heviesso, has his own sect and transforms into "Egun" or "Gu" throughout the African diaspora. In the village of Gbedala, he has only a few personal shrines, belonging to senior members of the original lineages of the village. Ogun is recognized by all, but with the enormous growth and power of Bangre, his influence is somewhat hampered in Ghana and Togo. Bangre is everywhere, growing in popularity, black-and-white striped costume, red or black fez, long beard, speaking Quranic verses, the mimetic version of everything romanticized as northern (and slave) by southern Ewes.

Bangre is the only gorovodu spirit who travels easily to and from the Sacred Forest and shrine. The Bangre pantheon is composed of anywhere from four to twelve different god objects, made from bells, antelope horns, slave shackles, iron tools, knives, and various gourds of northern origin. These god objects are repositories of cultural contact and encounters between Ewes and their northern slaves and family members. Lord Bangre is a guardian of the bush, a master hunter and military man, with northern Ghanaian and eastern Ivoirian roots as an earth god, not too different from Sakpata. The mythology around Bangre is extensive, and his "black" and "white" versions are structural placemarks for myth and ritual among the Dagari/Dagomba of Jack Goody's (1972) research. For Dannabang Kuwabong (2004, 6), Bangre epitomizes earth and prosperity in a harsh environment: "Bagre, as a religious and cultural mythopoeic narrative and performance, reflects a spiritual attitude to the environment. The environment *mo wi so,* kola is spiritually guarded through the rituals and sacrifices performed to the Tengbane or Mother Earth, the second most powerful deity after the supreme God, Nangmen."

Bangre, like his fictive brother Hevioso/Sàngó, asks for regular libations and animals because he controls the stars, clouds, and heavens. Like all kola nut gods it is *goro* or *bisi* that he requests most. Ogun, Adze, and Bangre reign over animals and birds and can be as sweet and fatherly as Saint Francis or as unrelenting as Lord Shiva. Goody's "Myth of Bagre" (1972) was an important text on African myths, even though it got little attention in the decades following its publication. Goody (2003, 81) himself called it his most important work: "Of all the things that I have worked on in my academic life, the one that I am most proud of is the account of Bagre ceremonies among the LoDagaa of northern Ghana, especially the transcription and translation of the recitation that I have called *The Myth of Bagre*."

Anthony Naaeke (2005, 2–10) has probed the text for the relationship between the Bagre myth and gender. While others have focused on the environment, myth, and cosmology. Bangre, like Kunde and the other indigenous gods, grew despite capitalism and Christianity, and most often right along with them (Mohr 2011).

In renowned Gorovodu shrines, such as those at Kpando, Lomé, Ho, and Aneho, prospective clients show up from throughout western Africa and beyond. My research details a wide range of people visiting Bangre: Burkinabes, Nigerians, Malians, and even some from Europe, Asia, and the Americas. They come to confront witchcraft and sorcery, to assist with childbirth, to find jobs, to escape persecution, and to travel abroad. Bangre is one of many children of Kunde and Ablewa, but he is the fiercest of characters, able to shape-shift into powerful bush animals, acting as hunter, warrior, policeman, soldier, and martyr. Like his paradigmatic doubles of Yewe provenance, Heviesso and Ogun, Bangre is a god of justice and uses his many sacred tools and elements to capture and punish violators of Gorovodu law (*ese*). It makes sense that the favorite son of Kunde would be a master of justice and combat. He uses a shield made of plant fibers and cowry shells, with woven ornaments and talismans; like the magical shield of Ogun/Egu, he is bullet proof. He also uses a wooden gun (*tokpui*) filled with sacred medicines drawn from the Sacred Forest and northern bush. He stalks his prey while marking his gun or skillfully tracks wild animals and witches before mimetically slicing their throats, snaring or trapping them, all played out in episodes of spirit possession by adepts. He defends against the passionate

Figure 3.3. The washing and preparation of Bangre god-object. Lome, Togo. Photograph by author.

envy of others and defends adepts against assassination or arrest at the hands of the secret police; hence, veneration of Bangre is growing, especially in one-party authoritarian Togo.

Bangre's multiplicity crosses real and imagined space and time, through his holistic construction, which includes the assemblage of many other gods and minor gods. These other gods are made of materials ranging from antelope and water buffalo horns to Fulani knives, Dagomba bells, and even bullets and pieces of military and police uniforms. Bangre himself is composed of a large circular bell with "Dagari roots," where the bells once were wrapped around magical baobab trees and used for initiation (Goody 1972, 112–113). As assistant priest, Sofo Amagbe, who is also a Mami Wata devotee and priest, once said in 2006, "I know he is not only one god but also several others. I don't understand how this is . . . but he is one man with many faces or one extended family of gods. Bangre is the hunter. When the hunter goes hunting, he does not go alone but with his tools. He puts his tools, his supplies, in a bag or sheaths them in his belt. That bag that holds the tools of the hunter, the weapons of Bangre, is Magazun. Sourougou, and Tsengue [related warrior/hunter spirits] are like tools that help him hunt" (personal conversation 2014).

CONCLUSION: SHRINE ETHNOGRAPHY, GLOBAL CONNECTIVITY, AND VODU IDENTITY

Shrines in Africa have long fascinated ethnographers, from E. E. Evans-Pritchard (1937) and Victor Witter Turner (1967) to Jack Goody (1972). The symbols and objects associated with the spirits are as diverse and multivocal as the persons serving them. This comparative study traverses four distinct but related shrines: ancient/modern, northern/southern, foreign/local. Timothy Insoll (2004, 105) writes that the term *shrine* fails to describe the range of structures and ideas included in its boundaries. Therefore, how we define shrines is "from above" and not from "within"—meaning these shrines are living breathing entities where the very cycle of life is engaged, performed, and interpreted. The field pivots toward "medicine shrines," especially in light of the rapid growth of medical anthropology and African archaeology more generally. Some shrines, such as Mami Wata and Mama Tchamba (slave spirit order), are not entirely medicinal, even though they can improve one's lot and well-being. Both Yewe and Tron spirits not only possess their devotees but also heal them with plants, epiphany, and transcendental manipulations. Although Kunde and Bangre are known as "medicine gods," Mami Wata and Sakpata also work on diagnosis, treatment, and well-being, albeit not through the black powder medicines of Gorovodu. Vodún healing plays a central role, fibers tying mortals to the worlds of ancestors and gods. The so-called medicine cults and shrines have continued to flourish into modernity precisely because of their ability to cross currents, mobile and resilient and successful by nature, bringing morality, healing, and ecstasy. In a context devoid of Western medicine and access to health care, medicinal shrines like Gorovodu and medicine gods like Kunde and Bangre save lives.

On equal footing with the medicine shrine are the Sacred Forests (Zogbe) that occupy many communities throughout the Bight of Benin. Whereas Sakpata and Mami Wata are of the earth and sea, Heviesso, Bangre, and Kunde are champions from the forest. Michael Sheridan (2008, 23) references these "sacred groves" throughout Africa as historical constructs with ongoing agency that escaped the functional and mechanistic perspective of "shrines as static tradition." B. T. James (2009, 41) has noted in relation to Hausa medicinal substances that medicinal power "is partly drawn from their interconnections to a wider framework of metaphorical associations and not simply inherent biomedical qualities of the constituent ingredients" (cited in Insoll 2011). Insoll (2011),

Goody (1967), and many others have also pointed out that these "medicines" do not work outside of the context of certain shrines, outside certain literal and symbolic contexts. The symbolic and "medical" spheres are not distinct realms of study, but rather occupy the same sphere for wellness.

Vodún shrines are not only unfinished but works in progress. According to Rush (2013, 32–33), "Transatlantic shrines are works in progress, eternally under construction, and accordingly, unfinished. The static nature of a shrine is misleading. Although a shrine used in Vodún may appear 'finished,' it continues to change in terms of both form and meaning. The form can expand rhizomatically each time a new offering is made, ranging from organic materials such as animal blood and animal parts, saliva, palm oil, fruit, and prepared foodstuffs to mass-produced items such as perfumes, powder, plastic dolls, candies, bottles of liquor, or what Cosentino (1995) calls 'disparate stuff.'"

For Blier (1996), *vo* among the Fòn translates "to relax" and *dun* means "to draw water." This also testifies to the pronounced vividness of both Da and Mami Wata along the coast. Rush (2013, 103–104) continues referencing Karen McCarthy Brown (2001): "According to KM Brown, this ceaselessly circling rainbow serpent connects Haitians, inextricably, to their long-lost transatlantic ancestors. The snake swallowing its own tail has become a transatlantic trope for protection, regeneration, and connection. That is, every time one witnesses a multicolored arc formed by the refraction of sunlight in a rainfall's mist, one is witness to and protected by Dan Aida Wedo's majestic instantaneity on both sides of the Atlantic." The same ouroboric symbol connecting Africa and the New World globally also connects north/south spirits locally within Togo and Benin.

What is Vodún? Why does it matter? How is it represented? How does a comparative and descriptive approach help us shed light on similarities and differences between and within Vodún? Vodún is an ancient ritualcentric belief system that matters because it develops, nurtures, and heals the entire lifeworld of its followers. The artisanship that goes into the creation of material culture is a testament to the deeply organic power of Vodún persons—themselves an intersection of past, present, and future worlds. In Gbedala, this "past world" includes the forced marriage of northern slaves (amefleflewo); these bought persons are now reified in regular commemorative rituals and accompanying consecrated objects. Sacred "slave jewelry" (*tchambagan*) is found or gifted and imbibed with medicinal power through prayer, plants, and other rites. The short ethnographic film compiled by me and Christian Vannier and linked here showcases the importance of Mama Tchamba and slave spirits to Togolese Gorovodu and Vodún.[5] Tchamba spirits are a pantheon dedicated to the memory of northern slaves (also a town in northern Togo) and a multiethnic symbolic category tied to Fulani and Hausa peoples who married into Ewe patrilines into the twentieth century.

The "bracelets" mimic shackles, and these often seemingly disparate sacred objects are found in the Mami Wata shrine or draped around the Bangre alter. These possessions originate in various forms swathed around Sakpata's head, strung from Mami Wata's entryway, or fastened to Kunde's and Bangre's god objects in the shrine and Sacred Forest. Symbols and sacred objects matter because they are the embodiment of the creed. They represent "myth in action" by giving agency to participants and constructing individual and collective interpretations and meanings. Devotees try to emulate their gods and capture spiritual essence through the materiality of the god objects and shrines and the epiphanies of possession trance and revelation. Meanwhile, Bangre and Kunde are made up of gunpowder, wild animal parts, bullet casings, and distinct plants—not exactly what you find at your local convenience store or typical open-air markets of Lomé, Accra, and Cotonou.

The reason people construct their gods with their own hands (manipulation) is because they want it to act on their behalf, just as they honor the spirits with many taboos, rites, and proscriptions. Like the adepts themselves, these gods and shrines share many similarities and distinctions regarding their personhood/godhood. These spirits are dynamic, mobile, and global. They are a testament to the African religious imagination: embedded, ecstatic, and magnificent. The fluid nature of these is all about spirit service, and these crosscurrents traverse symbolic and real borders while breaking down boundaries: ancient and modern, coastal and savanna, earth and water, human and divine, foreign and local, northern and southern, past and present. Devotees of Yewevodu and Gorovodu in contemporary Togo continue to honor and emulate their gods, revealing to the world a vibrant religious culture that has become a dominant aesthetic for the Black Atlantic world.

NOTES

1. The Tron of northern provenance are also called Gorovodus or Vodus in southern Togo. In Ghana, Tron is associated with Brekete. These gods also have other names like Atinga and Tigare, in such far-away places as Nigeria. For the purposes here, I am using Brekete, Tron, and Gorovodu interchangeably.

2. Mami Wata is not exactly Yewevodu since she is not of the original seven. However, like Sakpata (of earth) she is old and ancient and is present in communities where Sakpata/Aholu exists. Mama Zogbe (2007) has traced her roots to

predynastic Egypt when "Sybils," or prophetesses, reigned supreme throughout the ancient world. She is no doubt foreign but not necessarily distant, and her exact origin is debatable, with some saying Congo, Nigeria, South Africa, Brazil, India, Egypt, or Europe.

3. The highly contested term *fetish* has been taken up at length by others because of its inherent racial overtones (Pietz 1985, 5–17). Like the term *voodoo* (or *vudu*), it is used by Ewes, Minas, and other ethnic groups to refer to both spirits and sacred altars.

4. *Chasing the Spirit: Gorovodu in Southern Togo*. A film by Eric J. Montgomery and Christian N. Vannier. 66 min. Color. Detroit: CultureRealm Films (culturerealm.com), 2012. Available from Amazon.com. See Sakpata at 08:30.

5. "The Tchamba Order," part 4 of *Ethnography of a Shrine: Tchamba*, CultureRealm Films, posted on December 17, 2015, YouTube video, 05:40, https://www.youtube.com/watch?v=Ue-qmr35RrY.

REFERENCES

Allman, Jean, and John Parker. 2005. *Tongnaab: The History of a West African God*. Bloomington: Indiana University Press.

Barnes, Sandra T. 1997. "The Many Faces of Ogun: Introduction to the First Edition." In *Africa's Ogun: Old World and New*, edited by Sandra Barnes, 1–26. Bloomington: Indiana University Press.

Bastian, Misty L. 1997. "Married in the Water: Spirit Kin and Other Afflictions of Modernity in Southeastern Nigeria." *Journal of Religion in Africa* 27 (1): 116–134.

Baum, Robert M. 1999. *Shrines of the Slave Trade: Diola Religion and Society in Precolonial Senegambia*. Oxford: Oxford University Press.

Bay, Enda G. 2008. *Asen, Ancestors and Vodu: Tracing Change in African Art*. Chicago: University of Illinois Press.

Blier, Suzanne Preston. 1996. *African Vodún: Art, Psychology, and Power*. Chicago: University of Chicago Press.

Boon, James A. 1983. *Other Tribes, Other Scribes: Symbolic Anthropology in the Comparative Study of Cultures, Histories, Religions and Texts*. Cambridge: Cambridge University Press.

Cosentino, Donald J. 1995. "Imagine Heaven." In *The Sacred Arts of Haitian Vodou*, edited by the Los Angeles Fowler Museum of Cultural History, 25–55. Los Angeles: Fowler Museum of Cultural History.

Creed, Barbara. 1987. "From Here to Modernity: Feminism and Postmodernism." *Screen* 28 (2): 47–68.

Drewal, Henry John. 2009. "Material, Sensorial Religion the Case of Mami Wata." *Material Religion* 5 (2): 226–229.

Drewal, Henry John, Marilyn Houlberg, Bogumil Jewsiewicki, John W. Nunley, and Jill Salmons. 2008. "Mami Wata: Arts for Water Spirits in Africa and Its Diasporas." *African Arts* 41 (2): 60–83.
Evans-Pritchard, E. E. 1937. *Witchcraft, Oracles and Magic among the Azande.* Vol. 12. London: Oxford University Press.
Field, Margaret Joyce. 1960. *Search for Security: An Ethnopsychiatric Study of Rural Ghana.* New York: W. W. Norton.
Frank, Barbara. 1995. "Permitted and Prohibited Wealth: Commodity-Possessing Spirits, Economic Morals, and the Goddess Mami Wata in West Africa." *Ethnology* 34 (4): 331–346.
Friedson, Steven M. 2010. *Remains of Ritual: Northern Gods in a Southern Land.* Chicago: University of Chicago Press.
Gayibor, Nicoué. 1985. "L'aire culturelle aja-tado des origines à la fin du XVIIf siècle." PhD diss., University of Paris.
———. 1992. *Traditions historiques du Bas-Togo.* Vol. 1. Paris: Centre d'études linguistiques et historiques par la tradition orale.
Goody, Jack. 1972. *The Myth of the Bagre.* Oxford: Oxford University Press.
———. 2003. "The 'Civilizing Process' in Ghana." *European Journal of Sociology* 44 (1): 61–73.
Goody, Jack, and Esther Goody. 1967. "The Circulation of Women and Children in Northern Ghana." *Man* 2 (2): 226–248.
Greene, Sandra E. 2003. "Whispers and Silences: Explorations in African Oral History." *Africa Today* 50 (2): 41–53.
Herskovits, Melville J. 1938. *Dahomey: An Ancient West African Kingdom.* 2 vols. New York: J. J. Augustin.
Houlberg, Marilyn. 1996. "Sirens and Snakes: Water Spirits in the Arts of Haitian Vodou." *African Arts* 29 (2): 30.
Insoll, Timothy. 2004. *Archaeology, Ritual, Religion.* New York: Routledge.
———. 2011. "Substance and Materiality? The Archaeology of Talensi Medicine Shrines and Medicinal Practices." *Anthropology and Medicine* 18 (2): 181–203.
Insoll, Timothy, Rachel MacLean, and Benjamin Kankpeyeng. 2013. *Temporalizing Anthropology: Archaeology in the Talensi Tong Hills, Northern Ghana.* Leiden, Netherlands: Africa Magna Verlag.
James, B. T. 2009. "Broadening Interpretive Perspectives on Indigenous Healing: The Case of Bori Spirit Possession amongst the Hausa." MA thesis, University of Manchester.
Jell-Bahlsen, Sabine. 1994. "'This Native Something': Understanding and Acknowledging the African Experience." *Dialectical Anthropology* 19 (2-3): 373–386.
Kart, Susan. 2009. "Asen and Ancestors." *African Studies Review* 52 (1): 217–219.
Kuwabong, Dannabang. 2004. "Bagre: A Dagaaba Celebration of Environmental Balance between Humans and Non-Humans." *Journal of Dagaare Studies* 4:1–13.

Landry, Timothy R. 2016. "Incarnating Spirits, Composing Shrines, and Cooking Divine Power in Vodún." *Material Religion* 12 (1): 50–73.

Mbowura, Cletus K. 2013. "Constructing the Historicity of Chieftaincy among the Nawuri of Northern Ghana." *Contemporary Journal of African Studies* 1 (2): 21–44.

McCarthy Brown, Karen. 2001. *Mama Lola: A Vodou Priestess in Brooklyn.* Berkeley: University of California Press.

McGee, Adam Michael. 2014. "Imagined Voodoo: Terror, Sex, and Racism in American Popular Culture." PhD diss., Harvard University.

Mohr, Adam. 2011. "Capitalism, Chaos, and Christian Healing: Faith Tabernacle Congregation in Southern Colonial Ghana, 1918–26." *Journal of African History* 52 (1): 63–83.

Montgomery, Eric. 2016. "Syncretism in Vodu and Òrìsà." *Journal of Religion and Society* 2: 1–19.

———. 2017. "Visual 'Voodoo': Photo-Voice in Togo." *Visual Anthropology* 30 (4): 287–309.

———. 2018. "They Died in Blood: Morality and Communitas in Ewe Ritual." *Journal of Ritual Studies* 32 (1): 25–40.

———, ed. 2019. *Shackled Sentiments; Spirits, Slaves, and Memories in the African Diaspora.* Boston: Rowman and Littlefield.

———. 2019. "Slavery, Personhood, and Mimesis in Ewe Gorovodu and Mama Tchamba." In *Shackled Sentiments: Slaves, Spirits, and Memories in the African Diaspora*, edited by Eric Montgomery, 59–82. Boston: Rowman and Littlefield.

Montgomery, Eric, and Christian Vannier. 2017. *An Ethnography of a Vodu Shrine in Southern Togo: Of Spirit, Slave and Sea.* Leiden, Netherlands: Brill.

Naaeke, Anthony. 2005. "The Cultural Relevance of Myth: A Reader-Response Analysis of the Bagre Myth with Reference to the Role and Place of Women in the Dagaaba Society." *Journal of Dagaare Studies* 5:1–10.

Pietz, William. 1985. "The Problem of the Fetish, I." *RES: Anthropology and Aesthetics* 9 (1): 5–17.

Quiroz, Diana, Marc Sosef, and Tinde Van Andel. 2016. "Why Ritual Plant Use Has Ethnopharmacological Relevance." *Journal of Ethnopharmacology* 188:48–56.

Rosenthal, Judy. 1998. *Possession, Ecstasy, and Law in Ewe Voodoo.* Charlottesville: University of Virginia Press.

Rush, Dana. 2013. *Vodún in Coastal Bénin: Unfinished, Open-Ended, Global.* Nashville: Vanderbilt University Press.

Salmons, Jill. 1977. "Mammy Wata." *African Arts* 1:8–87.

Sastre, Robert. 1970. "Les Vodu dans la vie culturelle, sociale et politique du Sud-Dahomey." *Cahiers des religions africaines* 4 (8): 177–188.

Sheridan, Michael J. 2008. "The Dynamics of African Sacred Groves: Ecological, Social and Symbolic Processes." In *African Sacred Groves: Ecological Dynamics and Social Change*, edited by Michael Sheridan and Celia Nyamweru, 9–41. Athens: Ohio University Press.

Stöcklin, W. H. 1981. "Sakpata, a Contribution of the African Medicine Man to Smallpox Eradication." *Gesnerus* 39 (3–4): 405–415.

Sweet, James H. 2011. *Domingos Álvares, African Healing, and the Intellectual History of the Atlantic World*. Chapel Hill: University of North Carolina Press.

Turner, Victor Witter. 1967. *The Forest of Symbols: Aspects of Ndembu Ritual*. Ithaca, NY: Cornell University Press.

Vannier, Christian, and Eric J. Montgomery, 2015. "The Materia Medica of Vodu Practitioners in Southern Togo." *Applied Anthropologist* 35 (1): 31–38.

Venkatachalam, Meera. 2015. *Slavery, Memory and Religion in Southeastern Ghana, c. 1850–Present*. Cambridge: Cambridge University Press.

Wendl, Tobias. 2001. "Visions of Modernity in Ghana: Mami Wata Shrines, Photo Studios and Horror Films." *Visual Anthropology* 14 (3): 269–292.

Zannou, A., Rigobert C. Tossou, S. Vodouhè, Paul Richards, Paul C. Struik, J. Zoundjihékpon, Adam Ahanchédé, and V. Agbo. 2007. "Socio-cultural Factors Influencing and Maintaining Yam and Cowpea Diversity in Benin." *International Journal of Agricultural Sustainability* 5 (2–3): 140–160.

Zogbé, Mama. 2005. "Mami Wata." *Africa's Ancient God/dess Unveiled*. Atlanta: Mami Wata Healing Society.

ERIC J. MONTGOMERY is Assistant Professor of Anthropology at Michigan State University and faculty as well as Saperstein Senior Science and Peace Fellow in the Center for Peace and Conflict Studies at Wayne State University. He is coauthor of *An Ethnography of a Vodu Shrine in Southern Togo* and editor of *Shackled Sentiments: Slaves, Spirits, and Memories in the African Diaspora*.

FOUR

A PRAYER FOR A MUSLIM SPIRIT

Islam in Gorovodu

Christian Vannier

ISLAM CONSTITUTES a significant inspiration in West Africa's historical heritage defined by exchange, absorption, and adaptation. Yet Islam and "indigenous" religions have been conceptually kept apart in scholarship and other representations, a reflection of the needs and aspirations of colonialism and early ethnographers rather than cultural and geographical realities. Representations of North Africa and sub-Saharan Africa as virtually isolated from each other throughout history likely stems from colonial authorities seeking to distance West Africa from Islam and Islamic empires, in both past and present. This served to, first, represent colonized peoples as exotic cultural isolations standing outside history—and thus more capable of and receptive to modernization and proselytization—and, second, to conceptually isolate Muslim societies in the Near East and elsewhere that were viewed as military threats and subjects of colonial competition with other European states (Saul 2006, 4–6). In truth, African religious culture and Islamic religious culture have a relationship that is steeped in a lengthy history of contact and described by J. Lorand Matory (1994, 496) as "a mutually constitutive dialogue." Importantly, as Muslims slowly materialized across the Sahara into the West African forest belt, they did not introduce there a religion of the sword but rather a religion of trade, education, and ritual. There were no large-scale colonization or conquest pressures to convert (with the glaring exception of slavery), and so West Africans were typically free to convert to Islam "at their own pleasure" (Hunwick 2006, 17). Many found a new faith in Islam; many others did not. Even more common, many took on some symbols, codes, rituals, and other inspirations from Islam according to their own needs and aspirations while discarding others. The result was, and is, a religious pluralism that includes not only a fluid and dynamic interpretation of

Islam and what it means to be Muslim but a fluid and dynamic interpretation of African religious culture more generally.

AN ISLAMICIZED VODÚN

The first half of the twentieth century witnessed the rise and spread through contemporary Ghana and Togo of a ritual complex and pantheon of spirits called Gorovodu, also known as Brekete or Tron. Gorovodu, and the related Alafia or Attingali Vodún in Togo and Benin, share being labeled by academics as the "Islamic Vodún" (Rush 1999, 95), meaning they are ritual complexes that are embedded with symbols, practices, histories, and encounters that are conscious references to Islam. Today, Gorovodu is widely practiced in ethnic Ewe communities along the coast and Volta region of Ghana and Togo. In the early and mid-twentieth century, at the high tide and ebbing of colonialism, Gorovodu spread to this region from the Northern Territories (so named in the British Gold Coast colony) of Ghana and Togo as an early witch-finding cult but quickly developed into a powerful healing and ritual complex that displays numerous Islamic symbols and practices.

Ethnographies of Gorovodu situate many practices and symbols into a "romance of the north," to use Judy Rosenthal's (1998) appellation (see also Friedson 2009; Montgomery and Vannier 2017). Through dense histories of cultural and economic exchange, including slavery, communities along the coast exhibit a social fascination for real and imagined elements inherent to ethnic groups in the northern savanna territories of Ghana and Togo and the Sahel farther north in Mali, Niger, and Burkina Faso. Individuals and communities tap into the power of these northern, peripheral Others by making northern culture and ritual practice their own through mimesis and ritual economy. The "stylized elements" of northern culture become the "primary models for the aesthetics of Gorovodu" (Rosenthal 1998, 110), and today the Gorovodu ritual complex is ensconced in such northernisms. Many Gorovodu priests (*sofos*) insist the drum rhythms and dancing that serve as the foundation of Gorovodu ceremonial performance originated in the north and were brought south, likely by slaves. Ewe children are given northern or Muslim names. The Gorovodu spirits (*tro*, sing.; *trowo*, pl.) themselves originated in the north, and inside shrines, there is extensive *materia ethnographica* of imagined northern cultures. The names and secret names of the spirits are often northern in origin, representing the names of towns, trade routes, plants, spirits, or commodities. There is a cross-regional and cross-religious link between many sacred items of material culture in Ewe Gorovodu and among the nearby Guin-Mina

(Venkatachalam 2011, 2012). Qurans are often found in many shrines even though many cannot read them. Catholic rosaries and Muslim prayer beads are particularly pervasive and believed to have enormous power. Objects were made sacred through their northern histories (jewelry, weaponry, cookware, and clothing), which carry special symbolic potency.

Though not all northern societies are Muslim, Islam is the marker of "northern-ness" in coastal Ewe culture (Venkatachalam 2011, 255), and so what is "northern" is conjoined to what is "Muslim" in Gorovodu. The most visible aspects of this in Gorovodu are *salah* ceremonies. Salah (Arabic for "prayer") ceremonies are held regularly on Fridays (the Islamic holy day), or large-scale salah ceremonies (*salahga*) are held after *fetatrotro* ceremonies (large thanksgiving ceremonies) or when a shrine keeper determines it is important enough for the welfare and morality of the community to do so. Despite its name, a salah ceremony in Gorovodu is very much a Vodu affair, complete with call and response praise singing to the trowo, possession trance, dancing, and the playing of rhythms. However, salah ceremonies also display a wide array of Islamic elements. Depending on the size, occasion, and disposition of the shrine keeper, salah ceremonies may display the chanting of the *shahada*, performing of prostrations, and other Islam-derived practices.

According to Stephen Friedson (2009), salah became part of the Gorovodu ritual complex in the 1950s when the Gorovodu spirit Sunia Compo, accompanied by two bearded *imams* dressed in northern regalia, visited a senior priest (*sofoga*) in Ghana named Tosavi in a dream. The visitors taught Tosavi the prayers, songs, importance of almsgiving (*sadaqa*), and how to perform the prostrations (*rakat*). After the dream, "the parallel nature of Islam in [Gorovodu] was revealed, and a new kind of prayer was born from the dream of an old woman" (Friedson 2009, 46). From here, salah spread among Gorovodu shrines. Alessandra Brivio (2018, 11) states that salah was introduced to Gorovodu to celebrate the memory of Mama Seidou, an important early founder who is imagined as a mullah, or religious leader. I had the opportunity to interview two sofoga about the history of salah and the relation between Islam and Gorovodu more generally. One sofoga shook his head gravely and said, "No, stories like that are not true. Salah started from a session of the Vodu," he began. "When Dzreke did a session in homage to the Vodu in Yeji [Ghana], salah was part of that ceremony. It's been part of Gorovodu from the very beginning." Dzreke is considered a founder of Gorovodu earlier in the twentieth century, and according to the two sofoga I interviewed, salah and Islam have been presences in Gorovodu since the original founding. This sofoga's words lay bare a reality I explore in this chapter: Islamic-inspired ritual practices and symbols are not assimilations, absorptions, or add-ons that came after Gorovodu had been established as a recognized, distinct ritual complex. Rather, they are constitutive of the religious system itself. For certain, these practices and symbols are layered onto long-standing ritual practices that characterize those of Gbe speakers in the region more generally (e.g., the Ewe, Adja, Fon). But Gorovodu is new, carrying new meanings for practitioners that fit the contemporary era and are practical and effective in the contemporary era.

I argue that the emergence of Gorovodu as a ritual complex among ethnic Ewe practitioners in Togo and Ghana demonstrates the following: first, the Islamic-inspired symbols and materialities are constitutive of the ritual complex itself rather than some sort of addition or supplement to an existing system; second, such constitutive elements do not demonstrate the adoption of Islam into the cultural spheres of spirit service in Ewe communities along the coast but rather demonstrate the cumulative social experiences of engagements with Muslims and Islamic religious culture. From these arguments, I conclude that we must carefully consider the importance of historical encounters between those that serve the spirits and other religious, political, and economic systems in the Atlantic world.

A HISTORY OF ENCOUNTER AND ENGAGEMENT

West African societies first encountered Islam via traders who traveled from southern Morocco, the shortest crossing of the Sahara Desert, as early as the ninth century (Hunwick 2006, 15). By the sixteenth century, trade routes had opened from the Near East starting at Tripoli to Hausaland in Nigeria and from Lake Chad to Dar Fur and the Nile Valley. Once across, merchants and their religion traveled along an east-west axis through contemporary Senegal and Gambia and along the Sahel-savanna border (Saul 2006). These later routes greatly expanded trade and cultural exchange. Ivory, slaves, kola nuts, grain, and gold were traded northward, and salt, cloth, cowrie shells, and other items came south. Conversion throughout the Sahel region intensified along with trade, and by the latter half of the seventeenth century, Muslim scholars and merchants from Timbuktu and Hausalands were permanently settling between the Black and White Volta Rivers in contemporary Burkina Faso and northern Ghana.

In West Africa, Muslims settled in diasporic areas known as *zongos*, and by the eighteenth century, zongos and their markets were a fixture in most sizable towns throughout West Africa.[1] Muslims were merchants, scholars, diplomats, advisers, and councilors to chiefs and kings, technical specialists, and educated individuals (Saul 2006, 20). As scholars and councilors, an extensive source of Islamic influence came from books and literacy. Arabic was the principal language of literacy until the colonial period, and educated elites or their advisers intellectually deployed what was available to them, typically religious texts written in Arabic and transported by Muslims (Hunwick 2006, 20; Saul 2006, 15). The linguistic consequences are such that the Ewe language and others in West Africa deploy a considerable amount of Arabic loan words. Finally, Muslims were clerics who displayed extensive thaumaturgical abilities. Exchanges of esoteric knowledge and practice between Muslim and non-Muslim ritual specialists and the mutual influence they had on one another led to innovations in astrology and geomancy (Brenner 2000, 158). Louis Brenner (2000) gives the example of divination. The divination system known as Ifa among ethnic Yoruba in Nigeria and Benin likely originated from *khatt ar-raml*, a "sand writing" Muslim divination system present in the Dahomian courts of Abomey by the eighteenth century. At least one scholar argues that the Afa divination system, ubiquitous in Ewe communities and itself an offshoot of the Ifa system, derives its name from *al-fa'l*, Arabic for "good omen" or "fortune" (Saul 2006, 4). These histories are debatable. The point is that Islam in West Africa is not an exclusive, self-contained religion but rather a system with many elements that are easily recognizable to practitioners of indigenous religion. Divination, venerating ancestors with prayer and sacrifice, and fashioning amulets and charms for good fortune or protection against sorcery or witchcraft demonstrate a shared religious culture. Even today there is significant interplay between shrine keepers and Muslim clerics. Muslim specialists are well known for providing effective ritual services, and many non-Muslims patronize Muslim clerics for such services without any hint of conversion.

Turning attention to ethnic Ewe communities along the coast of southeast Ghana and Togo, indirect contact with Muslim merchants through mediating traders likely happened near the arrival of Islam in West Africa. More direct contact with northern Muslim societies first came via Ewe traders engaging slave merchants at slave markets that existed at the social border between the forest and the savanna between the eighteenth and nineteenth centuries (Venkatachalam 2011, 249). As a coastal ethnic group, the Ewe engaged extensively in the transatlantic slave trade. The trade in slaves was typically divided along gender lines. Men were most often sold into the transatlantic slave trade in exchange for European goods. Women were valued as domestic slaves, serving as wives, mothers, and workers in Ewe communities. Such women typically originated from the noncentralized hinterlands of the northern savanna, specifically ethnic Kabye, Hausa, Dagomba, Mossi, Yendi, and Tchamba peoples

(Montgomery and Vannier 2017; Rush 2011, 41; Wendl 1999). Though these cultural groups exhibited a great diversity in cultural ways of seeing and being, they were lumped together as "northern," which was imagined as imbibed with Islam. Whether or not slaves in Ewe communities in the nineteenth and early twentieth centuries were actually Muslims is less consequential than one may suppose. The northern territories were sites of cultural cohabitation where boundaries between Muslim and non-Muslim were porous and unstable. Given the lengthy history, most individuals taken from these areas were at the very least familiar with Islam. Slavery and slaves did not herald the imposition or adoption of Islamic-inspired ritual along the coast, and we cannot know to what extent Islam was known or acknowledged by Ewe communities at this time. Slavery did, no doubt, familiarize this Muslim Other and laid the groundwork for the dawn of the new spirits in the twentieth century.

The Savanna Spirits

In nearly every Gorovodu village, there exists a tranquil walled grove that serves as the setting for ecstatic ritual on any given evening. This grove is symbolic of the ancestral and ritual past and the distant northern desert, where slaves and the Gorovodus (trowo) originated. This Sacred Forest (*dzogbe*) is an imagined copy of all that is northern and foreign, a microcosm of the perception Ewe have of a distant and romanticized north (Rosenthal 1998). Life there is imagined as arid and transitory. People are imagined as nomadic and Muslim, with more intimate relationships with the spiritual realm (Brivio 2018, 14). During the early twentieth century, northern societies seemed less altered or affected by outside influences. Fertility rates were high. People adhered to traditional values in the face of European colonialism that wrought numerous ill effects in the south. New means of accumulation generated new social stratifications and their consequences: jealousy, conflict, and social disorder. Such epidemics as venereal disease, mental illness, and Spanish influenza (1919–1921) emerged in tandem with regional migration, social upheaval, and economic inequality. People along the coast internalized these events and developed worldviews regarding northern peoples and cultures that fused historical and contemporary cultural and economic experience. Given the associations of social inequality and disease with witchcraft, people reacted to their misfortunes by seeking new cosmologies based on morality, equality, and physical well-being. Kola nut cults from the Talensi, Mamprusi, and Gonja peoples from the Northern Territories quickly spread southward, then eastward and westward, until hundreds of shrines materialized throughout the Volta region (Brivio 2018, 2–3). Akan, Ewe, and Mina peoples saw northern religious culture as somehow harnessing a special power to defend against witchcraft and maintain order through healing and spirit possession. The paraphernalia, liturgy, rituals, religious training, and personality of northern spirits were embraced and made local in southern Ewe communities. These northern cults coalesced into what is known today as Gorovodu, a term that signifies several ideas at once: large corpus of ritual knowledge associated with Islamicized peoples of the northern savanna, the spirits that originally hailed from these territories, and the spirit objects residing in each shrine of growing religious networks in communities in the Volta region and along the coasts of Ghana and Togo.

These communities were receptive to new ritual systems and spiritual ways of knowing due to their rapid integration into the colonial economy and as a reaction to the economic move toward kola nut and cocoa cash cropping that opened new channels of wealth accumulation to individuals outside traditional socioeconomic hierarchies (Venkatachalam 2011, 250). The expansion of kola nut and cocoa brought new labor geographies and religious and ideological deregulation. Spirits benefitted from this expansion (Allman and Parker 2005, 48, 129) as new shrines, and the spirits and practices connected to them, migrated throughout the region via these new labor geographies. As Jack Goody (1986, 7–8, quoted in Baum 1999, 11) notes, the introduction of new shrines brought "new ideas, new prohibitions, new taboos, and were never 'more of the same' . . . introducing new evaluations of experience, sometimes have far-reaching effects on the political, moral, and cosmological order." The popularity of certain shrines and spirits were based primarily on spontaneous and pragmatic evaluation of efficacy. Character, personality, and practices of each spirit metamorphosed as new peoples took them into their communities. This migration was sped along by a rich history of ritual entrepreneurialism that drew many southerners on pilgrimages north to learn the rituals and gather the spirits to bring back south. Certain major movements coalesced into a kin-based pantheon by the mid-twentieth century and established a lasting presence that would eventually become globalized by the twenty-first century.

The 1920s and 1930s witnessed several antiwitchcraft/antimedicinal movements. Kunde and Sunia Kompo emerged during the Spanish influenza and were quickly followed by Tigare (later Bangede) and Nana Tongo (Allman and Parker 2005, 137). Kunde migrated farther south to the coast alongside Hausa traders, adopting many names, some to evade suppression by allied local and colonial elites and some through acculturation into new contexts: Brekete, Alafia (Hausa for "health"), and Goro. Sometime between 1928 and 1934, ritual entrepreneurs carried Kunde across the Volta River into French Togoland. These savanna spirits engaged the religious ecology of the coastal Ewe groups who at this time were a religious amalgam of Christian converts, Muslims, ancestor cults, and adherents of alternative ritual orders, such as Yewe, Afa, and Mami Wata. When Gorovodu first circulated in this context, it did not appear as a completely alien philosophy or way of seeing, but rather "it integrated into a cultural environment which was ready to take on the language" (Brivio 2008, 237). Adherents and worshippers of each spirit or religious system did not represent neatly bounded categories of practice and identity. Rather, they coexisted in overlapping matrixes of rites and beliefs.

An early migrant was Ablewa, a spirit and ritual complex that enjoyed immense popularity throughout southern Ghana and Togo as a witch finder. Considered dangerous to colonial control, Ablewa was outlawed in 1908 due to its mass adoption across cultures and geography (Rosenthal 1998, 85–88). Her subversiveness in the face of established belief systems and her ability to mobilize adherents caused the systematic destruction of her established shrines by colonial authorities and their Christian convert allies (Allman and Parker 2005, 131). Yet Ablewa persisted and grew. Along with her rise in reverence came direct inspirations from Islamic religious culture: the wearing of smocks and the red fez by priests and the designation of Friday as Ablewa's sacred day. These ritual practices and observances are hallmarks of northern cultures and their heavier contact with Islam. It is also with Ablewa that the ritual use of kola nut enters colonially recorded history (Allman and Parker 2005, 130). Finally, Ablewa heralded a period of intense mimetic adoption of northern ritual and accoutrements coinciding with an intensification of cultural exchange between the Islamicized north and the south. Cocoa production was expanding and, alongside it, infrastructure projects meant to aid cocoa's production and export. These projects and plantations required significant labor inputs, often filled by northern ethnic groups, including Muslims, who brought their customs, religion, and medicines (including kola nuts) with them.

By the 1970s, the kin-based pantheon of spirits and ritual complex known as Gorovodu came to the small community of Gbedala, Togo, where research for this chapter was conducted. A young sofo named Teteh established a shrine and, together with the spirits, began establishing a ritual constituency throughout the region. As the ritual complex grew, other shrines were established in the community, and new sofo and other ritual specialists were trained and professionalized. The new ritual complex quickly engaged the established ritual orders, such as Tchamba (slave ancestor veneration), which itself recognizes the

Islamicized religious culture of slaves kept in the community throughout the slavery era and more recent experiences with Evangelical Christianity.

PRAYERS TO A MUSLIM VODU: A SALAH CEREMONY IN GOROVODU

What is clear from this brief history is that Islamic symbols, practices, and materialities did not come directly to southern Ewe communities, through either conquest or proselytizing, but rather indirectly as influences or precoded in indigenous symbols and practices. They were adopted by communities and groups based on experience and efficacy. Elements viewed as indispensable or powerful were kept, elaborated on, or transformed. Those elements deemed redundant or unnecessary were discarded or significantly altered. Today, Islamic-inspired elements are so embedded in the daily ritual life of Gorovodu practitioners that they seem mundane and everyday. Yet there are moments when these elements come to the fore and are made explicit. The most recognizable moments are salah ceremonies.

Friedson (2009, 46) argues that salah is "the most overt expression of Islam in all of [Gorovodu]." There are two general types of salah ceremonies, regular and occasional. No doubt Friedson was referring to the salah ceremonies that followed large fetatrotro ceremonies (special feasts to serve and thank the spirits through large-scale animal sacrifice) or that are called together by senior shrine keepers on rare occurrences. Following many fetatrotro ceremonies, shrine keepers often host a large salah (salahga) to manifest in the community the law and discipline (i.e., sharia) that are the imagined strengths of Islam. Salahga are large undertakings, attended by women, men, and visitors from near and far. Ritual and symbolic expressions of Islam are made explicit as prayer mats were rolled out in the shrine's courtyard. Women wrapped white pagne cloths around their bodies and heads in mimetic performance of the hijab as men sat in attendance. A trained song leader (*ehadzito*) leds the group in singing the first part of the shahada, the repetitions of the *takbir*, and, finally, the repetitions of the *basmala*. Ceremony participants then prostrated themselves on the prayer mats and quietly sang a hymn to Nana Wango, the Grandmother Crocodile spirit of Gorovodu. Finally, the shahada was sung in praise as hands clapped and drums beat.

Similarities in practices and similar rigidity in moral codes of conduct have led to the ingestion of Islamic ritual practices into Gorovodu. Sofos and congregations draw on Islam, knowable here as a prescribed set of ritual practices, as a source of intense ritual power. Yet to say this ceremony is a mix of Islamic and Gorovodu practices would not be emic to local understandings. Salah are Gorovodu ceremonies in which participants embody the imagined morality and discipline of Islam by mimetically claiming certain ceremonial practices. Such occasional ceremonies are well documented elsewhere (Friedson 2009; Montgomery and Vannier 2017). Here, I am more interested in the rituals and symbols of the everyday that pervade Gorovodu and demonstrate deeply embedded engagements with Muslims. To this end, I detail a composite ethnographic sketch of regular salah performances that occur every Friday morning, the Muslim day of prayer, at Gorovodu shrines throughout the region. These regular performances lack many Muslim elements detailed above but lay bare the embeddedness of Islamic inspirations.

My research colleague and I were invited to a Salah ceremony on a Friday morning in July by the daughter (Auntie) of the late chief (*madza*) of the small Ewe fishing community of Gbedala, along the coast in southern Togo. Auntie carried herself in the manner of her late father. When he died, the lineage heads assembled and determined she was too young to assume chieftaincy of the community (*duko*), and so the senior Gorovodu priest (sofoga) of the largest shrine in the community took over the duties. Twenty-four years old that summer, Auntie was now the keeper of her own Gorovodu shrine and was a growing force in the community as a powerful sofo in her own right.

We arrived at her shrine at the appointed time of 10:30 a.m. to find the ceremony had already begun. A small group of women wrapped in white pagne cloths sat on wooden benches in the shrine's courtyard under the thatched roof that kept the sun away. Many women had infants strapped tightly to their backs, and a few wore white wraps on their heads mimeticizing the hijab. In the center of the courtyard was a circular cement slab embedded with cowry shells that formed a +. This was the site of Legba, master of the crossroads between this world and that of the spirits and ancestors. He must be saluted before any ceremony begins, a brief ritual that Auntie performed prior to our arrival. At the head of the group, sitting by the entrance to the shrine itself, was the drummer leading the rhythm with an *adodo* drum and a *bosomfo* (junior or assistant priest) acting as the ehadzito (song leader), leading the call and response prayers and keeping time with the *atoke* bell. These two young men led the praises to the Gorovodus. They sang out their call, and the women responded, beating wooden sticks to the rhythm of the adodo drum. We sat in plastic chairs that were quickly provided for us and other women who slowly made their way into participation in the ceremony. I was fortunate to have an expat member of the community named Angola sit next to me. Angola had migrated to Ghana years before for work yet was home visiting, and he enjoyed helping me out with translations and explanations. Hymns can be quite opaque to an outsider. Metaphors, histories, and polyvalent references make for a dense discursive maze.

As the rhythm, singing, and clapping continued, women started to stand in pairs and dance a line of traditional Ewe dance. Such dancing was playful, and women would invite or goad each other into a quick dance.

The bosofo called out, "Be truthful always!"

Participants responded, "Yes, only on top of the house can you look into the valley."

"Your mother and father invite you!" sang the bosofo.

"Yes, where the vodu [trowo] are, one cannot go without the truth!" responded the congregation.

Another sofoga arrived to participate in the salah. The bosofo took the opportunity to hand him the atoke bell, so he could stand and encourage the small congregation to sing louder and bolder to evoke the spirits to come to the ceremony.

After many stops and starts in the collective singing and rhythm, the spirits responded to the congregation. A reputable senior adept (tronsi) grasped the bosofo's wrist and stood, spinning rapidly in the throes of possession. Immediately, two *senterua*, women who act as managers of spirits that seize individuals in possession, came quickly to the woman's side and guided her spinning, so she would not run into the poles holding up the thatch roof or her fellow ceremony participants. A third woman grabbed a *buta* kettle and poured water on the spirit's wrists, hands, and then feet while the senterua held her and removed her earrings and hairpins. Buta kettles are standard at all Gorovodu ceremonies. Filled with water infused with plant medicines from the northern savanna purchased from merchants at zongos, buta kettles are known as "Muslim kettles." They are used to salute northern spirits either by sprinkling water at their feet or washing parts of their bodies, such as the wrists and hands, in mimetic performance of Muslim ablution. After the spirit was washed, it cried out to be released and spun again. The spirit went to each person in our circle of participants and shook their hands in greeting. She shook our hands like she did everyone else and then approached the senior sofoga who came late to the ceremony. They shook with both hands and had a whole conversation of welcome to each other before the spirit stood and allowed the bosofo to take her hands and allowing him to lead her into the shrine. The sofoga then assumed the duties of song leader as the singing intensified in celebration.

Shortly after the spirit went into the shrine, curiosity made me walk over and observe the inside of the shrine from the doorway. Auntie's Gorovodu

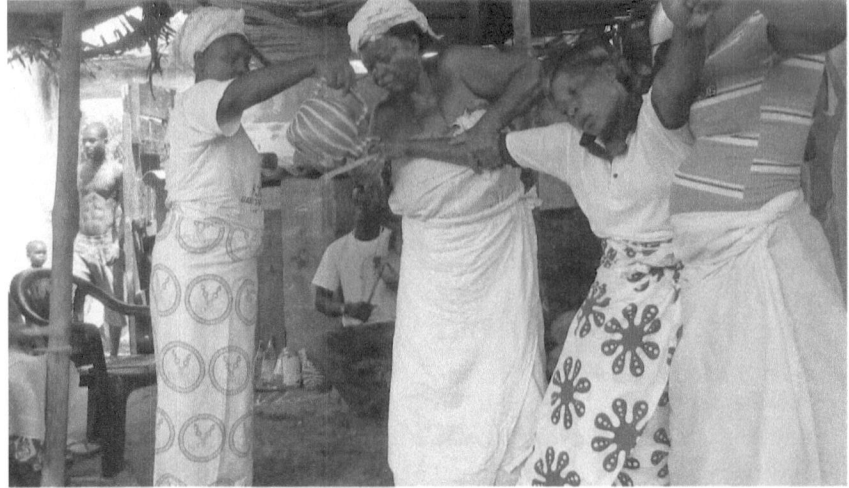

Figure 4.1. The spirit is pacified with *amatsi* medicinal water from the Muslim *buta* kettle.

shrine was small, clean, and beautifully adorned with murals and sacred accoutrements that hung on the walls and lay on the floor. Along the east wall were wooden chairs. Opposite them, the spirit fetishes, sitting in front of their individual white houses (*kpome*), lined the entire wall. Kunde and his father, Kadzanka, on the far left, his kpome was connected to that of his wife, Ablewa, who sat in her kpome with Kunde's mother, Allah. Next were their daughter, Sunia Kompo and then Sacra Bode, the dark slave and spirit of earth that hails from the northern savanna. Sacra Bode is the steed of Bangede, whose fetish sat directly in front of Sacra Bode. Bangede is the soldier, policeman, and hunter. He is depicted as a tall Muslim, and his spirit fetish is made with horsetail to symbolize the long beards of the pious. Finally, Nana Wango, Grandmother Crocodile, sat in her kpome with her riverman's paddles and other accoutrements in the opposite corner of the shrine. On the other side was a door leading to the small garden where plant medicines are cultivated.

The possessed tronsi was bent over deep at the waist in front of the Bangede spirit fetish while two senterua quickly removed her pagne cloth and adorned her in the accoutrements of Bangede. The tronsi was no longer herself. Bangede, the Muslim warrior and hunter of people, had seized control and demanded the accoutrements and materialities appropriate to him. He (Bangede) was wrapped in a red, white, and black cloth; *amatsi* (medicinal water) was poured on his neck in ablution, and a fez was put atop his head. Once adorned, Bangede turned to the door and motioned me out of the way. He came back to the

Figure 4.2. Murals depicting the spirits adorn the walls of the shrine.

courtyard to sing and dance with the congregation as the drummer drummed his rhythms and the congregation sang his praises. It was not long before another tronsi stood and began spinning. Kunde, father of the Gorovodu spirits, joined Bangede. The same two senterua quickly surrounded him (Kunde). Kunde did not greet everyone in the congregation but made straight for the sofoga, squatting in front of him while clasping his hands. Kunde had something to say since the conversation went on for some time. The sofoga nodded again and again, repeating that he heard, understood, and thanked Kunde. Kunde then stood and went into the shrine with Bangede a few steps behind.

"We are the riders of lions [dzata]," shouted the sofoga, acting as the ehadzito, in direct reference to Kunde.

"Yes! We are unconcerned with your weapons," responded the congregation.

"We are the king of the night," came the call from the sofoga.

"Yes! Giraffe cannot hide from the children," came the response from the congregation.

When I peered again into the shrine, I saw Bangede and Kunde sitting and directing the preparation of plant medicines. The former ehadzito and another assistant priestess were busy gathering herbs and roots and tearing them into small bits, making a pile on a prayer mat. Once finished, they put the plant and root parts in a small cauldron and added soda water. Bangede stood and ordered the ehadzito to pour him ritual gin. The ehadzito quickly handed him a small glass and grabbed the bottle from behind the Bangede fetish. He poured

Figure 4.3. Bangede prepares the medicinal wash.

Bangede a tote of gin, and Bangede said a lengthy prayer over the cauldron before pouring it over the medicine. Bangede handed the glass to Kunde, who did the same, and then the bosofo himself said a prayer and then took the gin into his mouth and spat it like a cloud into the cauldron. Bangede ordered amatsi from the buta that sat upon Kunde's kpome to be added too. Ample baby powder and baby oil completed the medicinal bath. Satisfied, Bangede lifted the cauldron, and everyone returned outside to the ceremony. Upon coming back to the courtyard, the sofoga altered the call and response prayer:

"Vodus [trowo] open small gates that become big gates," he sang, throwing his hands in the air for emphasis.

"If you always pour the libation in the right way," sang the congregation as they watched the two spirits and accompanying bosofo pass through the center of courtyard.

The spirits took the cauldron just outside the courtyard and, making a + in the sand with the baby oil, set it down and dug a small hole next to it. The music had stopped since many women were no longer present. I thought the ceremony was over, but soon the congregation trickled back together with small infants and young toddlers. One by one, mothers brought their children over to the small hole to be washed by the medicine in the cauldron. Many children wailed while two bosofo tried to calm them long enough for the wash to be over and back into the arms of their mothers. Perhaps fourteen children lined up and washed in this manner, their mothers taking them home afterward.

Figure 4.4. The medicinal wash sits upon the crossroads next to the hold, which will be used as a makeshift bath.

The ceremony now complete, the atmosphere became jovial. The sofoga emerged from the shrine with the bottle of ritual gin and passed it around to those who desired quick refreshment with the spirits before returning to their duties. Angola sat in the same chair, fingering his beloved Muslim rosary that he had purchased in Accra. Fashioned with clay and glass, they are made in northern Nigeria and sold throughout West Africa. The rosary beads are bound with handmade leather and tend to have yellow and purple contrasts in them. People hold them in their hands and pray to Kunde like a Christian prays to Christ.

"You look confused," he said.

"I am," I said. "What happened?"

"There is disease coming, you know. Bangede came over the tronsi and told her in a vision. Bangede also told that sofoga from Benin and the bosofo of this shrine."

"Did Bangede order the medicine made?" I asked.

"Yes, Bangede is from the north. That medicine must be from the north because that is why Bangede was here, to help make that medicine. He said disease is coming and you must protect the children. Then he told them how to make the medicine, and they got their children. Now they will be protected."

"What disease is coming, and why was Kunde here too?" I asked pressingly.

"I do not know. You now know all that I now know," he replied with a shrug.

I laughed and took the tote of gin the sofoga offered to me. We stayed to interview some attendees, but everyone seemed tired or too busy with demands that had been delayed long enough. We packed our notebooks and cameras and went looking for a small meal and some rest. The sun was hot at one o'clock in the afternoon.

DISCUSSION

This ceremony was unique in that I did not observe at other ceremonies the exact order of events that I observed here. However, this ceremony was thematic to other salah ceremonies performed on other Fridays at other shrines in that it involved drum and bell rhythm making, call and response prayers, dancing, and possession by Gorovodu spirits whereby the spirits engaged ceremony participants. Also similar, the salah was attended primarily by women. Men are typically engaged in the fishing industry at this time, and so salah ceremonies are considered women's affairs. I use as my primary data a regular performance of salah to demonstrate that Gorovodu is foremost a ritual complex situated in local practices. As stated earlier, large formal salah ceremonies demonstrate overt mimetic performances of Islam, such as the shahada and takbir. Yet even this performance of salah demonstrates the deeply embedded nature of Islamic ritual in Gorovodu religious culture, and this regular "everyday" nature is a more powerful testament to the influence of Muslims and Islam on Ewe religious culture.

In a regular salah ceremony, the use of Friday, the wearing of white, the use of buta kettles, and other elements represent assemblages taken from Islam.[2] All other aspects, such as hymn lyrics, drumming, and possession are local Vodu affairs. We may borrow from Suzanne Preston Blier's (1988, 137) "primacy of assemblage" to argue salah is a ritual assemblage, a bringing together of ritual acts from Islam to create something entirely new, imbibed with new meanings for the new realities that called the assemblage together in the first place. Intentionality is key to assemblage (Rush 2013, 29), and mimesis, creative selection, and experimentation by innumerable actors create the meanings that give the assemblage social power. Hence, ritual assemblage results not in some bricolage of disparate practices but rather in original forms of meaning and practice that continually comport and adjust to new realties and challenges. Viewed this way, we are able to see "Islam" as a well of ritual resources from which Ewe Gorovodu practitioners can draw on, experiment, and create toward surviving and thriving in an increasingly pluralistic and cosmopolitan West Africa.

More generally, the primacy of assemblage reflects the composite character of ritual, pantheons, individual spirits, and shrines that is itself a hallmark of Vodún religious culture throughout the Atlantic world.[3] The aptitude for mimetic embrace of foreign people, spirits, rituals, materialities, and philosophies reflects the open-ended and perpetually pragmatic nature of Vodún shrines and practitioners (Brivio 2018, 16; Rush 2013, 12). This attribute continues to cause consternation among religious scholars and anthropologists that engage such religious cultures. For example, adequately naming the relationship between Islam and Gorovodu is quite difficult. It is not Islamic, para-Islamic, or pre-Islamic. For practitioners, there is no attempt to somehow reconcile the two ritual systems or create some sort of syncretism.[4] Salah ceremonies are generally analyzed through creative explorations of mimesis and mimetic performance (Friedson 2009; Kramer 1993; Montgomery and Vannier 2016, 2017; Rosenthal 1998). There is little more I am able to add to these discussions. Instead, I approach the influence of Islam on religious culture in southern Togo from a different perspective—namely, why did Gorovodu become established so quickly in Ewe communities along the coast and why does this "Islamic Vodún" continue to resonate and grow?

ISLAM AND CHRISTIANITY IN THE VODU IMAGINATION

As other scholars have noted, the Ewe "romance" with the cultures of the northern savanna and Sahel, which includes Muslim groups, is based on historical encounters and engagements (Friedson 2009; Montgomery and Vannier 2017; Rosenthal 1998). These encounters may be quite old, such as through trade and slavery; more recent, such as through colonialism; and even contemporary, through social engagements in markets, politics, and other activities. Though community members view Islam as a more recent religious addition than ancestor and local spirits, it is still viewed as more "African" than Christianity. Islam is viewed as disciplined, morally upright, communitycentric, and respectful of other people and groups. Christianity came much later from the seas to the south, along with colonialism, and so Islam was perceived as a northern-based resistance to southern-based oppression. Today, as Evangelicalism continues to establish itself in the region and demonize, belittle, and combat (sometimes violently) "indigenous" religions in its proselytize, Ewe Gorovodu adherents offer much more praise toward Muslims than they do to Christians. Muslims typically do no proselytizing, keeping instead at an aloof distance (Friedson 2009, 49–50), so Muslims and Islam more generally are held in greater esteem. As one sofoga told me, "We can do most things with Christians, but we can do all things with Muslims. The only difference between Islam and Vodu is the blood we are using."

According to sofoga in the community, Islam and Christianity have "similar faces" in that they believe in one spirit, one sacred pathway. However, he was also quick to note differences, especially semantic and procedural differences in the way in which rituals and prayers are enacted. Christians do not sacrifice; they do not butcher animals properly, with proper ritual and respect paid to the animal; and they do not kneel when they pray, contrasting the prostration in Islam with the "side to side" chants of spiritual Christianity. Contrarily, Muslims are viewed as similar in their ritual practices to Vodu. Likewise, Muslims are rigid in their moral codes. Christians are viewed as less moral than *vodunsi* or Muslims because of their lack of rigid religious law. Furthermore, the lack of immediate spiritual reward and punishment leads to immorality because there are no powerful deterrents. Since they lack rigid law, Christians are considered by many in the community as more prone to alcoholism and greed. Furthermore, as the sofoga continued,

> Christianity is immoral because they have abortions. The *yovo* [whites or foreigners] only see economics and think a lot of kids is a bad thing. When Christians do immoral things, there is no punishment. The Tron will punish you. The Tron say don't have *n'bia* [jealousy]. If you follow that, it is said you will be blessed. Kunde is not subject to the intricacies of this world. He is a dog, and like a dog, if you feed him and treat him as your companion, he will be a most faithful companion. If you do not, he will bite you and injure or even kill you.

If one breaks Vodu law, he or she must face punishment, which the Tron will mete out accordingly without discretion or discrimination. Jesus, it is viewed, will always forgive. Stories are often told of a vodunsi who becomes a serial transgressor or severely breaks the law and quickly converts to Christianity to beg forgiveness from Christ and so avoid spiritual punishment by the Tron. The stories mesh well with local experiences of proselytizing by foreigners but generally end with the transgressor horribly punished through disease or accident. Sharia law is seen as parallel to the law of Kunde. Similar to Vodu law, there is little room for forgiveness in certain interpretations of sharia. One must face punishment when a law has been transgressed. The law of Kunde is not about forgiveness; it is about the truth. From truth comes justice. Hence, many tronsi and sofo believe Christians have no respect—for themselves, other people, other beings, and especially their own history and culture. This is made most obvious in the eyes of vodunsi through the centrality of forgiveness in Christianity.

Whereas local views of Christianity stem from experiences with Christians, so it is with Islam and Muslims. Ritual practices and symbols in Gorovodu do not display Islam in an orthodox sense but rather a generalized Islam through which Islamic religious culture as expressed by African Muslims is made transparent and assimilated. Islam did not come to the West African forests abruptly or violently but instead came via traveling, trading, teaching, and settling. These Muslims brought more with them than what is commonly understood as orthodox Islam. They introduced new forms of divination, astronomy, and magic to the region. Christianity was, and in many ways remains, a different experience. Christianity came as the partner of new, more intense forms of slavery and violence, of the imposition of new economic ways of seeing and being, of conquest and control. New spirits and ritual powers that drew on Islam, Christianity's age-old adversary, could be spiritually tapped by ritual specialists, empowering constituents to resist the disease, witchcraft, and social conflict wrought by European and other Western exploits. The result is not an Islamic or some variety of para-Islamic identity but rather the emergence of a new and distinct Vodu identity, one that strengthens and invigorates itself through affiliation with and assimilation of African Islam.

CONCLUSION: ISLAM AND VODÚN

Gorovodu provides the scholar of Vodún and Vodún-related ritual complexes a compelling study of the ritual interactions between those that serve the spirits and the other religious systems that these individuals and communities encounter. Such ceremonies as salah are experiences of cumulative encounters and exchanges. Such willingness to assimilate practices and materialities of the Other gives Gorovodu and other Vodún-inspired systems an "unfinished aesthetic" (Rush 2013, 30). In such a system, items or practices that become or are viewed as ineffective or impractical are discarded. Those that are effective and practical are added onto or grow in significance. This perpetual evaluation of its own practices and those it encounters makes Gorovodu, and other Afro-Atlantic systems, dynamic, adaptable, ephemeral, yet constant or always there. This means the presence of Islamic-inspired ritual and symbolism in Gorovodu represents no more the adoption of foreign, exotic, or outside influences than the adoption of Oyo (Yoruba) inspired ritual and symbolism in modern Vodún in Benin.

The implications of this research are that more attention should be paid to the influence of Islamic religious culture on Afro-Atlantic religions and ritual complexes more generally. Early studies sought to conceptually isolate "tribal Africa" from time and space to analyze them as special relics from other eras, untouched, for better or worse, by the outside world, including by Muslims. No doubt numerous Muslims were sold into the transatlantic slave trade and established their agency in North and South America, and the potential influences of Islam on local religious culture has been noted in the Caribbean (Stewart 2005, 252). The sheer diversity of ritual practices, symbols, and materialities present in both African Islam and Atlantic Vodún requires more careful attention to their manifestations, best accomplished by a multisited ethnographic approach that conceptualizes the Afro-Atlantic world as a continuum of meaning making that is mobile, ever evolving, and drawing on deep wells of experience and encounter.

NOTES

1. The Ashanti government maintained zongos in their kingdom by the eighteenth century, and Ouagadougou was ruled by a Muslim king by the end of the same (Saul 2006, 17).
2. There are other practices that are not directly part of my analysis but important all the same in representing assemblages assimilated from Islam, such as food taboos demanded by different spirits in exchange for spiritual service, which often reflect dietary preferences or taboos of Muslims, or that children are often given Arabic names in addition to local naming practices.
3. I use the term *Vodún* here to denote the numerous denominations and orders that proliferate in the Atlantic world.
4. See Freidson 2009, 65. Eric Montgomery (2016) argues that such concepts as syncretism, hybridization, or creolization are too often politicized and denigrate the religious systems to which the concepts are applied and that definitions are usually either too broad or too narrow to adequately describe Afro-Atlantic religions. Douglas J. Falen (this volume), however, argues that syncretism is the "blending of elements from multiple cultures." Vodún represents this conscious blending of elements.

REFERENCES

Allman, Jean, and John Parker. 2005. *Tongnaab: The History of a West African Spirit*. Bloomington: Indiana University Press.

Baum, Robert M. 1999. *Shrines of the Slave Trade: Diola Religion and Society in Precolonial Senegambia*. Oxford: Oxford University Press.

Blier, Suzanne Preston. 1988. "Melville J. Herskovits and the Arts of Ancient Dahomey." *Res: Anthropology and Art* 16:124–142.

Brenner, Louis. 2000. "Histories of Religion in Africa." *Journal of Religion in Africa* 30 (2): 143–167.

Brivio, Alessandra. 2008. "Le Tron Est un Vodou Propre: Vodou Entre Islam et Christianism." In *Le Vodou*, edited by Jacques Hainard, Philippe Mathez, and Olivier Schinz, 307–324. Geneve: Infolio.

———. 2018. "Gorovodu: The Genesis of a 'Hausa Vodun.'" *Journal of West African History* 4 (1): 1–26.

Friedson, Steven M. 2009. *Remains of Ritual: Northern Spirits in Southern Lands*. Chicago: University of Chicago Press.

Goody, Jack. 1986. *The Logic of Writing and the Organization of Society*. Cambridge: Cambridge University Press.

Kramer, Fritz. 1993. *The Red Fez: Art and Spirit Possession in Africa*. Translated by Malcolm Green. London: Verso.

Matory, J. Lorand. 1994. "Rival Empires: Islam and the Religions of Spirit Possession among the Oyo-Yoruba." *American Ethnologist* 21 (3): 495–515.

Montgomery, Eric. 2016. "Syncretism in Vodu and Orisha: An Anthropological Analysis." *Journal of Religion and Society* 18:1–23.

Montgomery, Eric, and Christian Vannier. 2017. *An Ethnography of a Vodu Shrine in Southern Togo: Of Spirit, Slave, and Sea*. Leiden, Netherlands: Brill.

Rosenthal, Judy. 1998. *Possession, Ecstasy, and Law in Ewe Voodoo*. Charlottesville: University Press of Virginia

Rush, Dana. 1999. "Eternal Potential: Chromolithographs in Vodunland." *African Arts* 32 (4): 60–75.

Saul, Mahir. 2006. "Islam and West African Anthropology." *Africa Today* 53 (1): 3–33.

Stewart, Dianne M. 2005. *Three Eyes for the Journey: African Dimensions of the Jamaican Religious Experience*. Oxford: Oxford University Press.

Vannier, Christian, and Eric Montgomery. 2016. "Sacred Slaves: Tchamba Vodu in Southern Togo." *Journal of Africana Religion* 4 (1): 104–127.

Venkatachalam, Meera. 2011. "Between the Umbrella and the Elephant: Elections, Ethnic Negotiations and the Politics of Spirit Possession in Teshi, Accra." *Africa* 81 (2): 248–268.

———. 2015. *Slavery, Memory and Religion in Southeastern Ghana, c. 1850–Present*. Cambridge: Cambridge University Press.

CHRISTIAN VANNIER is a lecturer in the Department of Behavioral Science at the University of Michigan, Flint. He is coauthor of *An Ethnography of a Vodu Shrine in Southern Togo* and coeditor of *Cultures of Doing Good: Anthropologists and NGOs*.

FIVE

WHERE HAVE ALL THE *OUNSI* GONE?

Karen Richman

"THERE ARE no *ounsi* anymore." *Ounsi* refers to the gendered role conferred at the end of a lengthy and elaborate sacred rite of passage. Mention of the ounsi role today in Ti Rivyè, Léogane, in Haiti, inevitably precipitates a comment on its disappearance. In 1983, when my ethnography began, a commonly stated view of the relationship between levels of ritual participation and gender was "every last woman is initiated" (*denye fi kanzo*). At that time, initiation rites for women to become ounsi and the performance of spectacular public rituals necessitating the ounsi's participation were among the most popular and populous communitywide events. Now the opposite assertion is heard: there are no ounsi anymore. The potential for exaggeration of the complete ubiquity or the total absence of ounsi notwithstanding, the perception of a dramatic shift is significant.

In this chapter, I endeavor to gauge these claims by situating them in the relation to the commodification of secular and ritual labor, monetization of religious power, migration, religious conversion, new norms of selfhood, gender, ideas of social mobility, and unremitting economic and ecological crises. These processes are associated, of course, with modernity, capitalist colonialism, and postcolonial "development." To understand how these forces converge in the particular case of the perceived rise and decline of ounsi in Ti Rivyè, I draw on my engagement over nearly four decades with a community anchored in Ti Rivyè and its outposts in North America, especially, Florida, New York, Montreal, the Caribbean (including Guadeloupe and Martinique), and South America, in particular, Brazil, French Guyana, and Chile.

RITUAL TRANSFORMATIONS: FROM KIN TO CONGREGATION AND HOME TO TEMPLE

"There aren't any ounsi anymore" (*nan pwen ounsi ankò*), a Ti Rivyè man said to me in 2016. His perception today that "there aren't any more ounsi" prompts the questions of whether ounsi were always ubiquitous and whether their numerical diminution is an ominous sign of decline. In the early 1980s, I repeatedly heard the statement, "Every last woman is *kanzo*." The fact that my friends chose to draw attention to the quantitative dominance of initiates suggested that they were drawing attention to the newness of the "tradition." Were they signaling a trend that supplanted a previous convention, one that was not uniformly endorsed as wholly positive?

In his mid-twentieth-century study, *Le Vaudou Haïtien* (Voodoo in Haiti), Alfred Métraux (1972) offered a point of departure for asking whether and when the trend toward near-universal women's initiation came about. His study of Haitian ritual practices privileged what he observed in or near the capital of Port-au-Prince. He did not pretend otherwise. He did not universalize the urban practices and pretend they were representative of all of Haiti. Nor did he portray the practices he observed as timeless traditions. He wrote, rather, "The little I was able to see of rural Vodou convinced me that it was poor in its ritual compared to the Vodou of the capital.... Vodou deserves to be studied not only as regards the survival of Dahomean and Congolese beliefs and practices, but also as a religious system born fairly recently from a fusion of many different elements" (Métraux 1972, 61). Métraux further asserted that "the domestic cult [was] losing importance daily to the profit of the small autonomous cult groups which grow up around sanctuaries [and are] more numerous and prosperous in Port-au-Prince" (60–61). The spectacular, codified styles of worship that were displacing the modest, kin-based practices of Haiti's peasants were relatively recent, Métraux suggested. Unfortunately, Métraux did not develop further his intriguing observation about the relationship of these innovations to modernity.

My ethnographic research in ("glocal") Léogane took up Métraux's notion that the congregational forms and practices authorized as Vodou were not some "authentic" African religion of the peasants (as if there ever were one), a position still dominant in studies of Haitian Vodou, but rather conventions of an evolving periurban institution. The capital city of Port-au-Prince swelled in the first half of the twentieth century, largely in response to its encounter with the centralization and development policies of the United States occupation, which formally lasted from 1915 to 1934. Vodou temples, which became anchors for neotraditional ritual practices, were owned and managed by a new cadre of professional priests, whose source of power derived from a lengthy and expensive initiation. The priest commanded a new congregational structure based on individual voluntary association unrelated to kinship (though kinship terms of address were used), elaborate and expensive rituals carried out by female initiates, and a marked separation between the roles of performer and spectator.

Métraux (1972, 236–242) observed this same congregational structure at a rite he attended in Ti Rivyè, Léogane, in the 1940s. He was escorted there by Odette Mennesson-Rigaud, a researcher associated with the government's Bureau d'Ethnologie, who served as a guide to foreign ethnographers and whose mobility mirrored and perhaps even enhanced the spread of the congregational Vodou form. Ironically, Métraux represented the ritual as an example of "countryside" forms, and he downplayed its modern features.

Although there was no documented history of religious change in Léogane prior to my own, there was an intriguing analysis of such change in the Cul de Sac Plain, whose history as an extractive sugarcane-producing lowland adjacent to the capital is intimately linked to Léogane's. Gerald Murray (1977, 1980) suggested that a major lever in the displacement of domestic ritual practice was the shift in ritual roles from charismatic, clairvoyant shaman to professional priest, known as a *houngan* or *gangan*, whose source of power derived from a lengthy and expensive initiation. The novice was (and is) said to "take the *ason*" (*pran ason*). The ason is the sacred gourd rattle and bell used to summon the spirits, who are called lwa or *sen* (saint). Through their exclusive use of the ason, the professional gangan created a monopoly on new forms of communication with the inherited gods. This innovation obviated preexisting channels of access to the lwa, dreams and possession, which were open, at least in principle, to everyone in the descent group. As a result, "possession . . . lost its oracular function" (Murray 1980, 300).[1]

During an eighteen-month residence in Ti Rivyè in 1983 and 1984, I interviewed many senior women and men, including ounsi and gangan ason. Faustin Amilcar, the de facto historian of Ti Rivyè and a close collaborator and friend in this research, insisted that I seek out Camolien Alexandre. Camolien was the oldest member of the community, who identified himself as a *moun* Florvil (born during the presidency of Florvil Hyppolite, 1889–1896). His keen memory and deep knowledge of local land tenure also brought notaries and attorneys to the elder's door inquiring about the history of land in disputes. In his ninth decade when I knew him, Camolien had developed a cynical view of the evolution of religious leadership and ritual communication in Ti Rivyè over the course of the century. Camolien's recollections added specific detail to what Faustin and several other elders had told me.

He recalled when ordinary people like his parents, rather than an elite few, "knew everything" (*papa m te konn tout bagay*) to protect and nurture themselves and their families. The gangan ason's consolidation of communication with the inherited lwa led to the countervailing decline of the unrestricted oracular function of possession. Camolien felt increasingly alienated from the organization of ritual practice, which he dismissed as a "business": "The gangan of the old days had real knowledge, but the gangan here have a lot of lies. Those gangan—they didn't give the ason. The lwa was the one who gave it to you. You went to get it under the water. That was called the Guinea ason. The ason these gangan give today is something you buy." (Gangan lontan te gen bon rezon men gangan isit gen anpil manti. Gangan sa yo, yo pa bay ason. Se lwa ki ba ou. Ou al pran ni anba dlo. Sa rele ason ginen. Ason gangan bay—se bagay achte.)

Although the gangan ason's new power was achieved (unrelated to status), it came to be substantialized by kinship ties to the descent group, the inherited land, and the lwa. An (inherited) lwa was said to be the one who asks the gangan to "take the ason" while Loko, another ancient African (Ginen) lwa, presides over the initiation. Moreover, "calling the lwa (and the dead) with the *ason*," came to be deemed necessary for the most important and "traditional" "authentic African" (*fran* Ginen) rituals involving the descent group, the ancestors, and their lwa.

In Ti Rivyè, the catalyst in the professionalization of ritual leadership was a charismatic and politically connected gangan ason named Misdor. One of Misdor's sons (also a gangan ason) estimated in a conversation with me that his father "gave the ason" to more than one hundred fifty "students" (*elèv*). Pointing to the temple where Misdor once presided, he said, "[My father] gave the ason to everyone [every gangan ason] here. Everything they know comes from this house." Misdor's influence on ritual practice in Ti Rivyè was also keenly felt in the incorporation of formalized ritual roles for women who were initiated through the rite of passage known as kanzo.

When I interviewed Camolien, the topic of kanzo seemed to exasperate him more than any other. In his view, the practice of kanzo was a racket for the gangan ason, who benefited not only from fees collected from the initiates but also from their unlimited supply of "free" labor whenever the gangan ason was hired to direct a descent group's rites. Camolien said:

> Long ago there weren't a lot of ounsi. My mother wasn't an ounsi. We didn't have people who were ounsi. My mother—they inherited the lwa; they

served the lwa. Now there is no lack of ounsi. It's so the gangan can make money, beat the drums, pay—long ago we didn't have this, all this nonsense. Now there is all this business. That's why I don't pay attention to them. (Lontan pat genyen anpil ounsi. Manman m pat ounsi. Nou pat gen mounn ounsi. Manman m—yo leve jwenn lwa, yo sèvant lwa. Kouniyè a pa manke ounsi. Se pou gangan fè lajan, bat tanbou, peye–Lontan pat gen bagay sa yo-- bann tenten sa yo. Kouniyè a gen tout komès sa. Konsa tou m pa okipe yo.)

The rigid gendering of temple roles in Camolien's view was a means for gangan ason to profit from both the initiation rites for women and their unpaid labor at ever more expensive and spectacular rituals for the remainder of their ritual lives. The ounsi would refer to the leader and disciplinarian as *papa*. This modern congregational structure instituted a gender hierarchy that contradicted women's otherwise high social status as autonomous traders (*machann*) wielding full control over their own economic affairs and as the owners of their own homes by virtue of the practice of matrilocal residence.

Camolien's critique of the gangan ason's dependence on the free labor of the ounsi brought to mind a sacred song lyric quoted by Métraux (1972, 165):

Vèvè-lò it is the *ounsi* who makes the *gangan*
Ounsi falls down; the *gangan* then gets up
Vèvè-lò it is the *ounsi* who makes the *gangan*.

Reinforcing the fixing of gender hierarchy into local congregational structures was a de facto prohibition on locally resident women becoming local ritual leaders as *manbo* ason equivalent to the men, who were gangan ason. In 1984, I asked a senior gangan ason (who was a "student" of Misdor's) why there were no manbo ason there. He responded, "Here, men take the ason here, and lwa dance in the heads of women" (Isit gason pran ason; lwa danse nan tèt fi). In fact, women came from elsewhere to take the ason, but they did not "practice" locally. Léogane's reputation as a "school" of "authentic" temple Vodou still continues to draw outsiders, women as well as men, who come there to take the ason and apply their professional credentials elsewhere.

The social expectation in the early 1980s that every woman go through kanzo notwithstanding, it was assumed that a lwa "claimed" (*reklame*) a woman to go through the rite of passage. The request conformed to the typical pattern of communication between spirits and those who serve them. The first mode involved the spirits' use of passive or auspicious symbolic techniques to communicate the call, for example, appearing in dreams, divination, or in possession-performance. Failure to respond in a timely manner inevitably led the spirit to feel neglected and to have to resort to more aggressive pressure—namely, by "holding" (*kenbe*) the person with a *maladi lwa* (spirit-caused illness). In the case of initiation, the venerated, Ginen spirit, Danbala Wedo, was usually the one holding a woman until she agreed to "lie down" for him. This gendered phrasing did not, however, symbolize sexuality as much as symbolic death in the transitional phase of the initiation, whose format echoed the tripartite rite of passage outlined by Van Gennep ([1909] 1960) and later elaborated by Victor Turner (1967). The novices lay prone for nine days in the altar room of the shrine in preparation for rebirth into a new identity, dressed in white cloth and treated as though they were delicate and vulnerable newborns.

In contrast to acute, unusual, life-threatening afflictions caused by gods of the "hot" or "bitter" pantheons, illnesses sent by Danbala and other members of his relatively "cooler" and "sweeter" pantheon, which was called the Vodou pantheon, tended to be nonacute and chronic. The symptoms of the latter, common afflictions were diffuse enough to accommodate a broad constellation of symptoms, which nevertheless responded to one, and only one, remedy: kanzo.[2] The novices' confinement ended with a cheerful and festive rite of incorporation. The novices emerged from the altar room dressed in crisp, new dresses of sky blue but still under cover of large straw hats and towels (owing to their vulnerable and liminal state). The introduction of the new ounsi novices was always greeted with a complementary welcome, as is typical in the final reincorporation phase of a rite of passage. While standing among relatives and friends attending their emergence, I recall hearing flattering comments as to how healthy and fattened up the women appeared.

Even by local standards (elsewhere in Léogane), this particular Ti Rivyè community had a reputation of being especially disposed toward the kanzo, evidence especially of the impact of Misdor and his sons. I heard it said in 1983 that "every woman was initiated" (*denye fi kanzo*) by completing the ten-day rite of passage. The estimation certainly exaggerated the rate but indicated the significance of a trend that was still perceived as new. Our census of all households in the community demonstrated that fully half of the adult women had gone through this expensive rite of passage, and the majority had done so within the past decade. Some ounsi novices were young girls who had not yet been "claimed" to get initiated but rather accompanied their mothers into the altar room at a reduced price and with the expectation that the girls would eventually need to kanzo. Ironically, it was not unusual for ounsi to (pay to) submit to the kanzo ordeal a second time, it having been divined that immunization conferred by the first initiation had lost its effectiveness.

In the early 1980s, most local gangan ason conducted annual kanzo rites between June and October. The pace was so intense that the period was called "kanzo season" (*sezon kanzo*). One gangan ason was holding three kanzo a year to accommodate all of the ailing women needing to be "cured." The public ceremonies and dances accompanying the retreat of the novices, and their emergence as ounsi at the end of the rite of passage, were the most popular and frequent social events. They were carried out by scores of white-clad ounsi and attended by many more of their relatives. Initiation rites were also competitive occasions for the gangan ason and their ounsi. People ranked the kanzo according to the "heat" of the music and dancing, the refinement of the ritual, how many attended, the generosity and etiquette of the hosts and hostesses, and so on (see Deren 1953, 161). The conspicuous expenditure of financial resources for kanzo represented a significant social achievement, for they included fees to the gangan ason, drummers, a lay Catholic priest, and the novice's ritual "mother" and purchases of ritual objects, three sets of new garments, sacrificial victims, various offerings, and food and beverages to be served to scores of guests on four separate public occasions. Not to be ignored as a cost was the loss of the novice's labor for almost two months, which meant, of course, forgoing income or compensating someone else to take her place.

The direct and indirect costs of kanzo were shouldered by the migrant brothers, fathers, and sons of the initiates. It is likely that the migrants' ability and willingness to help heal (and affirm the gendered identities of) their female kin by financing their initiations of female kin with dollars earned abroad contributed to their escalating price. The relationship between mobile labor production (migration) and ritual reproduction is the focus of the next section.

MIGRATION, ECONOMIC CRISIS, AND DEMOGRAPHIC IMPLOSION

The modern style of congregational practice described above spread from Port-au-Prince to the densely settled lowlands of Cul de Sac and Léogane as these areas were undergoing massive economic and social upheaval that culminated with massive out-migration of young people and especially young men. Encroachment on the lands and labor of small farmers during the U.S. occupation, the forced importation of foods that undermined the market for locally grown foods and ecological ruin contributed to wide abandonment of small food production. When life activity was still viable in Ti Rivyè in particular, planting fields and fishing complemented one another; activities in one domain could often offset temporary crises in the other. The decline of farming in coastal Ti Rivyè was sadly echoed in the decline of its once robust fishing economy. "There is no livelihood here" (*pa gen lavi isit*) was a refrain in virtually all my 1983 and 1984 interviews with Ti Rivyè's small farmers and fishermen. Today, however, the glaring absence of productive activity in the unsown fields and a lifeless shoreline are far more extreme.

The last quarter of the twentieth century—amid a project of neoliberal development imposed with renewed vigor by the United States, multilateral lenders like the World Bank and the International Monetary Fund, and their allies—represented a final turning point in the transformation of the people of Ti Rivyè from producers of food to producers of people for export and consumers of migrants' wage remittances and imported food. The crisis squeezing Haiti's population echoed throughout the region. During the 1970s, according to Barry Levine (1987), a higher proportion of the Caribbean population emigrated than did the peoples of any other world area. In Ti Rivyè, the desire to emigrate was widespread, but few families could afford the cost of emigration until the end of the decade, when the cost, character, and location of migration changed. News of the successful voyage of a sailboat from Haiti to Miami in 1978 inspired a massive exodus of young men. Since they took their own small fishing sailboats, the cost of migration was low enough to make it possible for many to "take the *kanntè*" (pran kanntè). With word flowing home reporting not only how to navigate a successful voyage (without benefit of a motor) to Miami but also with the possibility of remaining and being allowed to work in the United States, albeit under onerous, unpredictable conditions, more residents, and notably more women, increasingly took to the sea. US Coast Guard cutters policing the Windward Passage between Cuba and Haiti interrupted the flow in 1982, but by then Ti Rivyè had contributed the bulk of their young adult men and a significant portion of their young women to the migration. As our census of all the households in 1983 revealed, the few able-bodied men who remained had tried to leave or, having failed, were exploring other routes to emigrate again (Richman 2005).

Ti Rivyè began to function as the moral and material anchor of a mobile, transnational community, 20 percent of whose members were "outside," primarily in Palm Beach and Broward Counties of Florida (*Mayami* was their term for this location). Everyday discourse naturalized the symbiotic interdependence between the kin members located "outside" (*deyò*) and "over there" (*lòt bò a*) and those "at home" (*lakay*). Their Kreyòl adages at the time further reinforced the spatial distribution of "life" and "life activity or livelihood." Life (*vi*) was inside, at home, but the "means to life" (*lavi*) were located outside. "To live in Haiti, you have to pursue livelihood Outside" (Viv an Ayiti, chache lavi Deyò). This statement was a common adage in the 1980s. Children who grew up at home supported in part by money earned abroad expected one day to "leave in search of a livelihood for their family" (chache lavi pou fanmi yo). When little Nason, now a grown man, was ten years old, for example, in 1984, he told me that one day he would "go over there" to search for a livelihood for his grandmother and his family. He had a picture of his future occupation: "working" and, more specifically, "cutting plantains." But, to his great frustration, his grandmother (an ounsi) was the one who left for the Outside—she returned for about two months every year—until her final return in 2014, at age eighty-nine, when she was buried. Men like Nason represent Ti Rivyè's first significant generation who grew up living at home and relying on relatives working outside. They know their migrant kin through the internet and WhatsApp cell phone calls and the parents' rare visits. Most expect to join their parents "over there," but funding and immigration policy—two variable factors—determine if and when they will get a visa.

In spite of the migrants' efforts, however, the residents left in Ti Rivyè feel that their poverty is deepening. The cost of living has escalated as more and more imported foods become staples. Despite the magnitude of remittances that have continued to go home since the exodus, those left at home often claim, "Pa gen lajan" (there is no money). When I interview gangan ason about the reason for the decline in initiation rites and in ritual activity, the primary reason they offer is "there is no money." They point to the high cost of basic foods—all imported—and of education for children: "Lavi vin chè" (life became expensive). The ritual leaders imply that even if women had the willingness to become initiated as ounsi, they lack the ability to do so. Even if others had the volition to sponsor rituals, they have no money left over to spend on rituals. (The issue of the many who do not have the volition to do so is discussed in another section of this chapter.)

This paradox is the fate of former colonized and small producer societies newly consigned to raising people for export and importing remittances and food. Haitian migrants' wage remittances reached an estimated $2.358 billion in 2016, accounting for 33.6 percent of the GDP according to the remittance expert Manuel Orozco (2018). As scholars have demonstrated, the monies migrants send home cannot fully compensate home families for the investments in the migrant's upbringing or the loss of their labor at home. Labor migration reproduces the impoverished means of producing raw labor for export to benefit capital; it does not reverse the economic decline and only intensifies the desire to leave (Kindleberger 1967).

In this light, the massive maritime exodus of young men and women "searching for a livelihood for their families" (chache lavi pou fanmi yo) apparently provided only a temporary reprieve to the growing rural economic crisis. Signs of potential recovery appeared in the scale of ritual production during the 1980s. Migrants who were willing infused money into the ritual system to fund women's kanzo initiations and the increasingly spectacular rituals requiring their participation, including the ever more elaborate mortuary rites as described by Elizabeth McAlister (this volume). The corollary sign of promising activity was the construction boom in spacious abodes for the living, the spirits, and the dead alike (Richman 2018). Migrants represented their transnational ties and their families' rising statuses through the construction of showy new houses (to use during vacations and to share with kin), new houses for the spirits (*kay lwa*) and large above-ground tombs decorated with ceramic tile and forged iron for themselves and their kin's final resting place. Inevitably, the vulnerabilities below these showy surfaces reveal themselves. Today, some of the beautiful houses are vacant or only partially occupied, monuments to the faded dream of a better life back home. Others are suspended in midconstruction, never to be completed. They stand like amputated concrete figures languishing on the landscape. Some of the shrines built by migrants are closed and abandoned. Indeed, where have all the ounsi gone?

Even though the maritime migration to Florida lasted less than four years (1978–1982), it hastened the pace of longer-term demographic shifts. The United States' immigration policy allowed the newcomers to establish authorized temporary status, which they transmuted to permanent residency after passage of the Immigration Reform and Control Act of 1986. With permanent residency, Ti Rivyè natives, like so many Haitian "entrants" (as their status classified them), quickly mobilized to begin sending for their family members. (They were also allowed finally to return home for visits without jeopardizing their precarious temporary status.) Many became naturalized citizens to hasten the timetable to bring family members into the United States, and if the United States border was closed to them, the map of possible relocations of their kin extended far beyond the United States. They considered other destinations in Canada, the Caribbean, and South America. Chile was a popular destination as of this writing. Tireless pursuit of knowledge about new migration opportunities and flexible exploitation of simultaneous, multilateral, local and global, collectivist strategies has kept families in perpetual and potential transit out of Ti Rivyè.

All the while, the Ti Rivyè mooring in Broward and Palm Beach Counties has become an established settlement as the anchor in Ti Rivyè has gradually loosened and threatens to float away. Ti Rivyè natives living as permanent residents and citizens in south Florida (and elsewhere as outposts of the south Florida anchor) now say without hesitation, "Everyone is here, now," and "There is no one left back home." The claim implies that all of their relatives have emigrated or they are in the process of emigrating. As for ounsi, the implication is that they, too, have left home and they are unlikely to return often if at all.

IMAGINED FUTURES AND THE AFFECTIVE MODERNITY OF YOUTH LEFT AT HOME

Migration is not the only factor contributing to the perception by those in the diaspora that "there is no one left" in Ti Rivyè. The population is in fact declining not only because of emigration but also because of the growing practice of modern citizenship that calls for delaying or limiting having children. The remaining population of Ti Rivyè is dwindling of its own accord. The fertility rate of the country, at 2.42, is only slightly above replacement rate (of 2.33), echoing the low birth rates in other parts of the Caribbean, including Jamaica and the Bahamas, as well as Europe, North America, and Japan. As anthropologists tracking the population implosion in these states have demonstrated, economic and social precarity strongly affects the strategies of young adults to limit or refrain entirely from having children (Allison 2013; Douglass 2005). Many of the Ti Rivyè children I have watched grow up since the 1980s have yet to become parents.

The young adults in Ti Rivyè who await a secure income and professional employment are nevertheless aware of the structural limitations on those aspirations. They may be educated and even have earned technical degrees to prepare them for jobs in nursing, communications, and engineering, but they cannot find employment. Their boredom mirrors that of swaths of youth facing a crisis of mediated stagnation and overproduction across the globe (O'Neill 2017). The twenty-nine-year-old daughter of a farmer and a vendor, whom I have known since she was born, for example, responded to a question on my written survey occupation. She reframed the question to situate individual work opportunity in its proper social and structural context: "My people don't do anything" (Moun mwen yo pa fè anyen). Meanwhile, she and her age cohort anticipate joining their own parents and relatives outside, but funding and immigration policy—two variable factors—determine if and when they will get a visa. Raised to leave, many are waiting at home. They are at rest and restless. Their productive energies center on planning a way out, gathering information, planning a route, and mustering funding from relatives abroad.

Nonetheless, the young adults imagine their futures through a lens shaped by local and global media in which the youth are an autonomous social category.[3] The lyrics of politically engaged Haitian popular music promote youth futures as a national priority. The young women and men of Ti Rivyè have attended school, thanks to their parents' labor outside, which has shaped their expectations of mobility. In contrast, their parents grew up before "youth" was a ratified social identity; when the privilege of formal education was rare, large families with minimal formal education suited their small farming and fisheries modes of production.

"Affective modernity" (Hirsch 2004) is increasingly at odds with the practice of organized religion generally, and it is likely even more incompatible with the concept of ounsi kanzo.[4] Young adults globally have responded to their precarious, imagined futures by turning away from religious affiliation, belief in a Supreme Being, and participation in organized religious rituals. Young Haitians are no exception (Pew Research Center 2018). As a gangan ason I have known for several decades explained to me recently, "The elders [who served lwa] are gone, and the young aren't interested." Indeed, many of the younger generation of adults regard *sèvis lwa* as backward and irrelevant to modern lives. Some talk about it as a waste of money to enrich manipulative gangan ason. If they have resources, they may be loath to give them to their kin to be "wasted" on useless ritual. They doubt the reality of the lwa's power either to improve their lives or afflict them as punishment for neglect. Doubt about the reality of spiritual affliction is another factor contributing to the decline of ounsi; women submitted to the call to kanzo to lift affliction sent by the spirit patron of the kanzo rite, Danbala Wedo, or another lwa in his pantheon. The range of symptoms associated with this type of affliction was so diffuse that it appeared to cover most forms of chronic ailment. Perhaps the sheer breadth of these chronic systems contributed to their being attributed to other causes.

For those who still believe in the relevance and efficaciousness of sèvis lwa, the subservient, gendered role of ounsi holds little appeal. A thirty-something gangan from Ti Rivyè averred on this point during our conversation in 2017. "If they [women] are 'still in it' [*toujou ladan n*] at all, they do not want to be ounsi; they want to be ritual leaders, or *manbo*." Whereas during the 1980s, there were hardly any local manbo ason, the "field" has modestly opened up to women: there are two manbo ason in the area (and about ten gangan ason).

Women and men occasionally still come to Ti Rivyè to pursue initiation into professional ritual leadership as manbo ason; the provision of professional ritual training remains an attractive, cutting-edge resource of the ritual economy. For example, a woman of Haitian descent based in New York went through the training to become a manbo ason under the guidance of a Ti Rivyè gangan ason. The process unfolded over two years and involved several virtual (internet and cellular phone) and physical visits. She promoted her acquisition of the ason and her professional credentials as a Vodou priestess and healer in social media and through colorful printed posters, one of which was displayed on an interior wall of the shrine before she completed the final stage of the rite of passage in 2015.

It is important to acknowledge that engagement in sèvis lwa and initiation into the ranks of ounsi presumes Catholic practice and affiliation. All rituals oriented to the lwa include Catholic practices, and the rite of passage into ounsi status necessitates attendance at mass. In view of its status as the religion of progress and modernity, in contrast to the image of Catholicism as conservative and hierarchical, Protestant evangelical rhetoric has had a pronounced impact on the representation of Vodou as premodern and backward as opposed to merely evil, a rhetoric that may influence affectively modern selves, regardless of their religious affiliation. In the next part of the chapter, I turn to the influence the encounter with Protestant Christianity has had on the diminution of the public practice of serving spirits and on the formal, public role of ounsi kanzo.

PROTESTANT CONVERSION, VISIBILITY, AND THE DISAPPEARANCE OF OUNSI

Roman Catholicism was the official religion of the colony of St. Domingue, and in 1804 it became the state religion of the republic of Haiti. Catholicism reigned as Haiti's only official religion for nearly two centuries. When the Haitian state recognized Protestantism in 1985, it belatedly acknowledged the significant realignment of the nation's religious identification. At that point, estimates of Protestant conversion were around one-fourth to one-third of the population. Today, it is possible that more than half (of those who affiliate with an organized religion) are Protestant.[5] The expansion of Protestant missionization in Haiti was closely linked to intensified United States–led development in the 1970s. The sociologist Charles-Poisset Romain (1986) claimed that missionization in Haiti during the 1970s was more intense than anywhere else in the hemisphere, that Haiti witnessed more proliferation of sects during that period than any other country. The Haitian government under control of François Duvalier welcomed the missionaries who offered to perform some of the work of the state while ignoring the state's violent and corrupt policies, which accomplished Duvalier's strategy of undermining the power of the state Catholic church (Courlander and Bastien 1966; Nichols 1970). With material and administrative support from the United States, faith-based organizations systematically covered the geography of the country, establishing churches, free education, and feeding programs that reached the poorest segments of the population. The malnourished pupils were "fed" North American Protestant faith and cultural discourses.

Fred Conway (1978), who conducted ethnographic fieldwork in southern Haiti in the 1970s, noted that the North American missionary presence was so pervasive that he was taken for a Protestant missionary. Through his history of the establishment of various mission churches and the wry comments of the villagers who observed those projects, Conway (1978) depicts the mutual utilitarianism of American missionaries and Haitian pastors, with the missionaries' quantitative desire for more converts and the Haitians' quest for American patronage, a decent job, prestige, and a visa to the United States. While pointing to Protestant missions, Conway's interlocutors told him, "The country is becoming more and more civilized," in contrast to the backwardness blamed on peasant Vodou. Several converts frankly told Conway that their conversion was a contribution to "development" (172).

According to Conway, people understood that Americans "needed" converts, and they were willing to pay for them. No one benefitted more from their "needs" to build missions and count disciples than the pastors. The clergy was and remains today one of the few "jobs" for men in rural areas. Romain (1986, 144) comments that "tout protestant est à la fois pasteur et missionnaire." The speech practice of addressing any male evangelical as "paste" reinforced this assumption. The success of the pastors reflected the convergence of the fluid, informal, lay, and entrepreneurial character of the evangelical practice with local values regarding leadership and spiritual power—namely, diffuse leadership, charismatic and spontaneous power, and an intense distrust of authority and bureaucracies. The religion welcomed the man who aspired to have a congregation, began by praying with two or three people, and eventually built a congregation.

In its gendered hierarchy, exclusive opportunities for males with charismatic appeal, and entrepreneurial ambition, there were obvious similarities to temple Vodou, which already was mirroring "modern" Protestant congregations when it developed in the early to mid-twentieth century in and around the capital. In both systems, women are slowly being welcomed into congregational leadership. A key difference between them was and remains Protestantism's identification with modernity and upward mobility, both figuratively and literally. For in addition to the social and economic boost of satisfying an American missionary organization's needs was the real possibility of a visa to the United

States and the opportunity to establish a congregation catering to the increasing "market" population of Haitian immigrants, which swelled after the late 1970s. Indeed, the miracle of the visa to the United States, the fruit of mission sponsorship, has been a frequent theme in pastors' narratives delivered from the pulpits of Haitian ethnic churches established in the United States (Richman 2008).

Haitian immigrants' religious adaptations are hardly unique and align with those of previous immigrants in the establishment of ethnic congregations headed by clergy ministering in both the immigrants' language and English (Warner and Wittner 1998). The Catholic church was slower to accommodate the newcomers, but Haitian Protestant churches flexibly accompanied Haitian immigrants' mobilities, offering numerous options for worship in Kreyòl and English (Richman 2005b).

To assess the effects of "the Protestant turn" on spiritual belief and magical/ritual practices, it is important to remember the instrumentalist and pluralistic orientations of West African Vodu and Vodún, as described by Venise N. Abidijou, Douglas J. Falen, Timothy Landry, Eric Montgomery, and Christian Vanier in this volume. These epistemologies laid the foundation for the "variety" of Vodou, to invoke an analogous linguistic term, that first developed in colonial Saint Domingue (Rey, this volume). Regardless of sectarian separatist or ascetic rhetoric and behavior, the fundamental pragmatism and flexibility of Vodu/Vodún/Vodou continues to influence Haitians' attitudes toward ritual power and religious affiliation. In the middle of the twentieth century, Métraux (1953, 1959) noted the tactical use of conversion as an act of revolt against lwa more than half a century ago, before the postwar expansion of Pentecostals in the country. Métraux explained how the act of conversion represented "a magic circle" of protection from discipline by lwa. He quoted what a person told him in Marbial: "If you want the (lwa) to leave you in peace, become a Protestant." Conversion was one of the few socially appropriate tactics available to a servitor. Métraux (1959, 352) added the insight that "no doubt it is the challenging attitude adopted by Protestants towards the (lwa) which has finally convinced the peasants that this religion confers upon its adepts a sort of supernatural immunity."

Métraux's analysis of the instrumental use of conversion closely echoed the internal Protestant critique. The Haitian Protestant theologian Roger Dorsainville had previously lamented that a "true conviction and profound commitment to be saved" were "rarely" the reason people converted. "Protestantism," he asserted, "is pursued as a superior *wanga* (magical power), the pastor is like a more powerful sorcerer" (L'Evangile est also recherché comme un "ouanga" supérieur, le prédicateur est comme un bocor puissant) (cited in Pressoir 1942, 8). The magic circle also protects the convert from very real fear of sorcery, a social weapon long used by peasants throughout the world to limit individualism and greed and enforce the reciprocity symbolized and enforced through sèvis lwa. Thus, a former ounsi, who migrated to south Florida from Ti Rivyè, told me after her conversion in the mid-1990s, "As soon as you convert, nothing can harm you" (Depi ou konvèti, anyen pa ka fè ou). It is important to underscore that her new religion has neither replaced nor diminished her belief in the reality of sorcerers' powers. "Le mal existe" (evil exists), she added (invoking a French register for emphasis in an otherwise Kreyòl conversation). Christianity persuaded her that it offered the most protective armor against evil forces.

Conversion did not, nor could it, require a profound change in belief. But it required, then as now, a visible disavowal of Catholic and sèvis lwa practices and the public physical destruction of associated sacred objects. It forbade attendance at all Catholic worship and all rituals related to the worship of lwa. Serving lwa is a fundamentally communal practice. It is not practiced in secret. Where temple Vodou has overtaken domestic practices, as in Ti Rivyè since the mid-twentieth century at least, it requires the ritual labor corps of ounsi and musicians under the leadership of gangan or manbo ason. Few Protestants would dare to be seen in the vicinity of their family's worship or "feeding" of their lwa. The increase in converts has inevitably affected a corresponding decrease in attendance at rituals and numbers of willing and eligible ounsi.

It is widely suspected that converts, who would not dare to step foot at a communal sèvis lwa, continue in private the practice of magic, sorcery, and countersorcery. Protestants are known to secretly patronize gangan who control this "market." While living in a Ti Rivyè hamlet, I had been curious about the strangers who occasionally appeared, asking for Joiecius, a senior gangan ason. They would wait patiently on the gallery of his wife's house until he arrived, and then they would follow him out of the yard. I finally asked the ritual leader who those strangers were. "They're Protestants," he told me, as if I were the only one who did not already know that obvious fact. "They come from the capital city." Pepe, another prestigious gangan ason, said to me, "If they say they convert so nothing can harm them, then why do they come to see gangan? And why do they have sacred things hidden in their houses?" In a curious echo of Dorsainville's 1940s lament about converts seeking stronger *wanga* (charms and spells) from Protestant pastors, Pepe displayed his begrudging admiration for his Protestant counterparts when he further asserted that "Pastors get wanga [charms and spells] and *dyab* [money-making powers), which they plant at the front of their yards, so when foreign missionaries pass by, they will notice them and give them money and send them to the States. They have to fill their churches to satisfy their sponsors. And they are good talkers, too." As Joiecius also told me, "It's a business; it's so they can make money" (Se yon biznis; se pou yo fè kòb). His claim echoed the critique of "the business" offered to Fred Conway by observers of Protestant strategies in southern Haiti. But the critique could equally apply to his own profession, recalling Camolien's cynical critique of the development of the gangan ason "trade" in Ti Rivyè.

The gangan ason I have known and interviewed repeatedly over the past four decades are loath to admit that the Protestant "trade" has affected their own. During my 1983–1984 research, I did occasionally witness the ritual leaders' public acknowledgment of this correlation. In one instance, the gangan ason, addressing the spirit, Ezili Dantò, who had "mounted" an ounsi at a large "feeding" in her honor, complained to the spirit, "Everyone around here is converting. There are only a few of us left, but we'll never stop serving the lwa." He might have added, "With the help of our migrant emissaries as long as they don't convert."

CONCLUSION

This discussion of the commercialization of ritual roles and practices began with the aged Camolien Alexandre's cynical history of "the business" of temple Vodou articulated by Camolien. To my surprise, in 2017 I was transported thirty-five years back to Camolien's little house and the sound of the venerable old man's voice. This time, I was sitting with the residents of the matrilineal yard (*lakou*) I have since 1983 called my home "over there," and to which I have returned year after year to document and capture their history. A middle-aged woman who looked vaguely familiar came passing through. She introduced her cousins and me. I was surprised when she launched into a critique of all of the ritual labor she had provided to enrich a certain prominent gangan ason without receiving any payment. She had been initiated as an ounsi as a young woman at the temple he oversaw. The long-term (and former?) ounsi was, in effect, reframing a ritual relationship that had been putatively untainted by monetary affairs as a crass commercial transaction. The timing of her complaint ten years after the death of the gangan ason was particularly ironic because there is so little ritual labor for ounsi to do anymore. Today, there is not enough activity to merit an earmarked "kanzo season." The temples no longer regularly sponsor annual rites of passage for women; the numbers of initiates are a fraction of what they were in the 1980s.

In the early 1980s, the ritual structure that mediated the circulation of Ti Rivyè's only remaining viable economic resource—labor—was not a timeless traditional pattern but rather a recent innovation. During the 1940s, a few professional gangan rose to prominence, whose authority was based on a new source of power, a lengthy and expensive initiation rite to "take the ason" (pran ason), the sacred gourd rattle and bell used to "communicate with the lwa." The professional gangan ason incorporated formalized performance roles associated with urban shrines, and they introduced new rituals that were nevertheless classified and perceived as unchanging, "authentic African" (fran Ginen) traditions practiced and transmitted by the "African" founders of the descent groups. The increasingly elaborate "services for the lwa" required the participation of corps of initiated women "servitors" (ounsi), along with singing, dancing, drumming, flag bearing, processionals, animal sacrifice, and copious offerings of costly imported foods and drinks. Thus, despite its authority as an ancient African practice, this form was a reinvented tradition that developed in response to major social and economic upheaval in the plains of Haiti, which culminated in the transformation of the free-holding peasants into producers of migrant laborers and consumers of wage remittances. The children of ounsi who today resist or reject the ritual roles of their mothers are not abandoning traditional Vodou, as if it ever existed, but rather a modern, monetized form whose adaptations to broader socioeconomic processes both mirrored and paved the way for encroachment by another and seemingly even more modern religion. The adaptation to commercialization of ritual, professional ritual leadership and congregational forms inevitably made temple Vodou more vulnerable to Protestant critiques of the financially corrupt and backward, not to mention evil, religion.

From the perspective of the complex dynamic within and about modernity, the relative abundance of ritual roles for women and practices associated with the rise of profitable temple Vodou are not signs of the health of the system. By contrast, these shifts occurred in the wake of an extended encounter with a U.S. military and administrative occupation, which contributed to loss of land to small farmers, land concentration, monocrop production of sugarcane on large plantations, and (low) wage labor. Increased importation of food and other products to compete with local production further undermined the agricultural system. The society turned to transnational migration to cope with these concomitant onslaughts.

The commodification of ritual authority, relationships, and roles described here could thus be seen as flexibly adapting to these shifts. As Giafferi-Dombre and other contributors to this volume plainly demonstrate, Vodou's antifundamentalist flexibility and resilience are undoubtedly the keys to its efficacy. But in appropriating certain of modernity's monetized techniques, perhaps the ritual system was inadvertently sowing different seeds of vulnerability. The reproduction of that ritual system would depend on the perpetuity of both a continuous supply of novices and a constant source of funds for rites of passage unfettered by completing claims. As a result of the inexorable demise of agriculture and fisheries, that money would have to come from outside, from deyò. Moreover, the migrants would have to maintain continued confidence in the system of sèvis lwa, too, in its effectiveness in keeping them and their kin healthy and safe from symbolic spiritual and human aggression. But the unremitting economic crisis at home and abroad would challenge that guarantee. Ironically, the relatively recent ritual practices associated with kanzo, particularly the fixing of lower-ranked gender roles, would come to appear to some as truly backward and even irrelevant to their imagined modern, upwardly mobile futures.

NOTES

1. The loss of the oracular function of possession in Cul de Sac had already been mentioned (in passing) by Harold Courlander, who conducted his research between 1937 and 1955, in Cul de Sac and Port-au-Prince. Courlander quoted one aged man from Belladère who was quite cynical of the rise of the gangan ason. The man's analysis of what had changed was that people could no longer talk to their inherited lwa (except by means of the professional priest): "Some of the things that are going on down there in the Plain (of the Cul de Sac) are not right. They are not the old way. In the old days, we did things differently. We did not *always* run to the *houngan*. The *grande famille* knew how to talk to the (*lwa*). Up here we don't do things the way they do them down below in the city" (Courlander 1960, 71–72).

2. Our census of all the households in the community in 1983–1984 (Richman 2005) included questions about ritual affiliation. The senior woman in each house was asked whether she was an ounsi, where she got initiated, her age at the time, the name of the gangan ason leading the rite of passage, and his relationship to her. (The same series of questions was asked about any other ounsi in her immediate family [mother, sister, child].) The next question posed to her was "Why did you get initiated?" The uniform response was "I was sick." The seventy-one respondents identified headache as the most common ailment leading to the decision to kanzo (41%), followed by respiratory problems (11%), fever (10%), digestive ailments (10%), sudden blindness (9%), sudden weight loss (4%), and other suffering (15%), including toothache, hearing loss, emotional crises, and pain in body and limbs.

This study raises the question of whether the sheer range of symptoms associated with this type of affliction was so diffuse that it appeared to cover most forms of chronic ailment. Perhaps the sheer breadth of these chronic systems contributed to their being attributed to other causes.

3. Examples of songs promoting youth futures as a pressing national priority are Wyclef Jean's "Piwo" (2014) and Kreyòl La's 2018 Carnival recording "Anlè Anlè Net."

4. The medical anthropologist Jennifer Hirsch (2004) has used the term "affective modernity" to describe Mexicans' new ideology influencing their sense of themselves as cosmopolitan (in this case with respect to marriage and sexuality) even as they maintained some behaviors that they themselves characterized as outmoded and backward.

5. The results of our recent, random survey conducted in Léogane in 2017 covering 550 households indicate that slightly more than half of the sample identify as Protestant. We presented our findings at the 2018 annual meetings of the Haitian Studies Association in Port-au-Prince in November (Richman et al. 2018).

REFERENCES

Allison, Anne, 2013. *Precarious Japan*. Chapel Hill, NC: Duke University Press.
Conway, Frederick. 1978. "Pentecostalism in the Context of Haitian Religion and Health Practice." PhD diss., American University.
Courlander, Harold. 1960. *The Drum and the Hoe: Life and Lore of the Haitian People*. Berkeley: University of California Press.
Deren, Maya. 1953. *Divine Horsemen: The Living Gods of Haiti*. London: McPherson.
Hirsch, Jennifer. 2004. *A Courtship after Marriage*. Berkeley: University of California Press.
Jean, Wyclef, 2014. "Piwo." Accessed October 1, 2021. https://www.youtube.com/watch?v=skWjudTI5TI.
Kindleberger, Charles. 1967. *Europe's Postwar Growth: The Role of Labor Supply*. Cambridge, MA: Harvard University Press.
Kreyol La. 2020. "Anlè Anlè Net [Karnival 2018]." MP3 audio. Track 8 on *Domination*, Self-release.
Métraux, Alfred. 1953a. "Médecine et Vodou en Haïti." *Acta Tropica* 10:28–68.
———. 1954–1955. "Le Noël Vodou en Haïti." *Bulletin de la Société Neuchâteloise de Géographie* 51:95–118.
———. (1959) 1972. *Voodoo in Haiti*. Translated by Hugo Charteris. New York: Schocken Books.
Murray, Gerald. 1970. "Women in Perdition: Ritual Fertility Control in Haiti." In *Culture, Natality and Family Planning*, edited by John Marshall and Steven Polgar, 59–78. Chapel Hill: University of North Carolina Press.

———. 1980. "Population Pressure, Land Tenure and Voodoo: The Economics of Haitian Peasant Ritual." In *Beyond the Myths of Culture: Essays in Cultural Materialism*, edited by E. Ross, 295–321. New York: Academic Press.
O'Neill, Bruce. 2017. *The Space of Boredom: Homelessness in the Slowing Global Order*. Durham, NC: Duke University Press.
Pew Research Center. 2018. *The Age Gap in Religion around the World*. Washington, DC, June 13, 2018. https://www.pewforum.org/2018/06/13/the-age-gap-in-religion-around-the-world/.
Pressoir, Catts. 1942. "L'Etat Actuel des Missions Protestantes en Haïti." Lecture given on Bible Sunday at St. Paul's Church. December 13, 1942.
Richman, Karen, 2005a. *Migration and Vodou*. Gainesville: University Press of Florida.
———. 2005b. "The Protestant Ethic and the Dis-spirit of Vodou." In *Immigrant Faiths: Transforming Religious Life in America*, edited by Karen Leonard, Alex Stepick, Manuel Vasquez, and Jennifer Holdaway, 165–187. Lanham, MD: Alta Mira.
———. 2008a. "Innocent Imitations? Authenticity and Mimesis in Haitian Vodou Art, Tourism and Anthropology." *Ethnohistory* 55 (2): 203–228.
———. 2008b. "A More Powerful Sorcerer: Conversion and Capital in the Haitian Diaspora." *New West Indian Guide* 81 (1–2): 1–43.
———. 2018. "Mortuary Rites and Social Dramas in Léogâne, Haiti." In *Passages and Afterworlds: Anthropological Perspectives on Death and Mortuary Rituals in the Caribbean*, edited by Maarit Forde and Yanique Hume, 139–158. Durham, NC: Duke University Press.
Richman, Karen, Jean Benoît Gede, Lamar Presuma, and Edson Jean. 2018. "A Safe House: An Interdisciplinary Tèt Ansanm." Paper presented at the Thirtieth Annual Conference of the Haitian Studies Association, Port-au-Prince, Haiti, November 9, 2018.
Romain, Charles. 1986. *Le Protestantisme Dans La Société Haïtienne*. Port-au-Prince: Henri Deschamps.
Turner, Victor. 1967. *The Forest of Symbols*. Ithaca, NY: Cornell University Press.
van Gennep, Arnold. (1909) 1960. *The Rites of Passage*. Translated by Monika Vizedom and Gabrielle Caffee. Chicago: University of Chicago Press.
Warner, R. Stephen, and Judith Wittner. 1998. *Gatherings in Diaspora: Religious Communities and the New Immigration*. Philadelphia: Temple University Press.

KAREN RICHMAN is Director for Undergraduate Studies at the Institute for Latino Studies and concurrent faculty in the Departments of Romance Languages and Anthropology at the University of Notre Dame. She is author of *Migration and Vodou*.

SIX

SAILING BETWEEN LOCAL AND GLOBAL

Vodou in the Modern and Contemporary Arts of Haiti

Natacha Giafferi-Dombre

THIS CHAPTER approaches a question at the heart of the artistic practice in Haiti, particularly Vodou or para-Vodou art: What is, or could be, the function of art in contemporary Haiti? Art writ large is a practice that is not supposed to exist in vernacular language but is one of the most recognized modes of cultural expression in the country, in a postcolonial context where Vodou is also the formulation of a discourse on the encounter with the Other. Scholars are tempted to consider Haiti's aesthetic production through the framework of authenticity, wondering whether and when an art object expressed a genuinely local imagination or responded to a foreign desire of exoticism. The country's economic and political subordination to former colonial and predatory powers cannot be ignored by any Haitian citizen, and particularly the artists, where protest is ingrained. In this sense, the initial shock of the American occupation (1915–1934) was decisive in what Carlo Avierl Célius (2008) calls "the invention of Haitian art" in the 1940s. Born out of the War of Independence, Haitian nationalism was stirred up once again by the experience of American imperialism depriving the young republic of its autonomy. Turning to Indigénisme, first in literature (the *Revue Indigène* published its first issue in 1927) and then in the arts, as a mode of cultural affirmation and resistance, the Haitian elites stopped imitating Europeans and dove into their own popular imagination, stories and tales, investing their culture's astonishing competence of flexibility and resiliency. The ethnographer Jean Price-Mars (2020), notably, insisted on the value of Vodou and the necessity to overcome the division between the people and the elite in this regard. From the painters Hector Hyppolite and Robert Saint-Brice to its most contemporary and globalized manifestations, Haitian art has been consistent with Vodou's tradition of incorporation and flexibility, core themes of this volume, when faced with unequal culture contact. Haitian art is an intelligent adaptation to the foreign or local upper-class demand for primitive/traditional/rural/Vodou art as well as to the lack of any other national production at present available other than the "production of migrants" (Richman 2008a). Rather than leaving the country, artists have the possibility to stay and produce one of the last remaining artifacts: art, be it paintings, beaded ceremonial flags, metal sculptures, or the more recent trash or recycled art also practiced in various African countries. This chapter assesses Haitian art and Vodou as artists sail between the local and global in contemporary times.

In the days of Saint-Domingue as a French colony, as at the time of American occupation or in today's postcolonial republic, Vodou's continued power and efficacy lies in its capacity to incorporate adversity or foreign elements and perpetually recontextualize itself. The observable commodification of popular and religious art is a result of the capitalist mode of consumption and circulation of art in the world (see Benoît and Delpuech 2015) that prolongs the colonial gaze Haitians had so fiercely fought since the ancien régime. It is also a sign of resilience and economic adaptation to a situation of growing poverty and economic inequality, in which making art and living from it is an art in itself, requiring careful observation of the demand since production comes at a cost that must be covered. Creation is not free but subject to the market, and this is true for the most independent productions. Thus, what Karen Richman (2008b) calls "the contradiction between mimetic reciprocity and a discourse of authenticity" should be our guideline throughout this text and any excursions into Haitian art territories.

In this chapter, I develop three main points: First, Vodou is plainly a twenty-first-century religion, global, always evolving, equipped with an aesthetic compatible with foreign-born popular cultures. Second, its artistic manifestations show a continuous tension between the desire for a national expression and the thirst for foreign movements, Western or not (Cuban *real maravilloso*, French surrealism, outsider art, *arte povera*, or recycled art), resolving into the creative appropriation of these foreign artistic movements. Third, Vodou-influenced arts have undergone a desacralization concomitant with the commodification of religious symbols and pictures while, at the same time, maintaining the capacity to inject a sense of spirituality into collective struggles and intimate interrogations embodied in works of art. Duplicity generally conveys negative connotations, but we might want to consider looking at Vodou's fluidity as a force of resilience that has enabled it, until recently, to resolve the inherent contradiction of its singular place in history. However, we must be aware of the limits of this capacity for resilience because Vodou itself is structurally affected by "the commodification of secular and ritual labor, monetization of religious power, migration, religious conversion [and] new norms of selfhood," as Karen Richman argues in this volume.

A RELIGION IN FLUX: RUPTURE AND HETEROGENEITY

If we envisage the notion of flux that manifests in processes of globalization as the guide to our reflection and consider the circulation of people and images across the globe as the common contemporary paradigm, we need to consider how these cultural encounters interact with the construction of identities. Haiti, as a colonial project and later as a small country under the influence of powerful nations, has had to adapt to imposed political and economic rules while trying to assert its existence as an independent republic. During the nineteenth and twentieth centuries, elites, Black or mulatto, adopted European cultural and religious values as vectors and signs of progress and looked at the rural, Vodouist masses with apparent contempt. As demonstrated elsewhere in this volume, Haitian Vodou is the product of repeated cultural encounters leading to the accumulative incorporation of religious elements—West African, Central African, Islamic, Christian—first in Africa, then in Saint-Domingue, and finally in the postcolony of the Republic of Haiti. By allowing a certain degree of heterodoxy and blending in its rituals, pantheons, and aesthetics, Haitian Vodou protects its core, inherited values—a strategy also observed in carnivalized Indo-Shia Islam *muharram* performances in Trinidad, escaping the double pitfall of isolationism/syncretism or a collective assimilation to the dominant Creole culture (Korom 2003). Maintaining West African Vodun's integrative capacity in its engagement with a Westernized America, Haitian Vodou preserves the ability to create new narratives and spiritual tools along inevitable evolutions. Their use of the power of the religious imagination (Appadurai 1996; Fernandez 1982) helps postcolonial nations cope with their enduring subalternity and rearrange their peripheral relation to centers upon which they are dependent. While staying faithful to its multilayered, multicultural memory, Haitian Vodou continues to aggregate and adapt extraneous elements out of the ruptures experienced by its believers. A continuity in discontinuity, it is by tradition innovative, an antonymous phenomenon shaped out of perpetual negotiations between its core system of meaning and the necessity to adjust to new circumstances. Haitian Vodou is not a passive receptor of novelties but emphasizes the mastery, deconstruction, and feeding on adversary energies. Its history shows a tremendous variety of external

Figure 6.1. *Maitre Grand Bois*, by Rockville. The tree to which Saint Sebastian / Grand Bois is tied symbolically sums up the wild, sacred spaces of the forest. Photograph by author.

influences, inputs, or borrowings. Sidney Mintz (1977) notably demonstrated how the expansion of capitalism always induced local responses and could not reduce the Caribbean to a mere effect of globalizing markets.

POP CULTURE AND VODOU: AN EFFECTIVE BRICOLAGE

Not only is Haitian Vodou open to foreign cults or divinities when deemed necessary, but it also integrates elements from the profane. Pop culture, for example, is a great source of inspiration for the Vodou synthesis. Haitian Vodou is a sacred-producing machine: once a profane element enters Vodou, it becomes part of a sacred ensemble where it functions as a cog, a lexical signifier of the

Vodou language. What could be seen as an effect of the triumph of capitalism around the globe could also be envisioned as a creative rephrasing of traditional figures, "show[ing] signs of local agency in the face of hegemonic influence" (see Falen, this volume). The local use of images born in the United States in the consumer culture of Disney and Hollywood does not necessarily mean a total loss of cultural autonomy. The American entertainment industry itself borrows from Haitian characters, such as Bawon Samdi or the *zonbi* (turning the latter into the domestic figure of the "zombie" that expresses American fears and obsessions, even the mystification of "gothic tropes"), and sends back its own idols: actors, pop singers, and rappers. Some of these representations or commodity fetishes are retained and appropriated locally because they carry perceived useful values (see Montgomery 2019). The street artists in charge of decorating collective transportation vehicles, whose profits depend on their success with travelers, transcribe these images of personal achievement, strength, or beauty into local aesthetics, blending typically Western representations into local shapes and colors. Buses and *tap tap*, once solely decorated with biblical or mystical phrases or pictures, now display North American movie or music stars accessible through cable or local TV and returning migrants. According to an article recently published by the Minustah,[1] the United Nations Stabilization Mission in Haiti, the Haitian street art of public transportation that appeared in the early 1940s only developed references to Vodou lwa (divinities) or their Catholic counterparts until the 1980s. The decorating artist Oldy Joël Auguste champions the style he was acquainted with and complains that these newly imported characters "don't reflect the Haitian culture" (Minustah 2013). But the newness is only apparent, since the fusion of these characters from cinema, itself a form of mythology, with Haitian deities is facilitated by the formal approach of cultural appropriation. If seductive, long-haired women from the American cinema industry are particularly pervasive in the representations of Ezili Freda (a lwa of femininity), Ogou (a lwa of warfare, metal, and fire) is easily recognized under the appearance of Rambo, while "Bawon Samedi is a large plastic statue of Darth Vader" (Cosentino 1995b, 408). Haitian Vodou is characterized by the same unfinished, work-in-progress nature as Vodùn in Africa (see Montgomery, this volume), and so imagery and other symbolic aspects of Haitian Vodou are open to the introduction of seemingly new materials.

Haiti is not an isolated country. Global popular culture currently developing throughout the world is bringing new modes of consumption as well as a new definition of reality and virtuality. In the *Nouvelliste*, the main Haitian newspaper since 1898, a mother interviewed for the occasion complained that her child kept asking her for a Halloween costume instead of celebrating the traditional Day of the Dead (Fèt Gede), which goes along with propitiatory offerings.[2] The child's teacher had planted this seed, as did the local merchants importing these goods, from the United States or South America. Another novelty in the celebration of November 1 and 2 is the Gede Fest. Subtitled "Twin Sisters Reunited" and jointly organized by the leader of the Vodou-rock band RAM and hotel keeper Richard Morse in the cities of Port-au-Prince, Jacmel, and New Orleans, it aims at underlining the common cultural features of these Haitian and American cities, invoking the historical presence of fugitive French colonials and their slaves in the aftermath of the revolution. With dances and a visit to the cemetery, it aspires to attract more tourists. The Cult of the Dead, already a local commercial occasion for street peddlers hawking goods to cemetery visitors, is becoming an investable attraction. Katherine Smith, whose main fieldwork is the Grand Cemetery of Port-au-Prince, reminds us that Sydney Mintz and Michel-Rolph Trouillot (1995, 43, quoted in Smith 2012, 94) had noted that, back under the presidency of the nationalist and *noiriste* Dumarsais Estimé, "Vodou became folklore; and folklore could be sold." This observation remains true today. Along with literature, Haitian art—considered inseparable from Vodou to such an extent that artists are struggling to propose other artistic universes to buyers and critics—is one of the few productive exports still operational in Haiti because Vodou remains a powerful resource, whether as a "cult" or as a cultural reference. It has been a marker of identity since the beginning of the twentieth century (the first novels depicting popular myths and traditions date back to 1902 and 1906: *La Vengeance de Mama* by Frédéric Marcelin and *Mimola* by Antoine Innocent [Clormeus 2012]) and more recently as a claimed element of sociopolitical struggle.

AN EVOLVING CONSTRUCTION OF VODOU AS PRACTICE AND REPRESENTATIONS

Vodou, as a practice and as a pantheon, is dynamic and has undergone intense change over the last two hundred years. In the twentieth century, intense urbanization and economic migration altered this kin-based religion, independent in the realization of most of its rituals, into a more congregational structure, led by male (*oungan*) or female (*mambo*) professional priests and served by a corps of servants / spirit wives (*ounsi*) who perform, dance, and sing during ceremonies (Richman 2008a). The spectacular dimension grew in importance, with ceremonies taking the appearance of "art happenings" and financial costs increasing accordingly. Richman (2008a) argues that spirit shrines became anchors for

SAILING BETWEEN LOCAL AND GLOBAL 145

Figure 6.2. A *drapo* by Nadine Fortilus. Note the borrowing of the "all-seeing eye" Masonic symbol. Photograph by author.

neotraditional religious practices, and migration reshaped the dual structure of the Vodou pantheon, constructing an imagined Guinean authenticity through the demonization of the Petro spirits. Besides these major structural changes, some additions can be noted that also result from engagement with the West. But they appeared at a time when Haitian society was not so deeply disaggregated and could choose to adopt or adapt foreign cults or rites. One example I will highlight is Freemasonry.

FREEMASONS, GEDE, AND THE NAPOLEONIC MILITARY ART OF FLAGS

On many occasions, Vodouists adopt Western sources of power or prestige they deem useful to their personal practice. As in Benin today (see Falen, this volume), Freemasonry has been considered of mystical interest to Vodouists since colonial times. It manifests most evidently in the representation of many preeminent lwa, such as Bawon Lakwa, entirely dressed as a master Mason, or Danbala Wedo, represented on a *drapo* (ceremonial flag) "as an undulating snake ... wearing the miter of the Irish Saint Patrick marked with the masonic 'G' for Grand Master" (Cosentino 1995a, 46). The square and the compass, the all-seeing eye, the five-pointed star, among others, are omnipresent in the arts of Vodou. Katherine Smith (2019) draws a comparative line between this Masonic imagery and that of the lwa Gede, whose skulls, tombs, black suits, or black-and-white shrines bear a very direct, easily noticeable resemblance to the Masons' ritual attire and attributes.[3]

Other features derive from military encounters and result from the association of the signs of religious power with military regalia. For example, the military expedition led between 1801 and 1803 by Napoleon Bonaparte introduced new objects of power. The Napoleonic armies left a lasting, tangible memory, not only as unjust attackers on the freedom of formerly enslaved Africans but also as the bearers of a specific military aesthetic. Patrick Polk (1995, 338; 2012, 128) identified this heritage in the Haitian arts of ritual banners, or drapo (from the French *drapeau*, or "flag"), observing the correlations in their ritualized use, their dimensions, background motifs, and the use of colors. The impact of the Leclerc military expedition is also observable in liturgical roles and terminologies. The *commandant de la place*, or *laplas*, leading the flags parade, indicate that profound military references in Haitian culture do not solely rely on the memory of the Army of Independence and the consecutive militarization of the society in the nineteenth century but also on the borrowing of the enemy's insignia during the Leclerc expedition. As for the Masonic insignia, they were all the better integrated, Polk explains, as they presented visual correspondences with the Dahomean royal insignia: the skulls of the *tohosu*, a divine category of ancestors in Dahomey. Polk (2012, 130) asks and answers, "Dahomean, Catholic, Masonic? None of these are mutually exclusive artistic wellsprings." There was a "persistence of the ancient Adja-Fon aesthetic of *assemblage* which remains the 'purest' link between the religious art of Haiti and Africa" (43).

The arts of Vodou provide us with an instructive example of how Haitian culture functions, illustrating its accumulative strategy. Just as Vodou altars associated objects gathered from a wide range of cultural sources, so too do contemporary drapo makers employ images and stylistic elements from Catholicism, Freemasonry, North American popular culture, Taino culture, and African sources. As Cosentino (1995, 25) writes, "All of Vodou's disparate elements came together in the context of colonial slavery to create a dynamic cultural *mélange* whose powers of appropriation and re-contextualization continue to shape and influence the way *Vodouisants* serve the spirits."

ART AND RELIGION AS CULTURAL TOOLS OF RESILIENCY

Artistic productions enable us to understand the physiognomy and functioning of the culture in which they emerge. Individual answers to the observation of daily life or universal issues, artworks still bring to the forefront collective questionings. They constitute a useful and direct narrative of the struggles and self-narratives of a nation. When the oungan and painter André Pierre dresses his lwa in eighteenth-century aristocratic clothes, or when the contemporary artist Edouard Duval-Carrié displaces the *Embarquement pour Cythère* by Antoine Watteau in the Vodou context of the lwa Ezili Freda, all dressed in pink, they exert a criticism of colonial history and today's society altogether. Joan (Colin) Dayan (1995) underlines the importance of this colonial register of representation and insists on the anthropomorphism of the lwa in Haiti in contrast to the old Dahomean deities. She wonders if Christianity and the circulation of Catholic images might have brought this identification to the human figure (Dayan 1995, 244), which is central to the representation of Haitian Vodou.

Caribbean aesthetics bear the mark of a broad intercontinental cross-fertilization manifesting from the first Indo-Euro-African contacts, extending previous intracontinental culture and cultural fusions in Africa. As a concept, culture usually bears the risk of substantivism. In Haiti, it is rather a snapshot of ongoing transformations. When globalization and capitalist consumerism influence cultures, they also give rise to responses, innovations, and inventions. When the artists of the Atis Rezistans collective (discussed at the end of this chapter) use car parts or cereals packages or when the "naïve" painters use hardboard and car paint, they make an inventory of the country as they morally and physically experience it.

Thus, when Haiti found itself isolated by the international embargo decreed in 1990 following the coup against President Jean-Bertrand Aristide, artists who could no longer import such materials as canvases, paints, or sequins embarked on an art of recuperation that still defines current practices. It was this isolation that led to the return of sculpture, long considered a fetish, both during the colony and during the anti-Vodou religious campaign of 1939–1942. "During this campaign any sculpted or three-dimensional object was assimilated to superstition. Thus, many Haitians were unable to distinguish the sacred from the profane when it came to sculpture, whether in the artisanal or artistic field," wrote Sterlin Ulysse (2017). If painting, and particularly the art of portraiture, dominated during the French colony and throughout the nineteenth century, sculpture, associated with Vodou, remained hidden for a long time. Its recent public reappearance allows it to renew the link with "sculpture, a priority art in non-Muslim Africa" (Michel Philippe Lerebours, quoted in Ulysse 2017).

In what we might call para-Vodou art or Vodou-inspired art—rather than Vodou art, as it is not designed for the temples but uses Vodou as a cultural reference—we have an opportunity to assess how the process at stake reflects itself in the practice and application of art. The constant to and from between the temple space, with its own Creolized aesthetic production, and the marketable art creation demonstrates how Vodou as religion accompanies rather than formats the daily life of Haitians. In the same way as the Mexican popular ex-votos integrate the preoccupations of their sponsors (prostitutes, transgender people, or small drug peddlers), Vodou aesthetics incorporate the social changes of its faithful. In many temples, the ritual flags are now no more than a piece of Chinese industrially made sequined fabric that only reflects the shininess and the color attributes of the lwa represented. The "traditional" hand-sequined flags have long been sold primarily to local or foreign art lovers. For the believer, what is important is the performance and the function of the object. The demand for functionality leaves room for a formal invention provided that the production is not intended for the temple. Thus, from the 1970s, the Vodou priest and artist Pierrot Barra and his wife, Marie Cassaise, created art objects that he called "Vodou Things" and sold them in the Iron Market in Port-au-Prince. He was inspired both by the visions sent to him by his various personal lwa and by the industrial materials he found around him: sequins, mirrors, and dolls whose parts he dismantled. If it is difficult to classify this work, which tends strongly toward outsider art, it is not less the authentic representative of a sacred art inherited from African Vodou practices. His example has inspired such younger artists as Dubréus Lhérisson and David Boyer, who took their first steps in Vodou art in Vodou temples, at oungan Ti Bout's sequined flags atelier, and then in Barra's studio. The art practice can therefore be disconnected from an active practice of Vodou and be conceived as a purely professional activity, but very often it accompanies an intense religious implication and an intimate knowledge of the religion.

ART, A FOREIGN BUT OPERATIVE NOTION

"To this day, Creole has no term to designate what the Western civilization qualifies as 'art'. Vodou culture holds the notion of what is 'beautiful' as a primarily driving quality," writes Rachel Beauvoir-Dominique (2005, 60). In her

Figure 6.3. Rose-Marie Desruisseau, *Ceremony for Gede*. The painter presents in her work the female sex as a positive force, which joins the position of the vodou toward sexuality. Photograph by author.

Figure 6.4. *Drapo*, by Nadine Fortilus. This representation mixes various divinities (Dambalah, Aida Wedo) around one Christian (nineteenth-century German) chromolithography very widespread in Africa, where it features Mami Wata. Photograph by author.

Intellectual History of Vodou Thought, Alessandra Benedicty-Kokken (2015, 231) goes further: "In Vodou art does not exist." Carlo A. Célius (2015) prefers to talk about "fields of artistic creation" rather than "art" to designate the "forms of crystallization" of a society's visions at a given moment. If indeed the notion does not exist as such in Vodou, the religion is at the origin of many aesthetic forms that Haitian culture has appropriated to make art. The relation between art and Vodou has always been fertile. Art is "a real guidebook to the religion," exclaims Randall Morris (1995, 394) about the metal work of Georges Liautaud. Both are heterogeneous and integrative, and both need one another to express themselves. Just like Christian institutions united with the state after the 1861 Concordat had relied on chromolithographs, the "Facebook for the divine" according to Cosentino (1998), Vodou had used these simple images as a visual support to incarnate the diversity of its pantheon. The Virgin Mary, St. Jacques, and St. Gérard were quickly adopted by the population, who, instead of deepening its Roman Catholic faith, fixed representations of the many lwa of Vodou under the traits of the saints. This is how, without the church's permission, they began to cover the walls of the *ounfò*, or temple, with Christian figures.

The aesthetic expressions belonging to or extending the sphere of religious activity reflect the fundamental bricolage theorized by Claude Lévi-Strauss (1962) in *La Pensée Sauvage*. The artistic production—either deriving from, pertaining to, or evoking Vodou—expresses its constitutive integrative nature. Thus, the observation of the artistic field should permit us to infer the functioning of ongoing changes in Haiti's religious identity.

Paradoxically, 1940s Haitian art was born from a desacralization of Vodou aesthetics. From the invention of Indigénisme, Vodou images and practices were taken out of the temples. Shows were organized, and dances were made into folklore. Indeed, "folklore could be sold." The state itself saw in the theatricality of Vodou the possibility of financial income during the vogue of Haiti as a place for North American tourism—through the presidency of the Duvalier father and son and following the advent of the Castro regime in Cuba. If Vodou artifacts had been destroyed during the antisuperstitious Campagne des rejetés or Campagne anti-vodou of 1939–1942—a skillful recuperation by the Catholic church of a spontaneous movement of peasants rejecting Vodou through fear of witchcraft or secret societies or to free themselves from the persecution of a spirit and the high costs of ceremonies—if hundreds of temples and thousands of sacred objects had been smashed or burned by the police, these same objects, or what was left of them, had now become items of monetary value, worthy of entering foreign public or private collections. The fact that the American dancer and choreographer Katherine Dunham and her company came repeatedly in the 1940s and 1950s, promoting African-inspired choreographies, certainly helped integrate Vodou music and dance into the field of the acceptable cultural phenomena. Vodou, once a hidden reality, had become an acclaimed element of national identity, and this, paradoxically, was partially due to engagements with foreign artists and research institutions.

According to Michel Philippe Lerebours (2018) there exists a logical link between the recognition of Vodou and the outburst of painting in 1946. He suggests two main factors: the switch to a figurative style in religious Vodou art, showing the lwa in action, and the arrival of tourists, ready for anything new and sensational. The political interest of Dumarsais Estimé in North American tourism permitted the experiment to last. Private collections were born, and galleries opened to satisfy this demand for "authenticity." The fact that this authenticity was precisely crafted is the reflection of a historical inequality.

The trend for the popular was settled, and no tourist henceforth would buy any work of art that bore the trace of the academy. The indigenous modernity that had been promoted since the 1930s had eclipsed any form of potential equality between Haitian and Western artists. The more naive, the better. Of course, the painters were less than naive. Perhaps their buyers were, in that they were unaware of the complex nature of their acquisitions. As new themes emerged in the fine arts, coming from subalterns living in adverse conditions (peasants, inhabitants of poor neighborhoods), Vodou practices, still forbidden and punishable by law since the Campagne des rejetés, were becoming the center of the new aesthetics; and so, from secrecy, Vodou went on to become a major and accepted category of artistic creation. It was detached from the actual religious practice to the point that objects could be created that evoke Vodou without ever being intended for anything other than being sold to audiences of local or foreign amateurs. The artists of the 1940s, known as the "Haitian Renaissance" and counting such eminent personalities as André Pierre or Hector Hyppolite, were not making Vodou art but a secular version of it. Their activity was distinct from their personal relation to the lwa, and they were using their fine knowledge of Vodou codes to carve out a place for themselves in the global art market.

AUTHENTICITY AND AMBIGUITY

An object may be an art piece or a scientific artifact, but its ontology relies on its contextualization. In Haiti, the category of Vodou art stems from exchanges between the secular and the sacred sphere. The evocation of religion and mystique in art meets international, mainly Western, demand. The question of authenticity should then be brought with caution. One case, called the *"bizango* guards' affair," deciphered by Catherine Benoît and André Delpuech (2015), illustrates this problematic use of the concept. Observing that "since 2007, countless so-called *bizango* statues, named after a secret society in Haiti, have emerged on the international art market" (136), they tried to trace the genealogy of this flourishing yet mysterious production. Their author came out to be a living artist named Dubréus Lhérisson, not an eighteenth- or nineteenth-century ritual specialist that supposedly made the statues. Still Benoît and Delpuech consider that the question of authenticity is not relevant in a context where, "indeed, sticking to the dichotomy ritual piece / work of art not only prevents to think

Figure 6.5. Paintings on recovered materials showing various entities, made by junior members of Atis Rezistans. Note the copresence of a commercial naive painting. Photograph by author.

the fluidity of the life of an object, but also the reality of the commodification of local objects under the influence of the capitalist expansion of the Western mode of consumption of objects" (149). More pertinent to them in this affair is the "spectacularization of Vodou for tourist and commercial purposes" (150). For them, the modes of othering realized through the presentation, the curating options, and the narrations offered to the public reveal the permanence of a colonial gaze (on this matter, see Frohnapfel 2021).

THE SACRED FLAGS: FROM TEMPLES TO GALLERIES

The sequined Vodou flags called drapo were shaped by repeated engagements of African-derived traditions with Brazil and Europe. Bel Air, the popular historical center of Port-au-Prince, has been harboring beading workshops since at least the 1950s, and Tina Girouard (1994) recalled the story of Tibout (Ceus St-Louis) and Boss To (Joseph Fortine). Having observed the sequined and beaded costumes of the Brazilian troupe opening the 1950 Carnival, Tibout borrowed their ornate style and adapted it not only to Rara (street festival) procession costumes but also to Vodou divinities' banners, until then only lightly adorned. This marked the beginning of a commercial practice, paralleling and even outnumbering the sequined flags designed for temples.

A Vodou flag used to be a simple piece of fabric depicting the lwa or its corresponding vèvè—a geometrical drawing symbolizing the spirit—and is both reminiscent of West African textile iconography as well as of French *militaria*. The motives that frame the representation of the lwa were inspired by the background motifs used in the colors of Napoleonic colonial regiments (Polk 1995, 338). The European embroidery imported to Saint-Domingue later came to be mixed with the Afro-Brazilian taste for shiny fabrics discovered by Haitians at the 1950 Port-au-Prince Carnival. Of course, the beads are no more of European manufactured glass, once traded in Africa for human beings, but are plastic and come from China. They lost their prestige but still carry the memory of an exchange system where a human could be equated to a sack of beads.

Eminently global, the art of sequins stands in between two worlds, sacred and secular. In the Vodou liturgy, the drapo are there to call the spirits to enter the space of the ounfò, and they mark the limit of both sacred and secular spaces. Thanks to illustrations contained in books like the one written by Tina Girouard (1994), the embroiderers who had lost or left their job in factories that exploited their labor in the 1980s could find a new financial resource and a more rewarding activity by embroidering Vodou flags for the international art market. Most Haitians would not buy any such flag to decorate their home, but the *blan*, the foreigners, "are crazy about mystical things," observes the flag maker Madame Moreau.[4] And the globalized elite, concerned about the defense and representation of Haiti's national culture, is now displaying the best of this local production in its living rooms.

VODOU AND PARA-VODOU ART: SEDUCTIONS AND POWER RELATIONS

The history of an indigenous painting culture has been attested to Haiti since the beginning of the nineteenth century. The first painters were nonfigurative, performing simple symbolic decorations in Vodou temples. When it gradually moved toward more figuration, it diversified its supports and undertook to copy the canvases present in the colonists' and the freemen's homes. Two types of subjects were mainly determined by the high cost of materials: the presidents/monarchs and the military were the subject of many portraits (Lerebours 1981), and religious painting, especially in the form of ex-voto, abounded. But these productions looked toward Europe and adorned the salons of the powerful, who, despite the success of the War of Independence, continued to take France as a cultural model. It was a matter of persuading the European nations of Haiti's membership in the human race, so long disputed by the institution of slavery. Then, in the late 1940s, the facilitation of American tourism on the island offered painters an economic outlet and determined their aesthetic orientations. Indeed, interest in this so-called native art was immediate and lasting. Today, in auction sales as in art galleries, the preference for figurative paintings showing the standard peasant or Vodou scenes continues to be privileged. Indigénisme did not go against the tastes of Western art collectors for whom Haiti represents, just like it did to sixteenth-century European navigators, a fantasized place of tropical luxuriance and biblical simplicity.

THE SELF, THE OTHER, AND THE MIRROR

Vodou aesthetics bear the religion's complexity and fundamental heterogeneity. The fruit of repeated and unequal cultural encounters, these aesthetics are simultaneously sincere and mimetic. Benoît and Delpuech (2015) urge us to go beyond the notion of authenticity. The very nature of Haitian history, cumulating economic dependency into political domination, obviously makes this category partly obsolete. The American art lover Dewitt Peters had been intrigued by the talent of Hector Hyppolite, then a poor oungan, as well as by Georges Liautaud, a gifted blacksmith who sculpted splendid cemetery iron crosses. Backed by local intellectuals and benefiting from the logistic support of the Haitian American Institute and the Haitian government, a public art center, the Centre d'Art, opened in 1944. If Peters did not train these men, their encounter and his support have forged the careers of these and many other brilliant creators, invited to liberate their inner vision along the line of popular and religious Vodou aesthetics then in vogue in the United States.

Other continental Americans intervened in the process of the creation of Haitian painting as it is internationally known. The "primitive" and "mystical" painting that flourished at the Centre d'Art would never have appeared in broad daylight, in the deplorable context of the anti-Vodou campaign, without the exhibition that was presented at the center in 1945 by the Cuban critic José Gómez Sicre. It is this same Sicre, supported by his compatriot Wilfredo Lam and by André Breton, who helped legitimize a new generation of mystic artists painting mystical scenes, Vodou characters, esoteric dreams, and the like.

The Cuban painters who showed their art to the Haitian public shared with their Caribbean neighbor the aesthetic of magical realism and the strong influence of French surrealism. A new hybrid was born called "Voodoo surrealism." For André Breton, Hyppolite was a surrealist, and as an oungan, his access to the supernatural was considered by the French writer, in search of magic in his artistic practice, a legitimate source of inspiration. Both Sicre and Breton found in Haiti what inspired them at the moment, superimposing upon the country's actual production their own search for authenticity and primitivism. This had lasting consequences on art in Haiti, since then labeled as "primitive art." One must remember all the efforts made by such Haitian intellectuals as Anténor Firmin at the end of the nineteenth century to escape the primitivist gaze in order to taste the irony of this enthusiastic welcome given to Vodou's manifestations in art by foreigners in 1945. Firmin's "Of the Equality of Human Races: Positivist Anthropology," published in 1885, had been an answer to Count de Gobineau's infamous racist thesis, "Essay on the Inequality of the Human Races" (1853). Firmin's brilliant essay was part of a national effort to fight the country's political isolation on the international scene, highlighting and valuing African-derived cultural and physical traits. His scientific work put Haiti at the head of the fight against racial prejudice across the globe. This fight for equality, already championed during the War of Independence, is another aspect of Haiti's important role on the international stage, despite its poverty and small size. Alongside literature, Haitian artistic production contributes to the nation's international significance.

Karen Richman (2008b, 203) addresses the birth of modern Haitian art from the angle of the mimesis, considering the relationship between the foreign buyer and the local producer: "During the 1940s, worker-artists in urban Haiti imitated foreign entrepreneurs' imitations of their imagined essence. . . . The industry of Vodou art, like other national folk-art modes of production, typically manages to contain the contradiction between mimetic reciprocity and a discourse of authenticity."

Artists have found themselves both accomplices and victims of an unequal and false situation, adapting Vodou symbols to the international art marketplace often without being fully aware of its boundaries, values, and functions abroad. Artists who were also Vodou priests, Richman analyzes, would be presented as ahistoric painters, as "shamans" protecting the group from the evil spirits. The insistence that she notes, for example, in the narratives contemporary to that period, on the use by Hyppolite of a chicken feather as a brush before he was presented with more modern material at the Centre d'Art is particularly significant of the role play that was at stake in the artist-mentor relationship that was evolving.

For Richman (2008b, 204), this "mimetic interplay" included "European and North American tourists, ethnographers, local cultural entrepreneurs, and artists in Port-au-Prince." She suggests that in many cases the inclusion of the Vodou pantheon is an example of gamesmanship in which artists catered to the tastes for the "exotic" expressed by many foreign buyers. This can be said of the painting as well as the drapo handicraft that developed along the lines of a globalized market including North America and Europe, seduced by the decorative and suggestive qualities of this craft.

HAITI AND THE WEST THROUGH THE DEAD EYES OF A SKULL

Artistic practices in Haiti have not yet emancipated themselves from an ambiguous relationship with the West. One of the reasons for this is that buyers remain largely Western, and the most important acquisitions, due to a lack of operational local museums, are done by Western institutions. From Hector Hyppolite to contemporary André Eugène, Jean Hérard Celeur or Guyodo (for a detailed understanding of contemporary artists' respective positions toward Vodou, see Frohnapfel 2021), references to Vodou indicate the centrality of an ancestral religious practice and the celebration of collective struggles. Alternatively, they derive, at least in part, from a commercial strategy, the neobaroque skulls covered with pearls and trimmings of Dubréus Lhérisson's echoing Damian Hirst's diamond-paved trimmings.

The confusion of ritual and profane genres is another trait of contemporary Haitian art, as opposed to what was defined as Haitian art until then: genre scenes, scenes of daily rural or urban life, high-ranking personalities' portraits. The recurrent use of Vodou's symbols and imagery as well as the voluntary confusion of the ritual and the profane have been on display at several exhibitions, primarily *The Sacred Arts of Vodou* at the University of California, Los Angeles, which opened the Vodou aesthetic to an ever-growing circle of amateurs and onlookers in 1995. Since in 2009, the *Ghetto Biennial* has been held in Port-au-Prince, inviting foreign artists and visitors to evolve in the midst of a staggering accumulation of heteroclite works presented by urban artists in the ruins of a once prosperous commercial district. These creations, though trending toward cosmopolitanism, offer a critical reading of the economic and political condition these artists are faced with locally. Once again, visitors from developed nations are attracted to primitive, transgressive qualities ascribed to the Other, a renewed form of "Savage Slot" (Trouillot 2003).

The spectacularization of Vodou as a form of thrilling exoticism echoes other types of extreme or alternative tourism, such as tours in South African ghettos, Brazilian favelas, or disused areas of former Soviet Republics. In Haiti, visiting a deprived area strongly affected by the 2010 earthquake has been coupled with the artistic tourism experience. Is the biennale another form of disaster tourism? How should we relate it to the notion of authenticity? How do the actors, local and foreign, interact with one another? One particular answer lies in the performance, at the Third Ghetto Biennale entitled *Decentering the Market and Other Tales of Progress*, of an English artist, Katy Beinart, that raised several issues of anthropological interest. Dressed as a mambo, a Vodou priestess, she made a performance consisting in the tracing of a vèvè with salt, a material the local oungan and artist Papa Da (Alphonse Jean Junior) told her not to use but finally agreed to, considering that this was her quest and her decision. Playing with the fantasy of both being an ethnographer and going native, she cites the art critic Hal Foster (1996), overriding the fact that he precisely doubted that the methods of ethnography could be imported into art (in the present case, they were just played out). With Papa Da blessing her vèvè, in her own words "complicit in the ersatz theatricality of this invented hybrid ritual-performance," the biennale had become a healing place for a foreign artist investigating her own identity ("personal ancestral link to salt").[5] For this visiting artist, doing art in Haiti meant mimicking the aesthetic expression of Vodou for the purpose of a personal objective rooted in a distant history. Vodou rituals do look like art performances: there is the music, the singing and dancing, the costumes, the drawing of the vèvè and *minokan* (the central vèvè drawn around the sacred pole, or *poto-mitan*), and the lights. Indeed, the qualities of ancestrality and modernity seem to blend in Vodou's present actualizations. But the recurrence and centrality of the pattern of *fatra*, the "waste," from which the recycling artists of Atis Rezistans create, tell us as much of Vodou and the sacred force attached to the detritus and the broken and the sentiment of being peripheral and discarded in the world. Bonding the human remains and the debris from the garbage, these improvised magicians try to repair the torn fabric of their history. "Price-Mars associated Bawon Samdi with an urban, invented saint," notes Katherine Smith (2012, 90) in her "Genealogies of Gede," bringing our attention to the context in which the Gede family of spirits attained its full popularity: US occupation. It was thus the imposed contact with the American occupying troops that brought the Gede family to the forefront of the Haitian religious and artistic scene.

RESISTING PIRATES OF THE CARIBBEAN: RELATIONAL AESTHETICS

The Ghetto Biennale is the emanation of a Port-au-Prince collective of "salvage" or "trash artists" called Atis Rezistans (Artists' Resistance) living and working in a block adjacent to the Grand Rue.[6] Unlike most folk artists, who have very little direct contact with foreigners and often sell their work through galleries or local intermediaries, Atis Rezistans have both personal and professional relationships with foreign artists, curators, and researchers who actively support them, visit them, and invite them abroad. The construction of this collective project is thus multisited, although the creation of works of art (sculptures, installations, happenings) is carried out on-site in Haiti. Reinforcing this dialogue with foreign actors is the holding of the biennale, in or around the squatted compound where Atis Rezistans has taken its quarters, developing along a provocative and stimulating proposition: "The Americans send us their trash, we use it and transform it, then sell it back to them to put in their living rooms."[7] The collective has succeeded in attracting young artists from all over the world to the biennale, considering that they had too often, for financial or administrative reasons, been prevented from accompanying their work abroad. Through their integration of urban, liberating, and provocative aesthetic forms that enthrall Western audiences, as well as through the importation of the contemporary forms of artists' squat, readymade installation or performance, these actors achieved direct access to the far-away world of contemporary art collectors and galleries. These acts allow them to exist in the contemporary art world. The collective's artists have thus short-circuited, also by making a smart use of the resources offered by social networks, the unequal and hierarchical distribution of the resources devoted to artists in Haiti.

According to their English cocurator, the photographer Leah Gordon, "For myself, another point of departure was 'The Radicant' by Nicolas Bourriaud and his concept of the global artist as 'homo viator'. . . . In fact, for the 2nd Ghetto Biennale, one of the participating artists, Jason Metcalf, had the chapter on Creolisation from 'The Radicant' translated into Kreyol and distributed throughout the neighborhood. Travel, for the majority of the global community, usually takes the form of forced migration or illegal immigration. The Ghetto Biennale was an attempt to open a dialogue about this within the international art world."[8]

A media success, the enterprise has yet been criticized for its inability to achieve the goals it set for itself, notably creating a genuine equality between the participants. Caitlin Elizabeth Lennon, investigating in 2012, the year following the second biennale, alleged that the democratic utopia of collaborative work between local and invited artists had a negative effect because the parts brought together had varying agendas (selling / not selling, criticizing the art industry / wanting to enter it, etc.). Lennon (2012, 39) adds, "An examination of the 2011 Ghetto Biennale projects will show that in fact the exhibition's

Figure 6.6. In the yard of Atis Rezistans, where the works of individual artists are collectively and anonymously displayed. Here, a possible Dambalah Wedo (cf. the miter of Saint Patrick) carries a double-headed fetus that evokes the Marassa. Photograph by author.

construction mimics the neoliberal rhetoric of globalization seen throughout modern art. While the tension between 'colonizer' and 'colonized' seems simultaneously and continuously subverted, it still remains veiled under the euphoric sentiment of the Biennale."

Still, the Haitian artists of the biennale succeeded in commenting upon their trauma and "transform the debris of Haiti's failing economy into a critical commentary on the issues of isolation and marginality faced by the developing world" (Lennon 2012, 24). Furthermore, by recycling and rearranging various imported materials, they used the integrative approach of Vodou and its relation to metal and human remains. Like many religions, Vodou sacralizes detritus, and detritus has to do with the sacred (Douglas 1966). Here, the *Homo faber* is also a *Homo sacer*, and the men and women at work try to give a signification to their sense of being left over just like the debris they assemble into anthropomorphic figures (gods, monsters). Even leftover cadavers (bones, skulls, hair) are used in composite works (see Dubréus Lhérisson, Jean Hérard Céleur, and even more notably Jean-Claude Saintilus), invoking the magic inherent to such bodily "objects" and fetishizing the partial aspect in the rubbish (bits of heads, of arms, of wheelchairs, of cooling fans, etc.). Through this creative bricolage, they revive the capacity of Vodou inspiration to make sense of scattered parts and bring them together in collective totems and protective figures installed in the street. Among these inspiring figures are the revered Bawon Lakwa and Gede family.

NEGOTIATED IDENTITIES IN MIGRATION AND THE COLONIZATION OF IMAGINARIES

If Bawon Samdi proliferates in international popular culture, from B movies to rock music, Gede has remained specifically Haitian. According to many scholars since Karen McCarthy Brown (2001), Gede might even be the spirit most loved by Haitians and the "most revealing personification of the *pèp ayisyan* (Haitian people)" (Smith 2012, 98). If he looks like, and can be, a celebration of hypermasculinity, it is most profoundly a celebration of life impulse, of libido, over death. In this sense, the omnipresence of phallic sculptures in the compound of Atis Rezistans, which preexisted the 2010 earthquake but developed all the more thereafter, can be considered both as a comment and a reaction to the tragic situation endured by Haitians in general, including the poor artists who live in this deprived area. The figuration of penises and the use of human skulls taken from the cemetery associate signs traditionally elaborated in Vodou (Beasley 2010) and appreciated by Westerners. The center and the periphery are thus glued together and exchanging respective flux—money and international recognition on one side and intriguing art products on the other. Now the gigantic sculptures of Jean Hérard Céleur, André Eugène, or Guyodo reign over the district and its denizens.[9] Let us hope, with McCarthy Brown (2001, 19), that Gede, whose "special talent lies in viewing the facts of life from refreshing new perspectives," will once again permit Haitian art to bring new visions to the front.

If many artists in Haiti deal with the issue of globalization and resort to Vodou's aesthetic or symbolic qualities, we might want to consider the case of Haitian American artists like Vladimir Cybil Charlier. Raised between Queens and Haiti, she interrogates the notions of diasporic identities, history, and religion through works that mix symbols of her two places of belonging. Her visual clashes tell the complex story of her multiple affiliations. Her series *Haiti Meets Harlem*, for example, places the face of Malcom X on Ogou/St-Jacques's body or that of Billie Holiday on Ezili's. And the Vodou twins (*marasa*) incarnate the special relationship that animated Jean-Michel Basquiat and Andy Warhol in her *Marassa Andy and Basquiat*. She is in search of "a new space," arguing that "there is no fixed identity nowadays.... There is the pervasive influence of American culture abroad."[10] Noting this "visual fluidity" at work in her art, Vladimir Cybil Charlier insists that what is true for the artist is true for anybody who had to "renegotiate and reinvent their culture because of migration—or immigration. That is the story of America." Interested in the vèvè as "cultural markers," whom she calls "our parameters," she combines them with the very American art of graffiti. Her work is defined by her double filiation, just like the lwa who, according to Donald Cosentino, travel without green cards.[11]

Jean-Michel Basquiat himself, often pejoratively counted as a Haitian artist, once said his cultural memory was in Africa but at the same time following him everywhere. In a globalized world, the subjects have to find their way through exile, a sometimes-internalized self-exile where one is stuck in a country of little opportunity. When Duval-Carrié represents his *Imagined Landscapes*, he chooses to figure them as Minnie and Mickey Mouse, as Batman, Donald Duck, Mister Potato-Head, Marie-Antoinette, even putting Christopher Columbus at the prow (*After Bierstad, the Landing of Columbus*, 2013). The colonization of the imaginary continues from that of the bodies and the soil, here represented by a distant military ship waiting in the bay like the real German, and later American, warships did in the nineteenth and twentieth century to impose their will on the little young republic. When the lwa Ezili Dantor gets off the plane, she is surrounded by two American MPs whose helmets are barred by a Red Cross emblem (*Erzulie as a Migrant*). The whole Vodou family—at least its main figures—is depicted under the traits of migrants on an overcrowded ship (*Migration of the Spirits*). Just like Ulysses's voyage, this story speaks to what humans have to endure to find home and define themselves, while the artist affirms his efforts toward individual agency.

CONCLUSION

Possession rituals, by transposing on a religious ground human hardships and struggles, put into collectively intelligible narratives the destiny of a nation. Similarly, the practice and the showing of art formulate the interrogations of a moment in relation to a common heritage, playing with representations and symbols understood by the whole community. In Haiti as in other places of the Black Atlantic, shrines and works of art alike have become places of memorial activation (Apter and Derby 2010), and Vodou is still a resource appreciated by artists for its ability to mobilize and convey concepts. As the *kòd lonbrit* (umbilical cord) of every Haitian is buried under a tree, which connects him or her to the land of his or her *ras* (ancestors) whether in New York, Montreal, Paris, or French Guiana, Vodou symbolism helps the person to orient himself or herself in his or her earthly journey. It functions as a cultural digesting machine, ambiguous and versatile, alternatively discriminated and celebrated, authentic and fabricated, and this plasticity makes it eminently compatible with artistic work.

We have quickly flown over three major characteristics of its influence on the arts: the ability to make sense out of foreign elements and global pop culture; the capacity to undergo commodification without losing its spiritual resources; and the art of playing with the persistent colonial gaze and Western projections, at some point turning them into a commercial advantage. Vodou has always been helpful to its devotees by guiding them through the oceans of modern and now contemporary worlds, providing them the necessary duplicity they need to carve a place for themselves—halfway between local and global, here and there, now and then.

NOTES

1. Minustah, "'Tap Tap': L'art sur Roues Haïtien," May 13, 2013, https://minustah.unmissions.org/%C2%AB-tap-tap-%C2%BB-l%E2%80%99art-sur-roues-ha%C3%AFtien.
2. Staff, *Le Nouvelliste*, November 2, 2018.
3. Filmmaker and writer Maya Deren noted an association between Masonry and Ogou and pleaded for a unifying role of the Mason order in *Divine Horsemen: The Living Gods of Haiti* (New York: Vanguard, 1953).
4. See Madame Moreau in Giafferi-Dombre, 2018.
5. Katy Beinart, "Goute Sel," *Salted Earth* (blog), January 5, 2014, https://saltedearth.net/2014/01/05/goute-sel/.
6. "Relational aesthetics," a concept developed by the French critic Nicolas Bourriaud ([1998] 2002), defends the idea that contemporary art can propose new visions to a society and have an effect on it. Art, says Bourriaud, "is modeling possible universes" (13).
7. Maksaens Denis, dir., *E Pluribus Unum* (DVD), 2006, cited in Gordon, 109.
8. "The Biennial Questionnaire: Leah Gordon," *ArtReview*, November 20, 2013, https://artreview.com/previews/the_biennial_questionnaire_leah_gordon/.
9. Post-Katrina New Orleans manifested similar artistic responses, using comparable funereal imagery and the same references to the protective power of the phallus in street sculptures (Wehmeyer 2012, 156).
10. Vladimir Cybil, interview by Jerry Philogene, *Bomb*, no. 90 (January 1, 2005), https://bombmagazine.org/articles/vladimir-cybil/.
11. See "Gods without Greencards: Haiti, History and the Lwa in the Paintings of Edouard Duval-Carrié and André Pierre," a talk given by Donald Cosentino at Brown University, April 18, 2011.

REFERENCES

Appadurai, Arjun. 1996. *Modernity at Large: The Cultural Consequences of Globalization*. Minneapolis: University of Minnesota Press.

Apter, Andrew, and Lauren Derby. 2010. *Activating the Past: History and Memory in the Black Atlantic World*. Newcastle upon Tyne: Cambridge Scholars.

Beasley, Myron. 2010. "Vodou, Penises and Bones: Ritual Performance of Death and Eroticism in the Cemetery and the Junk Yards of Port-au-Prince." *Performance Research: A Journal of the Performing Arts* 15 (1): 41–47.

Beauvoir-Dominique, Rachel. 2005. "Libérer le double, la beauté sera convulsive." *Gradhiva* 1:57–69.

Benedicty-Kokken, Alessandra. 2015. *Spirit Possession in French, Haitian, and Vodou Thought: An Intellectual History*. New York: Lexington Books.

Benoît, Catherine, and André Delpuech. 2015. "Trois capitaines pour un empereur! Histoires de *bizango*." *Gradhiva* 2:130–155.

Bourriaud, Nicolas. (1998) 2002. *Relational Aesthetics*. Paris: Les Presses du Réel.

Célius, Carlo Avierl. 2008. *Langage plastique et énonciation identitaire: l'invention de l'art haïtien*. Laval, Canada: Presses de l'Université de Laval.

Cleophat, Nixon. 2019. "Vodou as the Embryo and Marker of Haitian Sociohistorical Identity." In *Shackled Sentiments: Slaves, Spirits, and Memories in the African Diaspora*, edited by Eric Montgomery, 21-40. New York: Lexington Books.

Clormeus, Lewis Ampidu. 2012. "À propos de la seconde campagne antisuperstitieuse en Haïti (1911–1912). Contribution à une historiographie." *Histoire, monde et cultures religieuses* 24:105–130.

Coll. 2000. "Les graffitistes du vodou." In *Haïti, Anges et Démons*, 85–95. Paris: Hoebecke/La Halle Saint-Pierre.

Cosentino, Donald. 1995a. "Imagine Heaven." In *The Sacred Arts of Haitian Vodou*, edited by the Los Angeles Fowler Museum of Cultural History, 22–59. Los Angeles: Fowler Museum of Cultural History.

———. 1995b. "Envoi. The Gedes and Bawon Samdi." In *The Sacred Arts of Haitian Vodou*, edited by the Los Angeles Fowler Museum of Cultural History, 399–415. Los Angeles: Fowler Museum of Cultural History.

———. 1998. *Vodou Things: The Art of Pierrot Barra et Marie Cassaise*. Jackson: University Press of Mississippi.

Dayan, Joan. 1995. *Haiti, History and the Gods*. Berkeley: University of California Press.

Douglas, Mary. 1966. *Purity and Danger: An Analysis of Concepts of Pollution and Taboo*. New York: Routledge.

Fernandez, James W. 1982. *Bwiti: An Ethnography of the Religious Imagination in Africa*. Princeton, NJ: Princeton University Press.

Fetnan, Rime. 2017. "Le curator en ethnographe: usages de l'anthropologie dans deux expositions internationales d'art contemporain." *ICOFOM Study Series* 45:57–69.

Firmin, Anténor. (1885) 2002. *The Equality of Human Races: Positivist Anthropology*. Champaign: Illinois University Press.

Foster, Hal. 1996. *The Return of the Real: The Avant-Garde at the End of the Century*. Cambridge, MA: MIT Press.

Frohnapfel, David. 2021. *Alleviate Objects: Intersectional Entanglement and Progressive Racism in Caribbean Art*. Bielefeld, Germany: Transcript.

Giafferi-Dombre, Natacha, dir. 2015. *Jen fi parey mwen (Girls like Me)*. Jacques Bartoli / Haitian Resource Development Foundation. Weston, FL.

———, dir. 2018. *Create!* Jacques Bartoli / Haitian Resource Development Foundation. Weston, FL.

Girouard, Tina. 1994. *Sequin Artists of Haiti*. New Orleans: Contemporary Arts Center.

Gordon, Leah. 2012. "Gede: The Poster Boy for Vodou." In *In Extremis: Death and Life in 21st-Century Haitian Art*, 101–113. Los Angeles: Fowler Museum of Cultural History.

Gradhiva. 2015. "Quelques aspects de la nouvelle scène artistique d'Haïti." *Gradhiva* 21:104–129.

Korom, Frank J. 2003. *Hosay Trinidad: Muharram Performances in an Indo-Caribbean Diaspora*. Philadelphia: University of Pennsylvania Press.

Lennon, Elizabeth. 2012. *The Ghetto Biennale: Art and Agency in a Haitian Context*. MA thesis, Louisiana State University.

McCarthy Brown, Karen. 2001. *Mama Lola: A Vodou Priestess in Brooklyn*. Berkeley: University of California Press.

Métraux, Alfred. 1958. *Le Vaudou haïtien*. Paris: Gallimard.

Mintz, Sidney W. 1977. "The So-Called World-System: Local Initiative and Local Response." *Dialectical Anthropology* 2 (2): 254–255.

Minustah (Mission des Nations Unies pour la stabilisation en Haïti). 2013. "'Tap Tap': L'art sur Roues Haïtien." May 13, 2013. Accessed October 7, 2021. https://minustah.unmissions.org/%C2%AB-tap-tap-%C2%BB-l%E2%80%99art-sur-roues-ha%C3%AFtien.

Montgomery, Eric James. 2019. "Gothic 'Voodoo' in Africa and Haiti." *eTropic* 18 (1). Accessed October 6, 2021. https://journals.jcu.edu.au/etropic/article/view/3666.

Morris, Randall. 1995. "The Style of His Hand: The Iron Art of Georges Liautaud." In *The Sacred Arts of Haitian Vodou*, edited by the Los Angeles Fowler Museum of Cultural History, 383–395. Los Angeles: Fowler Museum of Cultural History.

Polk, Patrick A. 1995 "Sacred Banners and the Divine Cavalry Charge." In *The Sacred Arts of Haitian Vodou*, edited by the Los Angeles Fowler Museum of Cultural History, 325–347. Los Angeles: Fowler Museum of Cultural History.

———. 2012. "Remember You Must Die! Gede Banners, Memento Mori, and the Fine Arts of Facing Death." In *In Extremis: Death and Life in 21st-Century Haitian Art*, 11–41. Los Angeles: Fowler Museum of Cultural History.

Price-Mars, Jean. (1928) 2020. *Ainsi Par L'Oncle*. Montreal: Mémoire d'Encrier.

Richman, Karen. 2008a. *Migration and Vodou*. Gainesville: University Press of Florida.

———. 2008b. "Innocent Imitations? Authenticity and Mimesis in Haitian Vodou Art, Tourism, and Anthropology." *Ethnohistory* 55 (2): 203–223.

Rush, Dana. 2011. "In Remembrance of Slavery: Tchamba Vodun." *African Arts* 44 (1): 40–51.

———. 2013. *Vodun in Coastal Benin: Unfinished, Open-Ended, Global*. Nashville: Vanderbilt University Press.

Smith, Katherine. 2012. "Genealogies of Gede." In *In Extremis: Death and Life in 21st-Century Haitian Art*, 85–99. Los Angeles: Fowler Museum of Cultural History.

———. 2019a. "Freemasonry in Vodou Flags: Atlantic History and Haitian Art." In *Sacred Diagrams: Haitian Vodou Flags from the Gessen Collection*, 12–13. Tampa, FL: Tampa Museum of Art.

———. 2019b. "Saint-Jean Baptiste, Haitian Vodou and the Masonic Imagery." In *Freemasonry and the Visual Arts from the Eighteenth Century Forward: Historical and Global Perspectives*, edited by Reva Wolf and Alisa Luxenberg, 243–262. London: Bloomsbury Academic.

Trouillot, Michel-Rolph. 2003. "Anthropology and the Savage Slot: The Poetics and Politics of Otherness." In *Global Transformations: Anthropology and the Modern World*, edited by Michael Trouillot, 7–28. New York: Palgrave Macmillan.

Ulysse, Sterlin. 2017. "La difficile acceptation de la sculpture dans l'art contemporain en haïti, vestige de la campagne antisuperstitieuse." In *Pensée afrocaribéenne et (psycho)traumatismes de l'esclavage et de la colonisation—Toubiyon twoma Lesklavaj ak Kolonizasyon: Dangoyaj Panse Afwo-Krayobeyen*, edited by Judite Blanc and Serge Madhere. Québec City: Collection Ayiti, Éditions Science et Bien Commun. Accessed October 6, 2021. https://scienceetbiencommun.pressbooks.pub/psychologieafricaine/.

Wehmeyer, Stephen C. 2012. "Playing Dead: The Northside Skull and Bone Gang." In *In Extremis: Death and Life in 21st Century Haitian Art*, 143–159. Los Angeles: Fowler Museum of Cultural History.

NATACHA GIAFFERI-DOMBRE is an independent researcher and translator, member of the PIND (Punk Is Not Dead) research group (Tours University, France), and author of *Une ethnologue à Port-au-Prince: Question de couleur et luttes pour le classement socio-racial dans la capitale haïtienne*.

PART TWO

Engagement

SEVEN

TAKING HOLD OF A FAITH

Jeffrey Anderson

IN 1885, Jean Montanée died. In a time when the deaths of African American men rarely garnered any attention, Montanée became the subject of a biographical obituary in the popular *Harper's Weekly*. Its author was no less a personage than Lafcadio Hearn.[1] The somewhat misleading title of the piece, "The Last of the Voudoos," made clear the reason for the exceptional attention. Hearn (1885, 726) elaborated, explaining, "In the death ... New Orleans lost, at the end of August, the most extraordinary African character that ever obtained celebrity within her limits," adding that although Montanée had not truly been the last of his faith in the city, he had been the final "really important figure." Alongside Montanée's religion—understood by the journalist as simply magic—and the consequent respect in which believers held him, it was his international heritage and experience that made him worthy of memorial. After an introductory paragraph that described his subject's importance, Hearn spent the next two explaining that Montanée had been born in Senegal, likely into the Bamana people, before being kidnapped by a Spanish slave trader and soon finding himself as a cook in Cuba. There his master freed him, after which he became a ship's cook, traveling widely, as Hearn put it, "in both hemispheres" (727). Finally, he settled in New Orleans, where he took on work, first as a cotton roller and later as a professional diviner. Even after settling down, however, Montanée continued to embody a host of cultures. He would always display his Bamana ethnicity by three parallel curved scars extending down each cheek from temple to edge of lips. His desk, meanwhile, was adorned with a picture of the Virgin Mary, an elephant tusk, and shells from Africa—probably cowries—that he used to tell fortunes. Moreover, his clients of both African and European heritage helped him to live the

Figure 7.1. Magical wares in a Senegalese marabout's shop. Senegalese men and women made up most of the early French colonial Louisiana's slave population. Unsurprisingly, some of the items in this selection of magical goods resemble those used in the supernatural work of New Orleans's historical Voodoo practitioners.

American dream of becoming a rich man during his heyday. His wealth allowed him to support a collection of wives, one of whom, reported Hearn, was a white woman. Finally, though Hearn seems not to have realized it, the faith with which Montanée had become so associated was most strongly influenced by the Bight of Benin region of Africa, not his former Senegalese homeland (726–727; see also Gomez 1998, 55–57).

Though Hearn depicted Montanée as a man distinctly embodying globalism, he asserted, perhaps unconsciously, that he was a figure who belonged to a particular place and people. In the first sentence of the article, for instance, Hearn stated that it was New Orleans that suffered from Montanée's decease. Elsewhere in the obituary, Hearn identified the precise location of the home of the supposed "Last Voudoo" and indicated the respect he held throughout the city by referencing excitement generated by his crossing of Canal Street to visit the American section of New Orleans. More subtly, he described Montanée's children playing on the *banquette*, a word used in New Orleans for a sidewalk or boardwalk (727; see also Valdman 2010, 58). In addition to depicting Jean Montanée as a possession of New Orleans, Hearn also made it clear that his place within the city was among the African American population. Though the journalist acknowledged that some whites had paid for his subject's divinatory services, he described them as having been driven by "curiosity or doubt." His Black followers, on the other hand, had sought him out for his "predictions and counsel" (727).

Hearn's dual vision of Voodoo, or at least one of its best-known practitioners, as a global phenomenon as well as one bound to a specific locale and race, finds itself expressed in modern scholarly and popular conversations about the religion. Unlike the famous journalist, however, since the early twentieth century, scholars, believers, and popular authors have tended to lay claim to Voodoo for a particular region, race, or other restricted category. In short, alongside widespread recognition of the historically decentralized and global nature of Mississippi River valley Voodoo and its many cousins—including Haitian Vodou and West African Vodún—modern notions like identity, including but not limited to Afrocentrism and nationalism, have increasingly persuaded a variety of scholars and believers to assert authority of varying degrees of exclusivity over the faith. Mississippi valley Voodoo, moreover, is arguably even more malleable than its ancestors and New World relations because it is not a living tradition in a conventional sense, having dissipated as a full-fledged religion during the 1940s.[2] Though these competing claims to Voodoo are problematic exercises in contested historic memory and can seem to dispute the religion's far-flung, multicultural heritage, their very existence reflects a history and continued appeal steeped in globalism.

THE GLOBE IN THE MISSISSIPPI RIVER VALLEY

By any measure, Voodoo's history embodies globalism. As happened elsewhere, Europeans' desire to exploit the resources of the New World using unfree labor shaped the environment that would give rise to the faith. In the Mississippi River valley, the French were the principal actors during the huge Louisiana colony's early days. To supply their plantations with labor, settlers initially purchased the greatest number of slaves from the port of Ouidah, a home of Vodún and an independent state until it fell to the expansionist Kingdom of Dahomey in 1727. By the 1720s, however, the French had begun to buy growing numbers of African bondspersons from Senegambia. By 1743, approximately two-thirds of the dark-skinned inhabitants of the area came from the latter region, while most of the rest hailed from what is now Benin and its neighbors (Hall 1992, 57–95, 382–397). Once the Spanish acquired the region in 1763, following France's disastrous loss in the Seven Years' War, slave imports shifted dramatically, with by far the largest single cohort arriving from West Central Africa. According to the historian Michael Gomez, the number imported into the future state of Louisiana was so great during the post-French period that West Central Africans came to account for 35.8 percent of the total imports between 1720 and 1820 (Gomez 1998, 137; Hall 2005, 42–44).[3]

Further globalization of the region followed the United States' acquisition of the Louisiana Territory in 1803. Anglo-American immigrants, of course, introduced their own bondspersons with them. Some had come from African homelands familiar to many slaves already living in the territory. Others originated among groups not well represented along the Mississippi River, such as the Igbo, or had spent their entire lives working Americans' land (Hall 2005, 175–177). In addition to slaves brought by American settlers, a large number of immigrants from the former French colony of Saint-Domingue arrived between 1791 and 1815, bringing additional bondspersons with them. Their numbers peaked in 1809–1810 after the Spanish expelled many from Cuba, where they had earlier attempted to make a home following the outbreak of the Haitian Revolution. All told, somewhere between 15,000 and 20,000 arrived, with as many as nine-tenths settling in and around New Orleans. By way of perspective, the entire population of the city had amounted to a mere 8,000 individuals in 1799 (Dessens 2007, 1, 27–29).

These varied peoples shaped a Creole faith that in many ways resembled Haitian Vodou. At the risk of sounding passé, it is safe to state that, as is true of the Haitian faith, the deities of Voodoo were the descendants of African originals. Among the most important were Blanc Dani, Papa Lébat, and Assonquer. The first two are easily recognizable as having developed from Dan and Legba of the Bight of Benin and roughly corresponding to Vodou's Danbala and Papa Legba. Assonquer, meanwhile, was probably none other than the healing god Osanyin of the Yoruba, who had developed in Haiti as Ossange (Cable 1880, 99, 101, 182, 184, 253, 257, 447; Ellis 1894, 79; Pitkin 1904, 194, 196; Scheu 2011, 89, 174–175; Thompson 1983, 42–51, 166–167). Also, like Vodou, Voodoo embraced spirits, such as Grand Zombi and Jean Macouloumba, whose origin lay in West Central Africa, well outside the Bight of Benin. There is, however, no evidence that the concept of *nanchons* (Nago or Yoruba spirits) was to be found the Mississippi valley. Likewise, some of the reputed deities of the Mississippi valley, such as Jean Macouloumba, appear to have no clear parallel in Haiti ("Dance" 1896, 2; Pitkin 1904, 275–276, 282–285; "Tribulations" 1863, 1; "Voudooism" 1890, 10). Other features of both the Haitian and Mississippi valley faiths included a shared reverence for the spirits of the dead, initiatory ceremonies, and a prominent place for magic (Breaux and McKinney n.d., 1–3; McKinney n.d., 1, 8).[4]

Figure 7.2. A Vodun shrine in Ouidah. Note the serpentine *vodu* that adorn it. Spirits like these were the direct ancestors of Voodoo's Blanc Dani and Haiti's Danbala.

Encounters between distinct African peoples and their faiths did not occur in isolation. For example, in Louisiana, Voodoo drew upon European magical traditions, incorporating the French grimoire *Les secrets merveilleux de la magie naturelle du Petit Albert*, popularly known as the *'Tit Albert*, into their practice (Anderson 2005, 56). Likewise, as happened across the New World, Catholicism interacted freely with African faiths. In colonial French Louisiana, the 1724 version of the Code Noir required that all slaves receive instruction in Catholicism (Spear 2014, 53–72). American immigrants brought their own predominantly Protestant forms of Christianity with them. It should come as no surprise that candles, incense, holy water, Bibles, and other Christian paraphernalia had made their way into Voodoo by at least the early twentieth century (Hyatt 1970–1978, 744–745, 747–749, 772, 834, 852). Also, as was true in other African diasporic religions, deities that had originated in Africa had taken on the alter egos of Catholic saints by the late nineteenth century. In New Orleans, for instance, Papa Lébat was also St. Peter, and Blanc Dani was Michael the Archangel (Dédé 1939, 2; Pitkin 1904, 194, 196).

A persistent Native American presence also helped to shape Voodoo. During the nineteenth century, Choctaws, Houmas, and Chitimachas were common visitors to New Orleans, and their presence was probably even more frequent during the previous century ("Indians in the Life of New Orleans" n.d.; Latrobe 1986, 71). Marie Laveau, the city's most famous Voodoo practitioner, reportedly bought herbs from such visitors, presumably for professional use (Dédé n.d., 2–3). Similarly, one of her associates, James Alexander, was commonly known as "Indian Jim" because of his claims to Native American ancestry (Hobley 1941, 3; Michinard 1940, 1). According to the folklorist Mary Alicia Owen, Native American influence was even more pronounced in Missouri Voodoo, where its most famous practitioner, "King" Alexander, claimed to be half Cherokee. Moreover, per Owen, the most honored spirit in its pantheon was Grandfather Rattlesnake, who appears to have been a Creole version of Vodún's Dan that had taken on the characteristics of a Native American spirit, much as New Orleans's Blanc Dani merged Dan and the Archangel Michael (Owen 1892, 236–237; 241; 1893, 224; 1898, 313–314).

Unlike its many New and Old World relations, however, Voodoo is not a living tradition in the conventional sense. To be sure, the hoodoo associated with the religion is alive and well, and aspects of the faith survive within New Orleans's Spiritual Churches (Jacobs and Kaslow 1991, 30–48, 74, 125–148, 209). Nevertheless, the most recent evidence of initiations comes from the files of the Louisiana Writers' Project, which operated during the late 1930s and early 1940s. The last unambiguous references to the religion's deities appear in the same sources.[5]

Despite the disappearance of the historical religion from the Mississippi River valley, a substantial number of New Orleanians practice various reconstructed forms of Voodoo or other African diasporic faiths, linking them to the city's cultural heritage. As was true of the earlier manifestation of the faith, the modern versions are themselves global in heritage. The city's most prominent Voodoo leader is Sallie Ann Glassman, a white woman of Jewish background from the American Northeast. She underwent initiation as a mambo in Haitian Vodou. Her interpretation of the religion, however, is unique in that she honors the spirit of New Orleans's most famous historical Voodoo priestess, Marie Laveau, and because she does not perform animal sacrifices, using yoga to offer her own life forces to the lwa instead. Another practitioner, Priestess Miriam, is a Mississippian African American from a Baptist background whose interest in Voodoo grew out of her involvement with a Spiritual Church and her relationship with Oswan Chamani, a practitioner of the Belizean form of obeah. The website for her Voodoo Spiritual Temple, however, references Fon Vodún and

Haitian Vodou while describing itself as serving those seeking aid from "Afrocentric American Voodooism, the Grand Spirits of New Orleans Voodoo, and the Great Universal Spiritual Tradition" (Voodoo Spiritual Temple n.d.; Anderson 2005, 142–144). Another prominent contributor to the city's African diasporic culture is Nana Sula Spirit. She was born and grew up in New Jersey but became an initiate in Akan religion and the Yoruba Ifa/orisha faith before moving to New Orleans. There, she operates the Temple of Light–Ile' de Coin-Coin, which she built to honor Marie Therese Coin-Coin a prominent Creole of color and planter from near Natchitoches, Louisiana (Nana Sula Spirit n.d.).

The global nature of Mississippi valley Voodoo did not originate in North America, however. One could argue, for instance, that Haitian Vodou with its nations of lwa and pervasive use of Catholic iconography has a more obviously global heritage than did the sorts found in New Orleans and Missouri (Métraux 1972, 85–86). At the same time, the varieties present along the Bight of Benin were inherently global in outlook if not heritage. Beninese Vodún and Togolese Vodu, for example, do not appear to have ever had a closed pantheon, adopting and even creating deities over time. As an informant with whom I spoke in 2015 put it, Togo's Vodu pantheon today consists of *natural* deities who have always lived on the land where they are worshipped and *found* deities who came from elsewhere or came into being at particular points in time. By way of illustration, the anthropologist Melville Herskovits ([1938] 1967, 2:103–104) recorded that such important deities as Mawu Lisa and Dan were said by his informants to be eighteenth-century additions to the religion of Dahomey. An extremely popular deity called Tron is a more recent member of the faith (Landry 2019, 6, 105). Significantly, Vodún and Vodu's embrace of new gods is not confined to those of African origin. Mami Wata, for instance, a mermaid-like spirit found along the coast, draws from the European concepts of mermaids (Drewal 2008, 33–41, 89–101). I have personally visited shrines dedicated to Hindu deities as well as others occupied by gods themselves considered to be Muslim.

The African faiths are global in more than just the deities they serve. They also invite initiates from a variety of backgrounds. Timothy R. Landry's (2018, 4, 91–93) monograph *Vodún: Secrecy and the Search for Divine Power* examines this phenomenon in considerable depth, determining that tourism has become a driving force in the religion as foreign visitors to the region seek initiation as a means of attachment to a divinity as well as an authenticating experience. Though my own fieldwork has been much less extensive, I found myself urged to undergo initiation to Dan upon two occasions. Though most accounts of this openness to outsiders come from recent years, it was almost certainly present in earlier iterations of the faith, which helps to explain why large numbers of whites were participating in New Orleans Voodoo rituals by the late nineteenth century (Roberts 2015, 5–8, 80–102). In sum, like the various related faiths of the Bight of Benin and the New World, Mississippi valley Voodoo has proven to be remarkably global in both composition and openness.

CLAIMING A FAITH

Set against this convergence of global cultures has been a trend toward claims of ownership of the religion. This concept is easily illustrated by two of my own experiences publishing a reference work entitled *The Voodoo Encyclopedia: Magic, Ritual, and Religion*. In 2013, while collecting and revising entries for the volume, three colleagues—whom I respect immensely—reached out to suggest that I change the spelling of the religion's name to reflect the Haitian Kreyòl orthography, one of them entitling the subject of her email "Voodoo [sic] Encyclopedia." Three years later, I presented a copy of the finished work to Dada Daagbo Hounon Houna II, who claims the position of supreme chief of Vodún in Benin, as a thank-you gift for his assistance with some research I had been conducting. As he accepted the present with thanks, he noted that it should have been written in French and have used *Vodún* in place of *Voodoo*.

There was probably more than one reason behind each suggestion. The recommendations could have simply come from familiarity. The three colleagues, for example, were all associated with the Congress of Santa Barbara (KOSANBA), an association of scholars who study and advocate for Haitian Vodou. Hounon Houna II, meanwhile, claims leadership of Beninese Vodún (see Center for Black Studies Research UC Santa Barbara n.d.; Royal Palace of Hounon Houna II n.d.). Seeing the use of the word *Voodoo* might simply have struck some or all of them as an error, especially considering that my familiarity with them was because of their own areas of expertise. In at least some cases, however, their request for changes in spelling were doubtless intended to distance serious examination of the religion from the negative stereotypes associated with the term *Voodoo* (see Long 2002). At the same time, arguing that these terms, which typically reference a Haitian and an African religion, respectively, should be employed to describe a Mississippi valley religion, is an assertion—conscious or unconscious—of ownership over the North American belief system. In effect, they asserted that the faith's historical links to Haiti and Benin justified subsuming it within their respective realms of scholarly and religious authority.

Despite Mississippi valley Voodoo's global history and openness, it has been a contested symbol of identity for much of its history. The situation has been aided by the fact that the faith had largely faded away as an intact religion by the 1940s, but even prior to this, it had become a symbol claimed or assigned as a marker of identity. As one would expect, during its earliest recorded history in the Mississippi River valley, the religion had such negative connotations that few other than practitioners would have claimed ownership. Most often, when authors assigned possession of the faith, they did so with an eye to attributing vice. An 1850 article, for instance, addressed Voodoo as a social ill that corrupted slaves by bringing them into contact with "disorderly free negroes and mischievous whites," attributing its power to African Americans' "peculiar fascination in everything which has a tinge of mystery and superstition" (*Daily Picayune* 1850, 2). On those rare occasions when one proved bold enough to proclaim their ownership of the faith—as several did in a quest to reclaim a confiscated divine image in the same year—they were apt to find themselves mocked. The chief article that discussed the events involving the image described what it called an "assemblage of negrodom" causing the courtroom to smell so badly that "civet alone could be an antidote" (*New Orleans Weekly Delta* 1850, 345). In such a racist social milieu, claiming any link to the religion, much less possession of it, was perilous.

A profound shift in the valuation of Black ownership of Voodoo began during the 1930s with the publication of Zora Neale Hurston's (1931) "Hoodoo in America," a lengthy article that appeared in the *Journal of American Folklore*. It was the first significant American work to claim Voodoo—called "hoodoo" and defined as "magic practices" by its author—as an honorable aspect of African American culture worthy of celebration (317). Rather than condemning it as superstition confined to the ignorant, Hurston claimed it as part of African American culture "wherever any number of Negroes are found in America" (318). She went on to describe a series of initiations and rituals in which she claimed to have participated, recount stories about powerful practitioners of the past, and even produce what she implied was a series of orally preserved formulas passed down from the great Marie Laveau, New Orleans's most famous Voodoo priestess. For Hurston, Voodoo was empowering and liberating, an aspect of African American culture to be claimed enthusiastically. Much of the Voodoo material later appeared in her 1935 collection of folklore, *Mules and Men*, which has seen a much broader readership than her scholarly article. Sadly, much of the information presented by Hurston misrepresented its sources or was simple fabrication. Nevertheless, Hurston's viewpoint on the proper ownership of Voodoo has become normative (Anderson 2019, 75–81).[6]

The vehicle for the shift was largely literary in nature. A series of popular authors, beginning with Alice Walker, found inspiration in *Mules and Men*. The result has been a flowering of literature and other art forms in which Voodoo and other manifestations of African diasporic religion and magic have been firmly claimed as expressions of what it means to be African American (Anderson 2019, 75–81). Examples range from the highly intellectual and literary novels and poetry of Ishmael Reed and Arthur Flowers (see Kouhoutek 2019; Schroeder 2002) to the 2009 animated Disney musical, *Princess and the Frog*, which depicts Voodoo as both the cause and cure of a transformative curse in early twentieth-century Black New Orleans. Such images of the religion have propelled African American–specific claims of it into the realm of scholarship.

A prime example of scholarly claims on the faith is Katrina Hazzard-Donald's (2013) *Mojo Workin': The Old African American Hoodoo System*. Though the primary focus of the book is what its author refers to as "black belt traditional Hoodoo," she also briefly addresses Voodoo, generally treating it as distinct from hoodoo but sometimes more like an idiosyncratic regional version of it.[7] In the latter approach, she was preceded by Hurston as well as by many historical practitioners of Voodoo. As she puts it, her claim on hoodoo and, by extension, Voodoo is important because "hoodoo, for African Americans, is embodied historical memory linking them back through time to previous generations and ultimately to their African past. It is also a paradigm for approaching both the world and all areas of social life" (4). As part of her claims for the ownership of hoodoo by African Americans, she rejects any entitlement of non–African Americans to the practice, describing changes to the tradition, especially those made in pursuit of profit, as creating an inauthentic "snake-oil" version (16, 106–115).

Race has not been the only grounds for claiming the faith. In contrast to my three colleagues and the Hounon Houna II, who asserted that ownership of Voodoo resides with Haiti or Benin, as well as those who maintain that it properly belongs to African Americans, a wide range of authors have claimed that the religion properly belonged to the city of New Orleans. George Washington Cable's ([1880] 2001) historical novel *The Grandissimes*, for instance, used Voodoo in its efforts to depict the foreignness of New Orleans to the experience of its fictional protagonist, Joseph Frowenfeld, an American who travels to the newly acquired city following the Louisiana Purchase. He also used its supposed practice by whites in the city as part of his critique of nineteenth-century racial mores. Helen Pitkin (1904) would feature Voodoo even more prominently in *Angel by Brevet: A Story of Modern New Orleans*, using the religion as a means of emphasizing what she called its "color," meaning local distinctiveness. Cable's and Pitkin's approaches have set the tone for fictional depictions of New Orleans ever since.

Figure 7.3. Offerings in a tomb in New Orleans's St. Louis No. 2 Cemetery. This particular graveyard was once the burial place of Marie Comtesse, a famous nineteenth-century Voodoo priestess. That her last resting place continues to be honored speaks to the survival of hoodoo and continued cultural resonance of Voodoo.

Others would make less subtle claims on Voodoo for New Orleans in the era's nonfiction. In most cases, writers accepted and even emphasized that Voodoo was primarily the domain of the city's Black inhabitants, but their purpose in referencing the religion at all was to assert that it belonged to New Orleans as part of its unique character. In 1885, the members of the city's press published the *Historical Sketch Book and Guide to New Orleans and Environs*, a handbook for early tourists, which includes, as chapter 26, an account of a journalist's visit to a St. John's Eve Voodoo ceremony (Coleman 1885). The book's title page states that it contains "Exhaustive Accounts of the Traditions, Historical Legends, and Remarkable Localities of the Creole City," a list of categories that clearly indicated their claim on Voodoo as a key aspect of New Orleans's urban personality. Likewise, Henry Castellanos's ([1895] 2006) publication *New Orleans as It Was: Episodes of Louisiana Life* claimed Voodoo as a defining feature of the Crescent City. Castellanos, who denigrated the religion as "peculiar idolatry" defined by a "stupid creed and bestial rites," nevertheless portrayed it as a universally known aspect of "local history" (90). Despite devoting an entire chapter to Voodoo in his reminiscences of New Orleans's days gone by, he closed his account by expressing his hope that the faith would be "forever wiped out of existence" (101). Others would follow who had a much less condemnatory approach to the subject, including Lyle Saxon ([1933] 1989), whose *Fabulous New Orleans* has chapters on both Voodoo Queen Marie Laveau and the religion in general. He was certainly not free of the racism found in Castellanos, though he toned it down somewhat, depicting African Americans as merely "intensely emotional" and given to "childlike credulity" (239). Still, for him, Voodoo was a feature of what he called New Orleans's "Gaudy Age" and most "picturesque period" (167, 169).

The height of the drive to claim Voodoo as distinctively New Orleanian came with the advent of the Federal Writers' Project (FWP) in 1935. Though its primary purpose was to provide work to unemployed writers, their job was to produce literature that fostered nationalism by emphasizing the country's various regional, racial, and ethnic cultures, which had been unified through the forces of democracy and capitalism (Penkower 1977, 1–29, 238–248). To further this goal, the agency produced state and city guidebooks, including ones for Louisiana and New Orleans. The *New Orleans City Guide* references Voodoo in its sections on folkways and religion and described the community of Buras, Louisiana, as being particularly tied to it (FWP 1938, 58–66, 83, 175). The Louisiana guidebook included its own information on the religion in roughly the same places (FWP 1941, 98–100, 133). A third FWP book, *Gumbo Ya-Ya: A Collection of Louisiana Folk Tales*, appeared after the program itself had ended. As one might expect, it contained many references to Voodoo scattered throughout the volume. The city's claim on the religion was made clear in the dust jacket that accompanied one printing, which proclaimed, "Here are stories that made New Orleans a legend among cities" (Saxon et al. 1945, e.g., 68, 168, 242–243, 248–249).

A fourth book, Robert Tallant's (1946) *Voodoo in New Orleans*, drew from the work of FWP employs to create the most enduring treatment of the religion. As the most readily available work on the faith, it went on to inform almost all other accounts of Voodoo prior to the twenty-first century. Though Tallant further toned down the racist characterizations of the religion that mar so much of what came before, condescension and general sensationalism remain pervasive. A good example was his groundless statement that all Voodoo ceremonies involved the drinking of blood, after which he went on to successively state that there was no evidence of human sacrifice in Louisiana and then to imply that perhaps it happened after all (15). Despite its flaws, *Voodoo in New Orleans* is a very readable book and went further than any other work to foster the development of the city's pervasive Voodoo tourist ambience, represented by shops for sightseers, such as Marie Laveau's House of Voodoo; the Historic New Orleans Voodoo Museum; businesses that aimed for authenticity, like the New Orleans Healing Center and Voodoo Authentica; street artists; and a host of nondescript souvenir shops that included Voodoo dolls among their wares.

While the assertions of ownership on behalf of African Americans and particular geographies have proven the most persistent, there are a variety of opposing viewpoints. The empowering image of Voodoo claimed by Hurston and the many who have followed her lead has exposed the faith to both broader and narrower claims of ownership. Kodi Roberts (2015), for example, vigorously argues against understanding Voodoo as an African American religion in his *Voodoo and Power: The Politics of Religion in New Orleans, 1881–1940*. It was, he claimed, a multicultural creation that properly belonged to the disempowered among both Black and white people in New Orleans, who took hold of it as a way to seize control of their lives in an era defined by many layers of injustice (6–7, 11, 86–102, 194–197).

In contrast to Roberts, some have laid claim to the empowerment supposedly offered by Voodoo for smaller populations. In one extreme case, Brenda Marie Osbey (2011) used her article "Why We Can't Talk to You about Voodoo" to assert that Voodoo properly belongs to African American women native to New Orleans, denying that the faith can even be discussed with outsiders and thereby dismissing any claims the religion might have to a global identity. Biographers of Marie Laveau, such as Martha Ward and Ina Fandrich, are more typical, however. Fandrich (2005), for instance, argues that Voodoo was a liberating "African-based religious tradition" (148) and a feminized faith, stating "essentially this tradition appears to have been a women's religion" (117). She went on to claim that this nexus proved empowering not only to the free women who dominated the religion's leadership but in Marie Laveau's case, helped to undermine slavery by providing her with the ability to purchase slaves in order to free them and by giving her the means to be involved in "underground abolitionist activity" (163). Ward (2004) expressed much the same sentiments in her biography of Laveau, once again treating Voodoo as belonging to women, generally those of African descent, and operating for their benefit. The author, however, situated herself alongside the many white women who have been attracted to the religion over the years (xiii–xiv, 78–92).

CONCLUSION

Modern popular and scholarly interpretation of Mississippi valley Voodoo is an interesting study in the malleability of historical memory. While virtually no one disagrees that Voodoo has roots in many cultures from different parts of the globe, most authors intentionally or subconsciously claim it for a particular geographical space or lineage or for a restricted population. Those who claim it on behalf of Haiti or Benin emphasize key aspects of its historical development to claim a nationalistic authority over its interpretation, a development very much in keeping with the pervasive melding of Vodou and nationalism in modern Haiti.[8] Those who assert New Orleans's hold on the faith, meanwhile, generally do so to promote Crescent City exceptionalism, a concept cherished both by individuals who identify with the city as well as those hoping to profit from its local color. Theses that describe the religion as belonging to races, classes, or genders, meanwhile, tend to view it through the lens of social ideologies—ranging from outright racism to Hurston's latent Afrocentrism or the feminism of Fandrich—that promise either suppression or empowerment to those who own Voodoo.

Every claim on Voodoo has its problematic aspects. Maintaining that it was a religion belonging to New Orleans, for instance, ignores its demonstrable presence elsewhere, most notably Missouri.[9] Claims that it belongs exclusively to African Americans must excise the well-documented participation of whites in Voodoo as both worshippers in communal ceremonies and clients of prominent practitioners. Those who see it as the possession of the underprivileged in general risk deemphasizing its strong African heritage as well as the fact that a number of its more successful practitioners, including Jean Montanée, strain the definition of what it meant to be disadvantaged. At the same time, to ignore these competing assertions of ownership risks surrendering Voodoo to today's New Age / postmodern culture that condones picking and choosing those aspects of religion that suit one's individual predilections and risks subsuming Voodoo within a vague and insipid Western spirituality (Anderson 2005, 140–144).

Symbols, one of which the historical Voodoo of the Mississippi valley has become, are always open to interpretation. That there is no long-established body of believers to sort authenticity from that which is less than genuine doubtless contributes to the fact that so many interpretations can compete but nevertheless coexist. Without an authoritative body, there can be no definitive claim to ownership. In such a milieu, contested meanings are the norm, not the exception. Moreover, each of the viewpoints sampled above has some truth to it. After all, the religion *was* historically practiced primarily by women, African

Americans, and the underprivileged. Moreover, all three categories found a home in many individual practitioners. Likewise, while it is impossible to determine whether the majority of practitioners lived in New Orleans, the city was certainly the best attested center of the faith.

One recent popular author and initiate of Haitian Vodou, Kenaz Filan (2011), took up the task of teaching readers how to practice the Mississippi valley religion in his *New Orleans Voodoo Handbook*. After stating that those who claim modern Voodoo traditions were a creation of a "few bored white folks" are not entirely wrong, and acknowledging that "there may not have been a survival of Haitian Vodou that persists to the present day in the Louisiana backwoods and bayous," he goes on to state that "New Orleans Voodoo is a freeform system of worship" (1–2). From a historical perspective, he almost certainly would have been incorrect, but when one reads his explanation as an analogy for modern interpretations of the faith, he hits the mark. The many competing, often plausible—if sometimes contradictory—claims to the religion speak to its global nature. That modern scholars, popular authors, and Voodoo revivalists from different parts of the country—rich, poor, male, female, Black, and white—identify with the religion testifies to the fact that there is more to it than a narrow definition confining it to a particular race, class, gender, or locale. The seeds of each interpretation rest in its history, and it is at least as global in its modern appeal as it was in its historical development.

NOTES

1. For an excellent discussion of the life and writings of Lafcadio Hearn, a journalist and writer of fiction who played a pivotal role in shaping popular perceptions of both New Orleans and Japan, see Starr 2001, xi–xxvi.

2. While Caribbean faiths, such as Haitian Vodou and Cuban Santería, have maintained a pantheon, complex theology, and initiation- and experience-based hierarchies, these disappeared from the records of Mississippi valley Voodoo after World War II. Even during the late 1930s, few knew how to conduct initiation ceremonies, and the identities of deities were largely forgotten. Such survivals from the faith alongside its continued cultural relevance later inspired the many modern Voodoo congregations in the Crescent City. Leaders of these groups tend to have been initiated into an African diasporic religion, most commonly in Haiti or West Africa, but have established themselves in New Orleans because of its historical ties to Voodoo.

3. A host of excellent scholarship on the interplay of cultures in the Atlantic world has appeared in recent decades. Among the key works in this field have

been Robert Farris Thompson's (1983) *Flash of the Spirit: African and Afro-American Arts and Philosophy* and John K. Thornton's (1992) *Africa and Africans in the Making of the Atlantic World, 1400–1680*.

4. Unfortunately, many of the earliest reference to Voodoo's deities appear in works of fiction. While independent sources collected at a later date generally verify their existence, one must guard against taking these works of fiction and their descriptions of the religion of Voodoo at face value.

5. Not all agree with my assessment. The most prominent scholar to propose an alternative interpretation is Kodi A. Roberts (2015). In *Voodoo and Power: The Politics of Religion in New Orleans, 1881–1940*, he argues that the Spiritual Churches that developed in twentieth-century New Orleans are a manifestation of the faith, which he posits took on the trappings of Christian congregations as a strategy for escaping persecution.

6. While it is necessary to take Hurston with a grain of salt, especially the more sensational portions of her writings, she did record many aspects of genuine hoodoo lore regarding the use of plants, the prominence of Marie Laveau, the existence of initiations, and the like.

7. For examples of the latter approach see Hazzard-Donal 2013, 39, where she notes that hoodoo and Voodoo were often indistinguishable for both practitioners and observers, and 126–127, where she discusses the rarity of candles outside of hoodoo in the New Orleans area. Though Hazzard-Donald does not delve deeply into the connections between hoodoo and Voodoo, she argued that hoodoo was a religion itself, rendering the idea that Voodoo was a subset of a broader African American faith a tenable one (2–4).

8. When I visited Haiti in 2017 to learn about modern Vodou, for instance, a great many practitioners began their explanation of the religion by recounting an explanation of how Vodou was the driving force in the movement to overthrown slavery and the French and frequently continued by describing it as the basis of their national culture.

9. The works of the folklorist Mary Alicia Owen provide some of the best data on this otherwise poorly documented branch of the religion.

REFERENCES

Anderson, Jeffrey. 2005. *Conjure in African American Society*. Baton Rouge: Louisiana State University Press.

———. 2019. "Guiding Myths: Zora Neale Hurston and Her Impact on Hoodoo and Voodoo Scholarship." In *Voodoo, Hoodoo and Conjure in African American Literature*, edited by James S. Mellis, 69–83. Jefferson, NC: McFarland.

Breaux, Hazel, and Robert McKinney. n.d. "Hoodoo Opening Ceremony." Louisiana Writers' Project, Federal Writers' Project, Cammie G. Henry

Research Center, Watson Memorial Library, Northwestern State University, Natchitoches, LA, box 3-C-1, folder 44.

Cable, George Washington. (1880) 2001. *The Grandissimes: A Story of Creole Life*. With an introduction by W. Kenneth Holditch. Gretna, LA: Publican.

Castellanos, Henry C. (1895) 2006. *New Orleans as It Was*. Louisiana paperback ed. With an introduction by Judith Kelleher Schafer. Baton Rouge: Louisiana State University Press.

Center for Black Studies Research UC Santa Barbara. n.d. "Haitian Studies>KOSANBA." Accessed September 9, 2020. https://www.cbsr.ucsb.edu/research/haitian-studies/kosanba.

Coleman, William Head. 1885. *Historical Sketch Book and Guide to New Orleans and Environs: with Map. Illustrated with Many Original Engravings; and Containing Exhaustive Accounts of the Traditions, Historical Legends, and Remarkable Localities of the Creole City*. New York: W. H. Coleman.

Daily Picayune. 1850. "Unlawful Assemblies." July 31, 1850, 2.

———. 1890. "Voudooism." June 22, 1890, 10.

Dédé, Maria. 1939. Interview by Robert McKinney and Arguedas. New Orleans, LA, July 9, 1939. Louisiana Writers' Project, Federal Writers' Project, Cammie G. Henry Research Center, Watson Memorial Library, Northwestern State University, Natchitoches, LA, folder 533.

———. n.d. Interview by [Robert] McKinney. New Orleans, LA. Louisiana Writers' Project, Federal Writers' Project, Cammie G. Henry Research Center, Watson Memorial Library, Northwestern State University, Natchitoches, LA, folder 25.

Dessens, Nathalie. 2007. *From Saint-Domingue to New Orleans: Migration and Influences*. Gainesville: University Press of Florida.

Drewal, Henry John. 2008. *Mami Wata: Arts for Water Spirits in Africa and Its Diaspora*. Los Angeles: Fowler Museum at UCLA.

Ellis, Alfred Burdon. 1894. *The Yoruba-Speaking Peoples of the Slave Coast of West Africa*. London: Chapman and Hall.

Fandrich, Ina Johanna. 2005. *The Mysterious Voodoo Queen, Marie Laveaux: A Study of Powerful Female Leadership in Nineteenth-Century New Orleans*. New York: Routledge.

Federal Writers' Project. 1938. *New Orleans City Guide*. American Guide Series. Boston: Houghton Mifflin. https://archive.org/details/neworleanscityoowritmiss/page/n5/mode/2up.

———. 1941. *Louisiana: A Guide to the State*. American Guide Series. New York: Hastings House.

Filan, Kenaz. 2011. *The New Orleans Voodoo Handbook*. Rochester, VT: Destiny Books.

Gomez, Michael A. 1998. *Exchanging Our Country Marks: The Transformation of African Identities in the Colonial and Antebellum South*. Chapel Hill: University of North Carolina Press.

Hall, Gwendolyn Midlo. 1992. *Africans in Colonial Louisiana: The Development of Afro-Creole Culture in the Eighteenth Century.* Baton Rouge: Louisiana State University Press.

———. 2005. *Slavery and African Ethnicities in the Americas: Restoring the Links.* Chapel Hill: University of North Carolina Press.

Hazzard-Donald, Katrina. 2013. *Mojo Workin': The Old African American Hoodoo System.* Urbana: University of Illinois Press.

Hearn, Lafcadio. 1885. "The Last of the Voudoos." *Harper's Weekly* 29 (November 7): 726–727.

Herskovits, Melville J. (1938) 1967. *Dahomey: An Ancient West African Kingdom.* 2 vols. New York: J. J. Augustin. Reprint, Evanston, IL: Northwestern University Press.

Hobley, Nathan H. January 1941. Interview by Zoe Posey, New Orleans, LA. Louisiana Writers' Project, Federal Writers' Project, Cammie G. Henry Research Center, Watson Memorial Library, Northwestern State University, Natchitoches, LA, box 3-C-1, folder 44.

Hurston, Zora Neale. 1931. "Hoodoo in America." *Journal of American Folklore* 44:317–417.

Hyatt, Harry Middleton. 1970–1978. *Hoodoo-Conjuration-Witchcraft-Rootwork.* 5 vols. Memoirs of the Alma Egan Hyatt Foundation. Hannibal, MO: Western.

"Indians in the Life of New Orleans." n.d. Louisiana Writers' Project, Federal Writers' Project, Cammie G. Henry Research Center, Watson Memorial Library, Northwestern State University, Natchitoches, LA, folder 95.

Jacobs, Claude F., and Andrew J. Kaslow. 1991. *The Spiritual Churches of New Orleans: Origins, Beliefs, and Rituals of an African-American Religion.* Knoxville: University of Tennessee Press.

Kohoutek, Karen Joan. 2019. "The Mumbo Jumbo Kathedral: HooDoo and Voodoo in the 'Work' of Ishmael Reed." In *Voodoo, Hoodoo and Conjure in African American Literature,* edited by James S. Mellis, 149–160. Jefferson, NC: McFarland.

Landry, Timothy R. *Vodún: Secrecy and the Search for Divine Power.* Philadelphia: University of Pennsylvania Press.

Latrobe, John H. B. 1986. *Southern Travels: Journal of John H. B. Latrobe, 1834.* Edited and with an introduction by Samuel Wilson, with a preface by Stanton Frazar. New Orleans: Historic New Orleans Collection.

Long, Carolyn Morrow. 2002. "Perceptions of New Orleans Voodoo: Sin, Fraud, Entertainment, and Religion." *Nova Religio: The Journal of Alternative and Emergent Religions* 6 (1): 86–101.

L'Union. 1863. "Tribulations des Voudous." August 1, 1863, 1.

McKinney, Robert. n.d. "Popular Gris-Gris among Present Day Hoodoo Queens." Louisiana Writers' Project, Federal Writers' Project, Cammie G.

Henry Research Center, Watson Memorial Library, Northwestern State University, Natchitoches, LA, box 3-C-1, folder 44.

Métraux, Alfred. 1972. *Voodoo in Haiti*. Translated by Hugo Charteris and with an introduction by Sidney W. Mintz. New York: Schocken Books.

Michinard, Henriette. 1940. "About Voodoo: Dr. James Alexander—'Indian Jim.'" Interview of intimate of Tony Lafon by Henriette Michinard, New Orleans, LA, August 1940. Louisiana Writers' Project, Federal Writers' Project, Cammie G. Henry Research Center, Watson Memorial Library, Northwestern State University, Natchitoches, LA, box 3-C-1, folder 44.

Nana Sula Spirit. n.d. "Temple of Light." Accessed September 3, 2020. https://www.sulaspirit.com/temple-of-light.

New Orleans Weekly Delta. 1850. "The Virgin of the Voudous." August 12, 1850, 345.

Osbey, Brenda Marie. 2011. "Why We Can't Talk to You about Voodoo." *Southern Literary Journal* 43 (Spring): 1–11.

Owen, Mary Alicia. 1892. "Among the Voodoos." In *The International Folk-lore Congress 1891: Papers and Transactions*, 230–248. London: David Nutt.

———. 1893. *Old Rabbit, the Voodoo and Other Sorcerers*. With an introduction by Charles Godfrey Leland and with illustrations by Juliette A. Owen and Louis Wain. London: T. Fisher Unwin.

Penkower, Monty Noam. 1977. *The Federal Writers' Project: A Study in Government Patronage of the Arts*. Urbana: University of Illinois Press.

Pitkin, Helen. 1904. *An Angel by Brevet: A Story of Modern New Orleans*. Philadelphia: J. B. Lippincott.

Roberts, Kodi A. 2015. *Voodoo and Power: The Politics of Religion in New Orleans, 1881–1940*. Baton Rouge: Louisiana State University.

Royal Palace of Hounon Houna II. n.d. "About Us." Accessed September 9, 2020. https://www.hounonhouna2.org/.

Saxon, Lyle. (1933) 1989. *Fabulous New Orleans*. Gretna, LA: Pelican Publishing Company.

Saxon, Lyle, Robert Tallant, and Edward Dreyer. 1945. *Gumbo Ya-Ya: A Collection of Louisiana Folk Tales*. New York: Bonanza Books.

Scheu, Patricia [Mambo Vye Zo Komande LaMenfo]. 2011. *Serving the Spirits: The Religion of Vodou*. Philadelphia: published by author.

Schroeder, Patricia R. 2002. "Arthur Flowers, Zora Neale Hurtson, and the 'Literary Hoodoo' Tradition." *African American Review* 36:263–272.

Spear, Jennifer M. 2014. *Race, Sex, and Social Order in Early New Orleans*. Baltimore: Johns Hopkins University Press.

Starr, Frederick, ed. 2001. *Inventing New Orleans: Writings of Lafcadio Hearn*. Jackson: University of Mississippi Press.

Tallant, Robert. 1946. *Voodoo in New Orleans*. New York: Macmillan.

Thompson, Robert Farris. 1983. *Flash of the Spirit: African and Afro-American Art and Philosophy.* New York: Random House.

Thornton, John K. 1992 *Africa and Africans in the Making of the Atlantic World, 1400–1680.* Cambridge: Cambridge University Press.

Times-Democrat. 1896. "Dance of the Voodoos." June 24, 1896, 2.

Valdman, Albert, and Kevin J. Rottet, eds. 2010. *Dictionary of Louisiana French as Spoken in Cajun, Creole, and American Indian Communities.* Jackson: University Press of Mississippi.

"Voodooism." 1898. In *The International Folk-lore Congress of the World's Columbian Exposition, July 1893.* Archives of the International Folk-Lore Association, vol. 1, edited by Helen Wheeler Bassett and Frederick Starr, 313–326. Chicago: Charles H. Sergel.

Voodoo Spiritual Temple. n.d. "About." Accessed September 3, 2020. https://voodoospiritualtemple.org/about.

Ward, Martha. 2004. *Voodoo Queen: The Spirited Lives of Marie Laveau.* Jackson, MS: University Press of Mississippi.

JEFFREY Anderson is Associate Professor of History at the University of Louisiana, Monroe. He is author of *Conjure in African American Society* and editor of *The Voodoo Encyclopedia: Magic, Ritual, and Religion.*

EIGHT

THE PHYSIC(S)ALITY OF VODÚN AND THE (MIS)BEHAVIOR OF MATTER

Venise N. Adjibodou

ENGAGEMENT, AS outlined in the introduction to this volume, refers to the relationships between humans and spirits that constitute the core of lived religion in Vodún and its related worldviews in West Africa, the Caribbean, and the Americas. Engagement encapsulates the epistemological, ritual, socioeconomic, ontological, and emotional exchanges within and beyond the temple or shrine. The first half of this volume illuminates the centuries-long cross-cultural encounters that (re)generate human-spirit activity across time. As Eric Montgomery explains in this volume (chap. 3), old and new spirits find place in contemporary worship by providing healing to populations underserved by their local health care system. Montgomery cites "the African religious imagination" for the fluid, layered meanings, and applications of Vodun. Christian Vannier, also in this volume, argues that religious practices reveal a collective account of interactions between coastal communities and northern Muslims. Islamic practice, therefore, becomes endogenous to Vodún. Historical and ethnographic approaches to African religions procure remarkable insights. Nevertheless, it can be difficult to engage a central component of Vodún: spirits cocreate rituals and practices. Notice the grammatical structure in the preceding clause; spirits are the subject, the actor. How, then, can researchers examine spirits as agential participants?

The question highlights an epistemological bias in academe that privileges Western knowledge systems. There exists an assumption that no measurable proof of spirit agency withstands Western scientific investigation. The assumption that a Western scientific method is the only viable episteme through which humans can understand phenomena arises from six hundred years of anti-Black racism designed to denigrate African humanity and Africans' contributions to human history (Kendi 2016). The consequences of global white-supremacist ideologies include reducing Vodún to devil worship or patronizing African knowledge systems by categorizing them as incomplete and inadequate scientific tools. Such prejudice overlooks the physics-defying phenomena transpiring during some Vodún rituals. Rather than leave these questions unaddressed, it is imperative for researchers to engage Vodún as a science and resist the implicit assumptions undergirding methods for academic research into Africana religions. Just as Vodún's flexibility and resilience has enabled it to expand despite colonialism and religious oppression, so too must the methods, lenses, and approaches in religious studies, anthropology, and Africana studies expand their dimensions to include marginalized yet invaluable knowledge systems.

This chapter explores two Vodún rituals conducted by two different practitioners that produce the same empirical outcome: a bloodless chicken whose blood disappears before the knife pierces the fowl's body. One ritual occurs in Agata, Benin, in 2008; the other takes place in Philadelphia, Pennsylvania, in 2018. I use pseudonyms to protect the practitioners' identities. The data's graphic nature serves neither to exoticize Vodún nor to depict the religion as grotesque. Instead, the similarities between these two events motivate my decision to analyze them. The event in 2008 seemed to me an anomaly. I had not, prior to that moment nor since then, witnessed any Vodún offering in which the animal's blood disappears. For this reason, the event in 2018 surprised me. The outcome I observed ten years prior could be replicated. The method changed, but the empirical data remain the same. Ontological inquiries arise from each case. I argue that Vodún rituals are technologies and Vodún is a science. This is no metaphor since what is at issue in both case studies is the behavior of matter. The epistemology and mechanics of Vodún as a science represent a necessary direction for future research in the materiality of African religions.

Edith Turner (1993, 11) encouraged anthropologists to grapple with the question "What are spirits?" and noted, "There seems to be a force field between the anthropologist and her or his subject matter making it impossible for her or him to come close to it, a kind of religious frigidity." Turner pinpoints the epistemological incongruence between academe and the myriad non-Western epistemologies among the communities that many anthropologists and scholars of religion study. This incongruence is an effect of what Bonaventura de Sousa Santos (2014, 165) calls metonymic reason, "a kind of reason that claims to be the only form of rationality and therefore does not exert itself to discover other kinds of rationality." Sousa Santos argues that Western knowledge is a type of metonymic reason. It "claims to be exclusive, complete, and universal, even though it is merely one of the logics of rationality that exist in the world and prevails only in the strata of the world compromised by Western modernity" (168). Furthermore, he argues that modern science is a knowledge "that does not know well enough the limits of what it allows one to know of the experience of the world and knows even less well the other kinds of knowledge that share with it the epistemological diversity of the world" (111). Western epistemology deems all knowledges except itself nonexistent. In doing so, knowledges belonging to indigenous people become inert and invisible. They can neither comment on contemporary problems nor propose solutions.

My contribution to this edited volume emerges from my strong desire to contest epistemicide, to create theories and methods contradicting this process. I take seriously Paulin Hountondji's (2009, 129) admonition "to develop first and foremost an African-based tradition of knowledge in all disciplines," a tradition whose agenda arises from African societies. Vodún poses hard questions to Western science, and pursuing the answers revitalizes the value that indigenous knowledge systems offer studies on materiality. Since Eurocentric knowledge is metonymic, it must partner with forms of knowing and knowledges beyond itself to ascertain the lived religious experiences that function as epistemological resources for African people. Indigenous knowledge and forms of knowing are at the core of the events recounted in these case studies. Therefore, a hybrid epistemological foundation becomes crucial to the theorization of matter in Vodún.

Additionally, the questions posed in this chapter converge with the ontological turn in anthropology that Eduardo Viveiros de Castro initiated (Castro 2015; Henare, Holbraad, and Wastell 2007; Holbraad 2017; Kohn 2013). Castro argues that anthropologists should examine the questions indigenous concepts present and see what description of the world these concepts provide. "The domain of concepts," in his view, "does not coincide with subjects' cognitive faculties or internal states: concepts are intellectual objects or events, not mental states or attributes" (Castro 2013, 484). A bloodless chicken, as a concept, produces a description of the world in which matter behaves counter to quantum physics. Castro pursues such concepts because he finds the things indigenous people think. "The concepts they deploy, the 'descriptions' they produce, are very different to our own—and thus that the world described by these concepts is very different to ours" (2013, 485). The case studies presented below, however, trouble the conceptual differences between the "native's" world and the anthropologist's world. In both cases, the bloodless chickens are material objects visible to the researcher and to the consultants; they are data points that pull toward themselves the boundaries of each observer's epistemology such that the concept of a bloodless chicken is no longer an "indigenous concept" but a human one.

Last, the researcher's and the consultant's sensoriums play a significant role in bridging Western epistemologies and Vodún epistemologies (Brivio 2018; Drewal 1996; 1988; Egonwa 2008; Rosenthal 2010; Rush 2008; 2001³).[1] Both knowledges value the body's senses: sight, touch, hearing, smell, and taste. In Vodún, as in Yoruba orisha tradition, practitioners value an internal sense some have called ESP or intuition (Drewal 2005). This internal sense, however, bears less significance in the cases evaluated here. The bloodless chickens are ascertainable through sound, touch, smell, and sight. The case studies offered here pivot on visual perception. James J. Gibson argues that visual perception involves *affordances*.[2] "The *affordances* of the environment," he argues, "are what it *offers* the animal, what it *provides* or *furnishes*, either for good or ill" (Gibson 2014, 119, original author's emphasis). For Gibson, "animal" refers to humans and nonhuman species. Therefore, his idea mobilizes the question: What do bloodless chickens, and the tactile processes by which they emerge, provide or furnish a study on the materiality of Vodún? If, as Gibson claims, "a niche is a set of affordances" and "the niche implies a kind of animal, and an animal implies a kind of niche" (120), what does the materiality of a bloodless chicken tell the human animal about its constitution and about its relationship to space and visible matter?

New possibilities for the theorization of materiality in Vodún await. To be clear: these case studies are not about belief; they did not happen because the consultant and the researcher decided "to exit the world of logical positivism" and don a unique "state of mind" that Dana Rush (1999, 61) refers to as "Vodúnland." To the contrary, these events produced data perceived through sight, hearing, smell, and touch. The change in the chicken's state defies Western scientific laws about the behavior of matter. Blood, according to physics and chemistry, cannot simply disappear from view. Yet visual perception during each ritual generates affordances that offer opportunities to integrate indigenous knowledge into an analysis of ritual and materiality.

CASE STUDY #1: A HEN FOR ADÉLÉKÈ

Mobolaji became a *bɔkonɔn*, a diviner, while visiting his hometown, Porto-Novo, Benin, a few years ago.[3] In addition to learning how to consult the Fa, Vodún's most significant form of knowing past, present, and future events, Mobolaji learned how to supplicate and wield a powerful, red, female divinity named Adélékè.[4] To say the deity is "red" means her vibration is hot and of the earth, in contrast to divinities who are "white," cool, and usually from the water. He acquired this divinity from an elderly diviner in Sakete, Benin. The spirit's physical emanation is a small calabash packed to the brim with substances and wrapped tightly in three pieces of fabric: one red, one black, and one white. The white fabric covers the exterior. Numerous taut red and black threads crisscross each half of the calabash to secure the fabric tightly over the container's contents. The fine threads create another tactile layer to the deity's embodiment.

Mobolaji brought the vodún to southwest Philadelphia to assist a man suffering from sexual dysfunction. The man claimed his problems began after he decided to leave his wife, at which point she threatened him by saying if he left her, he would never be able to penetrate another woman. He left his wife anyway. A few months later, he noticed he could not perform sexually. This client called Mobolaji because he suspected an African spiritual power might be the cause behind his physical problem. Mobolaji later explained to me that Adélékè told him she needed a ritual sacrifice—a red hen—to heal the client. The bɔkɔnɔn took his client to a live poultry store just outside Philadelphia, where the client purchased one red hen. That evening, the bɔkɔnɔn bent his body to the floor and held the live hen with his right hand while he used his left hand to place Adélékè (the small calabash wrapped in fabric) atop the hen's body. During the ritual, Mobolaji used his hands to determine the feel of the hen's flesh, to sense its pulse, muscular structure, breath, and movement. He could smell the feathered creature's odor.

The hen nudged Mobolaji's hands with her wings, wiggled her head, and briefly stuck out her feet. The bird did not make any sounds indicating pain or discomfort. As the bɔkɔnɔn prayed to counteract the curses and spiritual problems facing his client, he called the divinity's name and said the curse's negativity should return to whoever sent it toward his client. Mobolaji invoked Adélékè to take the blood from the chicken, and, consequently, whoever attempted to harm his client would also lose their blood. He tapped the calabash seven times with his left hand to wake the divinity, seven times because the divinity is female. As he tapped it, Mobolaji commanded the spirit to stand up and take the offering. He spat on the spirit three times to give her his own acɛ (power) (Abiodun 1994; Kossou 1983).[5] The bɔkɔnɔn later explained to me he received a specific acɛ to make the spirit take the blood of the animal he offers. The spirit was taking longer to react, so he spat on her to remind her he has the authority to command her to accept the offering, to make the spirit to cause her to accept the offering faster. After spitting his acɛ onto Adélékè, Mobolaji gently jostled the hen's body. Its head flopped up and down; its feathers and feet were still. Mobolaji patted the hen's head gently to see if it would respond. He turned the hen's head to see it if would open its eyes. Its eyes remained closed, and its limp neck could not support its head. His visual perception further enabled him to determine when the hen ceased to resist and to determine when its physical posture seemed lifeless. Mobolaji then cast the hen's body on the floor and put down Adéléké. Only at this moment did Mobolaji pick up a large kitchen knife and cut the chicken.[6] He found no blood in the hen's body. Mobolaji's sensorium enabled him to know when the desired outcome had occurred. He used his ears to hear the chicken's clucking and the sound of the animal's movement. The information collected through his body confirmed for Mobolaji the hen had died. Similarly, seeing the inside of the chicken's body and recognizing the absence of blood confirms for him that the concept of a bloodless chicken is an empirical data point. His sensory data support the veracity of an indigenous concept Mobolaji uses to describe the world.

Do not let the bloodless chicken distract from the questions it generates. What agents are responsible for the blood's disappearance? Did the blood shift form, location, or both? If it changed form, what did it become? If it changed place, where did it go? Furthermore, what agents are responsible for these causes and effects? What kind of action happened here? In other words, what are we looking at? These questions should drive new explorations in Vodún materiality but answering them may remain nearly impossible if the researcher relies only on Western frameworks. Adéléké's hen illustrates the (mis)behavior of matter, its defiance of the laws of physics known to Western science. When matter breaks the rules in Western epistemology, it becomes difficult to classify. Furthermore, in anthropology and religious studies, Adéléké's hen is a prime "X-file," the type of event researchers in African religions avoid discussing lest they lose credibility for seeming to argue the "imaginary" is "Real" (Apter 2017, 288). The conundrum, I propose, is an issue of visual perception and epistemological location. The ritual suggests Adéléké is a more-than-human actor who responds to Mobolaji's codified actions. Nevertheless, the mechanics behind Adéléké's participation remain a mystery to the client. The affordance scholars have missed, however, is the offer to interpret such events as technological displays. The event presents a unique descriptive statement: Vodún shrines are technological devices; Vodún rituals are a type of technology; and Vodún is a science.

In religious studies and anthropology, to visually perceive an event like Adéléké's hen is an affordance offering definitions of ritual. James J. Gibson's theory of affordances considers what a perceived object offers a person. According to Gibson (2014, 126), objects have numerous affordances, but people usually see only the affordances they find most useful. A researcher may or may not pay attention to an event like a ritual whose outcome defies physics. "The affordance of something does *not change* as the need of the observer changes. The observer may or may not perceive or attend to the affordance, but the affordance, being invariant, is always there to be perceived.... The object offers what it does because of what it is" (126). Regardless of whether a researcher takes seriously his or her own or a consultant's embodied knowledge, methodological killjoys like a phenomenon Western science cannot explain "[are] always there to be perceived"; they afford the study of religion new theoretical horizons "because of what it is" (130, original author's emphasis). As Ronald Grimes (2014, 40) surmises, rituals are "grounded in ultimate concerns; posit more-than-human actors; have the least permeable, most vigorously defended boundaries; are often surrounded by obfuscation, mystification, and other processes that inhibit criticism." Mobolaji and his client use this ritual to engage a grave ultimate concern about the war between good and evil in his client's life. Not only is the client's reproductive health at stake, but also the curse his ex-wife placed on him threatens his ability to live in security and peace. The ritual posits more-than-human actors by suggesting Adéléké is an actor who produces causes and effects. It also suggests humans and spirits engage one another to produce transdimensional transformations of the self. The vodún active during the ritual not only repaired the client's physical ailment, but Adéléké improved his spiritual health by removing the curse that attacked him spiritually. As Alissa Jordan states in this volume (chap. 8), "Our body selves transmute along with our tasks, practices, and interactions. We eat, we drink, we meet others, we zone out, we discover ourselves, or others unearth our own capacities in ways that deeply transform us; in short, we are affected, we affect others, and all of this is made possible through the expressive, fleshy, and shifting matrix of embodied being." Vodún rituals, effectually, serve as transdimensional intersections where multiple ontological modes and affective states intertwine. In this case study, human bodies, a chicken, Adéléké, and the vital force (aεɛ) inhabiting them contribute to the ritual's transformative power.

The new definition made possible by this ritual is the ability to perceive the "vigorously defended boundaries" (Grimes 2014) as rules of physics. Instead of concluding sociocultural beliefs govern the ritual and its interpretation, the chicken's death suggests Vodún rituals illustrate the (mis)behavior of matter Western science cannot grasp on its own. Scholars could reclassify rituals by removing them from the mystical and placing them in the taxonomy of the scientific. Grimes's definition would have to adjust to this maneuver. Ritual may still imply the presence of nonhuman actors and indeed attend to life's most pressing concerns. Ritual also, however, becomes an embodiment of cosmological rules redefining the behavior of matter, a scientific practice requiring non-Western epistemology to comprehend and evaluate it. The science of Vodún rituals, thus, becomes a new direction for material studies of African religions.

VODÚN SHRINES ARE TECHNOLOGICAL DEVICES

When Mobolaji and I debriefed the event, he referred to the calabash named Adéléke as a shed in which the spirit resides. He mentioned that only people initiated into this divinity can see the spirit outside of her shed. As he offered me a closer look at Adéléke's calabash, he tapped the lower portion three times before opening it to ensure the spirit was not outside of the calabash.[7] The calabash's convex openings are packed tightly with substances. The spirit can emerge from the substance and remain visible to initiated people. For the noninitiated eye, the calabash's contents remain concealed by fabric. Mobolaji compared the tapping to a knock on someone's bedroom door; a person knocks to ensure they do not catch the resident by surprise. In his view, the calabash is a room where the spirit resides. The blood she consumes, he suggests, enters this room. Later in our conversation, Mobolaji confirmed the calabash is not simply a residence, but it is also the spirit's physical body. The calabash itself functions as a liminal space connecting the vodún to the human realm, much like the sacred forests in Timothy Landry's contribution to this volume (chap. 10). Landry notes that a sacred leaf called *agègbè* "represents its own world through shared experiences with Vodúnisants and demonstrates important life lessons. *Agègbè* is an agentive being or person. . . . The *agègbè*-person, when in a relationship with a human-person, exists between the forested world of spirits and the cultivated world of humans." Similarly, Adéléke's calabash facilitates the spirit's engagement with human beings and with matter in the human dimension. As body and shed, the calabash visually demarcates a boundary between the spirit dimension and the human dimension.

Mobolaji's comment that the calabash serves as Adéléke's room or shed implies the calabash is a space.[8] In addition, as Mobolaji points out, the calabash is the vodún's body, thereby suggesting the acε in the calabash and the substances packed into it collectively constitute a substantive entity known as the female Adéléke. The calabash and its ingredients "work" because of cooperation among agentic matter. Yet one could also perceive the calabash as a device. The vodún-as-vibration, the spirit in its immaterial form, uses the calabash to participate in transactions with human beings. To this latter point, the calabash is the device Adéléke uses to retrieve and store matter.

In Vodún, the spirits are agents in a classical sense. They are actors who produce causes and effects. The vodún participates in this event in two ontological forms: as a vibration, or spirit; and as a material form perceived as a calabash. Both the vodún-as-vibration and the calabash-as-vodún are part of the scientific process in the event described above. Here the vodún uses the device to consume matter. Insofar as the vodún have bodies, they are said to eat. Eating is an organism's process of breaking down a substance into microparticles (nutrients) its body can extract and use. Eating is one of many human behaviors the vodún are said to demonstrate. Eating, however, may also reference the transformation of matter, the breaking down of earthly substances into new (at times, imperceptible) states. In Mobolaji's words, Adélékè "sucks" the animal's essence. "To suck" refers to a vacuum-like extraction or removal of a substance from one place and into another. On one hand, Adélékè functions as an invisible, agentic force who manipulates the chicken's blood. On the other hand, the calabash, considered Adélékè's "room" and "body," doubles as a mechanical device. In both instances, Adélékè, as vibration, body, and device, causes matter to change place and form. Consumption, therefore, is the transposition of matter. *How* the vodún in any ontological state achieves this result requires further research into the scientific intersections of acɛ, the *odu* (sacred geomantic signs within Fa divination), agency, and matter.

To say the vodún are vibrations means the vodún are frequencies or waves. The wave-particle duality known in Western physics claims waves can behave like particles and particles can behave like waves ("The Uncertainty Principle" 2016). Therefore, one may ascertain the vodún as particle-like waves as well as wavelike particles. As such, one must ask: Particles of what? Acɛ. In Vodún, all matter contains acɛ, the "powerful and essential part of a being," its "vital principle" (Agossou 1972, 29, my translation). All matter has agentic capacity (Alaimo 2008; Bennett 2009; 2010; Coole 2005).[9] From an African indigenous epistemological purview, the periodic table of elements known in Western science has yet to grasp this aspect of matter. One could thus envision a visual diagram like a periodic table of elements that describes each element's acɛ and use indigenous knowledge systems to classify how that acɛ forms with other acɛ to produce specific objects, effects, or states. Just as Western science concludes atoms share electrons to form molecular bonds, Vodún science contains a theory about how the acɛ in one substance interacts or bonds with the acɛ in another substance. The vibrations known as spirits, vodún, could appear as elements on a new diagram because they are particle-like and wavelike entities containing distinct acɛ.

At the same time, a shrine, as the physical body of a spirit, illustrates the bonds formed between the vital principles in various substances when humans combine specific objects to create the acɛ known as a specific vodún. For example, the calabash Mobolaji claims is Adélékè's body and Adélékè's shed consists of material the old man in Sakete, Benin, combined purposefully. The substances inside contain specific acɛ that, once combined and activated through Vodún scientific processes, generate another type of acɛ: the vodún or particle-like wave known as "Adéléke." Combining substances to create a shrine or to conduct a ritual operates in ways similar to chemistry. Each substance has its chemical properties. When combined and processed according to specific African technological processes, predictable material outcomes occur. Western science states chemical reactions change the bonds in a molecule. To make blood invisible to the eye would require breaking down the substance through chemical processes. But the event described above does not involve chemical reactions as understood in Western chemistry. Nevertheless, the blood becomes undetectable to human senses. At stake is the recognition of a lacuna in Western knowledge. This gap may be responsible for the epistemological and hermeneutical incongruity between how anthropologists and scholars of religion interpret Vodún rituals and how Vodún practitioners interpret them. Whereas Western science cannot explain the bloodless chicken, rethinking the vodún through African indigenous knowledge systems provides new principles with which to describe the (mis)behavior of matter. Incorporating indigenous knowledge systems into the dominant epistemology of our time will broaden the scope of the information human beings have amassed about the material world.

SOCIOCOSMIC RELATIONSHIPS AND MATERIAL BONDS IN VODÚN RITUALS

Applying indigenous knowledge systems to an interpretation of ritual results in new perspectives on a long-studied subject. It is beyond the scope of this essay to review the arc of theoretical perspectives on ritual and, by extension, practice; however, other scholars have written on this topic (Apter 2007; Bell 1992; 1997; Grimes 2014). Instead, I will consider the changes that indigenous knowledge brings to certain definitions of ritual in anthropology and religious studies. For instance, in cultural anthropology, ritual consists of a couple of integral components. First, ritual is "a stylized performance that symbolically enacts and maintains a social order" (Welsch 2018). Whereas the social order in this definition pertains to relationships among humans, a bloodless chicken, as an African indigenous concept, points to a set of sociocosmic relationships. Sociocosmic relationships are the bonds between human and nonhuman agential entities established and nurtured by transactions across space and time. These bonds are social in the sense that they require actors to negotiate their agency and create causes in response to another actor's effects and affect. These bonds are cosmic because they conjoin entities spanning the entire ontological range within Vodún cosmology. Rituals are one kind of transaction informing a relationship between a human and a vodún. On one hand, the ritual for Adéléké described above exemplifies the power dynamics in the relationship between Mobolaji and Adéléké. He has the acɛ to command the spirit to obey his directions (e.g., accept the chicken by removing its essence). On the other hand, Mobolaji's need to spit his acɛ onto the calabash to command the vodún evinces Adéléké's ability to resist Mobolaji's command and deny his request. Their sociocosmic relationship indicates a vodún may use its agency to alter the anticipated course of events.

Second, "rituals are repetitive, culturally marked as special, and often involve magical thinking" (Welsch 2018). Mobolaji's interactions with Adéléké render tangible, sensory outcomes. There is no magic; rather, the conversion of the hen's blood from a visible substance to a substance removed from sight is a scientific feat. To reduce the ritual to a culturally relative object erases the contributions indigenous knowledge systems like Vodún offer to the hegemonic narratives Western science presents as fact. I neither suggest Western science is wrong nor suggest Western science has become invalid. To the contrary, the data from this ritual indicate Western science remains incomplete so long as African forms of knowing and African knowledge systems remain marginalized in scientific research. Moreover, the case of Adéléké's hen stands out as epistemologically relevant because it informs the client's knowledge. The event instructs the client on how matter can change and which agents achieve those effects.

Ritualization, a theory Catherine Bell (1992) advanced in religious studies, becomes an incomplete framework when it is applied to rituals that produce material transpositions Western science cannot explain. Bell (1992, 74) defines ritualization as "a matter of various culturally specific strategies for setting some activities off from others, for creating and privileging a qualitative distinction between the 'sacred' and the 'profane,' and for ascribing such distinctions to realities thought to transcend the powers of human actors." Adéléké's bloodless hen, on the other hand, indicates Vodún rituals distinguish scientific acts from nonscientific acts. Remember, spirits in Vodún may be perceived as particle-like entities that bond with the acɛ in other substances to form predictable changes in material states. The bloodless chicken points to the merging of agentic matter. The objects used in the ritual to supplicate Adéléké each play a part in producing the change in the hen's ontological condition. The acɛ in these items converge. Moreover, the specialized acɛ Mobolaji possesses combines with the vital force in the ritual's ingredients to activate Adélékè. Vodún rituals are culturally specific, but one should remember the observable data points in this case study constitute a critique of the conclusions Western science presents. Whereas Western scientific methods are considered the standard for testing and verifying an observation, Vodún science proves Western thinking has not grasped all there is to know about material states. An epistemological collaboration between Western science and Vodún science necessitates reciprocal respect between both knowledges. Vodún science offers insightful commentary on the human constitution and the human body's situatedness in the world. Vodún science proposes humans consist of the same agentic matter comprising natural and synthetic objects. Acε, or the vital principle in all things, is something integral to yet beyond the nanoparticles at the core of every atom (e.g., quarks, leptons, and bosons). The elements constituting human flesh share the same agentic capacity as the elements in all other substances. To be human is to be imbricated in limitless interconnection. Humans are porous: we contain vital energy, and we are, by extension, one type of technology through which this vital energy acts on the world.

Effectually, ritual generates embodied knowledge, and the data points collected experientially offer the observer new conclusions. First, the human dimension and the more-than-human dimension are enfolded domains such that humans and spirits operate in the same social and spatiotemporal location. Second, the transposition of matter through Vodún rituals involves scientific principles applicable to the immediate material environment contextualizing human bodies. Third, human bodies are catalytic instruments in Vodún science. Whether spitting acε to expedite a vodún's response or using one's hands to combine substances to make an empowered object, human bodies remain integral to scientific processes in Vodún. Reinterpreting the body is an important first step to reinterpreting ritual.

CASE STUDY #2: A HEN FOR AIDOHOUEDO

In 2008, I visited Temple Guda Fli Gbé at the Bankole family's compound in Agata, just outside Porto-Novo. The family's youngest child, Hounon Ogundipo, is the temple's priest. Hounon Ogundipo conducted a ritual offering to Aidohouedo, the rainbow serpent deity associated with marine spirits. It was a simple, diurnal offering with very few mechanics. The *hounon*'s father, a few adepts, and I knelt on the temple's mosaic floor while Hounon Ogundipo laid out a short, blue Islamic prayer mat and lit three white candles. He secured the candles to the floor by standing each one in a small pool of melted wax.

Afterward, the priest held the hen upside down in the air with his right hand and slowly began to sing a song to Aidohouedo. The hen clucked and fluttered as we joined him in song. Hounon Ogundipo held a knife in his left hand, but he had not yet used it. He held the chicken in the air and shook it gently as he sang. With each passing lyric, the chicken resisted less and, eventually, its wings stopped flapping. As we concluded the song in a whisper, I noticed the chicken did not hold up its head when Hounon Ogundipo brought it toward the ground. The bird lay limp in his hands. Only at this point did he bring the knife to the fowl's larynx. But there was no need to fret over the animal's suffering. When the knife finally opened the hen's body, the bird's flesh was dry. There was no blood. The knife came out clean.

A materialist approach to religion, as developed by Manuel A. Vásquez (2011), requires methodological agnosticism. Methodological agnosticism enables anthropologists and scholars of religion to avoid the questions of whether spirits are ontologically real and focus instead on the material effects spirits have within communities in specific spaces at particular times. A scholar interested in the materiality of religion should pursue the psychological, biological, environmental, sociocultural, and historical effects mobilizing practices described as religious.[10] Vásquez's approach, unfortunately, prohibits scholars from reckoning with the scientific components within African indigenous religions. Vodún knowledge and Vodún forms of knowing attribute the blood's disappearance to Aidohouedo, a rainbow serpent of prosperity associated with the Mami Wata. In this knowledge system, however, the vodun are more than spirits. The entity known as Aidohouedo constitutes a particular acε that interacts with the priest's acε to transpose matter. In Vodún, a practitioner will at times undergo a specific ritual designed to ensure a particular vodun will accept offerings and commands from the practitioner's hand. In the case of Aidohouedo's hen, the vodún clearly agrees to transform the blood of the chicken in Hounon Ogundipo's hands. There may be a complementary relationship between the acε in the vodún, the acε in the priest's hand, and the acε on the priest's tongue. Note that Hounon Ogundipo prayed and sang a song to this particular divinity prior to the hen's transformation. Speech acts, thus, constitute another key component in the mechanics of Vodún science.

A striking difference between the case of Adéléké's hen and Aidohouedo's hen is the vodún in the former case study has a body. Adéléké's calabash serves as a container for the invisible vibration and functions as the device through which Adéléké participates in transactions with humans. Aidohouedo, on the other hand, does not become manifest in a material form visible to the eye or accessible to the priest's hands. The serpent deity does not use a device to transpose matter. As argued above, human bodies catalyze the transposition of matter in Vodún. Aidohouedo's invisibility and immateriality, however, indicates the vodún are chemically active forces despite their intangibility. A vodún-as-vibration consists of particles of acɛ that participate in molecular interactions with matter. This is the chemical activity Aidohouedo participates in to transpose the chicken's blood. Aidohouedo, as a wavelike particle, behaves like a force; it enacts a push or pull on another object. The vodún's force becomes ascertainable through the blood's disappearance. Again, how a song, a prayer, and candlelight result in the removal of a hen's blood remains unclear. It is the challenge for material studies in Vodún.

Scholars would do well to pursue Vodún as a science in and of itself rather than as a *metaphor* for science. Douglas Falen's (2018) research on *aze*, or witchcraft, in Benin illuminates the scientific metaphors Beninese use to describe good and bad aze. Falen (2018, 61) notes, "Beninese equate Western technological inventions with African mystical powers, giving rise to informants' explicit analogies between 'white people's witchcraft' and 'African science.'" Alas, "Beninese do not necessarily equate science solely with benevolent practical technology, because they conceive of both science and *aze* as tools or instruments of power that are guided by the moral disposition of those who wield them rather than by an inherent quality in the tool" (187). Falen's conclusions confirm Beninese frequently use Western technology as a metaphor for African concepts of power. Nonetheless, these metaphorical references should not lead scholars to omit empirical data illustrating Vodún science. Falen states he cannot prove whether people who claim to be victims of witchcraft have suffered consequences wrought via supernatural powers (101–102). Aidohouedo's bloodless chicken and Adéléké's bloodless hen, in contrast, are observable data points that confirm Vodún rituals transform matter through methods unknown to Western science; neither chemistry, physics, nor biology explain how these transformations occur. "African science" is not merely a euphemism; the transposition of matter substantiates Vodún's role as a scientific epistemological category. Visual perception of the bloodless chicken affords a reinterpretation of Falen's data: Beninese may frequently explain *African scientific observations* to Westerners in Western technological terms. As such, "electrical currents, vibrations, waves, and signals" may not be concepts belonging only to Western societies (63). New directions in Vodún studies should continue exploring African indigenous frameworks that explain the concepts at the core of empirical—not metaphorical—African science.

CONCLUSION

The evidence in these case studies indicates a need for another epistemology, another record and rubric for encounters with the material world. The science behind the transformation of matter in Vodún is a necessary direction for future studies on materiality in African religions. Indigenous knowledge within Vodún will provide the concepts researchers need when reporting on Vodún as a science. Furthermore, the physic(s)ality of Vodún knowledge, the learning about the (mis)behavior of matter through one's sensorium, should direct new theoretical engagements with materiality in Vodún. Of course, to proceed with such a research plan would ask scholars to engage the biases undergirding their research proposals, methodologies, and arguments. A new boldness reflective of Vodún's audacity to endure, its fluid embrace of coexisting worldviews, and its resistance against anti-Black bias must imbue new research on materiality in Vodun.

NOTES

1. I reference multiple Vodún epistemologies because the knowledge in Vodún changes depending on its cultural and temporal location. Similar to the perpetual evolution in Vodún iconography Dana Rush (2013) describes as the religion's "unfinished" quality, I recognize Vodún knowledge continually expands as Vodún practitioners glean new understandings from personal experiences and from interactions with other cultures.

2. Webb Keane has written extensively about *ethical affordances*, and he has contributed much literature along the ethical turn in anthropology. The ethics involved in the case studies I examine will require future exploration. While Keane's (2016, 27) writings directed me toward Gibson's theories, it is clear these instances about bloodless chickens concern something very different from the "aspects of people's experiences and perceptions that they might draw on in the process of making ethical evaluations and decisions, whether consciously or not." For more on ethical affordances, see Keane 2014; 2018.

3. All the consultants' names and the name of the temple where I collected the second case study are pseudonyms.

4. Adéléké has both male and female manifestations. Mobolaji works with both, but this particular ritual involved only the female Adéléké.

5. The term *acɛ* in Vodún is the same as *ase* in Yoruba. Both terms refer to power, vital force, empowered speech, and an animating force, among other things.

6. As with most Vodún offerings, the participants in this ritual plucked, cleaned, and cooked the chicken afterward. They shared the meal as part of the process of sharing the offering with the spirit, Adéléké.

7. I still could not see its contents because they were covered by fabric.

8. Parsing these ideas offers a new comment on whether shrines are spaces or bodies. Whereas Eric Montgomery and Christian Vannier (2017) use "shrine" to describe the spaces where Vodún rituals and practices happen, Timothy Landry (2016) argues that the word should only apply to the material forms that operate as a spirit's body. Judy Rosenthal (2005) has used the term to describe spaces, the bodies of spirits, and the bodies of women who experience possession trance.

9. In this way, new materialism becomes useful for thinking about agency and matter in Vodún. New materialism, like Vodún, displaces anthropocentric perspectives on agency and recognizes all things—living and nonliving—have a force and a capacity to act upon, within, through, and against entities in the world (Alaimo 2008; Bennett 2009; Coole and Frost 2010).

10. Vasquez (2011, 8) argues that scholars of religion should treat "religion as the open-ended product of the discursive and nondiscursive practices of embodied individuals, that is, individuals who exist in particular times and spaces. These individuals are embedded in nature and culture, and drawing from and conditioned by their ecological, biological, psychological, and sociocultural resources, they construct multiple identities and practices, some of which come to be designated, often through contestation, as religious at particular junctures."

REFERENCES

Abiodun, Rowland. 1994. "Understanding Yoruba Art and Aesthetics." *African Arts* 27 (3): 68–78.

Agossou, Jacob Medewale. 1972. *Gbɛtɔ Et Gbedótó = L'homme Et Le Dieu Créateur Selon Les Sud-Dahoméens : De La Dialectique De Participation Vitale à Une Théologie Anthropocentrique*. Paris: Beauchesne.

Alaimo, Stacy. 2008. "Trans-Corporeal Feminisms and the Ethical Space of Nature." In *Material Feminisms*, edited by Stacy Alaimo and Susan Heckman, 237–264. Bloomington: Indiana University Press.

Apter, Andrew. 2007. *Beyond Words: Discourse and Critical Agency in Africa*. Chicago: University of Chicago Press.

———. 2017. "Ethnographic X-Files and Holbraad's Double-Bind: Reflections on an Ontological Turn of Events." *HAU: Journal of Ethnographic Theory* 7 (1): 287–302.

Bell, Catherine. 1992. *Ritual Theory, Ritual Practice*. New York: Oxford University Press.

———. 1997. *Ritual: Perspectives and Dimensions*. New York: Oxford University Press.

Bennett, Jane. 2009. *Vibrant Matter: A Political Ecology of Things*. Durham, NC: Duke University Press.

———. 2010. "A Vitalist Stopover on the Way to a New Materialism." In *New Materialisms: Ontology, Agency, and Politics*, edited by Diana Coole and Samantha Frost, 47–69. Durham, NC: Duke University Press.
Brivio, Alessandra. 2018. "Gorovodu: The Genesis of a 'Hausa Vodún.'" *Journal of West African History* 4 (1): 1–26.
Castro, Eduardo Viveiros de. 2013. "The Relative Native." Translated by Julia Sauma and Martin Holbraad. *HAU: Journal of Ethnographic Theory* 3 (3): 473–502.
———. 2015. *The Relative Native: Essays on Indigenous Conceptual Worlds*. Chicago: Hau Books.
Claffey, Patrick. 2007. *Christian Churches in Dahomey Benin: A Study of Their Sociopolitical Role*. Leiden, Netherlands: Brill.
Coole, Diana. 2005. "Rethinking Agency: A Phenomenological Approach to Embodiment and Agentic Capacities." *Political Studies* 53 (1): 124–142.
Coole, Diana, and Samantha Frost, eds. 2010. *New Materialisms: Ontology, Agency, and Politics*. Durham, NC: Duke University Press.
Drewal, Henry John. 1988. "Performing the Other: Mami Wata Worship in Africa." *TDR* 32 (2): 160–185.
———. 1996. "Mami Wata Shrines: Exotica and the Construction of Self." In *African Material Culture*, edited by Mary Jo Arnoldi and Kris L. Hardin, 308–333. Bloomington: Indiana University Press.
———. 2005. "Senses in Understandings of Art." *African Arts* 38 (2): 1–96.
Egonwa, Osa D. 2008. "The Mami-Wata Phenomenon: 'Old Wine in New Skin.'" In *Sacred Waters: Arts for Mami Wata and Other Divinities in Africa and the Diaspora*, edited by Henry John Drewal, 217–227. Bloomington: Indiana University Press.
Ellis, Stephen, and Gerrie ter Haar. 2004. *Worlds of Power: Religious Thought and Political Practice in Africa*. New York: Oxford University Press.
Falen, Douglas J. 2016. "Vodún, Spiritual Insecurity, and Religious Importation in Benin." *Journal of Religion in Africa* 46 (4): 453–483. https://proxy.library.upenn.edu:2101/10.1163/15700666-12341195.
———. 2018. *African Science: Witchcraft, Vodún, and Healing in Southern Benin*. Madison: University of Wisconsin Press.
Gibson, James J. "The Theory of Affordances (1979)." In *The People, Place, and Space Reader*, edited by Jen Jack Giesking and William Mangold with Cindi Katz, Setha Low, and Susan Saegert, 56–60. London: Routledge, 2014.
Grimes, Ronald L. 2014. "Appendix 15: Major Claims of *The Craft of Ritual Studies*." In *The Craft of Ritual Studies*, 391. New York: Oxford University Press.
Henare, Amiria J. M., Martin Holbraad, and Sari Wastell, eds. 2007. *Thinking through Things: Theorising Artefacts Ethnographically*. London: Routledge.
Holbraad, Martin. 2017. *The Ontological Turn: An Anthropological Exposition*. Cambridge: Cambridge University Press.

Hountondji, Paulin J. 2009. "Knowledge of Africa, Knowledge by Africans: Two Perspectives on African Studies." *RCCS Annual Review*, no. 1, 121–131. Accessed December 1, 2018. http://journals.openedition.org/rccsar/174.

Keane, Webb. 2014. "Affordances and Reflexivity in Ethical Life: An Ethnographic Stance." *Anthropological Theory* 14 (1): 3–26.

———. 2016. *Ethical Life: Its Natural and Social Histories*. Princeton, NJ: Princeton University Press.

———. 2018. "Perspectives on Affordances, or the Anthropologically Real." *HAU: Journal of Ethnographic Theory* 8 (1/2): 27–38.

Kendi, Ibram X. 2017. *Stamped from the Beginning: The Definitive History of Racist Ideas in America*. New York: Random House.

Kohn, Eduardo. 2013. *How Forests Think: Toward an Anthropology beyond the Human*. Berkeley: University of California Press.

Kossou, Basile Toussaint. 1983. *SE et GBE: dynamique de l'existence chez les Fon*. Paris: Pensée Universelle.

Landry, Timothy R. 2016. "Incarnating Spirits, Composing Shrines, and Cooking Divine Power in Vodún." *Material Religion* 12 (1): 50–73. https://doi.org/10.1080/17432200.2015.1120086.

Montgomery, Eric J., and Christian Vannier. 2017. *An Ethnography of a Vodu Shrine in Southern Togo: Of Spirit, Slave, and Sea*. London: Brill.

Rosenthal, Judy. 2005. "Foreign Spirits inside the Family." In *Women on the Verge of Home*, edited by Bilinda Straight, 149–174. Albany: State University of New York Press.

———. 2010. "Vodu Angels of History: Ghana, Togo, Benin." In *Activating the Past: History and Memory in the Black Atlantic World*, edited by Andrew Apter and Lauren Derby, 157–184. Cambridge: Cambridge Scholars.

Rush, Dana. 1999. "Eternal Potential: Chromolithographs in Vodúnland." *African Arts* 32 (4): 61. http://www.jstor.org/stable/3337669.

———. 2008. "The Idea of 'India' in West African Vodún Art and Thought." In *India in Africa, Africa in India: Indian Ocean Cosmopolitanisms*, edited by John C. Hawley, 149–180. Bloomington: Indiana University Press.

———. 2013. *Vodún in Coastal Bénin: Unfinished, Open-Ended, Global*. Nashville: Vanderbilt University Press.

Soothill, Jane E. 2007. *Gender, Social Change, and Spiritual Power: Charismatic Christianity in Ghana*. Leiden, Netherlands: Brill.

Sousa Santos, Bonaventura de. 2014. *Epistemologies of the South: Justice against Epistemicide*. Boulder, CO: Paradigm.

Tall, Emmanuelle Kadya. "On representation and power: portrait of a vodún leader in present-day Benin." *Africa: The Journal of the International African Institute*, vol. 84, 2014, pp. 246–268. Project MUSE, muse.jhu.edu/article/551451.

"The Uncertainty Principle." 2016. *Stanford Encyclopedia of Philosophy*. Accessed April 8, 2018. https://plato.stanford.edu/entries/qt-uncertainty/#InteHeisUnceRela.

Turner, Edith. B. 1993. "The Reality of Spirits: A Tabooed or Permitted Field of Study?" *Anthropology of Consciousness*, no. 4, 9–12. https://proxy.library.upenn.edu:2101/10.1525/ac.1993.4.1.9.

Vásquez, Manuel A. 2011. *More than Belief: A Materialist Theory of Religion*. New York: Oxford University Press.

Welsch, Robert L. 2018. "ritual." In *A Dictionary of Cultural Anthropology*. Oxford: Oxford University Press. Accessed December 1, 2018. http://proxy.library.upenn.edu:2400/view/10.1093/acref/9780191836688.001.0001/acref-9780191836688-e-316.

VENISE N. ADJIBODOU is an independent scholar with a PhD from the University of Pennsylvania. She is a Diversity, Equity, and Inclusion practitioner and a learning and development specialist.

NINE

VODOU SKINS

Making Bodily Surfaces Social in Haitian Vodou Infant Care

Alissa Jordan

INTRODUCTION

In Sou Lapwen, the mattress that I sleep on bows down in the center. Those who have mattresses here have mattresses that bow down like this, pulling occupants inward. So, the night passes. People roll to center and then again moving away from each other in the heat. It is a strange dance given to the stars that shine through the holes in the *tòl* (corrugated metal) roof. But our faces, hands, and limbs are pressed into bedsheets that are clean and fresh smelling—like all fabric, rigorously, fastidiously clean. Our bodies like the sheets are freshly washed, and on Tuesdays the scent of perfume wafts in from Manbo (priestess) Nel's bed, where she sleeps alone, mandated by her marriage to the lwa (spirits). Using the perfume, she makes the house pleasant, calling out to the other residents of Sou Lapwen, those spirits who are invisible, busily working, but eager for tenderness.

The mattresses carry all these motions: the taking on and off of sheets, the bodies rolling, the faces pressed against the surfaces, the sweat-filled dreams, the urine where babies have slept and been moved and cradled and rocked back to sleep. When we change the covers, we embarrassingly see the lines, the marks, the stains of bodies over the years. It offers up the memory of sleeping flesh.

The pillows are repositories of past motions and movements, those now forgotten but through which once before we measured out our lives. They are stuffed with old clothes, which in their great age have become light, soft, and as fragile as tissue paper. When the seam on a side rips, colors and patterns of past years peek out: sections of cotton and silky thread that have been finished by time, thinned out by the bodies that wore them, the sun that beat on them while hanging to dry, the hands that pulled and pushed the soap through their fibers.

Between the mattress and the box frame, held up by crumbling concrete blocks, we store the nicest pieces of our clothing: the dresses, the funeral clothing, the buttoned shirts and trousers and sweaters, all carefully folded on the seams so that after several months they will still be flat from the weight of our bodies and still smell freshly of the wash when they were placed. Where the mattress dips downward, we layer clothing in greater quantity to try and even out the surface. At first it will work. It will fill in the spots where the mattress bows, and we will fall into each other less, until new patterns of our motions appear.

The surface of the world is shaped by traces of the living and here, the dead and gone, the living and gone, and the dead and here. The world is filled with shadows both of friends and enemies living beside us. On and on these things and these traces and these persons *go*, incorporating one another and sinking in, getting lost in one another, going into and under the mattresses we sleep on.

***

With its philosophical attention to permutations of flesh and feeling, Haitian Vodou makes important connections between the skin that people are in and their (many) selves. In the process of becoming a person in Haitian Vodou, one undergoes a number of collaborative projects that socialize the surfaces of bodies. Many of these activities are ostensibly used to protect and shore bodies up against emotions, energies, and other risks that can invade them. These practices also have the effect of creating skins, surfaces, and bodies themselves as vital social sites where care (and likewise neglect) is communicated and received.

Alma Gottlieb (2000, 2015), working with Beng infants and caretakers in Cote d'Ivoire, critically addressed infancy as key to understanding processes of bodily enculturation, embodiment, and habit in Beng religious thought. Gottlieb (2000) argued that infants and caregivers had much to teach ethnographers about social worlds, about human places within them, and about the way that new beings become human. Across many sites in the Afro-Atlantic, the period between conception and the end of early childhood is a ritually intense period that includes a condensed panoply of naming practices, ecological introductions, security measures, daily bodily care, and much more. This chapter explores the important social projects of cleansing, shaping, and healing skin in Haitian Vodou, which families and communities use from infancy onward to shape themselves and one another into vibrant, social, thriving members of a society.

In Haitian folk medicine, bodies are permeable and extendable. They connect humans to one another as well as nonhuman beings, such as the lwa, materials, energies, forces, and climates. Nixon Cleophat (this volume) identifies this permeability and interconnectedness as part of Haitian Vodou's liberatory ecotheology, which posits that the fates of both human and nonhuman beings are deeply intertwined. Human waists, backs, and wombs can open and close, heads can heat up or cool down, breast milk can be either nourishing or toxic, and blood can be fine or go bad (Farmer 1988; Laguerre 1987; Murray and Álvarez 1979). Bodies, in short, are not the unified and stable entities imagined by the rugged individualism of neoliberalism but are shifting biosocial creations that are tightly knit out of the relations between persons, places, things, environments, beings, times, histories, and dreams. As J. Lorand Matory (2009) argues, people who practice and follow Afro-Creole religions in the African diaspora have long explored selfhood as something that is multiple, transnational, and relational—not individuals but "the many." Followers of these religions have engaged in a complex, lived theorization of human identity and physical being as something that is multisited, multinational, and multidimensional (Matory 2009). "The many" is not some abstracted theorization of humankind's place in the cosmos but an everyday phenomenological theorization of human beings as shared selves in rich, multilocal, and transnational environs.

In this chapter, I treat infancy as a critical period where babies and caregivers learn both to be interconnected and to instill this interconnectedness into future generations. I specifically explore how collective practices of bathing, of satiating hunger, and of healing illness are used to shape infants (and others) into social beings whose bodies and selves are mutually entangled with those of their families.

ON INFANCY IN SOU LAPWEN

Sou Lapwen is a valley town in the arrondissement of Arcahaie, Haiti, nestled at the base of a mountain. It is a town where small Evangelical churches pop up alongside brightly colored Haitian Vodou *peristils* (center pole of shrine), where many residents refer to themselves as *poko konveti* (not yet converted). In Sou Lapwen, where there are no more than five hundred residents, households are organized by *lakou* (family courtyard), with extended families sharing a cooking pot. In Sou Lapwen, health and well-being can be particularly elusive goals, and this is especially true for infants and children. In a survey I conducted with residents between 2013 and 2014, families reported that 24 percent of the children who were born living to them died within the first six years. Those who survived these harrowing odds—that is, the other 76 percent of children—bore the marks of the fights their families and communities waged against death. The evidence of these battles was laid out in scars, in the color and texture of hair, and in the complex emotional tangles left in a body that survived a world that one's sibling could not.

So common, so repetitive are these battles against infant illness and disease that early childhood itself could be characterized as the rhythm created by the diagnosis, interventions, healings, and care used to keep babies alive. That rhythm, like the rhythm of sleep, is tapped out on skin from other skin, leaving its marks on surfaces all over the world. All this is preface to say that the children who grew up in my midst were not well during their infancy and toddler years. Even the ones I thought of as healthy, like Waglet, strong and willful and fat, have mothers like Ninev, who can recount for you the waxing and waning of his life-force during those first years. Ninev can remind you how illness and death came for her child, many times, but she and her family and all the lwa managed to hold him tight to this world. Though the skill of the lwa, the healings, and the manbo are unquestioned, the possibility of things having gone otherwise haunts her dreams still.

BODILY ATTENTIONS

When I was living in the Nel's lakou, I sometimes shared the same room with Ninev, and I would hear her fretting about Waglet's illnesses late into the night, long after he was asleep. Not speaking openly about it, keeping her words few, and chewing on her bottom lip, she would say, "Demenn nap fe yon te pou li" (Tomorrow, we will make tea for him) or "Demenn nap rasanble bagay pou li" (Tomorrow, we will assemble things for a remedy for him), all the late nights filled with the beat of "Demen … demen … demen" (tomorrow) on her frowning lips. I heard her voice, you see, but I didn't *listen* to it yet. Instead, I reassured myself, time after time: "But he is well. Waglet is fine, running around and energetic and strong." Hearing the calculating stillness of her thinking broken apart by suddenly spoken plans for the next day, I would brood over the incongruency of our experiences of "Fo" (Waglet). In those late-night sessions, I came to what I thought at first was an important, even enlightening realization: that wellness itself was suspicious for infants, that health itself is regarded with great unease for survivors. Soon I learned that this so-called realization would only ever strike an outsider as compelling. It held little truth and even less insight. For, time after time, Ninev's late-night vigils were followed—sometimes within hours, sometimes by a day, by the more obvious signs of illness that I knew how to recognize, illness that had been brewing all along.

I came to understand that the wellness I seemed to be perceiving was a dangerous mirage that could trick the untrained eye. Ninev like so many other of her women peers in Sou Lapwen had ways of reading the body, the color of children's eyes, the swell of their stomachs, long before the illness rose to the obvious surface of life. Time after time, a Waglet that had been well became, within five hours, twelve hours, eighteen hours, a Waglet drowning in the sweat of a fever, a Waglet covered in swollen, terrible blisters, a Waglet that suddenly stopped playing or eating. The biomedical model I took with me had trained me to read Ninev's late-night pronouncements of fear as superstitious and uninformed. It trained me to stop listening if I didn't see what she was talking about. So I would say to her: "Stop listening to that voice that tells you he is unwell. He is fine." And I slowly learned my lesson. She was wise enough to ignore me entirely. But I still feel the cold pangs of having told her to do otherwise.

The knowledge Ninev had built over a lifetime of being in a body, of observing bodies, of attending to the way that risks appear in bodies, was an expertise that the biomedical model missed entirely. Gradually, I learned to accept that the signs of illness and well-being buried in Waglet's flesh were in a language I could not read. Though clinics, doctors, and this young anthropologist misread it entirely, the lwa understood the language of Waglet's skin, and so too were Ninev, her mother, her aunts, and her cousins fluent in its suggestions, insinuations, and insistencies. Thus, my story of studying bodily care in Haiti is a story of releasing the assumptions I had about what bodies look like when they are well, about when illnesses begin and when they end, and about the perceptions and actions that make healing possible.

BATHS THAT SOCIALIZE SKIN

In Haitian Vodou, bodies themselves are permeable to one another, and in an important sense, they are shared. Emotions, relationships, experiences, conditions, and insecurities move through people and families, passing through skin, blood, and bone and affecting these on their way through (Caple James 2008; Farmer 1988). In this physiological system, illness as well as medicine can be absorbed by bodies in myriad ways, one critical way being through the surface of the skin. To avoid unwanted intrusions, to allow for smooth socializing, and to keep bodies healthy, skins and all manner of other surfaces must be rigorously maintained. Open dirt yards are fastidiously swept of leaves, walls are wiped down, and bodies are bathed. If infants are healthy, they are bathed daily, often twice or three times. When they are unhealthy or ill, these baths include ritual preparations of herbs and water that absorb medicine through the skin and prime the body for further healing.

Kras is the general residue that bodies are known to excrete in Haiti: the dead, dry, grayish skin cells that appear when you rub your hands together vigorously; the dandruff on your scalp; the oily, thick black coating on your skin that accumulates around your neck, collarbone, and upper backs; the smegma in the folds of labia or tucked within the foreskin of a penis; the discharge that can be squeezed out of the nipples of both men and women. The mark of a neglected child is an accumulation of kras, in contrast to an accumulation of dirt, soil, mud, and other dirty substances. Bathing is the joyful and healing task that caretakers teach to infants that rids bodies of kras. The same word, *benye* (to bathe), is used for routine body washing, summer beach days, or swimming in any body of water. Twice per day (at least), people firmly root themselves in the present moment as they touch, clean, manicure, and immerse their bodies in fresh, beautiful water.

FELDA'S BATH

When Fedna prepares Felda for a bath, she first draws the water from the local canal, brings it back to her house, and pours it into the bathing basin to leave in the sun. Clean water is not called "clean" or "good," it is called "beautiful," with a long drawn-out vowel: *dlo a bèl, lanmè a bèl* (the water is beautiful, the ocean is beautiful). On days that the canal water is dirty on account of rain, it is not simply an inconvenience; it is a disappointment that she and others refuse to bear. Luckily, a split leaf of cactus thrown into the water bucket will turn the water crystal clear. The gel within this single leaf attracts all the dirt and sediment from the water, grabbing it to itself and turning the water beautiful within twenty minutes. (This why so many cacti in town are quite poor specimens in the rainy season, with only one or two leaves left.)

In Felda's case, the bucket of water is emptied into a bright pink bathing tub that she enjoys immensely. This pink tub is special; it was a gift from Felda's father, and it is prettier than the bathing basins nearly everyone else uses, which are large metal dishes used for laundry (though the metal basins heat up water much better). Once the water is at least lukewarm, Fedna takes off the child's clothes and then soaps up a small cloth or loofah with bar soap. If the day is

Figure 9.1. Felda gets a bath.

particularly hot, she pulls the tub to the shade. Before placing Felda within the water, she holds her and drips water from the basin onto her belly to get her used to the temperature and feel. Felda usually kicks and smiles at this point, excited to get into the water. Then, Fedna places her in the tub, balancing her upright, so she leans over her front legs and doesn't look too wobbly. If she isn't sick or recovering from sickness, Fedna pours water over her head and chest as well as the rest of her body. If she is sick, she cleans her chest and head carefully with a rag that is wet, avoiding pouring water on these areas.

As Fedna gently spills water over Felda's body, she delights in it and usually laughs. Some babies, especially the youngest ones, fuss and sob when the water hits their skin, but caretakers continue assuring them it is all right, furrowing their brows sympathetically, and cleaning them in spite of the protest (one of the few times families or other caretakers carry on in the face of an angry baby).

After wetting Felda, her mother pulls out the soapy cloth and vigorously massages it in circular motions across their backs. This often throws Felda's balance off; her mother is prepared with her other arm, smartly planted on the bottom of the washing basin in front of Felda. When Fedna was younger and Felda was *tou nèf* (very new, very young; e.g., under five months of age), she held her hand open in front of Felda's chest, so she could more directly redirect her when she fell forward. This way, Fedna and other caretakers teach children to find their balance themselves, with guidance and redirection should they fall forward too far.

Moving from the back to the chest and then the arms, Fedna continues rubbing Felda with the towel while squeezing soap through it, making a delightful squeaking noise that women are the proud masters of. In this way, she progresses in circular motions across her body. She applies more pressure and leans in to check her work, in areas where kras accumulates the most: necks, upper backs, folds of skin on bellies, underarms, wrist folds, behind ears, between the legs, and between fingers and toes. She does each of these areas multiple times before moving on to the next. Finally, Felda is left to play a bit, should she so desire, or taken out if she has had enough of the bath. When Fedna takes her out, she lays her across her lap facing up, checking to see if Felda is truly clean. She rubs key points on Felda's skin with her fingers to ensure that no kras is lifted up and that she has done a good enough job. If no kras turns up, Fedna moves on to other realms of the body, checking Felda's eyes, cleaning out her nostrils, the sides of their mouth, perhaps retouching the areas behind their ears. Then Fedna moves on to powder Felda with sweet-scented clouds of white baby powder from a dish with a soft and fluffy poof. She especially focuses the powder on Felda's neck and her chest, her upper back, behind her ears, and between her legs.

Fedna continues to bathe Felda daily like this until she reaches two and a half years old, when she refuses to bathe in the small tub any longer. She, like many babies of her age, now wants to stand with her mother and her other caregivers who clean themselves standing up, emptying water onto themselves with cups, bending down to guide her through the process.[1] When children reach four or five and become more independent, they are given more freedom for the midday bath and are allowed to decide when and how to do it.[2] Usually this means they start bathing with older children, who run to the shallow parts of the canal in large groups and help the younger ones wash. Children of four or five can often be seen plodding along the white, dusty stone path with a towel and a tin can holding soap and a rag, yelling for the others who have run ahead of them. When these newly independent children return home, caretakers check to see how well they have bathed and scold those who are dirty (along with their siblings, who were expected to oversee the process).

When a child has gone too long without cleaning themselves during the day, or if they have accumulated kras due to some activity or mishap, they are usually derided in conversation but not directly spoken to. "Ou wè salòp sa?" (Do you see that slob?) Evelyn will jokingly say to me about her grandson, who is fully in hearing distance. "Ou wè kras sou li? Pa manyen l. Kòchon." (You see that filth on him? Don't touch him. Pig.) These comments made to other adults in earshot of children are intended to socially correct their habits, often sending embarrassed children back home for another round of bathing.

THE ETHNOGRAPHER LEARNS HOW TO BATHE

Bathing for other residents of Sou Lapwen is as fastidious as it is for children. Adults bathe at least twice a day (midday and evening) and sometimes thrice a day (in the morning as well), in addition to washing their faces, necks, and forearms first thing upon waking. If it is possible due to schedules, young women will try to bathe together for the longer, more leisurely midday bath, which happens during the hottest part of the day. With a cup, I would bathe myself with the other women, pouring water and then soaping up a loofah or handkerchief or the underwear we have worn. As a newcomer, and someone who had a very different approach to bathing (both in frequency and style), I had to be taught all the fundamentals of proper bathing. After watching me bathe in the haphazard way I had used my whole life, Ninev's cousin Maya was one of the first to tell me I needed to attend to my body more methodically. She showed me to focus on cleansing my forehead, hands, chest, inner and outer elbows, wrists, knees, ankles, hips, and bottom of the spine, which I was told to scrub very well. These sites are not only places where kras is known to accumulate but, relatedly, are sites of other kinds of bodily traffic. These locations are tended to in baptism, often with healing oils or ointments, in healing rites, in protective remedies, and in postmortem rituals.

Treating me like a child, Maya would rub my wrists and neck and scold me when I showed up with too much sweat at her house. The first time she said it, I thought her scold was a general comment. She extended her pointer finger, swiped at my neck, and presented it to me: "Ou we?" (You see?) she said. "Wi, pousye!" (Yes, dust!) I said, though I couldn't really see much of anything, and I gestured to the road. "Non, non," she chided, "Sa pa pousye. Se kras. Kras. Ou pa konn benyen." (No, no, that's not dust. That's kras. Kras. You don't bathe.) So I went back again, getting a little better each time.

In the final bath before bed, I would go to a walled-off section of earth with a bucket of water to bathe by myself. This last bath is often in the lakou and often alone, or at least only with children who come for a good dousing of water. It is not as social as the midday bath, though people still often talk to each other, shouting from their separate bathing spots. It is a necessary act that is much quicker, lasting no more than fifteen minutes, but it keeps the sheets clean, and it means the hot, tin-roofed room won't smell too quickly, and it means that the kras from my skin is fully washed away, so it doesn't rub onto someone else's body.

I soon realized that in spite of Maya's instructions, I was not washing well enough to the standards of my lakou. There was clearly something Maya hadn't told me. Ninev, her aunt Nel, and her goddaughter would chuckle a bit when I bathed with them in the confines of Nel's lakou. Then there were whispers. Then there were a few confusing but joking insults about my husband leaving me. I didn't make much of this until Nel confronted me about the issue one night, after the final bath of the day.

Nel began by explaining, as gently as she could, that although "ou fè kou ou ap benyen, men ou pap benyen *vre*" (although you are acting like you are bathing, you are not *really* bathing). Finally, Nel pulled an empty bucket over and sat upon it, fully clothed, while motioning as if she was cleaning her vagina with her hands, and I couldn't believe what I was saying. "Mwen konn lave l, wi!" (I wash that, of course!) I explained. But she shook her head, finally explaining, "Ou pran dlo ak de dwet ou, ou fouye yo andan, epi ou foubi tout andan, konprann?" (You take water with your two fingers, you push them up inside yourself, and you scrub all around, understand?) I couldn't believe it. "Douching?" I thought, "She wants me to douche?" I sat down on the edge of the mattress, held up by concrete blocks, and kicked a bit at the loose crumbles of concrete while explaining that I had never once put water up into my vagina or scrubbed the inside of my vagina in this way.

Nel was dead silent. I continued, speaking vaguely about how douching can increase the odds of infections and about how I was just fine and clean as I was. Nel continued to be silent. It was too dark to see if her cheeks went red, but she asked, "Ou pajanm te fè sa?" (You've never done that?) I shook my head. "Mwen pajanm fè sa." (I've never, ever done that.) And she looked a bit nauseated. This was how I learned of the kras that women and girls possess in their genitals (something men also possess, to a lesser degree) and the importance attached to appropriately cleaning them. She pleaded, "Fè l, ou dwe fè l." I responded firmly "Non," which led her to stare intently at me for a moment before leaving.

"Well," I thought, "so they'll make fun of me a bit for not doing it. I can take a joke." I expected that they would soon tire of the topic, but I was wrong. The problem kept escalating. By engaging with the family as an adoptive member of the courtyard, I had responsibilities. These responsibilities, furthermore, were not individualized; rather, my responsibility to my own body was in effect a responsibility to the bodies of others. Not a half day went by without Nel, Nanis, Ninev, or Gaen quizzically looking me over, offering me pointed comments and pleas to douche.

I approached these interventions by insisting, repeatedly, that I simply would not scrub the inside of my vagina, certainly not with the canal water. It could give me an infection, I explained to Nanis. Then I explained to Gaen how the female gynecologist that I saw in the United States spoke to me at length about the dangers of douching in her generation. Nonetheless, these protests fell on deaf ears. The kras and *dlo* (water) of the vagina, I learned, were bodily residues that were in the domain of basic hygiene and had nothing to do with doctors, gynecologists, or biomedicine. The fact that I had refused throughout my entire life to clean myself properly left them highly concerned for the state of my genital well-being, not to mention my sanity (given that poor hygiene was an important indication of mental illness in adults).

It occurred to me soon enough that their protests weren't simply about me and what I was doing but that they were also concerned, even frantic, about how this affected their perception of the lakou and their own cleanliness as a result. My lack of basic and decent hygiene was becoming not just a joke but a thorn in everyone's side. By not douching—regardless of the suitability of the available water sources—I was making the lakou, even the very bench I was sitting on, even the family I was a part of, dirtier than they had been before I arrived. And that was the final realization that shifted my thinking on the matter. My cleanliness, or lack thereof, was having real effects on how others were thinking about their bodies and about the lakou we were all a part of.

Still, I was determined not to do something that I was worried might sicken me, and I was too nervous about the state of water to trust even a half-hearted attempt. So I found a middle road. I decided to fake it. At night, before anyone else went to bed, I would slip into my room with a bucket, mimicking the sounds of skin and splashing water. At first, I found that Nel was indeed listening, and perhaps the others too, because she shouted cryptically through the wall: "Ou wè?" (You see (how much better it is)?) To which I splashed away and replied, "Wi!" Bodies may be social spaces, but there is also room for improvisation.

SHARING FOOD

Like practices of bathing, practices of eating and sharing food are deeply social ones. They are tied into the ways that bodies are expected to be nurtured by society, but also the ways we are expected to nurture our own bodies in order to care for society. Klejames was my first real lesson on food in Haiti, because he offered me the first lesson on food that challenged me in a deep way. I had already had a number of important interactions about *manje* (food) by the time little Klejames, a baby of three weeks old, came to the courtyard to live as Ninev's foster son. But all those lessons were the sort of lessons that are easy for ethnographers (and anyone, really) to accept: hot food is good for you, good food is a delight in life, you shouldn't make fun of the food someone offers you, and you shouldn't eat from the hands of someone you really don't trust. Klejames offered a different, more personal lesson about food: we eat together (even newborn babies).

Klejames came into the world in a less than ideal way, but certainly it was not one of the worst stories we knew of. He was born to an unwed Evangelical teenager from a neighboring town, who insisted that even with money or support, she and her parents would be unwilling to care for the baby, who would get them thrown out of their church. She was willing to keep in touch with afternoon visits two or three times a year, but that was it. She gave the baby to Ninev's cousin Carmelite, who could not take another infant on. So Carmelite brought Klejames and his mother to Ninev and Nel, who both spent all of three minutes deliberating over fostering him (whom they adopted a year later).

I bought a hefty load of formula as soon as it was clear the two-week old baby was going to be staying in Ninev's house. At first, everyone was eager for the milk. Even the adults ate it sprinkled in their porridge, and the young children ate it as powder on spoons the adults extended to them. However, after the first week, it became clear that no one wanted to use this formula as Klejames's only food source. Although he was still very small, Ninev, Gaen, and Ninev's children were passing him complex foods from their plates, including smashed beans and fermented rice.

Nel explained that as an orphan, Klejames had more complex needs for food. Orphans, she explained, should be fed strong, solid foods because if their mothers have already stopped breastfeeding, returning to milk-heavy diets would weaken or even kill the child as they had *gen tan pase sa* (already passed it; i.e., grown beyond it) and were coming to expect the comparably better nutrition of *bon manje* (good food). By giving newborns nutritious, home cooked food that the rest of the lakou would share (albeit in a different form), families seek to bulk up infants with something comparably more *fò* (strong) than breastmilk. Though it is seen as highly special and nutritious, and always fed to children for the first week or so after birth, breastmilk is also seen as lasting only a very short time in the body.

Adults and children fed Klejames as they fed the other infants; first, whoever held the dish would take a ceremonial bite from the infants' plate, making a show of how delicious the food is, and then begin feeding the infants while also offering food to hungry children nearby. Babies who fuss at this experience are playfully chided as *vizier* or *chich* (a cheap person) while caretakers continue apportioning food until everyone is as full as can be. The result of this practice is that infants come to understand and expect feeding to be a time of mutual care rather than an independent interaction with their caregiver. Furthermore, older infants and toddlers come to grasp bodily knowledge about hunger: that in any given situation, they are not the only ones who are hungry, and they are not the only ones who must be fed.

At three and a half months old, Klejames suffered his first serious illness. He was lazy and made less noise than normal; his eyes had a wincing look to them; he resisted being woken up. We applied *maskreti* (black castor) oil around the clock, blanketing his scalp and chest in a scented, oily film. He was getting shinier and shinier each time he was passed around the rooms of the lakou for a newer diagnosis or for new relatives, friends, and networks to be called in. His skin glowed and infused the air around him with a savory smell. Every time he drank formula, he had diarrhea. He cried, seemingly out of hunger, constantly. When offered food, he whipped his head back and forth to get away from the spoon or the nipple. The pattern seemed inalterable. I tried different brands to no avail. I escorted him on three different visits to doctors at three different clinics, which led to no help at all, just a (negative) HIV test and an inconclusive blood draw. Piles of soiled cloth diapers, soiled handkerchiefs, soiled pillowcases, and soiled blankets were stacked in the side of the lakou by laundry *kivets* (area), for Ninev was unable to keep up with washing them. He was going through ten a day. They couldn't be washed quickly enough to be replaced. He just alternated, bare-butt, on the laps of Ninev, Nanis, and Nel, and Felicie when she was around.

Even though formula didn't seem to be the root cause of the illness, it did encourage the worst of his symptoms—the vomiting, the diarrhea, and the fatigue. I kept buying formula, which was being passed to the other children without me knowing, as it was being phased out from his diet entirely. I saw some of it: how the formula was prepared and left to go bad, how other children were allowed more freedom in eating it. Clearly it wasn't working for him, so I tried to find food that would provide nutrition and which Ninev would be happy to share. At the same time, I was deeply concerned that the decision to not feed formula would have devastating consequences for Klejames, who was now in a state of constant sickness and whose body seemed to desperately need high-calorie nutrition. So I suggested not using milk-based formulas at all, instead finding a pharmacy in Arcahaie that had a package of soy formula for newborns. I stopped calling the formula *lèt* (milk) and now called it manje (food), thinking if I emphasized its nonmilk qualities, Ninev and Nel might be more inclined to it after the stomach upsets. The switch of formula and the change in language did not make a difference to the lakou or to Klejames. His low fever persisted, and his body broke out in awful boils again.

Figure 9.2. Ninev holds Klejames while Kafou extends his hand in greeting.

There was an important turning point one late afternoon, when Sidney, Ninev's nephew, stumbled into the house with a far-off look in his eyes. He scanned the lakou strangely. Nanis, from the back corner of Nel's house, saw him come in and dropped the pan she was washing as she shouted for Nathaima, her daughter. "Carry that chair, carry that chair for the lwa," Nanis shouted. Nanis ushered him slowly to the backyard, and on the way, he nodded salutes to Nathaima, Zhedd, Yvon, and Nel, who had been in the kitchen. He introduced himself as the lwa Kafou, greeted the lakou, and then asked to see Klejames (see fig. 9.2). He turned to the matter of his illness: "Sa se travay malfektè li ye . . . epi manje sa . . . manje sa, wi . . . manje sa pa bon pou li" (His illness is the work of a *malfektè* [sorcerer] . . . and food . . . *that food*. That food you are giving isn't good for the baby.) Nel inquired what food he was speaking of, with Ninev watching expectantly, and he responded, "Manje lèt . . . manje koule lèt la . . . li pap ka manje sa ankò si ou vle l geri. Pa bay li manje blanch menm." (The milky food . . . the food the color of milk. He won't improve if he eats any white food at all. Don't give him white food.)

Hearing this, my heart sank, and I felt hopeless. I knew how final the words of the lwa would be in the lakou, and I was still convinced this child of three months needed milk to grow strong and survive. I spoke out of turn, trying to plead with him, "Se pwa, wi, Mèt Kafou, e pa lèt, se pwa" (It's beans, Mèt Kafou, not milk, its beans.) The lwa twisted his face in scorn at the rudeness of my interruption. I went silent. Kafou looked at me with his eyes wide open as he swayed slightly back and forth: "Mwen deja di pa bay li, mwen di pa bay li, tande?" ("I already said not to give it to him, I said don't give it to him, do you hear?"). And that was the end of the formula debate. There were many remedies, with many lwa who attended, but no more milks. In spite of my fears, Klejames grew larger, and his eyes grew brighter each week, as he was tended to with teas, meaty broths, and local porridge mixed with fish and fat.

In the course of his struggles, commercial formula became entangled with the lwa of the crossroads, distant oungan (priests) from the mountains brought special onions to sweeten his mouth to food; dream messages with teas in them were brought to Nel, and diapers were soiled and cleansed of their watery contents until slowly but surely he began to improve (for a time). All of these actors and energies were put into figuring out how, when, and what Klejames needed to consume to survive his tumultuous infancy. His story is exceptional only in that it occurred in the courtyard of a manbo, but I have seen the same lwa visit other courtyards, asking after babies in the same way, across Sou Lapwen and the towns nearby. The lwa have much to say here, and they always have a good deal to say about food and babies.

An important lesson that they have taught me is that satiating hunger is not simply a biological act. Feelings of hunger and the satisfaction of hunger are deeply socialized in Haiti. Hunger is an emotion as palpable and externalized as anger, sadness, or fear.

Alta Mae Stevens (1995, 78), in an important study on the symbolism of food in Haitian Vodou, describes how sensations of hunger are emotionally related to the experience of anxiety. Stevens draws an example from the work of Karen McCarthy Brown (1991), who spoke of the relationship between hunger and anxiety for her key interlocutor, Alourdes, who "obsesses about food. She seems to be constantly hungry and constantly worried that no one will feed her. When food is provided, she picks at her meal and rarely admits she enjoys it" (Brown 1991, 44, cited in Stevens 1999, 126). Likewise, in Sou Lapwen, people experience anxiety and hunger (as well as food aversion) as part of the same emotional register. When someone is hungry-anxious, you can sense it in their restlessness, in their eyes that dart, in their repetitive bodily movements, such as yawning. When someone is anxious but does not claim to be hungry, food is still prescribed as an important calmative agent. Likewise, when one is hungry but does not claim to be anxious, reassurance, touch, and care can help treat the problem as well as food.

Working with Haitian Vodouisants in Tomazo in the 1970s, Maria Alvarèz and Gerald Murray (1981, 62) explored how the physiological experience of hunger was known to exacerbate and accelerate other illnesses. When a woman is pregnant or in the postpartum period, these problems increase exponentially. The emotional and physical damage caused by hunger can harm women, fetuses, and newborn babies in a variety of ways. In Sou Lapwen, as soon as a woman comes to know she is pregnant, her relationships with others change concerning food. Her survival and the survival of the fetus are not simply the mother's ultimate responsibility but are dependent upon a full community of others. This is in contrast with the model of individual responsibility presented by neoliberal and colonial models of being, which isolate mothers, fetuses, and newborns into tightly constrained pair bonds.

In Haiti, fetal and infant viability is the concern of not only the mother but also the father, aunts, uncles, friends, and partners that make up the extended lakou. When lakou fail to satiate the hunger of pregnant women and fetuses, they risk fetal illness and certain deformations of the skin. Marks on the cheek, forehead, or hand of newborns are considered testaments to these unsatisfied cravings, to prenatal histories of social neglect (see a discussion of such markings in Murray and Alvarèz 1979). In Sou Lapwen, no matter *where* a pregnant woman is when she and her fetus (through her) begin expressing hunger or anxiety, others who are around her are obligated to at least offer her food (though this does not mean she would be wise to always accept such gifts). For those friends and family who are well within one's trusted network, these acts of food provision to mother and unborn baby are a way of drawing infants and mothers more deeply into social webs of nourishment and care.

HEALING AND PROTECTING BODIES

Before birth, these efforts to connect with babies are mediated by and through mothers' bodies, but following birth, communities begin caring directly for the child that they feel they already know. One of the most important ways they participate in care is by doing what is necessary to protect mothers and babies from incursions of negative emotion and energy. This includes creating environments that shield mothers and babies from the deadly penetration of *frèdi* (cold), of such *move nanm* (evil forces or evil living energies) as *lougawou* (female shapeshifters), and of emotion. Aside from the more catastrophic effects of frèdi and move nanm, babies (and mothers) also are highly sensitive to the anger, sorrow, jealousy, judgment, and conflict of the world around them. Shock, anger, and jealousy can destroy a woman's milk supply, causing it to spoil or go to the mother's head (*lèt monte nan tèt li*). These emotions can also cause *move san* (bad blood), by poisoning the blood of infants and their mothers, creating a plethora of physical symptoms that can become serious quite quickly.

Although Haitian infants and toddlers are accustomed to sharing food with a wider circle of compatriots than American children, these circles of care have social order, as well as having their limits. While being taught to eat with other members of their lakou, Felda, Klejames, Waglet, Kamis, and Jemima were also simultaneously taught to avoid food from adults (and teenagers) they don't know well (even if these acquaintances were offering them food in Nel's courtyard). As children begin crawling and understanding some language, they are explicitly taught not to eat food outside the lakou (except with extended families) and not to touch things on the road (especially shiny pieces of money). Many children do not grasp the reason behind these lessons till they are much older, but the teachings are regularly drilled into infants by parents, older children, and other relatives. These caretakers are eager to chastise wandering arms that reach for food in the extended hand of a stranger or curious eyes that seek objects outside their own lakou, sometimes setting up the lesson to have the opportunity to correct them.

Thus, by the age of three or four, Nel recounted to me, any child in Sou Lapwen knows they shouldn't eat food from the hand of a stranger or a casual acquaintance. Likewise, at this age, they know not to pick up money or attractive trinkets they find on the road. Infants are told how these objects *gen mèt pa yo* (have their own owners), and thus picking them up is akin to stealing. These owners are not always human, not even *often* human. Objects found on the road belong either to the lwa, usually given to them as an offering from a *travay* (ritual work) of some kind, or they belong to (or they can themselves actually *be*) *malfèkte* (evildoers). Nel and other caretakers ensure that young children know this lesson before allowing them freedom to roam outside their homes. One way this lesson is taught is by sending children on short missions to purchase items from nearby (trusted) houses, such as an onion for dinner or a small sachet of sugar for coffee. Children of two and half are sent on their own with a five-gourdes coin or a bill tucked into their tiny fists. As they parade proudly to the designated house, caretakers watch them carefully from behind gates. If the toddler leans down to look at coins or objects on the road, adults shout at them to leave it and keep going. If they are successful, when they return, adults will applaud them for their behavior and their assistance. In both the case of avoiding food and avoiding valuable items, children are taught to limit their sharing (and their claims to objects) to members within their lakou and the lakou they are closest with.

Although there are plenty of reasons that all of these behaviors are risky for adults as well as children, the most salient reason for infants is that these behaviors are thought to expose them to the actions of lougawou. In Sou Lapwen, *lougawou* is the name assigned to a specific phenomenon, whereby an adult woman engages in extremely *cho* (hot) selling magic and either accidentally or purposefully becomes a shapeshifter that hungers for infant *nanm* (force, life energy). When infants fall sick with specific symptoms including rapid weight loss, seizures, listlessness, a special form of diarrhea, followed by widespread bodily swelling, a lougawou is uniformly thought to be the culprit. This kind of illness requires specialized treatment from manbo, oungan, *moun fey* (herbalists), or *bòkò* (ritual practitioners that specialize in hot magic), often requiring a combination of these. Although lougawou attacks are very common for infants in Sou Lapwen, the routine strategies that families and practitioners use to treat these attacks do not involve naming anyone as being responsible.[3]

In principle, lougawou are believed to be actual neighbor women (though rarely does anyone know who) that shed their human skin like clothing at night, revealing themselves as dogs that speak Creole, as donkeys as large as houses, as turkeys whose eyes burn with light, as crickets that glow bright red. In this form, they use their eyes and not their mouths as orifices, hooking into infants' bodies like a parasite. They are thus able to consume their nanm little by little, causing their bodies to shrivel up and shrink under a violent enchantment (although the end stage of the attack can result in bodily swelling). Lougawou swallow not with their mouths but with their eyes; they take bodies into themselves rather than nourish bodies outside of themselves. These reversals are as grotesque as they are fearsome; instead of swallowing in the normal way of a human, they digest infants by vomiting up their life-force (in the form of blood), which then is transformed into matches, fish, or wares that can be sold for a profit at the marketplace. This process of taking from infants rather than giving to them, of shrinking their bodies rather than expanding them, is a profound reversal from the ways that people in general are expected to nourish and grow infants.

Lougawou are known through the marks they leave on infants' bodies—thirst, diarrhea, seizures, and shrinking—as well as the things they do to caretakers' bodies, which are felt to be pressed down upon, enfeebled, immobilized during attacks. From the moment a woman is pregnant till a child reaches four or five years old, families engage in practices to avoid lougawou attacks and to teach children to do the same. As children outgrow their infancy and early childhood, they learn to become infant caretakers, ritual assistants, and active interpreters of bodily signs themselves, engaging with the issues raised by lougawou from the perspective of participants. Even before children reach an age when lougawou are no longer harmful, Nel explained, they grasp basic methods of protecting more vulnerable infants from lougawou attacks.

Even for infants and caretakers who escape outright attacks, lougawou still leave their indelible marks pressed upon their skin, their houses and spaces, their accoutrements, and their social networks. They are marked by the creative and ritual practices that are used to ballast them against attack, and they are marked by the human and nonhuman exchanges and networks that rally for their survival. For those who experienced outright attacks, the marks left upon their bodies (and those of their families), as well as their social spaces, are enormous. During my most intensive period in the field, between 2013 and 2015, four families in Sou Lapwen were so beleaguered by lougawou attacks that they relocated their entire families. These relocations were logistically complex due to the fact that Sou Lapwen was quite small and that there were no vacant or "unused" homes, meaning families had to relocate into others' lakou. In each of these four cases, relocation meant that families already struggling to put food on the table accepted a further drop in their livelihoods and living conditions to save their infants from what they saw as imminent death.

Yvna and Pierre still speak of how surprised and grateful they were when it became clear Wilner, their baby, would survive. When I met Wilner, he was eighteen months old but looked like an eleven-month-old given how wasted his body had been by illness. After working with Nel on herbal treatments and serums, Wilner gradually improved. With renewed belief that Wilner could overcome an attack that had been ongoing for more than a year, Yvna and Pierre began making preparations to leave their house, out of a fear that whatever lougawou had been attacking the house would now simply come back to make Wilner sick again. When I heard of this move, I was scared about the decision—the avocado tree, the rooms, the irrigation canal, the exterior kitchen, everything the family needed to scrape by was on that small plot of land! Nonetheless, Nel explained to me, it was the right decision—the only healthy decision to make. It was a decision that would buy Wilner's life back.

So Pierre and Yvna abandoned their existing home, and the intimate social ties of neighbors and nearby family, and moved to the opposite side of town to a one-room mud and daub hut at the back of a distant relative's property.

Wilner's health continued to improve after the move, and he started walking short distances at two and a half years. When I saw him at five years old, he was still wearing the matches and red string cross his father had made him. It had been threaded over, restrung too many times to count.

The familial shift necessitated by Wilner's illness, and that of the three other families who moved due to lougawou, was seen to reshape his body, helping it grow larger, fatter, stronger, and more capable given its distance from an attacking lougawou. In the process of this move and the requisite shifts in bodily habits, behaviors, and rhythms, Wilner's family and community located his body, his illness, and his recovery as critical for their own well-being. Cumulatively, these practices insisted both on the vulnerability of his body to neighborly violence and on the related familial maxim to protect him from further harm at a significant cost.

These affections, concretized in the figure of the lougawou, can contour daily life in unsettling and disruptive ways. Envy is one of the most dangerous emotions that infants can be exposed to, and it is also often said that this is the emotion that lougawou feel when they choose an infant to consume. The reason for this envy, according to Nel, Nanis, and others in Sou Lapwen, is that infants are so beautiful, sensual, and desirable. Seeing this sensual appeal, and the fat full-bellied care that infants receive, as well as the intense affection they arouse in caregivers, lougawou become envious of such energy and youth and desire to possess it themselves. Thus, families imagine that lougawou observe the care and affection that infants receive, the desire that families feel for babies, and that they in turn feel spikes of desire and envy so strong that they consume the child. It is the devastating consequences of such profound desires for possession, rather than any animosity, that is thought to animate lougawou actions.

CONCLUSION: INFANCY AND BODILY BECOMING

Throughout infancy, bodily acts of care, bodily risks, and bodily ideals are constantly interacting and tended to by a broad community of others. During this life period that all must go through, one's survival (and familial survival) is hardly assured. It is a time of intense longing and profound losses, when the fabric of human social existence is both most in need of shaping and most in need of protection. This chapter has addressed the interactive bodily techniques that work to produce the lived experience of "the many" and the phenomenological ecotheology that Nixon Cleophat outlines in this volume (chap. 11). Teaching bodily techniques of tending to skins and other surfaces, families teach children important methods of distinguishing their effects upon others and the world's effects upon themselves.

Such practices, coupled with a slew of other important rituals and bodily orientations in Afro-Creole religious practices, demonstrate that human bodies are profoundly interconnected, transnational spaces (Cleophat chap. 11; Matory 2009; Strongman 2008). To care for an infant is thus to look after the lakou-as-in-the-infant, to care for oneself-as-in-the-infant, the ancestors-as-in-the-infant, the future-as-in-the-infant, and so on, all in a way that is both tactile and spiritual.

In many African Atlantic metaphysics, bodily selves (human and otherwise) are complex assemblages of multiple forces, each of which carries forward distinct pasts, histories, vulnerabilities, and potentials into daily life. For humans, this lived condition means that we require extensive technical, spiritual, and material maintenance to survive. As Cleophat (this volume) demonstrates, great importance is placed on how both human and nonhuman bodies appear in social life, and how they relate to, pass through, or interact with others. Our bodily selves transmute along with our tasks, practices, and interactions. We eat, we drink, we meet others, we zone out, we discover ourselves, or others unearth our own capacities in ways that deeply transform us; in short, we are affected, we affect others, and all of this is made possible through the expressive, fleshy, and shifting matrix of embodied being. In Sou Lapwen, these changes and others can be understood and managed through the effects they leave on bodily surfaces, such as skins.

NOTES

1. It is more common to bathe with a woman in this manner for men are more prone to travel to the canal to bathe, often as they finish work in the fields or with animals.

2. An important exception to this pattern is on school days, when mothers, aunts, and cousins take important charge of their children's bath routine, so they can appear at school as fresh as possible.

3. The bodily experience of lougawou vis-à-vis infant attacks is by no means the extent of the phenomenon. Lougawou raise extensive, palpable tensions from reciprocity, to scapegoating, to social marginality, social continuance, and more (see, e.g., Alvàrez and Murray 1973). Along these lines of tension, townspeople and families explicitly engage with such important questions as injustice and loss: not only the injustice of failed and heart-wrenching battles to save infants from painful deaths but the profound social injustice of accusation.

REFERENCES

Alvarèz, Maria, and Gerald Murray. 1973. *Childbearing, Sickness and Ritual Healing in a Haitian Village.* Port-au-Prince: Division d'Hygiène Familiale.

———. 1981. *Socialization for Scarcity: Child Feeding Beliefs and Practices in a Haitian Village.* Port-au-Prince: USAID/Haiti.

Caple James, Erica. 2008. "Haunting Ghosts." In *Postcolonial Disorders*, 132–56. Berkeley: University of California Press.

Dayan, Joan. 1996. *Haiti, History, and the Gods.* Berkeley: University of California Press.

Farmer, P. 1988. "Bad Blood, Spoiled Milk: Bodily Fluids as Moral Barometers in Rural Haiti." *American Ethnologist* 15 (1): 62–83.

Gottlieb, Alma. 2000. "Where Have All the Babies Gone? Toward an Anthropology of Infants (and Their Caretakers)." *Anthropological Quarterly* 73 (3): 121–132.

———. 2015. *The Afterlife Is Where We Come From.* Chicago: University of Chicago Press.

Jordan, Alissa. 2016. "Atlas of Skins: A Sensual Map of Becoming Persons, Becoming Werewomen, and Becoming Zonbi in a Haitian Vodou Lakou." PhD diss., University of Florida.

Matory, James L. 2009. "The Many Who Dance in Me: Afro-Atlantic Ontology and the Problem with 'Transnationalism.'" In *Transnational Transcendence: Essays on Religion and Globalization*, 231–262. Berkeley: University of California Press.

McCarthy Brown, Karen. 1991. *Mama Lola: A Vodou Priestess in New York.* Berkeley: University of California Press.

———. 2006. "Afro-Caribbean Spirituality: A Haitian Case Study." In *Vodou in Haitian Life and Culture*, 1–26. Palgrave Macmillan: New York.

Stevens, Alta M. 1995. "Manje In Haitian Culture: The Symbolic Significance of Manje in Haitian Culture." *Journal of Haitian Studies* 1 (1): 75–88.

———. 1999. "Poison and Nurturance: Changing Food and Community Symbolism among Haitians in Oldtown, a New England City." *Journal of Haitian Studies* 5 (1): 20–28.

Strongman, Roberto. 2008. "The Afro-Diasporic Body in Haitian Vodou and the Transcending of Gendered Cartesian Corporeality." *Kunapipi* 30 (2): 4.

ALISSA JORDAN is Associate Director of the Center for Experimental Ethnography at the University of Pennsylvania.

TEN

SPIRITED FORESTS AND THE WEST AFRICAN FOREST COMPLEX

Timothy R. Landry

VODÚN, AS imagined by Western media and as some scholars have constructed it, does not exist. In Vodún, there are no set beliefs or practices; there are few established universal rules; and there is little in the way of continuity. As a religious classification, the term *Vodún* was used first by colonialists and missionaries to partition, condense, and homogenize a vast set of beliefs and practices that are—for the most part—formless, fluid, and heterogeneous. *Vodún*, the word that has come to index—and in some ways, reduce—the matrix of indigenous religious practices of Fon speakers in southern Benin, comes from the *gbè* group of Niger-Congo languages and may be defined as a "spirit," "god," "divinity," and perhaps most accurately as a "presence."[1] By framing Vodún as a singular religion, scholars have gained the ability to place Vodún into comparative conversations with such religions as Christianity and Islam. However, I contend that we do so at a great cost to our ability to understand the religious complex (Rush 2013). If Vodún is to be framed as a religion, it must be understood analytically as a religion of a thousand religions that is home to an incalculable, ever-growing number of presences, each with its own set of rituals, taboos, and truths. Complicating scholars' impulse to position Vodún as a religious category, *fɔngbè* does not have a noun for "religion." Instead, Fon speakers use the verb "to worship" (*sinsɛn*) and when speaking fɔngbè describe their religion as *vodúnsínsɛn* (literally, "spirit worship") and themselves as *vodúnsɛ̀ntɔ́* (literally, "one who follows a spirit's taboos").[2] In this way, Vodún provides the space for one to worship established vodún alongside emerging presences such as Christ, and even their own divine power made manifest as differences such as twinness, dwarfism, albinism, and even queerness (see Cleophat's chapter in this volume).[3]

Best understood as a complex of spirit cults or religions, Vodún is imbued with limitless possibilities. Vodúnisants do not simply believe in the panoply of spirit presences; they experience their realities during moments of spirit possession, learn from them during dreams and divinatory consultations, and nourish them and speak to them while visiting spirit shrines, the vodún's ritually created material presence in the earthly realm (Landry 2015). Vodún is empowered by its obscurity. Indeed, Vodún and its Caribbean derivatives have survived and even thrive in places around the world in part because of the religion's flexible, adaptable, and absorptive nature (see Giafferi-Dombre's chapter in this volume). To frame Vodún in a way that facilitates a deep, locally inspired understanding, I aim to produce a new lens through which scholars may engage with Vodún and its derivatives around the world. While I have echoed Vodún's indefinability elsewhere (Landry 2015, 2016, 2019), here I seek to challenge this premise by constructing a framework that tethers Vodún not to its flexible nature but to the ontological potency and symbolic primacy of the forest. By centering spirited or sacred forests in Benin (and, to a lesser extent, Haiti), I draw on theories of liminality, space, and material religion to develop a framework through which one might seek to understand Vodún's global success that extends beyond arguments focused primarily on the religion's flexibility.

The type of forest, which inspires my analysis, is the spirited, or so-called sacred, forest. Inspired by the anthropologist Paul Christopher Johnson, I use the term *spirited* to move away from the sacred-secular binary while also capturing the spiritual power of these particular spaces. Additionally, for Fon speakers, *spirited forest* is much more in line with the ways they understand sacredness. The most common translation of the French *sacre* (sacred) into fòngbè is *yɛhwenú*, meaning "spirit" (*yɛhwe*) "thing" (*nŭ*)—or "stuff of the spirits." Johnson (2014, 17) saw "spirited things" as being "things that are intercalated within the semiotic ideology of possession by spirits." While spirits in Benin often take control of—or possess—the bodies of their devotees, in this chapter I depart from Johnson in favor of how Fon speakers think of the so-called sacred and its relationship to objects and spirits. In so doing, I focus on the ways in which spirits possess—and therefore empower—not people but spaces and objects. As such, I am able to show how Vodúnisants are able to use secrecy to transform forests into places—or stuff—of power, wherein ritual grammar, social ontologies, and "social order" are all made manifest (Colson 1997).

In Benin, the generic forest is known as *zùn*. Spirited forests are those sections of forest that are demarcated, protected, and preserved as central focal points for the spirits. These forests are often marked as being powerful and therefore dangerously secret—allowing only initiates entrée.[4] These forests are typically named after the primary presence living within them. In this way, the sacred forest of Fá, the oracular spirit of knowledge, becomes *fázùn*; *sakpatázùn* is the sacred forest that has been set aside for Sakpatá, the vodún of the earth and of smallpox; and *vodúnzùn* is simply a generic spirited forest.[5] In Fonland, Vodún communities maintain social order through ritual secrecy, religious elders, and the gerontocracy, all of which has been codified in sacred—or powerful—places, objects, and beings. In the same way that Fon speakers use the term *acè* to describe social power, the right to act, and divine power, I use the term *sacred forest* to mean a forest of power, an acè-laden forest, or a forest animated specially by divine power. Here, I merge, as Fon speakers do, concepts of power and sacredness with places and presences, such as the vodún and their forests.

Spirited forest as a category is made analytically valuable by the way that practitioners of Vodún distinguish sacred forests from other forests. Indeed, with a skilled eye, one can see the otherwise invisible sacred forests that punctuate the Beninese landscape. Small forests are often found growing in the middle of agricultural fields; forest clusters are left to grow densely among trees that are cultivated and manicured; and walls, fences, and other permanent structures frequently protect groupings of powerful trees.

Despite the social salience of forests in Benin, scholars have paid little direct attention to understanding forests' social and symbolic value. More broadly, in anthropology, forests—and especially sacred forests—as beings that have the capacity to "represent the world" (Kohn 2013, 8) and as places of deep symbolic potency have received limited attention. When scholars have focused on sacred forests, they are often framed as relics of the past (Chevalier 1933; Fortes 1945; Frazer 1951; Omari 1990; Sibanda 1997); loci for environmental conservation and biodiversity (Berkes and Folke 2008; Djagoun et al. 2013; Dorm-Adzobu, Ampadu-Agyei, and Veit 1991; LeMay-Boucher, Noret, and Somville 2013); sites of pharmacological or sociomagical value (Verger 1995); or as key ritual symbols (Chouin 2008; Gottlieb 2008; Hughes 1994; Rival 1998; Siebert 2008; Turner 1967). Inspired by such anthropologists as Eduardo Kohn (2013), Graham Harvey (2005), and Donna Haraway (2008)—all of whom saw the ontological value of nonhuman cultural actors—I consider the forest an active being capable of collaborating with human Vodúnisants. As Kohn (2013, 1) so aptly put it, "Encounters with other kinds of beings force us to recognize the fact that seeing, representing, and perhaps knowing, even thinking, are not exclusively human affairs."

Indeed, it is by focusing on the ways in which folks encounter the forest and how the forest encounters its human interlocutors that I draw inspiration.

POWER FROM LIMINALITY

In 2011, while living in Benin, I was initiated as a priest of Fá, thereby becoming a diviner's apprentice. During my apprenticeship, I enjoyed many walks in the forest that surrounded Fátomè, the village in which I lived and worked.[6] During these outings I accompanied other diviners and sorcerers as we searched for leaves and forest objects (e.g., termite mound soil) to be used in ritual or magic. Each time I walked into the forest, I found that the air had thickened with humidity and the sometimes overpowering musty scent of leaves, flowers, and soil. The physical and metaphorical thickness of the forest deepened my breathing and changed the way I moved. Conscious of thorns, dangerous insects, and venomous snakes, I was taught to be keenly aware of where I walked or placed my hands. "Always look where you are grabbing," Jean, my initiator and mentor, would tell me while we picked the leaves he needed for ritual. The songs of birds, such as the *wŭtutú*, whose onomatopoeic cry is said to call the rain (these birds are tied to Xɛybyoso), filled the forest with sounds that over time moved from being unfamiliar to comforting. At the beginning of my apprenticeship, I experienced the forest as an intimidating and dangerous place. But Jean always encouraged me to embrace the forest's hidden power. He explained tirelessly to me and his other students the medical and magical power of leaves.

"Do you know this one?" Jean pointed.

"Umm, that's *agbègbé*!" I offered, excited that he pointed to a plant I actually knew.

"Good. What does it do?" Jean tested. I hesitated, embarrassed I could not remember.

Frustrated by my inability to recollect the names and powers of the leaves that he used every day, Jean grumbled, "I want you to be the best diviner in the United States! You need to learn this, Tim!"

While I performed many of Fá's rituals to his satisfaction and had developed a reputation for being a competent diviner, to Jean's disappointment, I was never able to master fully the power of leaves.

"I don't remember," I said, hanging my head while feeling wholly inadequate.

"If you respect agbègbé, it will teach you about the power of secrecy!" Jean reminded me.

For Jean and others like him, agbègbé does not index an esoteric mystery or operate as a result of the magical laws of sympathy. Instead, the plant represents its own world through shared experiences with Vodúnisants and demonstrates important life lessons. Agbègbé is an agentive being or person, like all the plants in the forest and like the forest itself (cf. Kohn 2013). The agbègbé-person, when in a relationship with a human person, exists between the forested world of spirits and the cultivated world of humans. At the margins, where the spirited forest meets the open forest, relationships help the spirited forest to blend with that of humans. Rituals, initiations, and acts of magic all depend on human-persons and plant-persons to collaborate. This partnership then destabilizes the boundaries that divide them in favor of shared representation and experiences. Indeed, drawing power from one's betweenness can be fruitful for anthropologists who are often betwixt and between two cultures, two languages, and two realities. But it is useful to consider how other social actors may also draw power from this state of being. As Paul Stoller (2009, 4) has shown, if beings can "draw strength from both sides of the between and breathe in the creative air of indeterminacy, we can find ourselves in a space of enormous growth, a space of power and creativity." Just as Jean and I could decide to pick agbègbé from the forest and take it home with us, agbègbé, caught between two worlds, can decide what lessons and mysteries to reveal and which to conceal once in our grasp.[7]

To many Fon speakers, the forest often deliberately influences the social worlds of humans. The forest's ability to act comes from the widely held assumption among practitioners of Vodún that the "world is full of people, only some of whom are human" (Harvey 2005, 17–18). Among Beninese Vodúnisants, the world is populated with agentive persons such as humans, spirits, animals, plants, minerals, and even the forest itself, all of whom interact with each other and affect the ways in which other persons in their social worlds experience the multidimensional world(s) around them. When anthropologists accept that personhood and agentive power extend beyond the human—and may operate apart from human-persons—an awareness of the forest's centrality to Vodún cosmology begins to emerge. The awareness of a diverse array of persons in Vodún is an ontological premise that permeates the religion's cosmology, which I argue is critical to understanding Vodún as a lived experience that extends beyond the needs, desires, and actions of human-persons. As Pazzi, one of Suzanne Preston Blier's (1998, 406n16) informants, said, "The forest . . . signifies the plentitude of the universe." While I have never spoken to Pazzi, I believe that the "plentitude" he mentions frames the forest as a place and as a person who is vibrant and empowered with the will to act. As Pazzi's quote seems to show, for Vodúnisants in Benin, the forest contains all of the powers of the universe and all the gifts that the cosmos has to offer to everyone, both human and nonhuman. Jean would often echo Pazzi's sentiment when he told his apprentices, "Any power you can imagine and any cure that you might need can be found in the forest. Everything we desire or will need is already here [in the forest]; we just need to find it."

For Beninese like Jean, everything that exists in the universe either already exists in the terrestrial world or, because of the forest's liminality and portal-like quality to the usually invisible spirit world, is obtainable in the forest itself. In this way, the forest embodies the full potential of the vodún both known and unknown, along with the limitless possibilities of magic and medicine.

One afternoon, while Jean and I were having a cold beer in a small roadside bar, we enjoyed a philosophical discussion wherein we unpacked the relationships that exist between the vodún and the forest.

"Can the vodún exist without the forest and leaves?" I asked Jean.

"The vodún *are* the forest and leaves," Jean emphasized.

"Literally?" I inquired.

"Yes. The leaves that we gather in the forest and the vodún are the same."

This conversation reminded me of a different discussion I had a few months prior with Aaron, a friend and Dàn (the serpent spirit of riches) priest who lives in Abomey, about two hours north of Ouidah. Discussing a similar topic as Jean and me, Aaron contended, "Vodún is nothing more than a way of making the natural power of leaves immortal."

Here, Aaron was suggesting that by incarnating vodún to earth by amalgamating leaves and other objects together, we are ensuring that the occult powers of leaves are eternal. Later, Aaron went on to say, "If a leaf that we need vanishes [becomes extinct], the shrines that we have now will ensure that the leaf's power will continue."

I left these two encounters with the understanding that the vodún and magic exist within, and are ontologically linked to, the forest. For many of my interlocutors, the forest is truly the center of the universe and the home of limitless potential. Simply put, without the forest, Vodún would cease to exist.

The life-force and occult power of the forest is made manifest and protected by a class of fairylike forest spirits known as *azizà*.

"You need to be careful about going into the forest," Jean would always warn. "If you find azizà, don't speak to them. They will trick you and take you into the deep forest, where you'll be lost. You'll never find your way back, and we won't be able to help you."

Azizà are presented as being both dangerous and necessary to the success of human life. In today's world, where Christianity and capitalism proliferate and affect the ways in which Beninese interact with the forest, there is a sense that azizà are particularly dangerous and angry. As Marc, a sorcerer living in Ouidah, once explained, "There was a time when azizà and humans worked together. If people needed to cure a disease, azizà would help them. If people needed a magical power, it was the azizà who would provide it. But as people converted to Christianity, the azizà have grown to distrust us. They don't like what we're doing to the forest. They dislike the plastic that's everywhere. They are angry with us, and because we take too much from the forest, the azizà no longer help us."

As this quote shows, Beninese now connect the rise in Christianity and the subsequent demonization of their indigenous beliefs and practices (e.g., Meyer 1999) with the withdrawal of azizà into the deep forest and away from where humans regularly live or venture. The azizà—and by extension the forest—have changed their relationship with humans from one of utility to one of irritation and trickery. There are stories of azizà stealing children and kidnapping forest goers, keeping them hidden for decades, and in some cases never returning their human captives to their families.

All we know about the azizà are what we learn from such stories as the one recounted by Marc. Yet, despite the proliferation of similar studies and their centrality to Vodún cosmology, and to the efficacy of ritual and magic, deep analysis and description of the azizà are nearly absent from the literature. Nevertheless, scholars have indicated two widely held attitudes among Fon speakers concerning the azizà: (1) humanity "is held to be indebted to the azizą̃ [sic] for magic" (Herskovits 1938, 262), and (2) the azizà are misshapen, ugly, and powerful. Azizà have also been described as "hairy ... deformed (monopedal), forest inhabitants [who are] the source of critical features of human technology and civilization" (Blier 1998, 85). Beninese have described azizà to me as being allusive, fairylike, winged, ugly, and mischievous. Just as E. E. Evans-Pritchard (1956, 131) saw twin births among the Nuer of the Sudan as a "special revelation of Spirit," for Fon speakers, the physical deformities of azizà point to their divine power indexing a trend in Vodún that I call the *apotheosis of difference*. Ontological anomalies such as twin births, dwarfism, albinism, melanism, and even queerness are all seen as evidence of divine presence.[8] In the case of azizà, their deformities, which can vary from telling to telling, mark them as divine and powerful. Their humanlike qualities position them as being a part of the world of humans, but their animallike qualities—their fur, wings, and claws—all mark them as beasts and creatures of the wild forest. Azizà are forever caught between the world of humans and the realm of the spirits. It is from this indeterminate status—betwixt and between human and spirit—that the azizà draw power and find purpose.

However conceived, they seem to mystify both Beninese Vodúnisants and scholars alike. Similar to Vodún itself, the azizà are allusive to both physical and intellectual apprehension. Trying to understand the oblique nature of the azizà, I asked Marc the simplest and perhaps most naive question I could conjure.

"Who are the azizà?" I began.

"They keep the forest's secrets," he replied matter-of-factly.

"Have they ever taught you magic?" I asked.

"They don't trust humans anymore. A long time ago, you could go into the forest to look for azizà if you needed something. When you found one, they would help you. They would tell you to combine this leaf with that feather and this rock. They would even give you the power to talk to animals, so you could ask the birds for their feathers without killing them. The birds would just give you one of their feathers because the azizà asked them to. But it's not like that anymore. Today, azizà hide and refuse to share their secrets. Humans have destroyed the forest and abused the powers that the azizà gave us. The magic is lost."

"Do you think it's lost forever?" I wondered aloud.

"That's up to the azizà," Marc said and shrugged. "It's their power to share— or not."

When leaves are used in magic and ritual, it is the azizà who are understood to have allowed their human interlocutors to use the forest's power to their benefit. Azizà are purported to teach the forest's mysteries to those they find worthy. As Jean once told me, "Using the forest, the azizà have the power to cure cancer and AIDS. They can teach us how to become invisible and how to teleport or fly without using witchcraft. They know magic that can render us bulletproof or allow us to breathe underwater. All of these powers live in the forest and all of these powers are known and protected by azizà."

As this quote shows, the power of the azizà and the forest are limitless, unimaginable, and possibly even unknowable. It is up to the forest and the azizà to share their riches with humanity. The link between the azizà, the forest, and the powers they each embody is complicated. In casual conversation, azizà are talked about as though they are small creatures who live in the forest. However, during conversations that are more philosophical, nearly every one of my informants merged the azizà and the forest into something that resembled a single entity. Blier (1998, 199) has argued that an azizà is "identified as an invisible being that resides deep within the recesses of the forest." However, I have found the relationship between azizà and the forest to be more complex than one of inhabitants and habitats. Many of my Beninese friends have described the azizà and the forest as being simultaneously dependent on each other and a part of each other. One Vodún priest even said, "The azizà are the forest's way of interacting with the world and everything in it beyond where its roots will allow it to go."

From this, one can see how those forest presences known as azizà may share what resembles a consciousness with the forest that allows the forest and azizà to converge in ways that are cosmologically, magically, and ritually meaningful. Put another way, the power of the azizà comes from their ontological connection to the forest. Their classification as a "deformed" and "ugly" spirit places them in a liminal space somewhere between forest, spirit, human, and god.

FORESTED SPACE

While capitalism has transformed the forest and all it contains into a commodity (Harper 2002; Sodikoff 2002; Tsing 2017), the forest remains central to the ways in which its devotees experience Vodún. Vodúnisants still need the forest to incarnate their spirits to earth and value the power of the ritual and magical power of the forest (Landry 2016). Indeed, shrines to those vodún who share the forest with the azizà dot the forestscape that surrounds many of Benin's villages and small towns.

Azizà are said to be *of* the forest. If we lose the forest, we also lose the azizà. Azizà are at once the forest in action, the forest's consciousness, and the manifestation of the forest's will. However, not all spirits are as unequivocally linked to the forest as the azizà. Like animals and plants, some of the vodún are said to live *in* the forest. They are born of the forest's power and embody the ontological essence of certain leaves and combination of leaves with other objects such as stones, feather, and animal remains (Landry 2016). Where azizà reflect the collective power of the forest, the vodún reflect fractions of that power that are consolidated into earthly shrines made by their human interlocutors.

The surrounding forest contains Fátomè's most powerful shrines. Some, such as Gbădù, Egúngún, Oró, Abìkú, and Zàngbètɔ, are hidden in forest groves and protected by barriers and strict rules of secrecy. Spirited forests (vodúnzùn) draw power from existing in a state between the domesticated village and the wild forest. Vodún groves may be surrounded by a deep unforgiving forest, a human-made wall of bricks or mud, or an insubstantial line of trees that serve only to visually obfuscate the hidden realm of the spirits from the everyday world of humans. These forests are not quite wild and not quite domesticated.

Only those men who are initiated into the cults may enter the forest domains of these presences. In the center of these groves always rests the presence itself (in the form of a shrine). Permeating outward from the shrine is the spirit's grove. Groves vary in size and, in most cases, are seen as dangerous as a result of the spirit's existence in the space itself. The grove is not a part of the spirit hidden at its core; nor is it a part of the forest that lies beyond its borders. In this way, the grove's liminality—between forest and presence—contributes to its power to garner power from both the presence it protects and the forest surrounding it. Worn paths lead to the groves' centers. Each marked by a shredded palm frond barrier (*azàn*). Whether we're talking about the precarious azàn that marks a forest path as secret and powerful or a more substantial brick or mud wall designed to cordon off space, the relationship between secrecy, power, and space is important to understanding how Vodúnisants relate to the forest. As Blier (1993, 185) points out, "In Benin ... fences [or other barriers] are a frequent visual metaphor that *announce* things identified in some way with mystery, secrecy, or power." Indeed, paying attention to enclosures and the demarcation of space are critical to the ways in which Vodúnisants experience ritual secrecy and the forest. In fɔngbè the word *kpá* means both "secret" and "enclosure" or "barrier." Understanding kpá also helps us to unpack the meaning found in compound words for secrecy, such as *kpánú* (meaning, "enclosed [or secret] thing") and *kpáxó* (meaning, "enclosed [or secret] speech"). These physical structures—no matter how large or how small—are in and of themselves vigilant preservers of secrecy and power (cf. Doris 2011). In so doing, they—in the words of Blier—"announce" the presence of secrecy, power, and danger. In these moments, the forest becomes a spirited thing (yɛhwenú) and one of the primary ways through which Vodúnisants develop relationships with beings that exist beyond the human.

***

"Are you ever tempted to enter the forest?" I asked Marie, one of Jean's wives.

"No!" she responded quickly. "I don't want to die or go blind!"

From dangerous wildlife, to the azizà, to the palm frond protected shrines, the forest is filled with both peril and power. While individuals rarely walk into the forest alone or without purpose, not all encounters with nonhuman presences are inherently dangerous. Around Fátomè, there are also shrines to such spirits as Dàn Wèkè and Sakpatá, whose shrines are not hidden, secret, or otherwise restricted. Anyone may approach these vodún to ask for help by offering prayers and sacrifice. Like all vodún, these spirits were materialized as shrines using leaves and blood sacrifice. Apart from the everyday physical and occult dangers of the forest, these shrines were welcoming and safe to anyone who was directed to visit them.

"Why are these shrines in the forest?" I asked Jean.

"Because this is where they live," Jean responded, perplexed at my question.

"Did they choose to live here?" I continued.

"Choose? No, it's just where they are. They were found here." Jean explained. "My great grandfather was hunting in the forest one afternoon and Dàn Wèkè revealed himself. He told my great-grandfather that he was here. So my grandfather performed the rituals and constructed this shrine helping Dàn Wèkè [to materialize]. Dàn Wèkè has been here ever since helping my family."

"Did the same thing happen with Sakpatá?" I inquired.

"Yes, of course. It happened at different times with all the spirits we have with us."

While the azizà are known to be a part of the forest by default, other vodún are often experienced when they reveal themselves to human interlocutors. For four generations, Dàn Wèkè has helped the residents of Fátomè, and the residents of Fátomè have fed and maintained Dàn Wèkè. Over time, this synergy has elevated the spirit to one of the area's most powerful serpent spirits, who is capable of bestowing wealth and riches to those who offer him food, drink, and prayer while approaching him with respect. Dàn Wèkè is not seen as being particularly dangerous. As such, the grove that surrounds this serpent spirit is not restricted; nor is it secured with walls or other barriers. Dàn's secrets lie not in the grove but under the ground. Generations ago, Dàn Wèkè's mysteries and powers were buried in the earth, and a visible shrine was installed on the surface—paradoxically hiding Dàn's secrets and announcing their presence. The forest floor is swept clean of debris, thereby marking the space as otherworldly—between forest and village and between human and presence.

Whether we are talking about restricted or open shrines, for many Beninese, the forest is the epicenter of occult power. It's a liminal place betwixt and between the dangerous realm of the spirits and the challenging world of humans. The forest opens portals to the other world and, in the world of humans, provides food and the ability to overcome life's obstacles. Azizà are said to capture human children and raise them as their own while teaching them the power of sorcery. Like the forest, which is neither the world of human or of spirits, the azizà are not of the world of humans or the world of the vodún. The forest and the azizà are inherently a part of both worlds and never fully formed in either. They have one hand in the world of spirits, where the mysteries of magic thrive, and one hand in the world of humans, where the mysteries of magic are desired. The realm of the vodún and the realm of humans are mediated through the forest and, by extension, through everyone's relationship with the azizà.

GBĂDÙ AND OTHER SPIRITED OBJECTS

Apart from the forest's ontological connection to azizà, the forest also serves as the proper home of Gbădù, the entity who is said by some to have combined the coolness of divine power (acè) with hotness of witchcraft (azĕ) to create the universe and everything in it. Fá diviners often describe Gbădù as being the nothingness that existed before something and the source of all other vodún, powers, and magic. She is the foundation of both divine power and the condensation of the universe's creative—yet volatile—power known as azĕ (witchcraft). Materially she is composed of a wide array of objects. A monkey stomach; parrot eggs; secret leaves; and bone fragments from elephants, lions, and leopards are all used to incarnate Gbădù to earth in her material shrine form (Landry 2016). These objects, and many others, are used to create the four small calabashes that make up her shrine. While more research needs to be done on the symbolic and ontological meaning of the different parts of Gbădù, I have a working hypothesis that breaks down the meaning of the four small calabashes that make up her shrine in order to explain her symbolic potency and social value.[9]

1. The first grapefruit-sized warty calabash is filled primarily with kaolin chalk (hwĕ). It embodies birth, the east, the place of the rising sun, and the first of 256 dù,[10] Gbe-Meji. Gbădù is said to have received this calabash from Măwŭ-Lisà, the creator vodún of the sky. The white color, its association with birth and the rising sun, and its connection to Măwŭ-Lisà (the white and cool vodún of creation) suggest that this calabash may index the social value of coolness, wellbeing, and goodness.
2. The second bumpy calabash is filled primarily with black charcoal (zokán). It represents death, the west, the place of the setting sun, and the second of the 256 dù, Yeku-Meji. Gbădù is said to have received this calabash from the ancestors and from Sakpatá, the vodún of the earth, smallpox, and modern-day incurable diseases (e.g., HIV/AIDS, cancer). The black color, its association with the setting sun, and its connection to Sakpatá all suggest that this calabash embodies the social importance of death, health, and family.
3. The third of the four calabashes is filled primarily with camwood, a red powdered wood from the "thunder tree" (sotín). It represents the north and the third of the 256 dù, Woli-Meji. Gbădù is said to have received

this calabash from Sogbó, the vodún of thunder and rain, and Gŭ, the vodún of fire, metal, and blacksmithing. Sogbó brings the rains, and Gŭ provides the metalsmithing necessary to build the agricultural tools need to farm and the weapons required to protect one's family resources. The blood-red color of this calabash indexes the divine living nature of the land. Its association to Sogbó and Gŭ points to the importance of agricultural strategy and subsistence. This calabash serves as a reminder that one's life is connected to the land and consequently centers the agricultural value of the symbiotic triadic relationship that exists between the earth, humanity, and the spirits—thereby expanding the notion of community beyond the human to include spirits and the earth itself.

4. The fourth of Gbădù's warty calabashes is filled with mud from the bottom of the sea (or, in some accounts, the river). It is represented by the south and the fourth of the 256 dù, Di-Meji. It is purported that this final calabash was a gift to Gbădù from Xù, the vodún of the sea. The ocean mud indexes the sea as the source of the vodún and reminds devotees of a mystical time before land when earth was an endless ocean. The ocean is the source of all life and indexical of the unknown, the mysterious, and the powerful.

Taken together, these four calabashes index those social values that are repeatedly highlighted in Vodún ritual and practice. For Fon Vodúnisants, and especially for Fá diviners, Gbădù embodies the social importance of (1) remaining cool, (2) health and the value of one's family, (3) the divine nature of the earth and its connection to their own subsistence, (4) the limitless power and mysterious potential of the vodún themselves. The anthropologist and famed scholar of Haitian Vodou Karen McCarthy Brown (1991) has argued that for Haitian Vodouisants their religion is first and foremost about healing one's family. While beyond the scope of this chapter, an analysis of Gbădù recognizes similar and durable themes found in Benin. This points to the possibility that healing and family might be themes worth exploring in more detail as scholars examine the ways in which Gbădù, and her forest home, might be important puzzle pieces to understanding Vodún in today's world.

No matter the accuracy of the aforementioned analysis, one thing is certain: Gbădù and her connection to the forest are important. When new initiates are introduced to her for the first time, it is an experience that is seen as a dangerous—yet important—part of a young man's coming of age. New initiates are introduced to Gbădù when they are brought to fázùn during their initiations. Here, they meet Gbădù and see her for the first time; they acquire the acè (the "power" or "right" to act) needed to perform divination; and they are allowed to consume acè (divine power), the term used to describe the she goats, ducks, hens, snails, and pigeons that were sacrificed to Gbădù and cooked.[11] Because young men are normally initiated in their early teens, consuming this meat is of particular interest to them as developing men.

After making sacrifices designed to ensure their safe entrance into the forest, initiation candidates are made to wash their eyes with a special protective medicine called Gbădùsìn (Gbădù's water/medicine), which contains shea butter, snail blood, and an array of secret leaves. Inoculated to risk, initiation candidates are led on their knees to a secluded vine-walled chamber. This forest room is Gbădù's inner sanctum and one of the most spirited spaces in Vodún. Entry into the room is strictly controlled; medicine must be poured into the eyes of anyone who enters; women are prohibited from entering; and all men must enter the room bare chested and wrapped in cloth around the waist. What happens in this chamber with the new initiate is secret. Nevertheless, it is widely known that this is where would-be diviners *become* diviners and where they are empowered with Gbădù's power to perform divination and speak to Fá. During my own initiation when I was introduced to Gbădù for the first time, Jean told me, "Tim, take a moment. Here you are, at the center of the universe. Before we continue, I want you to appreciate the seriousness of this moment."

In deep thought, and in the presence of Gbădù, my knees began to weaken, and tears welled up in my eyes. I reflected on Gbădù, the combustive creation of the cosmos, and the cultural and ritual potency of the space that Jean and his family entrusted to me. In this moment, the forest's power—and its sacredness—was more evident than ever. Gbădù's forest home makes her grove (fázùn) the center of the universe and the seat of all magical enchantments of divine and earthly presence. She is the wife of Fá, the source of his power, and the reason why Fá has the oracular power to know all that was, all that is, and all that will ever be. As such, one of the primary ways that one might observe the centrality of the forest is through Fá divination. Fá is the oracular spirit of destiny and the source of one of Vodún's most powerful forms of divination.

Fá divination uses 256 binary signs known as dù to peer into a person's past, resolve issues found in their present, and ensure a cool and balanced destiny-fulfilled future. Fá originally came to the Fon kingdom of Dahomey from Yorubaland in the 1720s (Bay 1998, 190). Since then, Fá has spread throughout the region, first serving the royal family and finally the populace. Fá (also known as Òrúnmìlà or Ifá to Yoruba speakers) is believed to have witnessed the creation of the universe and thus has knowledge of all possibilities.

As I mentioned, the forest around Fátomè is dotted with a dozen or so sacred groves, many of which are marked with shredded palm fronds (azàn). The azàn demarcates ritually curated parts of the forest as being especially powerful and liminal. It warns the uninitiated that what lies beyond the palm frond barrier is off limits and, if one is not inoculated by ritual initiation, volatile and perhaps deadly. One such place is fázùn, the forest of Fá. In 2011, Jean initiated Auguste, one of his sons who had just turned thirteen years old. To be initiated into Fá is to "receive Fá's forest" (Fázùnyí). Over the course of several days, initiation candidates eat the sacred foods of the forest, wash their bodies with fázùn's powerful leaves, and bury their hair deep in Fá's woods, having shaved their heads as part of their initiation. By merging their own personhood and destinies with that of the forest, initiates take the power of the forest into their bodies. But before Auguste was allowed to make this convergence, he first had to ask the forest for permission.

We all gathered just after sunset, the night before Auguste's initiation. Much of the village had assembled to watch Auguste follow his father, grandfather, older brothers, and cousins into the forest to seek approval from fázùn, Fá's sacred forest. Following a precession led by Daágbó, who carried the *fásèn*, the bokónɔ's (Fá diviner) sacred staff whose job it is to chase away death and misfortune (fig. 10.1). Once at fázùn's border, Auguste sacrificed a rooster to Lĕgbà, the vodún who opens the pathway to communication with the spirit world (fig. 10.2). He knelt at the entrance into fázùn—directly in front of the azàn while Jean poured libations of gin, water, and orange Fanta. Auguste placed a few coins onto the wet soil. Jean then pressed a kola nut to Auguste's forehead and asked, "Do you accept these offerings? May we come back tomorrow for Auguste's initiation?"

Jean tossed the four-lobed kola nut (*vì*) onto the ground. All four segments landed facing up.

"*Alăfíà!*" Jean shouted! "Fázùn has accepted the offerings!"

Moments like these are ubiquitous in Vodún. Representing its own will, the forest has the ability to refuse. While I never experienced a moment when the forest denied initiation to a seeker, I have been present when the forest asked for more sacrifices. During my own initiation, fázùn rebuffed my entry until I agreed to sacrifice an additional white she goat to Dàn Wèkè, the white serpent vodún of the universe. In the more than twenty initiations I observed and participated in, permission from the forest was always secured, albeit sometimes after intense and costly negotiations. In this way, the forest was an agentive presence whose permission was necessary to ensure the safety of those new initiates to ritually inoculate them to the forest's occult dangers.

Figure 10.1. The diviners of Fátomè leave the village for the sacred forest with the *fásèn* leading the way. Photograph by Timothy R. Landry, 2011.

In the case of Fá, the forest's danger is enhanced during initiations because of Gbădù's presence in the grove. Gbădù is understood to be the queen of the cosmic mothers (*mĭnɔna*), who uses azĕ (witchcraft) to protect the universe and enforce divine justice. As the keeper of azĕ, Gbădù is understood to be both the source of great occult power and fear. She is paradoxically the source of azĕ and one of the few entities that can protect from humans from its immense power. Within her womb rests the entire universe, and from her all things come.

Gbădù is experienced as being so dangerous that when an initiation is not in process, she is removed from fázùn and placed in a locked wooden box, which is in a locked room, found in a locked building, housed in a locked courtyard. Keeping her hidden behind four locks helps to mitigate any troubles one might incur by accidentally seeing her shrine. However, because Gbădù is believed to leave behind a residual radiation-like power in the grove where she resides during initiations, the forest is still off limits to noninitiates even when she's not there. Over time, objects such as the calabash of Gbădù accumulate power and authority (Doris 2011; Rubin 1974; Rush 2013). Constructed using leaves,

Figure 10.2. Offerings made prior to entering the forest. Photograph by Timothy R. Landry, 2011.

soils, sacrificial blood, and zoological curios, objects such as Gbădù become powerful assemblages of physical things and immaterial powers, energies, and residues (Blier 1988, 2004) These objects are protected and locked behind barriers. Their secrets are stored in the bodies of their human devotees and spirit interlocutors. These objects become condensations of tremendous occult powers that are protected by secrecy, housed in the forest, and experienced by human and nonhuman beings alike.

Gbădù's and Fá's connections to the forest are important as they collectively hold the keys to a person's well-being. Gbădù created the universe and therefore can shape one's fate in ways that no other vodún can, and Fá has the power to see one's destiny and ensure everyone who comes to him for guidance are living lives that are cool and fulfilled. In this way, not only is the forest important to Vodún cosmology; it is also the keeper of one's individual destiny. It is through the forest that Vodúnisants learn of their destiny through initiation, maintain their destinies through divination, contemplate the creation of their worlds, and ultimately achieve well-being in the world.

LIMINALITY, SPACE, AND OBJECTS—BEYOND AFRICA

While the forest is a critical experience and symbol for many practitioners of Vodún, the forest's centrality extends well beyond Fonland. In 2003 and 2004, I conducted research in Haiti among practitioners of Haitian Vodou (Landry 2008). During that time, I was initiated as priest of the religion (*houngan asogwe*).[12] On the sixth night of my initiation (kanzo) those of us who were to take the *ason* (pran ason[13]) were ushered out of the initiatory chamber (*djevo*) and into the sacred forest, where we would undergo a ceremony called *suleliye*. During this portion of the initiation, we were to meet a secret group of spirits (lwa), including Papa Loko Atisou, who would offer those he deemed worthy to take the ason from his hand, thereby becoming a priest or priestess of the spirits.[14] Suleliye is the ritual that makes the initiation candidate a priest in those Vodou houses that serve the spirits using the ason.[15] The ason is a small gourd that has been covered in a net of beads (and occasionally snake vertebrae) and adorned with a single bell. Like Gbădù, the ason is the condensation of power and authority. Made from a plant and retrieved from the forest itself, the ason is a representative of the forest's power and of Loko's supreme position among the lwa. Put another way, when a houngan or manbo shakes their ason to call or control the spirits, they do so with the power of the forest behind them (fig. 10.3). In these moments, the houngan/manbo, the ason, and the forest all merge to control the seen and unseen worlds of which they are all a part. Without the

Figure 10.3. Manbo with ason. Port-au-Prince, Haiti. Photograph by Timothy R. Landry, 2005.

forest, the suleliye cannot be performed, making it impossible to pass the ason onto new priests. As such, the suleliye and the forest are central to the proliferation of Vodou and to the service of lwa both in Haiti and in its diaspora.

While little can be said about the suleliye, it is widely known that the ritual confers the ason, that it is from Papa Loko's hand that the ason is given, and that the ritual must happen on the sacred ancestral land known as the *démembré* (Apter 2002). The démembré is normally uncultivated land where a sacred forest is allowed to grow and flourish. It is both the seat of the family and of the family's spirits. The démembré is fundamental to Vodou in Haiti and to the continuation of the family. As Patricia Scheu (2016, 207) describes, "It is on the *demembre* that the annual offerings are made to the family's lineage. Here is where the dead are buried and where the newborn members of a house are presented. Here is where the annual feedings of the spirits is done, and where the final rituals of life are performed."

It is for this reason that many Haitians living abroad have argued that initiations into Haitian Vodou must be done in Haiti and that those done elsewhere are ritually impossible and therefore invalid. As a Haitian American priestess of Vodou (manbo) once explained, "The démembré just can't be recreated elsewhere. It's intrinsic to relationship between the Haitian family and Haitian land. That just doesn't exist in New York City." I have met Haitian Vodouisants who reject all those initiations performed outside of Haiti, and I have met those that are more creative about the ways in which they interpret the rules that govern the authenticity of ritual—especially as it surrounds the initiation. In one remarkable case, Stefan, a houngan of Haitian Vodou living in the United States recreated the démembré by planting a silk cotton tree (*Ceiba pentandra*) in his US backyard using Haitian soil that he brought back from a trip to Haiti. While not all Vodouisants will agree with this solution, the ritually important tree, along with the imported Haitian soil, and the prayers and sacrifices made when planting the tree all coalesced—at least for this priest—to bring the allusive démembré to the United States.

When Stefan performs an initiation in the United States, he takes his initiation candidates to this tree—to this new démembré—where they will receive the ason from Loko, thereby taking the power of the forest into their hands. However, my own suileye was performed in Haiti. On the night I was to take the ason, we were veiled in a wide-brimmed straw hat that was adorned with a palm frond veil (*ayizan*) to prevent anyone from seeing our vulnerable preinitiated eyes. The palm fronds that now obscure our eyes in Haiti called back to the azàn that marked forest paths in southern Benin as dangerous and powerful.

"Why do we need to cover our eyes?" I asked.

"You're a baby. You're vulnerable. The ayizan protects you," Manbo Marie explained.

In Haiti, the ayizan marks one's body as different and protects the new initiate from outside harm. But it also protects the secrets of the kanzo and marks the initiates body as a secret (Johnson 2002) and powerful. In other words, the ayizan and the azàn both use leaves (palm fronds) to mark beings of power.

Marked paradoxically as vulnerable and dangerous, we left the djevo, dancing, and were quickly ushered out of the *peristyle* (Vodou temple) and into the street.

"Get in!" Manbo Marie said, pointing to an ambulance.

A member of Marie's Vodou house was a physician at one of the hospitals in Port-au-Prince, and he sent an ambulance for us. The ambulance allowed us to travel safely to the sacred forest during a time when the United Nations was enforcing a nightly curfew and stationing roadblocks all over the city—roadblocks that an ambulance could get through without being stopped or questioned.

"Everyone get down!" the driver shouted.

We were instructed to keep away from the windows. The sirens and flashing lights were actuated, and off we went, passing through two roadblocks to arrive at Marie's démembré. In Haiti, the winding Port-au-Prince streets were like the mysterious paths I traversed in the spirited forests found in Benin. For my first trip into the sacred forest in Benin, I was blindfolded, and for my first trip into the forest in Haiti, my head was on the floorboard of an ambulance. In both cases, the location of the forest was—at the time of my first encounter—just as it was meant to be, mysterious.

To calm my nerves, I tried to map the city in my head, and we blindly swerved and speed down the streets of Port-au-Prince. I was incredibly nervous about being caught. As the only foreigner in the group, the fear of being forcibly deported for breaking a UN curfew in the middle of my initiation made the twenty-minute ride seem to go on for hours. As Marie planned, we arrived safely and were instructed to disembark the ambulance. That evening, we met Papa Loko, took the ason, and eventually returned to the peristyle having had a profound experience in the sacred forest.

Later, long after the kanzo was completed, I asked Marie, "Why did you go through all of that trouble to transport us to the forest? Couldn't we have done the ceremony in the peristyle?"

"Did you want to be a real houngan?" Marie retorted. "Unless you want to be a fake houngan, the forest is required. You can't meet Papa Loko anywhere else," Marie explained in a fit of annoyance.

Like in Benin, the forest is central to the cosmology of Haitian Vodou. The kanzo cannot be performed successfully without leaves and the suleliye cannot be performed accurately without the forest. In Haiti, spirits (lwa) like Gran Bwa embody the mysteries of the forest, and the forest itself contains the secrets of the priesthood. In the Haitian diaspora, the forest retains centrality. Practitioners like Stefan innovate in ways that help them to recreate the démembré. Indeed, they use objects like trees and soil to bring Haiti and the forest to them. A quick internet search of media outlets, such as the *New York Post*, Gothamist, and the *Village Voice*, will reveal a decades-long history of Lucumí (Santeria) and Haitian Vodou rituals being performed in Brooklyn's Prospect Park. Cow tongues, severed goat heads, chicken carcasses, and other types of ritual paraphernalia have all been found in New York City's parks. As Vodún moves across the globe, the religion and its Caribbean derivatives finds themselves at home in some of the world's largest and most vibrant cities (Carr 2016; Castor 2017; Johnson 2007; Richman 2005). The cities' forested parks—designed for family outings, wooded walks, and picnics—have been transformed into the cities' most sacred and powerful sites. Without the barriers or permanent shrines that one might find in Benin, spaces such as Prospect Park become invisibly spirited. In the urban forests, the spirits walk among the uninitiated, their presence known only to a select few, and the parks take on a new, often concealed identity—that of the sacred forest, démembré, and vodúnzùn. Unbeknownst to the park's everyday users, the space—like so many forests in Benin and Haiti—become spirited stuff (yɛhwenú). Indeed, New York City parks like Prospect Park have been transformed into urban forests where rituals and sacrifices are performed and where spirits from faraway places find refuge. The vodún and the lwa have begun to animate new forests around the world and have maintained the forest's nature as the key to understanding the religion's cosmology. African diasporic religions, such as Lucumí and Candomblé, have also maintained the forest as a place of occult power and symbolic potency. When Fon- and Yoruba-speaking peoples were forcibly removed from their forest homes, they managed to maintain the forest's symbolic potency, indexing the forest's vital nature as the dominant experience for practitioners the world over.

CONCLUSION

In Benin, Yoruba and Fon spirits are often served in the same village. In these instances, it is the shared experience with the forest that binds them. Because both Yoruba and Fon societies are patrilineal and patrilocal, women tend to move into the homes of their husbands. As a result, in Fátomὲ while the women tend to come from both Fon and Yoruba families, the majority of the men in Fátomè are ethnically Yoruba but Fon speaking. The most important spirits (e.g., Fá, Gbădù, Gŭ, Xɛbyoso, Egúngún, Oró, Abìkú) that are found in Fátomè are all of Yoruba origin. However, Fon and Xwedá spirits are also present (e.g., Dàn Wèkè, Sakpatá, Măwŭ-Lisà, Hŏxò-vodún). I argue that the primary reason that spirits from nearby groups are so easily grafted into Fon, Yoruba, Ewe, Maxi, Ajă, and Xwedá worlds is because all these groups were born in the West African forest. For them, it is the forest that serves as a key experience and symbol that unites them, blurs their boundaries, and, in some ways, unifies their practices. Gbădù is one of the many spirits that are served in Nigeria, Benin, Togo, and Ghana and even among the diaspora in such places as Cuba, Trinidad, Brazil, Europe, and the United States. It is through the forest—with the use of leaves—that these presences are experienced, understood, and made manifest. The supremacy and unifying power of the forest as the key symbol and uniting experience of the complex of religions that I call the *West African forest complex* reaches well beyond West Africa. In such religions as Cuban Lucumí, Brazilian Candomblé, and Haitian Vodou, the forest maintains its importance, thereby linking most—if not all—African diasporic religions to the West African forest and therefore to each other.

Belief in the forest's power, as expressed in Benin, Haiti, and other places where West African forest religions have traveled, is maintained because the forest has proved itself to be effective. This focus on effectiveness is a key component of the Vodún worldview. To this point, in fɔngbè "to believe" is expressed as *dì*, which also means "to be efficacious." The forest is a place of occult power and the primary lens through which Beninese Vodúnisants and Haitian Vodouisants experience the spirit world. In so doing, they maintain relationships with those occult presences that have been purposefully and carefully maintained as being symbolically and ontologically central to their religious worldviews.

In the case of Benin, the forest and, by extension, the fairylike azizà are the paradoxical embodiments of the forest as dangerous and life-giving. It is in the forest that the cosmos's greatest threats reside, but it is from the forest that the universe's ultimate powers, magics, and gifts emerge to be used by the forest's human interlocutors. In Haiti, one may travel to the forest at great risk and at tremendous expense for the forest is necessary for the making of new priests and priestesses. Here, the forest is where one's ancestral connection to their land is maintained and where new priests are born. In New York City, Prospect Park has become an urban sacred forest where practitioners of the West African forest religions converge to perform initiations, revere their ancestors, and offer sacrifices to those spirits who traveled across the

Atlantic and now call the park home. The shared experience of the forest unifies those West African religions born in the forest with those African diasporic religions that now thrive in the African Americas. I call for scholars of African religions to acknowledge that Vodún as a religious category does not exist outside of its colonial history and that Vodún itself is a religious complex of hundreds, if not thousands, of different spirit cults—all with their own beliefs, practices, and rituals. By detangling Vodún from a tendency in the Western academy to unify vast practices under a single umbrella to gain the ability to compare and perhaps even to justify the existence of Vodún against Christianity, we in fact lose our ability to understand Vodún as it is meant to be experienced. My time in Benin, both as an anthropologist and as a diviner's apprentice, has convinced me that Vodún is best understood as a religious complex of cults wherein relationships with known presences are developed, maintained, and mediated through the forest as the religion's key symbol and primary mode of experience. By focusing on the forest complex, instead of separate so-called religions or spirit cults, we gain the remarkable ability to observe the ways in which West African forest religions and their Caribbean derivatives converge in places all over the world as they each filter their experiences and gain power from the forest—the seat of the divine power and of the full potential of the universe.

Forests, and especially spirited—or sacred—forests, lie at the heart of Vodún. As we have seen with the azizà, liminal spirited forests may operate as portals to an unseen world of powerful magic-teaching spirits. Gbădù has shown how, as the primordial center of the cosmos, the forest protects those key social values that permeate Vodún, such as coolness, family and health, subsistence, and the limitless power of the vodún. As we see in Haiti and the United States, in a global world, spirited forests reconstitute themselves as they travel across oceans and find new homes in cities, parks, and backyards. In their new homes, they conceal—and occasionally reveal—presences, powers, and secrets to those driven to listen. As I have attempted to show, it is through the forest that Vodún thrives, travels, and finds meaning. It is through the forest that everyday landscapes become powerful, sacred, and spirited. It is through the forest that Vodún finds its place in the world.

NOTES

1. I am thankful to Robert Thornton at the University of the Witwatersrand (South Africa) for suggesting "presence" as a possible translation.
2. This is also found in Haiti, where Haitian Vodou is known in Kreyòl as sevi lwa (literally, "spirit service").

3. One's status as a twin is believed to be a manifestation of Hŏxò-vodún; dwarfism, a manifestation of Tòxòsú; albinism, a manifestation of Măwŭ-Lisà; and queerness, as a manifestation of Mamíwátá. In all of these cases, individuals speak of "worshiping" their state of difference as evidence of being god-touched. In these ways, Vodún is system of religions wherein one's difference is not just celebrated; it is apotheosized.

4. While a spirited forest is most often protected by secrecy, this is not always the case. For Ouidah '92: The First International Festival of Vodun Arts and Cultures, portions of the forest known as Kpassé were opened to tourism. For more information, see Rush 2001.

5. When speaking French, the term *la forêt sacrée* (the sacred forest) is typically employed.

6. *Fátomè* is a pseudonym meaning "in the country of Fá."

7. The art historian Dana Rush also documents an interesting encounter with agbègbé. For her discussion of "Vodún as *Agbégbé* [sic]," see Rush 2013, 44–46.

8. Twin births are a manifestation of Hŏxò-vodún; dwarfism, of Tòxòsú; albinism, of Măwŭ-Lisà; melanism, of Gŭ; and queerness, of Mamíwátá.

9. Gbădù is incredibly secret. Access to her shrine is restricted, and the exact contents of her construction are restricted further still. The hypothesis I present here is the product of knowledge that I've gained as both an anthropologist and a diviner's apprentice. I've also been informed by the work of Bernard Maupoil (1943) and Jacques Bertho (1951). No serious attempt to understand Gbădù has since been made.

10. The word *dù* references the 256 signs used in Fá divination.

11. While cooking is normally a task performed by women, in the case of acè, only initiated men may prepare, touch, or consume this meat.

12. The Haitian Kreyòl word *houngan* comes from the Fon word *hungan*, meaning "chief of the spirits" (*hun*, "spirit"; *gan*, "chief"). The Haitian Kreyòl word *asogwe* comes from the Fon word *asogwe*, which indexes a large gourd that has been turned into a percussion instrument by covering the gourd with a net of macramé beads. When the beads clash against the side of the gourde, they make a staccato swishing sound that is indicative of the asogwe. As such, the Haitian Kreyòl phrase *houngan asogwe* comes from fɔngbè, meaning, "the chief of the spirits who owns the beaded rattle."

13. The Haitian Kreyòl word *ason* comes from the Fon word *ason*, which indexes a species of gourd that resembles the gourd used in Haiti to make the priestly rattle that Haitians call the ason.

14. Loko is a royal spirit still served in Ouidah, Benin. In Benin, Loko turned himself into an iroko tree to avoid being captured by slavers, thereby leaving his people without a king. In Haiti, this has been memorialized in his name, Loko

Atisou. *Atisou* comes from the Fon words meaning "man of the tree" (*atin*, "tree"; *su*, "man").

15. Not all Vodou houses uses the ason to serve the lwa. Ason lineage houses originated in Port-au-Prince and migrated south, while those houses that don't typically use the ason may be found north of Port-au-Prince.

REFERENCES

Apter, Andrew. 2002. "On African Origins: Creolization and Connaissance in Haitian Vodou." *American Ethnologist* 29 (2): 233–260.
Bay, Edna. 1998. *Wives of the Leopard: Gender, Politics, and Culture in the Kingdom of Dahomey*. Charlottesville: University of Virginia Press.
Berkes, Fikret, and Carl Folke. 1998. "Linking Social and Ecological Systems for Resilience and Sustainability." In *Linking Social and Ecological Systems: Management Practices and Social Mechanisms for Building Resilience*, edited by Fikret Berkes and Carl Folke, 1–25. Cambridge: Cambridge University Press.
Bertho, Jacques. 1951. "Le Gbadou Chez les Adja du Togo et du Dahomey." In *Comptes Rendus: Première Conférence Internationale des Africanistes de l'Ouest*, 2:331–350. Dakar: Institut Français d'Afrique Noire.
Blier, Suzanne Preston. 1988. "Melville J. Herskovits and the Arts of Ancient Dahomey." *Res: Anthropology and Art* 16:124–142.
———. 1993. "Art and Secret Agency: Concealment and Revelation in Artistic Expression." In *Secrecy: Art that Conceals and Reveals*, 181–194. New York: Museum for African Art.
———. 1995. *Vodun: Art, Psychology, and Power*. Chicago: University of Chicago Press.
———. 2004. "Assemblage: Aesthetic Expression and Social Experience in Danhomè." *Res: Anthropology and Art* 45:186–210.
Carr, C. Lynn. 2016. *A Year in White: Cultural Newcomers to Lukumi and Santería in the United States*. New Brunswick, NJ: Rutgers University Press.
Castor, N. Fadeke. 2017. *Spiritual Citizenship: Transnational Pathways from Black Power to Ifá in Trinidad*. Durham, NC: Duke University Press.
Chevalier, Auguste. 1933. "Les Bois Sacrés des Noirs de l'Afrique Tropicale comme Sanctuaries de le Nature." *Revue de la Société de Biogéographie*: 37–42.
Chouin, Gérard. 2008. "Archaeological Perspectives on Sacred Groves in Ghana." In *African Sacred Groves*, edited by Michael J. Sheridan and Celia Nyamweru, 178–194. Athens: University of Ohio Press.
Colson, Elizabeth. 1997. "Places of Power and Shrines of the Land." *Paideuma: Mitteilungen zur Kulturkunde* 43:47–57.
Djagoun, Chabi A. M. S., Hughes A. Akpona, Guy A. Mensah, Clive Nuttman, and Brice Sinsin. 2013. "Wild Mammals Trade for Zootherapeutic and Mythic

Purposes in Benin (West Africa): Capitalizing Species Involved, Provision Sources, and Implications for Conversation." In *Animals in Traditional Folk Medicine: Implications for Conservation*, edited by Rômulo Romeu Nóbrega Alves and Ierecê Lucena Rosa, 367–382. New York: Springer.

Doris, David T. 2011. *Vigilant Things: On Thieves, Yoruba Anti-Aesthetics, and the Strange Fates of Ordinary Objects in Nigeria*. Seattle: University of Washington Press.

Dorm-Adzobu, Clement, Okyeame Ampadu-Agyei, and Peter G. Veit. 1991. *Religious Beliefs and Environmental Protection: The Malshegu Sacred Grove in Northern Ghana*. New York: Center for International Development and Environment.

Evans-Pritchard, E. E. 1956. *Nuer Religion*. Oxford: Oxford University Press.

Fortes, Meyer. 1945. *The Dynamics of Clanship among the Tallensi*. London: Oxford University Press.

Frazer, James. 1951. *The Golden Bough*. Abridged ed. New York: Macmillan.

Gottlieb, Alma. 2008. "Loggers v. Spirits in the Beng Forest, Côte d'Ivoire: Competing Methods." In *African Sacred Groves*, edited by Michael J. Sheridan and Celia Nyamweru, 149–163. Athens: University of Ohio Press.

Haraway, Donna. 2008. *When Species Meet*. Minneapolis: University of Minnesota Press.

Harper, Janice. 2002. *Endangered Species: Health, Illness and Death among Madagascar's People of the Forest*. Durham, NC: Carolina Academic.

Harvey, Graham. 2005. *Animism: Respecting the Living World*. New York: Columbia University Press.

Herskovits, Melville J. 1938. *Dahomey: An Ancient West African Kingdom*. 2 vols. New York: J. J. Augustin.

Hughes, J. Donald. 1994. *Groves and Gardens, Parks and Paradises*. Baltimore: Johns Hopkins University Press.

Johnson, Paul Christopher. 2002. *Secrets, Gossip, and Gods: Transformation of Brazilian Candomblé*. Oxford: Oxford University Press.

———. 2007. *Diaspora Conversions: Black Carib Religion and the Recovery of Africa*. Berkeley: University of California Press.

———, ed. 2014. *Spirited Things: The Work of "Possession" in Afro-Atlantic Religions*. Chicago: University of Chicago Press.

Kenyatta, Jomo. 1965. *Facing Mt. Kenya*. New Delhi: Manohar.

Kohn, Eduardo. 2013. *How Forests Think: Toward an Anthropology beyond the Human*. Berkeley: University of California Press.

Landry, Timothy R. 2008. "Moving to Learn: Performance and Learning in Haitian Vodou." *Anthropology and Humanism* 33 (1/2): 53–65.

———. 2015. "Vodún, Globalization, and the Creative Layering of Belief in Southern Bénin." *Journal of Religion in Africa* 45 (2): 170–199.

———. 2016. "Incarnating Spirits, Composing Shrines, and Cooking Divine Power in Vodún." *Material Religion* 12 (1): 50–73.
———. 2019. *Vodún: Secrecy and the Search for Divine Power*. Philadelphia: University of Pennsylvania Press.
LeMay-Boucher, Philippe, Joël Noret, and Vincent Somville. 2013. "Facing Misfortune: Expenditures on Magico-religious Powers for Cure and Protection in Benin." *Journal of Africa Economics* 22 (2): 300–322.
McCarthy Brown, Karen. 1991. *Mama Lola: A Vodou Priestess in Brooklyn*. Berkeley: University of California Press.
Maupoil, Bernard. 1943. *Le Géomancie à l'Ancienne Côte des Escalves*. Paris: Institut d'Ethnologie.
Meyer, Birgit. 1999. *Translating the Devil: Religion and Modernity among the Ewe of Ghana*. Edinburgh: Edinburgh University Press.
Omari, Cuthbert. 1990. "Traditional African Land Ethics." In *Ethics of Environment and Development: Global Challenge, International Response*, edited by J. R. Engel and Joan Gibb Engel, 167–175. Tucson: University of Arizona Press.
Richman, Karen E. 2005. *Migration and Vodou*. Tallahassee: University Press of Florida.
Rival, Laura. 1998. *The Social Life of Trees: Anthropological Perspectives on Tree Symbolism*. Oxford: Oxford University Press.
Rubin, Arnold. 1974. *African Accumulative Sculpture: Power and Display*. New York: Pace Gallery.
Rush, Dana. 2001. "Contemporary Vodun Arts of Oudiah, Benin." *African Arts* 34 (4): 32–47.
———. 2013. *Vodun in Coastal Benin: Unfinished, Open-Ended, Global*. Nashville: Vanderbilt University Press.
Scheu, Patricia. 2016. "Oversouls and Egregores in Vodou: Esoteric Meaning in Land and Ritual." In *Vodou in the Haitian Experience: A Black Atlantic Perspective*, 193–208. Lanham, MD: Lexington Books.
Sibanda, Backson. 1997. "Governance and the Environment: The Role of African Religion in Sustainable Utilization of Natural Resources in Zimbabwe." *Forests, Trees and People Newsletter* 34:27–31.
Siebert, Ute. 2008. "Are Sacred Forests in Northern Bénin 'Traditional Conservation Areas'? Examples from the Bassila Region." In *African Sacred Groves*, edited by Michael J. Sheridan and Celia Nyamweru, 164–176. Athens: University of Ohio Press.
Sodikoff, Genese Marie. 2012. *Forest and Labor in Madagascar: From Colonial Concession to Global Biosphere*. Bloomington: Indiana University Press.
Stoller, Paul. 2009. *The Power of the Between: An Anthropological Odyssey*. Chicago: University of Chicago Press.

Tsing, Anna Lowenhaupt. 2017. *Mushroom at the End of the World: On the Possibility of Life in Capitalist Ruins*. Princeton, NJ: Princeton University Press.
Turner, Victor. 1967. *The Forest of Symbols: Aspects of Ndembu Ritual*. Ithaca, NY: Cornell University Press.
Verger, Pierre Fatumbi. 1995. *Ewé: The Use of Plants in Yoruba Society*. Rio de Janeiro: Odebrecht.

TIMOTHY R. LANDRY is Associate Professor of Anthropology and Religious Studies at Trinity College, Hartford, Connecticut. He is the author of *Vodún: Secrecy and the Search for Divine Power*, the winner of the 2019 Clifford Geertz Prize in the Anthropology of Religion.

ELEVEN

VODOU, AN INCLUSIVE EPISTEMOLOGY
Toward a Queer Ecotheology of Liberation

Nixon S. Cleophat

INTRODUCTION

"Syèl la konnen nou, se la tè n dwe respekte. Viv lwa yo!" So goes a verse of one of the Vodou ritual songs, which is recited at the beginning of a ceremony. The *adjenikon* (the head ritualist) often invites the congregation to sing this song as a reminder that a *fran* (authentic) Vodouyizan (Vodou practitioner) must live by the ethical precept that their existence is connected not only to the earthly but also natural realms. This verse is also an indication that the success of a Vodou ritual or ceremony lies in the affirmation that the essence of each *lwa* (Vodou divinity) is attached to the metaconnection between material and supernatural forces. For that reason, when singing this song, the ritualist must salute the western direction of the world, which mystically symbolizes the earthly dimension of the cosmos. However, the other three corners (north, air; south, water; east, fire) of the universe are saluted first. To my knowledge, there is no spiritual significance behind why the other elements are saluted first. But one thing that remains consistent is that in Vodou ritual, the four cardinal directions of the cosmos must be saluted and receive equal respect. This is similar to Native American spiritual tradition in which it is an ethical mandate that the personhood of "all things" in creation is recognized during any ritual performance. The lwa embody natural elements that give meaning to and make relevant the mysteries inherent in the supernatural world to the everydayness of the human person. In this capacity, Vodou is a spiritual tradition that affirms the dignity and worth of both the human person as well as nature. This chapter works to advance a queer, ecofriendly epistemology of Haitian Vodou.

In saluting the lwa, the Vodou ritualist venerates and celebrates both masculine and feminine energies in the universe. In Vodou, energy is neither void or neutral; natural forces are animated by energies that represent the wholeness of the cosmos both metaphysically and materially. Hence, the litany recited at the beginning of a Vodou ceremony requires the salutations of the four mystical directions of the universe. The Vodou community celebrates the interconnection of diverse forms of forces in nature. This ethic of interconnectedness propels me to contend that Vodou can be used as a framework for a theology of liberation investigating the intersections of ecology, gender, and sexuality.

This prayer song is not simply for spiritual acclamation or the veneration of the lwa. Rather, it is intended to make ecological ethics the basis of Vodou as well as the characteristics of the lwa. This dimension of Vodou makes its epistemology a liberating praxis for addressing issues related to ecology, gender, and sexuality. The verse above encourages the Vodouyizan not simply to honor the lwa as spiritual beings but also enable them to realize that the lwa are connected to diverse forms and manifestations of life. In times of drought and other natural disasters, such as the January 2010 earthquake, Vodou practitioners look to the lwa for guidance and relief, since each lwa is connected to a natural element.

This ecological dimension of Vodou has not been thoroughly investigated by scholars. It is true that such scholars as Patrick Bellegarde-Smith and Claudine Michel (2013) have written about the connection between Vodou divinities and natural forces, but they have not focused specifically on how Vodou ecological precepts can be used to address forms of oppression, such as sexism and homophobia. This chapter is one of the few scholarly works focusing on Vodou ecological principles as a paradigm for gender and sexual liberation.

Outside the Vodou world, there are a host of scholars who have done extensive research on the intersection of ecology and theological ethics. Over the past several decades, feminist scholars from various academic disciplines, such as theology, religious ethics, anthropology, and sociology, have made addressing ecological crisis and environmental degradation a socioethical endeavor. They have posited that any theological project that seeks to liberate the human person must be linked to the liberation of the planet (McFague 1979). Feminist scholars, such as Rosemary Ruether (2005), have relied on both Christian and "Pagan" traditions to highlight the importance of connecting the liberation of the human person, especially women, to that of the planet. Such scholars contend that oppression works in a weblike system and that patriarchal sexism and ecocide, like other forms of oppression, are interrelated. They are the result of the domination of power instituted by the dominant in history. Sally McFague (1979) explores this issue extensively in her groundbreaking book, *Models of God*, by adhering to the logic of the universe being the body of God to concienticize the human community. Recently, the womanist ethicist Melanie Harris (2017) takes this further by connecting the issue of ecology to gender and racial injustice. The difference between Harris's work and the other accounts on ecology is that she uses the African American historical experience to explicate how the issue of ecocide is deeply connected to racial and gender injustice.

Feminst and womanist scholars have contributed significantly to studies and research projects related to ecology and evirnomental justice. They have changed the discourse about liberation, which traditionally has been human-centric. Lacking in the scholarship of these scholars is the voice of indigenous African-based religions, such as Haitian Vodou. In addition, Greta Gaard (1997) contends the feminist approach to ecological work takes for granted the issue of sexuality. There seems to be an underlining perception that both gender and sexuality are interconnected when addressing ecological issues. Gaard utilizes a theoretical anthropological framework to address the shortcomings in eco-feminist thought, formulating an ecological theory that connects the issues of gender and sexuality as well as global oppression. Unlike the other feminist theorists, Gaard does not use a theological lens to examine the issue at stake.

In light of the aforementioned, this chapter is not a first. I am not the first scholar who is analyzing the issues of gender and sexuality in relation to the well-being of the natural world. Nonetheless, this work is among the few academic projects focused on Vodou's ecological precepts to address the issues of gender and sexuality in the Haitian socioreligious context. Importantly, this chapter provides a new insight on the ways in which gender and sexuality are examined in relation to ecology. The paradigm shift that this chapter proposes is a move beyond how scholars in the West talk about ecology and the environment in "scientific" terms and includes in the trajectory indigeneous cosmologies that have long called for a sacred relationship between humans and the earth. Relying on an Afrocentric theological epistemology, I maintain that connecting issues of gender and sexuality is a critical approach that can be used to address ecological injustice (Orabator 2018). In this chapter, I contend that Vodou's ethic of ecology goes beyond the speculation around the sacredness of nature or the environment but that the embodiment and sacredness of the natural world is made manifest in spiritual entities and energies, such as the lwa. I posit that Vodou embodies an ethical epistemology that links the liberation of nature and the human person. This is a directive for the affirmation of the well-being of the planet as well as the liberation of women and LGTBQ persons.

I highlight the fact that the lwa are physical manifestions of the natural world in a twofold fashion. First, I examine how different personalities and characteristics of the lwa speak to the diversity of natural elements. For example, a lwa like Danbala, the oldest Vodou divinity in the form of a python, who is associated with air and whose domain is the sky, requires his devotees to respect the natural elements associated with his being. Second, I argue that the lwa's beingness and essence are made manifest during possession. Whatever elements are associated with the lwa become visible when the lwa mount their reklame, the chosen ones. That is, the lwa do not simply represent nature; they also make nature tangible through possession. And when elements of nature become materialized through the lwa, they do not discrimate. Whatever human body that is available and worthy of being ridden becomes instantly a receptacle. In this regard, the manifestation of the lwa reveals that the human body is a performative site for natural elements and energies. I argue that Vodou's ecological ethics can be used to affirm the dignity and humanity of those who have been ostracized because of their gender or sexual orientation. It is the ecological association of each lwa that makes their manifestation on earth liberating.

In this chapter, I rely on various epistemologies, including those outside the field of theology. I divide the chapter into four sections. First, to understand the relationship between the lwa and the natural and physical world, I ciritcally examine mythology and cosmology as concepts that shed light on the ways in which the essence of the Vodou spirits relate to nature and how that relationship is manifest in the physical (human) embodiment. Second, I look into the ways that the characteristics of the lwas are perceiced and understood in Vodou rituals. Third, I evaluate how gender and sexuality are viewed in the greater Vodou community. Specifically, I investigate how Vodou ecological ethics create an inclusive space for women, homosexuals, lesbians, and trans persons. In this section, I not only address sexism and homophobia but also highlight how individuals who are disciminated against in both Haiti and the diaspora have been able to flourish interpersonally, spiritually, socially, and economically. Fourth, I examine the critical role of spirit possession in the affirmation of the humanity and dignity of the marginalized. Specifically, I underline how spirit possession not only makes natural energies tangible in ritual spaces but also constructs a libeartive praxis for the historically ostracized.

MYTHOLOGY AND COSMOLOGY IN VODOU: THE LWA AS ORNAMENTS OF NATURE AND MIRRORS FOR HUMANKIND

Vodou does not subscribe to a primordial fall of humankind as held in the Judeo-Christian creation myth. The history of humanity did not start with humans' first parents (Adam and Eve) disobeying the Creator of the cosmos. The destiny of this world was not turned into a tale of betrayal and condemnation because the first human persons disturbed the perfect state of harmony between God and humankind. Sin, according to Vodou mythology, did not enter the world because of humankind's awareness of their existence. There is no such thing as a concrete belief in a world that differentiates between good and evil. Bondye, the supreme benevolent divinity, according to Vodou mythology, did not establish any prohibitions that resticted access to natural forms of knowledge and awareness. Vodou mythology does not focus on a creation story that possibly was authored by a human person. Vodou's mythology speaks to the idea that myths contain "the primordial and pristine moral tradition of any given people" (Magesa 1997, 18). Through myths, we learn that the universe was not created by an all-powerful divine agent who became distraught with his or her own creation because of original sin. Like other African-derived religions, Vodou contends that the universe is full of spiritual energies in the forms of natural phenomena, such as the stars, the lwa, and animate and inanimate elements that are "directly related, and always interacting with [one another]" (Magesa 1997, 27), while also informing personhood and collective identity. The wholeness of the universe is grounded in the interrelatedness of all things in the universe. There is nothing in the universe that exists independently from other entities in nature and on earth. Laurenti Magesa defines this interrelatedness beautifully when he states, "The world of forces is held like a spider's web of which no single thread can be caused to vibrate without shaking the whole network" (Magesa 1997, 113). The universe, in essence, is a model of an organic whole composed of "supra-sensible or mystical correlations or participations" (Magesa 1997, 115).

Haitian Vodou does see humankind as the agent whom Bondye has put in charge to dominate humanity and nature (Cleophat 2016). The human person is not considered the steward of creation (Hurbon 1972). Humans were not put on earth to domesticate the animals, plants, and ecosystems. Humankind's role is attached to the mutual respect between humanity and nature, between humankind and the spiritual cosmos (Cleophat 2016). "The natural environment has its own claim on humanity and is to be respected in its own right" (Erskine 2005, 4). In Vodou, the human person is perceived as an additional element in creation, whose existence is attached to the natural order of the universe (Brown 2006). The human person, in this capacity, is not superior to other beings and nonbeings in the cosmos.

For humanity to be in harmony with the law of nature, there must be mutual-reciprocal relations between the cosmos, the metaphysical and material world, and the human person. This ecoethical principle does not only exist in Vodou; it is also prevalent in other indigenous religions. For example, according to John Mbiti (1969), in many West African traditional religions the human person is defined as the priest of creation. Humankind's role in relation to creation and humanity is not one that makes the human person the ruler of creation but a responsible agent that sees his or her existence and livelihood inseparable from the existence and condition of the cosmos (Mbiti 1969). Jacob Olupona (1999) takes this further by arguing that humans, in such African cosmogonies as the Yoruba, are not viewed as the stewards of creation, given that they are not superior to natural elements, such as leaves and rocks. In the African cosmology, animals, plants, humans, and minerals have been endowed with similar spiritual essence and worth. Both humankind and nature are "imbued divine essence" (Olupona 1999, 9).

This idea of creation is the foundation of Vodou, which mandates that humans rely less on a supreme divine ruler to make amends for their wrongdoing against creation, the cosmos, nature, and their fellow human persons. As found in many West African indigenous religions, the fulfillment of the ethic of the abundance of life lies in the understanding that the affirmation of the well-being of the human person and the natural world must take place in community. Failure to do so may lead to moral and spiritual consequences (Magesa 1997).

As Olupona (1999) maintains, for a human person to be considered trustworthy, they must be loyal and committed to the well-being of the earth. One who fails to follow this mandate is viewed as "one who betrays a sacred trust . . . [which, in return,] betrayed the Earth (*o dale*) and the ultimate punishment is mysterious death, which is also described as perishing in the Earth (*o bale lo*). . . . All the above go to prove that the Earth is a sacred entity whose trust is jealously guarded by the African people" (Olupona 1999, 181).

One of the ethical mandates to which Vodou practitioners must adhere is that they must relate human existence to everything in the cosmos, especially spiritual energy. Everything, whether the earth, trees, water, living beings, nonliving beings, animals, or human persons, is interrelated (Michel 2006). "The land, the family, and the spirits are, in a way, one and the same" (McCarthy Brown 1991, 98). Human essence and worth are not independent of natural phenomena and natural entities. Human existence depends on the well-being of other living and nonliving beings. Our role is to acknowledge the interdependence and interrelatedness of humankind and life outside the human sphere. By acknowledging this, humankind is able to affirm the sacredness of all things and beings in the universe. Human beings as well as other beings are manifestations of the divine (Brown 2006).

According to Mbiti (1969), one of the ecological precepts of African-derived religions is the recognition that the most supreme God is not alien to creation. There is not an estranged relationship between God and humanity, although God is often portrayed as the distant unmoved "Mover." However, when it comes to creation and nature, God's imprint is on everything in nature. In fact, in African-derived religions, such natural phenomena as the moon, the sky, thunder, and rain are not just the manifestations of the divine but also represent metaphysical characteristics of the essence and embodiment of God. Human life is understood to be connected to other forms of life, because God's creation is not compartmentalized. God has endowed everything in creation with equal worth (Mbiti 1969). Human life is not worthier than other forms of life. This idea corresponds to Yoruba cosmology wherein plants, animals, minerals, and humans have been endowed with the same level of worth and dignity. In Yoruba philosophy, nothing in the universe or earth is void. Everything is animated with soul and energy (Olupona 1999).

It is not a coincidence that Haitian Vodou defines life as an intertwined mystery, which can be explained in the kinship between all beings and nonbeings (Cleophat 2016). It is this very belief that convinced enslaved Africans to fight for collective freedom (Michel 2006). The enslaved did not only rely on Olorun, Olodumaré, or Nana Buluku (the supreme divinities in Vodún and Orisa in West African indigenous religions) or the spirits of their ancestors to be emancipated from European slavery and plantocracy; they also put great faith in the plants and herbs that fortified their physical strength and heightened their spiritual senses (Olupona 2013). Not only did they rely on the spirits of their ancestors but also the plants and herbs in their environment to create warfare weapons to fight the Napoleonic army and liberate themselves from chattel slavery (Cleophat 2016). They relied on the natural world for survival and self-care. It is no wonder that in all Vodou rituals there are *regleman* (ritual protocols) dedicated to the recognition of the interrelatedness of all beings and nonbeings in the community. In addition, the importance of libations and water are appropriate here. Whereas African religions offer water to trees and plants, Christians opt to cut down trees, mill them, and turn them into crosses. Sometimes, this deep sense of respect for the natural world is often misconstrued by outsiders, especially evangelical Christians, as being the worship of totems or objects (Cleophat 2016).

The ecofeminist Sallie McFague (1979, 118) captures Vodou's idea of the interdependence of the physical and natural word when she maintains: "We are, in the most profound ways, 'not our own': we belong, from the cells of our bodies to the finest creations of our minds, to the intricate, constantly changing cosmos. The ecosystem, of which we are part, is a whole: the rocks and waters, atmosphere and soil, plants, minerals, and human beings interact in a dynamic, mutually supportive way that make all talk of atomistic individualism indefensible."

OTHERWORDLY BEINGS: THE CHARACTERISTICS OF THE LWA

Unlike the Judeo-Christian creation narrative, the beginning of the cosmos commences with the history of the lwa. The world of the lwa predetermined the existence of the human world. The history of human life begins with natural processes and the essence of spiritual enegies. Creation started with the great cosmic egg of the rainbow serpent Danbala Wèdo (supreme snake divinity) and his counterpart Ayida Wèdo (female snake divinity) whom Bondye, "the Great Ancestor, the first Founder and Progenitor," gave the order to bring into existence all beings (Magesa 1997, 12). The creation myth in Vodou is not based on speculation of the the historical beginning of the world. Rather, most Vodouyizan do not interpret the creation story as a literal historical account, as many Christians believe. Rather, Vodou practitioners see the beginning of the cosmos being based on mythological creativity. For that reason, Vodou practitioners do not, for the most part, emphasize the story of the beginning of the world as being essential to their practice. To them, trying to comprehend something out of reach of human reality is a vain endeavor.

In the name *Danbala*, one finds the word *Da*, which in Fongbe (one of Benin's local languages) means the origin and essence of life (Deren 1953, 2). He is considered the beginning of movement both in the natural and physical world. Danbala's principles epitomize profound wisdom and understanding of the connection between human existence and the mystery in the universe. He represents the ancient past wherein all things in the universe were once intricately connected. He is the lwa who travels across the sky with Ayida Wèdo. Together, they generate and control the flow of the waters of heaven. Danbala's role as a sky divinity is extended on earth through his dominance over springs and rivers, which are heavenly waters that nourish and nurse the human race (Deren 1953).

As Maya Deren (1953, 3) states, "No man has ever witnessed the moment when life begins; it is in the moment of its ending that the limits of life, hence life itself, are manifest." It is a given that none of us know how the creation process of the world began, but through death, according to Vodou, humans encounter the cyclical nature of life. It is through death that one experiences the intersection of life and death. The story about creation becomes tangible at the time of death. There, the creation of the world becomes a transnatural phenomenon.

The story of Danbala and Ayida, regarding the process of creation, is similar to the Dogon creation story about the original order of creation. In the Dogon creation myth, "the creative process began with a primordial egg of the universe, divided into two placenta by its own internal vibration. Each placenta contained a pair of male and female twins ... each of which was equipped with two spiritual principles of the Supreme God" (Magesa 1997, 18). Both Danbala Wèdo and Ayida Wèdo represent the umbilical cord that unites all forms of life. They served as the blueprint of creation. In Danbala and Ayida, we encounter a dyad of the feminine and masculine (Bellegarde-Smith and Michel 2013). Together, they create life through the Marasas (the twin spirits). What is at the center of the Danbala and Ayida union is the creation of the world rooted in the union of masculine and feminine energy, affirming the divinity inherent in the beingness of all humans (Bellegarde-Smith and Michel 2013).

The Dogon concepts of Nommo (male) Amma (female) are similar to the principle of Marasa, which speaks to humankind's twinned nature: "half matter, half metaphysical, half mortal, half immortal, half human, half divine" (Deren 1953, 4). The Marasas are said to be the first children of Bondye, and their rite is considered the oldest spiritual tradition in Dahomean culture. Even though they are considered lwa, they are in a pantheon all by themselves. They, in essence, signify "firstness, newness, beginning, innocence" (Deren 1953, 4). They are the beginning of the history of the humanity. In the Marasas we can acknowledege that humans are part of a complex composite scheme that goes beyond dualitic existence and form. That is, the human person is not simply a product of male or female chromosomic makeup. And there is an in-between mystical element that contributes to the being and spirit of the human person.

Marasas, though representing duality, exemplify the idea of multiplicity and diverse forms of expression and being. They reveal that human life is not confined to a system of binarism that dichotomizes the being of the human person. The Marasas are not "to be separated into competitive, conflicting dualism. In Vodoun one and one make three; two and two make five; for the end of the equation is the third and fifth part, respectively, the relationship which makes all the parts meaningful" (Deren 1953, 2). The Marasas inform us that the essence of the human person is multidimensional. Humans are connected not only to the human experience but also to the metaphysical as well as natural processes. The Marasas are the origin of all the lwa as well as the beginning of the human race. They are the first cosmic reality that connects the spirit and human world. They are considered both the first parents as well as the first children of the human race (Deren 1953).

Just as the human body would be useless or essenceless without breath and blood flowing through it, in the same way, without the lwa nature and the universe would have been an "amoral mass of organic matter" with no relevance to the physical world (Deren 1953, 9). Without the existence of the lwa, physical (human) life would have been meaningless. Their energy animates and gives nature meaning. They represent elements in nature. They are earth, air, fire, and water. These natural elements have meanings and significance for Vodou practitioners, because through the lwa these natural elements become real as well as meaningful to humans. Because of the association between the lwa and natural elements, Vodou practitioners consider nature sacred, a holy tabernacle, the domain of divinities.

The lwa are not antithetical to the existence of Bondye. Each lwa represents a characteristic of Bondye. Even though Vodouists make mention of Bondye in their daily payers, similar to the other African-related supreme divinities, such as Olodumare (the Yoruba Supreme Being), Bondye seems to be removed from the daily ritual actvities of humans (Rey 2000). Bondye seems to leave it up to the lwa to assist humans in their daily ordeals and struggles. Thus, in Vodou, the idea of a Supreme Being "operates as a principle of ultimacy that gives an underlying unity to the multiplicity of deities and spirits: the many powers are understood to be aspects of, or intermediaries, for, the One God" (Ray 2000, 22). Bondye is the link between the lwa and humans, between nature and the physical world. The lwa are forces of nature, including the ocean, earth, fire, air, and death, for the achievement and fulfillment of the human, person living in harmony with the universe and the world beyond (Tinsley 2011).

Not only are the lwa the closest entities to Bondye; they are also the symbolic representations of nature. For exmaple Ogou, a lwa of might and justice, and the Petwo lwa (fierce Central African spirits with powerful healing skills) are associated with the element of fire (Deren 1953). Ogou (war and metal spirit) is the lwa that controls the element of fire; he prevents it from consuming humanity to ashes. While the lwa serve as intermediaries between Bondye and the human community, they are moral agents that make the invisible and mysterious visible and relatable in the human world.

They are "supernatural in the same sense that a principle is super-natural or abstract" (Deren 1953, 10).

THE LWA AS SYMBOLIC REPRESENTATIVES OF NATURE

Vodou's ecological ethic confirms that the universe and the being of the human person are connected. Humans exist as organic beings "in line with other energetic forces and spirits" (Bellegarde-Smith and Michel 2013, ii). In Vodou cosmology, nature does not work with dichotomies or polarities "but with dyads and with abiding balance and overarching equilibrium" (Bellegarde-Smith and Michel 2013, iii). The lwa, as representatives of nature, occupy different natural domains; they do not compete with one another for power and dominance. They do not allow their differences to create strife among them. They put their differences aside for the betterment of humankind and the well-being of nature. For example, if a *wanga* (spiritual work) is to be performed by a Rada lwa (West African–derived spirits), no Petwo lwa (lwa with diasporic and Central African roots in Haiti) will try to undermine the power of the Rada lwa. If anything, the Petwo lwa will bless a wonga performed by a Rada spirit.

This does not mean that Vodou does not celebrate differences and diverse forms of realities. On the contrary, Vodou embraces differences, but differences are not markers for competition or denial of essence for the sake of assigning more significance to a being or object over others. It is no surprise that Vodou and other Afro-derived spiritual traditions embrace the idea that both the feminine and the masculine have equal worth and that they complement each other. The union between Danbala and Ayida speaks to the idea of difference in Vodou being celebrated for the sake of life's affirmation. "In fact Danbala and Ayida as one, as gendered homornes, are housed in each of our own bodies" (Bellegarde-Smith and Michel 2013, 17). The lwa are "archetypes of energetic forces that embody gendered ideals, purposeful directions, and moral qualities" (Bellegarde-Smith and Michel 2013, 19).

When the humanity of a person is denied, it is not just the person who is affected but also the natural and spiritual orders attached to the spirit of that person (Cleophat 2016). Whatever happens, good or bad, to a human person also disturbs the universe and vice versa. When we pollute the air, it is not just the environment that we destroy; we also create an imbalance in the mystical realms of the spirits and our ancestors from whence we came (Deren 1953; Orabator 2018). Oppressing any human being who has been claimed by a deity like Danbala is an assault against the cosmological principle related to the nature and essence of Danbala, who is the "origin and essence of life . . . [who] is at once the ancient past and the assurance of the future" (Deren 1953, 11). Human liberation, therefore, must be linked to the liberation of the planet, because the being of the human person is connected to the spiritual energies and powers that reside in the cosmos. What we do to a human person does not just affect them; it also upsets and disrupts the natural processes of the universe. Similar to Rastafarian theology, in Vodou "the dignity of humanity is tied up with preserving and maintaining the dignity of the natural order. We cannot preserve the dignity of humanity when we destroy the unity of body and the natural order" (Erskine 2005, 39).

MASISI AND MADIVIN AS "DIVINE HORSEMEN"

In Vodou, the being of the human person is not simply attached to their physical makeup but also to a spiritual essence called *gwo bon nanj* (the big angel of the human person). While many may have associated this term with the soul of the human person, unlike the idea of the soul, this concept is not detached from our being. The gwo bon nanj is split into two realities that determine the moral compass of the human person (Montilus 1983). After death, the gwo bon nanj takes other spiritual forms, such as lwa that can come back to help the human community as moral agents. Its principle creates the psychic connection between the human person and the lwa (Deren 1953). This phenemenon, for lack of a better term, is called "possession." In Vodou, we use the term *spirit riding* or *mounting*, because the idea of "possession" connotes the invasion of a foreign spirit, which does not correlate with the democratic mutuality between the *serviteur*, "the possessed," and the lwa. As Joan Dayan (1997, 15) compellingly states,

> The language of possession, or *the crise de loa*—that moment when the [lwa] inhabits the head of his or her serviteur—articulate the reciprocal abiding of human and [the divine]. The "horse" is said to be mounted and ridden by the [lwa]. The event is not a matter of domination, but a kind of double movement of attenuation and expansion. For make no mistake about it, the [lwa] cannot appear in epiphany, cannot be made manifest on earth without the person who becomes the temporary receptacle or mount. And the possessed gives herself up to become an instrument in a social and collective drama.

The idea of possession in Vodou is not an invasion of a foreign entity on the physical site of the human person. Rather, it is a moment of mutuality and reciprocity that generates a mystical interconnectedness between the essence of the human person and metaphysical mysteries. It is in such mystical moment that the individual being mounted by a lwa transcends the human world into the spirit world.

Vodou welcomes everyone regardless of their gender, sexuality, or race. It is not surprising that women, same-gender-loving, and transgender persons are often attracted to and feel welcome in Vodou spaces and rituals from Africa to Haiti (McCarthy Brown 1991). It is not the marginalized that choose Vodou at their own will or out of sheer folly. Rather, the lwa themselves have made it their business to be a shield of protection for and affirmers of the dignity of the marginalized. Women are accepted by the lwa as equal to men because like men they are a product of nature. And nature does not discriminate against anything to which it gives birth. In Vodou ecological ethics, all things in the universe are created equal and interrelated.

Vodou celebrates female agency and autonomy because they embody the feminine mystical aspect of nature. Women are the descendants of the Ezili divinities. Vodou, unlike Christianity, does not associate the female primordial past with a vilified female ancestor, such as Eve. This is not to say that women who practice Vodou do not face discrimination from both Haitian society and the Vodou community. Despite this, the radical inclusiveness of Vodou creates space and empowers women spiritually, socially, and economically (Felima 2016). Deborah O'Neil and Terry Rey (2012) capture this reality vividly in their article "The Saint and Siren: Liberation Hagiography in a Haitian Village," by highlighting the ways in which women, especially those with Vodou sensibilities, in Bord de Mer de Limonade, a northern Haitian seaside village, relied on the Haitian-origin Catholic Saint Philomena for survival and strength. Women in Bord de Mer see Philomena as the "orchestrator of spiritual redemption and mediator" of [their] identity" (171). These women relate to Philomena because her story is one of resilience and survival in the face of a male-dominated society and religious status quo. Her story counteracts "decrees of male Catholic hierarchy" (177). "The villagers [in Bord de Mer de Limonade] adore their patroness, and she in turn helped them with the struggles of daily life" (177). Importantly, women find stories about such saints as Philomena appealing because their narratives mirror their own. Haitian women in such places as Bord de Mer understand the martyrdom of such saints because, like the typical Haitian woman, these female saint martyrs were once victims of violence and exploitation orchestrated by male supremacy and misogyny. The life of the Haitian peasant woman is misery. There is not a woman who hasn't been struck.

Importantly, the villagers, especially women, in Bord de Mer have not simply adopted Philomena as a Catholic saint. They have reappropriated and orally canonized her as a Vodou deity, such as La Sirèn, the supreme divinity of the sea, whom a great number of Vodouyizans see as a lwa who can alleviate the poverty and misery of the poor. La Sirèn, similar to other water divinities, is viewed as a transformer of and one who makes dreams come true for the oppressed. Water divinities such as La Sirèn "express the continuity of life among those not yet born, the living, and the living-timeless" (O'Neil and Rey 2012, 175). They link "ancient African senses of woman power and water power" and "[turn] poor ordinary women into community leaders and healers" (175).

One of the interesting aspects of the Philomena story is how her devotees, as Vodou practitioners, recontextualize her role in their daily life. It only makes sense that Saint Philomena would be regarded as a liberator of women and the least of these in Bord de Mer, given that her devotees rely on a Vodou spiritual hermeneutic to relate to her. In this capacity, these women see themselves in Saint Philomena, just like they do with Dantò, Freda and La Sirèn. They see Saint Philomena as part of a Vodou metamystical circle of female empowerment and liberation (see Montgomery in this volume).

As Maya Deren (1953, 12) maintains, Vodou salutes women as "the divinity of the dream," the destiny of humankind. Women, as the Ezilis embodied, have "the capacity to conceive beyond reality, to desire beyond adequacy, to create beyond need" (Deren 1953, 12). Haiti is a patriarchal society wherein women are often reminded that they are inferior to men; they are men's property, and their roles in society are to be wives, mistresses, and mothers (Brown 2001). But Vodou provides women with liberative alternatives. Because of Vodou, many women have gained economic power as well as social status (Felima 2016). The dynamism of the lwa provides a safe haven for women to escape daily sexist jokes or popular music that denigrates women and lowers them. In Eric Montgomery's *Shackled Sentiments*, Natacha Giafferi-Dombre (2019) took a different approach by alluding to the idea that it is not Vodou per se that is liberating to women but the mutual relationship between them and lwa, such as the Ezilis, that gives women the fortitude to stand against patriarchy and misogyny in Haitian society.

The Ezili divinities transcend human restrictive forces and realities that are hindrances to human development and flourishing. For that reason, *madivin* (lesbians) and *masisi* (effeminate gay men) found in the Ezilis an anchorage to forge their own sexual and gender identities. Ezili Freda (a rooted Dahomean Rada divinity) generates courage in those who live on the margins of society because of their gender and sexuality. Her being challenges Western hegemonic powers related to binaries around gender and sexuality (Tinsley 2011). The complexities around such lwa as Ezili Freda can be used as a lens to understand the issues of race, gender, and sexuality in society. The Ezilis embody divine forces of love, sexuality, gender, maternity, creativity, fertility, and gender fluidity. Through the Ezilis, sexually fluid women understand their bodies in relation to spirits, not simply through social circumstances (Tinsley 2011).

Masisi, in Vodou culture, are viewed as the proteges of the Ezilis, who embody grace, elegance, and creativity in their daily living in and interaction with the mundane world (Tinsley 2011). Masisi are regarded as children of Dantò (a Petwo diasporic female lwa), relying on her for spiritual protection, social uplifting, and economic survival (Felima 2016). Both Dantò and Freda also represent the history of colorism and class and gender oppression in Haiti. While Dantò is often depicted as the Black Madonna, who is closely connected to single motherhood, she is the patron lwa of poor Black women and lesbians (McCarthy Brown 2001). Dantò mirrors the story of the underprivileged in Haiti. In Dantò, women find groundedness and stability. In Dantò, women are encouraged to rely on nature for practical daily living. But also sometimes the fire element of Dantò can frighten women and other devotees who do not take care of themselves or their children. Yes, Dantò is motherly, but she is also full of maternal rage. "The maternal anger that is called into play when a mother must defend her children turned *Dantò* into a woman warrior during the slave revolution" (McCarthy Brown 2001, 188). We can still witness that maternal anger in her today when one of her children or any human being is being treated unfairly. Because Dantò is aware of the violence to which women are subject in Haitian society, especially when they are forced to stay in abusive domestic relationships, she is a fierce promoter and affirmer of female independence.

Freda is the opposite of Dantò. She epitomizes the ideals of the dominant *mulatta* socioeconomic class in Haiti. For example, Freda is often depicted as a fair skinned, wealthy childless lwa who has an affinity for luxury. The stories about Freda and Dantò speak to the history of colorism and classism in Haiti. Despite this, in the story of Freda all women's stories and the silenced voices of marginalized sexual groups such as masisi are heard and become visible (Tinsley 2011). The characteristics of the Ezilis challenge gender and sexual binaries, given that they embrace children of various sexual and gender identities.

The Ezilis do not discriminate against any human beings, regardless of their sexual orientations and gender affinities (Tinsley 2011). "Freda has a special relationship with effeminate gay men and is often considered their *mèt tèt* [the main spirit of the person]" (McAlister 2000, 133). It is important to keep in mind that Freda is not the only spirit who affirms the dignity of the sexually marginalized. Dantò is also a lwa on whom LGBTQ persons rely for affirmation of their gender and sexuality. It has been speculated that she is gender fluid and sexually open. She is neither male nor female. In some Vodou circles, she is perceived as an androgynous divinity. In other circles, she is viewed as the patroness of madivin and transgender persons. It is believed that masisi, madivin, and transgender individuals are blessed children of Dantò (McCarthy Brown 2001).

Vodou allows masisi to congregate and transform homophobic and sexist spaces into "communal yards and public squares" that, in the end, generate nonnormative gender and sexual formations (Tinsley 2011, 422). Vodou is not liberating to women, masisi, or madivin because of its theological ideologies. Rather, because it is guided by supernatural principles, such as the lwa, its ethics are inherently liberating. Although Vodou priests are entitled to interpret the characteristics and principles of the lwa in accordance with their outlooks on life, they are not intermediary agents between the lwa and the human community. "Lwa yo granmoun, yo fè sa yo vle" is a popular saying uttered often by Vodou practitioners to indicate that only the lwa can determine what is right or wrong for the human community. Still, the lwa must work in concert with both Bondye and natural cosmic processes to attend to human needs and wants. Vodou ethics are not based on religious ideologies. Vodou is not a religion whose laws and mandates are based on a sacred book, such as the Bible or Quran. Vodou ethics come from nature itself. Nature is the book on which Vodou practitioners rely to live holistically.

Like other African-derived religions, Vodou is more than a belief about life or a philosophy of how to live life directed by a sacred text. Vodou, to borrow Laurenti Magesa's (1997, 21) phrase, is a "way of life" or "life itself, where a distinction or separation is not made between [Vodou] and other areas of human existence." There is an intricate relationship between life itself and Vodou principles. For that reason, Vodou propels practitioners and followers to use Vodou to affirm, not denigrate, life, because denigrating the worth of a human person or natural entity signifies betraying the ethical fundamentals of Vodou.

TOWARD A QUEER VODOU ECOTHEOLOGY OF LIBERATION: "POSSESSION" AND THE TRANS/ FORMATION OF DESPISED BODIES

I use the term *possession* in this section for the sake of clarity and familiarity. However, I will also make reference to the term *mounting* to describe the encounter between the lwa and the human person. The term *possession* speaks more to the Western notion of the manifestation of spirit in the physical world. The term *possession* connotes that the body and spirit of the possessed is being invaded by an unfamiliar or foreign spirit. Possession seems to suggest that the person undergoing it does not have agency in the process of it. In this capacity, the lwa possessing the body of the human person would appear to violate their spiritual nature. It is this notion of spirit manifestation that makes Western religionists, especially conservative Christians, suspicious or skeptical about the idea of a spirit mounting the body of a human person under normal circumstances. Even charismatic Christian denominations, such as Pentecotalism, rarely use the term *possession* to describe the manifestation of the Holy Spirit, which is similar to the phenemenon of spirit in Haitian Vodou, except the Vodou divinities are more personable and interactive with the human community. The use of the word *possession* in Western religious circles denotes the manifestation of an entity with ill intention taking over someone's body for the sake of defiling them. For that reason, whenever someone is suspected of being under the influence of a spirit other than the Holy Spirit, *possession* is the term used to describe such experiences. The word *possession*, in this capacity, is associated with "demonic" spirit manifestation. Oftentimes, it is used to demonize ancestral religious traditions, such as Vodou, as religious sects that are led by demonic spiritual entities. Possession in Western theological parlance relates to the manifestations of spirits that are considered malevolent entities whose intentions are to cause harm to the human person.

In Vodou, however, the appearances of the lwa are not associated with "demonic" activities. Rather, their visitations are viewed as a special blessing bestowed on the human community. Upon the visitation of a lwa, the community of practitioners are priviledged not only to see nature embodied but also experience firsthand the visibility of the intersection between the divine and the human. The person being mounted by a lwa at that very moment becomes divine by the virtue of the essence of the lwa . So this manifestation does not denigrate the spiritual essence of the human person or devalue their worth. Rather, that individual who is seen as a reklame (chosen) becomes a host of honor, a *chwal* (divine horse[wo]man) who becomes a container of divine energy (Montgomery 2019). That is, metaphorically, that individual becomes a horse who is being ridden or mounted by a dignitary. "The metaphor is drawn from a horse and his rider and the actions and events which results are the expression of the will of the rider" (Deren 1953, 12). Such divine manifestation is not an act of the horse, it is entirely a divine performative act that turns the individual into a sacred instrument for "the reassurance and the instruction of the community" (Deren 1953, 12). Eric Montgomery (2019) took this further by positing that spirit possession as a metamystical performance reveals "past injustices to the forefront of the collective consciousness and is integral to the construction of individual identity.... Spirit possession offers bridges between the past/present, slaver/enslaved, traditional/modern, oppresser/oppressed."

Similar to the Yoruba tradition, in Vodou, even though humans are not considred supernatural beings, every human person by the virtue of the lwa has the potential to become a divinity (Abimbola 2006). In the process of possession, the lwa become the embodiment of the mounted. At this moment, the personality of the lwa becomes that of the possessed person. The gwo bon nanj (the main spirit) of the person is temporarily replaced by the spirit of the lwa (Deren 1953). The manifestation of a lwa makes it possible for a human person to attain divine status, even if it is temporary. The mounted at this point becomes a divine horse(wo)man. Montgomery's work on slave spirits among the Ewes of Togo confirms the phenomenon of metaphysical transformation that takes place during possession in African-derived religions, such as Haitian Vodou. Montgomery (2019, 87) defines the process of possession as an event beyond this world, wherein "men become women, children become adults, the powerless become powerful, and the master becomes the mastered." The slave spirits that are popular among the Adja-Ewes and Fons of southwestern Benin, like the Vodou deities, remind society that the spirits of those who died unjustly due to such social institutions as slavery are not gone and that the human community cannot live peacefully unless they do right by the spirits of the enslaved deceased as well as their progeny (Montgomery 2019).

Even though Vodou recognizes that there are malevolent spirits that can cause harm to the human spirit and body, the lwa are not in the same realm as the former. Vodou cosmology, like that of the Yoruba tradition, has two different categories of spirits: the lwa and *djabs* (malevolent spirits). The lwa is on the side of goodness and benevolence; though they may be forced to punish humans for wrongdoing, they are not by nature evil (Bellegarde-Smith and Michel 2013). They are supernatural entities whose intentions have been designed to help humans realize their full potential by bringing them close to the natural world as well as the ancestral (spirit) domain. On the other hand, the djabs, like the *ajogun* (antigoodness in Yoruba), are "irredeemably" and naturally evil entities who often wage war against humans and the lwa or orisa (Abimbola 2006). For example, any human acts such as sexism, homophobia, or ecocide that seem to be a threat to the dignity of the cosmos and the human person would be considered actions caused by the djabs, because anyone who is in close proximity of the essence of the lwa would not commit, support, or condone any acts or thoughts that are intended to devalue the worth of nature and the human person. Accordingly, it is a gross theological faux pas to associate the manifestation of a lwa with that of a djab, given that the lwa enter the bodies of the chosen during ceremonies not because they want to take away the agency of the mounted but because they want them to go beyond the human condition by becoming one with nature as well as the spirit world. Spirit manifestation is a selective endeavor. Although the lwa walk with all of us, they do not mount everyone. They mount the reklame. They choose who should become their divine horse(wo)men. This choice has nothing to do with one's socioeconomic status, educational background, gender, sexuality, or race.

In the process of being mounted by a lwa, the person mounted becomes the deity itself, but the shape and form of the body remains intact (Strongman 2008). This partly has to do with how the body is perceived in Vodou; the body of the mounted is seen as a worthy vessel that can be inhabited by both human and spiritual energies. During the manifestation of a lwa, the body of the reklame is "transmogrified" into the Vodou divinity that enters the body at that moment (Bellegarde-Smith and Michel 2013). This phenomenon provides a rare opportunity for the human community to interact with a divinity closely. This moment is never taken for granted. The community uses it to inquire about issues affecting them personally as well as seeking counsel from the lwa present. Similarly, in Adja-Fon traditition, "new spirits arise in times of crisis, and spirit mediumship is a powerful vehicle foe elevating contemporary concern and critiquing social and moral conditions" (Montgomery 2019, 93).

At this intersection, spirit does not discriminate. The lwa will mount any body, regardless of their gender and sexuality. They will make use of whatever reklame body to transmit messages from Ginen (the eschaological African mythical world of the ancestors, according to Haitian Vodou) to the human sphere. This moment brings both fear and relief. Those who have betrayed ethical codes of the community are often worried that the lwa will confront and discipline them publicly. The mounting of the lwa also brings a sense of comfort and healing to those who are experiencing hardship and needing the lwa to intervene on their behalf. At this critical crossroad, the sexuality and gender of the mounted becomes the least important aspect of their life.

Upon mounting the human body, the energy and characteractics of the lwa create a trans state of being of the person being mounted. For example, a woman who is being mounted by Ogou (spirit of war and justice) would exibit his characteristeristics related to the principles of justice, power, or strength (Deren 1953). "If a male [lwa] possesses a female devotee, the name of the [lwa] or the pronoun *he* will be used ... when referring to the acting subject responsible for all the events transpiring during that possession; and conversely if a female [lwa] possesses a male, the pronoun will be *she*" (Deren 1953, 111).

A woman who is mounted by male lwa such as Gede (the spirit of death and resurrection) will behave like a typical male Gede by gesturing that the baton Gede (the cane of Gede) is a symbolic phallus. At this point during the possession, this individual becomes a woman-turned-man (McAlister 2000). The mounted person exhibits a transformative stage of performance. A straight-acting man mounted by Gede, even though Gede's gender identity matches that of the man, would be extremely flamboyant in his demeanor, given that among Gede's traits is that he is "the ultimate drama queen in a divine theater of power and gender" (McAlister 2000, 144). Gede disrupts gender and sexual binaries every time he mounts a body. His manifestation on a woman body often alters the body in a translike state where the woman is neither male nor female, and the same can be said about him when he takes possession of a male body. The manifestation of the Gede lwa results in a corporeal regendering, a transcorporeal gender reassignment (Strongman 2008). The Gede lwa perform "an ambiguous gender scheme where both femininity and masculinity are parodied and ridiculed" (McAlister 2000, 145). He performs his theatrical tricks through satire and explicitly sexual jokes.

Gede is an affirmer of ambiguous sexual and gender identities. During possession, he not only disrupts dichotomies related to race, gender, sexuality, and class, but he also depoliticizes ritual spaces through his sexual gestures with his baton (symbol of Gede's huge phallus) and his tirade of *betiz* (profanities). Elizabeth McAlister (2000, 143) beautifully depicts Gede and his politics of gender and sexuality: "Gede opens a philosophical space for opposition and rejection of the suffering of the world through laughter. Gede are very much the spirits of slaves, but they can also be seen as transcendent mawon." Gede embodies the praxis of liberation transcending the human sphere. But the liberation generated during possession corresponds to a metaecological philosophy of freedom and equality wherein every natural phenomenon is perceived to have been endowed with the same and equal amount of dignity and worth.

CONCLUSION

In Vodou, the human person, especially one who is a reklame, is "kissed" by the Vodou divinities. A Vodouyizan, regardless of gender or sexual orientation, upon accepting their calling, as Bellegarde-Smith and Michel (2013) maintain, becomes *yon "nèg"* or a *"nègès" de konesans* (profound mystical knowledge), a wise Black human being, who has been the recipient of profound spiritual insight. A Vodouyizan, regardless of gender or sexual orientation, is a community healer and arbiter of justice. Someone who becomes a part of the Vodou system is anchored "beyond class structures, beyond skin color or wealth that the person might have amassed" (Bellegarde-Smith and Michel 2013, 466). As a healer, this individual does not require academic accolades. This individual is beyond this world—larger than life itself. By virtue of being a Vodouyizan, one benefits from admiration, respect, "and desire for amulation as a moral examplar who has achieved a level of spiritual development that sustains community" (467).

Spirit possession in Vodou proves the point that such scholars as Judith Butler (1988) have argued, that the body, upon assigning gender values and marks to it, is a performative stage on which different actors will transfom in accordance with the acts they are required to perfom. Possession is a way of knowing the self and embodiment of personhood beyond one's gender and sexuality. In that process, the body of the possessed becomes a fluid vessel. A male body can be transformed into female energy if the spirit possessing the individual holds masculine energy (Tinsley 2011). The body, according to Vodou aesthetic, is a malleable container whose essence can also be transferable to different objects, such as *kwi* (calabash plate), *govi* (small clay pot), and *kanari* (huge clay pot), associated with nature (Strongman 2008). The human body is a flexible self that can be transformed into multiple selves (Strongman 2008). The body is not confined or destined to the state of corporality. What we call the body is a metaillusion, and the value assigned to the body, especially in Western society, is a "historical idea" (Butler 1988, 521). Butler's (1988) theory of gender performance acknoweledges the possibilities that the human body can achieve as a historical and cultural phenomenon. But Vodou's ecological precepts take her theory further by not only affirming the cultural and historical possibilities that the body can attain in the here and now but also confirm that through the mounting of the lwa, the human body actually transcends those historical and cultural possibilities. The body, in this regard, attains a transcorporeal state of being wherein it is no longer confined to materiality. At this point, what it means to be a woman or a man is not simply a trained corporeal identity that one needs to surmount by rejecting the social mechanisms that have supported them. Through posession, the lwa disrupt the corporeal projection of gender and sex by turning marginalized bodies into divine transbeings.

The ethical dimension of the lwa lies in their ability to transcend the human soul and body and lead humans—namely, the oppressed—to self-empowerment and liberation. Gays and lesbians in Haiti, for instance, have been able to survive and resist violence, suffering, poverty, and natural catastrophes because they are the recipients of the grace and essence of the lwa. As in Rastafari, bodies that have been dehumanized should not be thought of as unworthy or associated with evils to which they have been subjected. Rather, they must be viewed as life-affirming sites of freedom in the here and now (Erskine 2005).

During the mounting of the lwa, an inseparable tie between the human body and the soul of the universe emerges. The body of the mounted, at this mystical intersection, becomes one with nature and the cosmos. This phenomenon creates a union between the human body and that of the universe. It is by being in touch with the cosmos that the bodies of the marginalized experience freedom from violence both in the past and present. When the lwa mount a human body, they transform it into a divine agent "capable of teaching, healing, and transcending the here and now" (McAlister 2000, 141). Since Vodou does not rely on a sacred text for ethical guidance or *konesans* (mystical knowledge), the body becomes not only a site for spirit manifestation but also a medium for the transmission of ethical communal messages. It is through the body that the mystè (mystery) embodied by the lwa becomes tangible. The body of the mounted becomes a sacred site, a holy tabernacle of the universe. As the Korean feminist theologian Chung Hyun Kyung (1994, 177) puts it so poetically, "The Cosmos is God's 'womb.' This intimate relationship between God and the cosmos is exploding with the seminal energy that generates and regenerates life. God energizes the cosmos, and the cosmos in return moves with the creator in a cosmic dance of exquisite balance of beauty."

The body of the mounted joins the mystical eternal dance between the lwa and natural energies. The mounting of the lwa on the bodies of women, masisi, madivin, and other sexually marginalized persons challenges the idea that their gender and sexual identities are against nature. The lwa as symbolic manifestations of nature affirm that sexually and genderly demonized bodies are not antithetical to (super)natural elements and processes. The manifestation of the lwa in the material world suggests that the liberation of the oppressed should be linked to the liberation of nature and vice versa (Gaard 1997). For example, when we associate abomination with a queer person who happens to be a reklame of a lwa, such as Danbala, we also devalue and fail to realize the natural essence that this devotee of Danbala personifies.

REFERENCES

Abimbola, Kola. 2006. *Yoruba Culture: A Philosophical Account*. Birmingham, UK: Iroko Academic.

Bellegarde-Smith, Patrick, and Claudine Michel. 2013. "Danbala/Ayida as Cosmic Prism: The Lwas as Trope for Understanding Metaphysics in Haitian Vodou and Beyond." *Africana Religions* 1 (4): 458–487.

Butler, Judith. 1988. "Performative Acts and Gender Construction: An Essay in Phenomenology and Feminist Theory." *Theatre Journal* 40 (4): 519–531.

Cleophat, Nixon. 2016. "Haitian Vodou: The Ethic of Social Sin and the Praxis of Liberation." In *Vodou in Haitian Memory: The Idea and Representation of Vodou in Haitian Imagination*, edited by Celucien L. Joseph and Nixon Shabalom Cleophat, 65–78. Lanham, MD: Lexington Books.

Dayan, Joan. 1997. "Vodoun, or the Voice of the Gods." In *Sacred Possessions: Vodou, Santeria, Obeah, and the Caribbean*, edited by Margarite Fernandez Olmos and Lizabeth Paravisini-Gebert, 5–31. New Brunswick, NJ: Rutgers University Press.

Deren, Maya. 1953. *Divine Horsemen: The Living Gods of Haiti*. Kingston, NJ: Mcpherson.

Erskine, Noel. 2005. *From Garvey to Marley: Rastafari Theology*. Gainesville: University Press of Florida.

Felima, Crystal Andrea. 2016. "The Econimics of Vodou: Haitian Women, Entrepreneurship, and Agency." In *Vodou in Haitian Memory: The Idea and Representation of Vodou in Haitian Imagination*, edited by Celucien L. Joseph and Nixon Shabalom Cleophat, 179–189. Lanham, MD: Lexington Books.

Friedson, Steven M. 2010. *Remains of Ritual: Northern Gods in a Southern Land*. Chicago: University of Chicago Press.

Gaard, Greta. 2004. *Toward a Queer Ecofeminism*. New Brunswick, NJ: Rutgers University Press.

Giafferi-Dombre, Natacha. 2019. "American Women Anthropologists of the Twentieth Century on Haitian Vodou: A Brief Overview." In *Shackled Sentiments: Slaves, Spirits, and Memories in the African Diaspora*, edited by Eric J. Montgomery, 3–20. Lanham, MD: Lexington Books.

Harris, Melanie. 2017. *Ecowomanism: African American Women and Earth-Honoring Faiths*. Maryknoll, NY: Orbis Books.

Hurbon, Laennec. 1972. *Dieu dans le Vaudou Haitien* [God in Haitian Vodou]. Paris: Maisonneuve & Larose.

Kyung, Chung Hyun. 1994. "Ecology, Feminism and African and Asian Spirituality: Towards a Spirituality of Eco-feminism." In *Ecotheology: Voices from the South and North*, edited by David G. Hallman, 177–181. Maryknoll, NY: Orbis Books.

Magesa, Laurenti. 1997. *African Religion: The Moral Traditions of Abundant Life*. Maryknoll, NY: Orbis Books.

Mbiti, John. 1969. *African Religions and Philosophy*. New York: Frederick A. Praeger.

McAlister, Elizabeth. 2000. "Love, Sex, and Gender Embodied: The Spirits of Haitian Vodou." In *Love, Sex, and Gender in World Religions*. The Library of Global Ethics and Religion, vol. 2, edited by Joseph Runzo and Nancy M. Martin, 128–145. Oxford: Oneworld.

McCarthy Brown, Karen. 2006. "Afro-Caribbean Spirituality: Haitian Case Study." In *Vodou in Haitian Life, Culture: Invisible Powers*, edited by Patrick Bellegarde-Smith and Claudine Michel, 1–26. New York: Palgrave Macmillan.

———. (1991) 2001. *Mama Lola: A Vodou Priestess in Brooklyn*. Berkeley: University of California Press.

McFague, Sallie. 1979. *Models of God*. Philadelphia: Fortress.

McKayin, Sam. 1994. "An Aboriginal Perspective on the Integrity of Creation." In *Ecotheology: Voices from South and North*, edited by David G. Hallman, 214–215. Maryknoll, NY: Orbis Books.

Michel, Claudine. 2006. "Vodou in Haiti: Way of Life and Mode of Survival." In *Vodou in Haitian Life, Culture: Invisible Powers*, by Patrick Bellegarde-Smith and Claudine Michel, 30–31. New York: Palgrave Macmillan.

Montgomery, Eric. 2019. *Shackled Sentiments: Slaves, Spirits, and Memories*. Lanham, MD: Lexington Books.

Olmos, Margarite Fernandez, and Lizabeth Paravisini-Gebert. 2011. *Creole Religions of the Caribbean: An Introduction from Vodou and Santeria to Obeah and Espiritismo*. New York: New York University Press.

Olupona, Jacob K. 1999. "African Religions and the Global Issues of Population, Consumption, and Ecology." In *Religious Perspectives on Population, Consumption, and Ecology*, edited by Harold Coward and Daniel C. Macguire, 175–199. Albany: SUNY Press.

———. 2013. *African Religions: A Very Short Introduction*. New York: Oxford University Press.

O'Neil, Deborah, and Terry Rey. 2012. "The Saint and Siren: Liberation Hagiography in a Haitian Village." *Studies in Religion* 41 (2): 166–186.

Platoff, Anne M. 2015. "Drapo Vodou: Sacred Standards of Haitian Vodou." *Flag Research Quarterly* 2 (3–4): 3–23.

Ray, Benjamin C. 2000. *African Religions: Symbol, Ritual, and Community*. 2nd ed. Upper Saddle River, NJ: Prentice Hall.

Ruether, Rosemary Radford. 2005. *Intergrating Ecofeminism, Globalization, and World Religions*. Lanham, MD: Rowman and Littlefield.

Strongman, Roberto. 2008. "Transcorporeality in Vodou." *Journal of Haitian Studies* 14 (2): 4–29.

Tinker, George. 1995. "The Full Circle of Liberation: An American Indian Theology of Place." In *Ecotheology: Voices from South and North*, edited by David G. Hallman, 218–224. Maryknoll, NY: Orbis Books.

Tinsley, Amise'eke Natasha. 2011. "Songs for Ezili: Vodou Espistemologies of (Trans)gender." *Feminist Studies* 37 (2): 417–436.

NIXON S. CLEOPHAT is Professor in the Department of Religion at Bloomfield College. He is coeditor of *Vodou in the Haitian Experience: A Black Atlantic Perspective* and *Critical Approaches to Religion: Race, Class, Sexuality, and Gender*.

TWELVE

NECROSCAPE AND DIASPORA

Making Ancestors in Haitian Vodou

Elizabeth McAlister

INTRODUCTION: RENT A NEW YORK
APARTMENT, BUY A HAITIAN TOMB

Frisner Augustin was a renowned Haitian drummer and was also my ritual brother for twenty-five years in a New York Vodou *sosyete* (congregation). He died suddenly in 2012 in Port-au-Prince, back in the neighborhood where he grew up. He held the rank of "priest of the drum" in the Afro-Haitian system called Vodou and was also a teacher of this complex and beautiful musical form. Ountò is the divine force of drumming and rhythmic language, and an Ountògi is someone devoted to the drum and its knowledge. Attending Frisner's last rites opened up a window onto the importance of the priesthood of the drum and got me thinking about how transnational migrants such as Frisner fare by dying in diaspora. Although Haitian mortuary rituals have been well described and analyzed by scholars, little has been written about these aspects of contemporary Vodou in the current age of transnational migration and diaspora, entanglements with the necropolitics of state interventions across borders, technology, rapid change, and people's resilience in adapting rituals in order to sustain them. Here I offer the term *necroscape* as a conceptual addition to the other "disjointed flows that are set in motion" through time and space with increased globalization: "ethnoscapes, mediascapes, technoscapes, financescapes," and religioscapes (Appadurai 1990, 6; McAlister 2005, 251). Necroscapes are flows of meaning and practices around death, including the shipping of human remains for burial across borders and the attendant theological, ritual, legal, financial, and logistical work needed for a proper burial.

Those who labored to produce the many Vodou funerary rituals for Frisner stood in a *kafou kat* (lit. "four crossroads"), a meeting of the four cardinal directions. This crossroads offers a fruitful way to describe the contours of the globalized Haitian necroscape. One axis, a cosmological, theological axis, was the watery line in Vodou thought, separating *la tè* (lit. "the earth") and *anba dlo* (lit. "underneath the water"), where the ancestral dead dwell. This line, sometimes referred to as *lamiwa* (the mirror), separates the living from the ancestors in Ginen, a mythic sacred Africa. Ginen refers to the Africa from which the Afro-Haitian ancestors were transported during the slave trade yet figures more as a cosmological ancestral home and a place of purification that exists outside of historical time and space. Frisner was a product of Ginen in all its guises, a descendent of enslaved and self-liberated Africans who was also a priest of the drum called and initiated by Ginen spirits, according to their wishes, who played at their pleasure. Considering his life, spiritual story, and death theologically is to understand rich and important dimensions of Afro-Haitian cosmology. But limiting the discussion to this aspect of his story, as fascinating as it is, risks painting a romantic view of a complicated life and a tragic death.

The other axis of this crossroads where Frisner lived out his life is the axis of material realities faced by transnational Caribbean migrants who live their lives embedded in social relationships across two nations. The last quarter of the twentieth century, during which Frisner migrated to New York City and traveled to Haiti whenever he could, is characterized by neoliberalism. This entails a shrinking of the social safety net, deregulation, and an emphasis on the individual. Neoliberalism cocreates anti-Blackness, violence against Black people, and the continuing extraction of their wealth long after colonial-era societies have permutated into new deadly and predatory necropolitical forms. Saidiya Hartman (2008, 6) sums up the situation succinctly: "This is the afterlife of slavery—skewed life chances, limited access to health and education, premature death, incarceration, and impoverishment." Caribbean societies were created out of the violence of the slave system and continue to be shaped by neocolonialism, predatory politics, state violence, and natural disasters (Forde 2018, 3). In turn, recent ethnographic attention to Caribbean mortuary practices has illuminated the importance of the dead, the ancestors, and the preservation of historical memory in funerary rites in a world shaped by anti-Black violence (Brown 2008; Forde and Hume 2018). The new necroscapes created by diasporic life, including the challenge of shipping human remains and holding proper funerary rituals, arise from and profoundly contour the disproportionately deadly conditions Haitians face.

These challenges call people to both resilience and flexibility in their engagements with the exigencies of tending to their dead properly under profoundly difficult circumstances.

To be sure, a thread within this latter scholarship in literature and philosophy also celebrates Black knowledge, survival, and joy. Christina Sharpe (2016), writing in *In the Wake: On Blackness and Being*, speaks excruciatingly about the many meanings of the word "wake" in the Black experience. Wakes are funerary rituals that allow for the religious "keeping watch with the dead." Wakes are also the tracks left on the water's surface by a ship, such as a slave ship, as well as the "consequences of something, in the line of flight and/or sight, awakening, and consciousness" (Sharpe 2016, 18). She focuses on the themes of the slave ship's hold, the womb, and the coffle, in ways that echo throughout Vodou ritualizing. We can see below in the Vodou rebirth rituals these common elements of containment, the symbolic roping together of initiates into a coffle, of stripping and social death in a symbolic womb as tomb, and of a watery passage to a new state or condition, followed by a rebirth. Haitian people have ingeniously refashioned elements of the death-dealing disaster that was kidnapping and enslavement into forms of deep knowledge, empowerment, and healing. The cosmology and attendant rituals form a kind of "wake work," or "ways to live in the wake of slavery, in slavery's afterlives, to survive (and more) the afterlife of property." In Sharpe's (2016, 50) philosophical sense of the term, "wake work" becomes "a mode of inhabiting *and* rupturing this episteme with our known lived and un/imaginable lives."

Vodou transformation rituals embody and enact themes of containment, the coffle, death, and rebirth by way of returning under the water to Africa. The labor of producing Frisner's funerary rituals as a form of wake work pointed directly back to his ritual rebirth as a drummer-priest, since one cannot understand the end of the cycle of life without attending its beginning. Viewing Frisner's life could be traced as a spiritual biography, best understood with attention to both axes presented here: the ontological and the material. His autobiography was both a cosmological engagement with the divine and a testament to the life of an artist and teacher who forged rich and joyful relationships despite his position in a world of virulent anti-Black and anti-immigrant racism. He lived for nearly four decades in New York City while nurturing close connections with his Haitian homeland. He died suddenly of a stroke one night at the age of sixty-four in postearthquake Port-au-Prince, in the chaos of sleeping in a tent with friends who had survived the catastrophe. Had he been in a house, with electricity and lights, it might have been clear to others that something was wrong, and he might have survived.

Still, there was no doubt in my mind that Frisner wanted to leave the planet from Haitian soil. My guess is that one reason for this is that he knew his funerary rites would be done correctly. Mortuary rituals have long been of keen interest to scholars of Afro-Atlantic history, since they seem to have endured even in societies where other religious elements were wiped out in what Jon Butler (1992) calls a spiritual holocaust for African American peoples. Funerary rituals and arts were an area where the enslaved were allowed some agency. Or as one historian put it better, these mortuary "freedoms" were "traded for the more powerful unfreedoms" of slavery (Potter 1991, 98). The relative liberty to perform complex funerary rites was part of the colonial necropolitical exchange, as it were. One aspect of the afterlife of slavery is the way that people incorporate its tropes and symbols into ritual memory, in a form of wake work that attends to the shapes of the past as well as the imperative to "keep watch" with and aid the transformation of the dead. The slave ship and its close containment, being tied to others in strict ritual discipline, and transformation into a servant—this time a servant of ancestral divinities—underlie the structure of initiation, and the funerary rituals are its undoing.

Haitian funerary rites have been discussed at different lengths in the ethnographic literature (Beauvoir 2008a; Comhaire-Sylvain 1959; Daniels 2017; Danticat 2010; Deren 1953; Métraux 1946; Richman 2018; Smith 2010). Only Edwidge Danticat (2010) and Karen Richman (2018) treat funerals in terms of the realities of diasporic life. Given both the high financial costs and enormous bureaucratic burdens imposed by states on shipping corpses internationally, there can be no doubt that performing the elaborate funerary rituals that are the ideal in Vodou are contingent, flexible, and subject to great obstacles.

Generally speaking, Haitians value being buried on Haitian soil, and most Haitians prefer burial to cremation. Burial on family land was the norm until the steady collapse of the agriculture sector forced so many into the capital. Now burial in the capital cemetery is second best (Daniels 2017, 966). This means that *dyaspora* (lit. "diaspora," meaning, someone living outside of Haiti) send their loved ones back home for burial when it is financially possible. But the process is expensive, and the bureaucracy is complex (Danticat 2010). The Haitian Embassy in the US must approve the shipping, which requires that families must gather the death certificate, a burial permit, a passport for the deceased (even if it is expired), proof of registration with an American funeral home, a letter of embalming, and a notarized letter of noncontagious disease (the fees for these papers cost approximately US$350 in 2018). Caskets must be specially sealed for air transportation, and a letter must be presented from the funeral home in Haiti that will receive the body at the airport. The body must be shipped by a funeral home that is a "known shipper," and only a few airlines provide this service; most bodies go on American Airlines. The cost of shipping is an average of US$7,000, not including the price the Haitian funeral parlor will charge to collect the body and store it, about US$2,500. Waiting for family members throughout the diaspora to assemble in Haiti for the funeral is expensive also, as keeping a body cold at the proper temperature can cost up to US$65 each day, and more in the provinces. In 2012, funerals in Haiti cost an average of $5,000, and interest rates for loans against them could rise to 150 percent (McFadden 2017). Set against the average Haitian income of $850 per year, these costs are impossible to afford for most living in Haiti and expensive for family in the diaspora as well. A burial insurance industry has grown over the past decades, and people both in Haiti and abroad pay each month for themselves and their parents to have a big funeral and be buried in Haiti. In 2019, as of this writing, the director of a funeral home popular in the Haitian community in Brooklyn estimated that five bodies leave John F. Kennedy airport for Port-au-Prince each week.

Frisner was a transnational religious artist, someone who lived with one foot in each of two countries. He brought religious musical knowledge and a brilliant pedagogy in teaching drumming from Haiti to the creative youth of New York and brought musicians, anthropologists, and remittances back to Haiti. Frisner generated a circuit of exchange of rhythms and tradition, money, goods, relationships, and sex, which eventually produced lifelong partnerships and children, as well as dance troupes, doctoral dissertations, books, and albums.[1] He was awarded the National Heritage Fellowship from the National Endowment for the Arts and numerous other artistic awards. Living frugally in Brooklyn allowed him to send remittances to his sister and other family members when he could. And with a kind of nostalgia for the future, he wanted to retire in Haiti, to die and to be buried there with the proper rituals done on his behalf. Who but a true transnational would pay rent on an apartment in Brooklyn but build and own a family tomb in Port-au-Prince?[2] (See fig. 12.1.)

THE MAKING OF A PRIEST OF THE DRUM:
WOMB AND WATER

Nobody did more than Frisner Augustin to develop a serious method for teaching Haitian drumming. He taught numerous apprentices who went on to make careers in this specialized niche. He recounted his life as a sacred story in which the spirits played the starring roles, and he served at their pleasure, embellishing each of their specific rhythms with his signature virtuosity. For Frisner, playing

Figure 12.1. Frisner Augustin pours a libation on the tomb he built for his family in the Gran Simitye, Port-au-Prince, Haiti. Photograph by Chantal Regnault, 1998.

and teaching Haitian folklore and Afro-Creole religious music was a calling, a charge, a passion, and a gift bequeathed to him by the ancestors (see also Michel 1996, 288). His nickname, "Ti-kèlèp," was an onomatopoeia for the galloping sound of the *boula*, known as the "baby" drum that holds down the rhythm and crosscuts the other drums' voices. The stories he told of his life often featured his ancestral spirits and the special protection they offered him. When it came time for him to be buried, it fell to his ritual elders to perform the important rituals that would attend to these special relationships properly.

Frisner was born in Port-au-Prince "sou Estimé," or "under the regime of Dumarsais Estimé," phrased in the way of older Haitians that marks birth dates by presidential era. It was the spring of 1948, and his mother Andrea gave birth to him in the shade under a tree outside the general hospital of Port-au-Prince while waiting for a hospital bed. After birthing her healthy infant, she took him home a few blocks away to the one-room shack she shared with his father (Wilcken 2012, 8). Frisner grew up there in the quartier behind the capital city's Grand Cimetière, which, by the time he brought me and other drumming students back to visit in the early 1980s as a successful maestro and teacher, had become a labyrinth of impoverished side streets called *koridò* (corridors) passable only on foot. He was often hungry as a child and more out of school than in it for want of tuition. He made himself useful in the Koridò Djòn (John's corridor) as a bright and outgoing young kid who could be trusted to do errands for the adults and carry them out properly. This most powerful household in the quartier was in fact a Vodou temple, headed by the Vodou priest Djòn himself. Apprenticing himself to the drummers of the Vodou society, Frisner spent his teenaged years developing into one of the most promising young percussionists in the country (fig. 12.2).

During this period, Frisner was a reklame, "reclaimed" by the spirits (McAlister 1993). He dreamed that two female spirits appeared and promised him sacred protection in exchange for marriage. Ezili Freda and Ezili Dantò would become his spirit wives later in New York City. In a wedding ceremony, each *mistè* (lit. "mystery") appeared in person, "dancing in the head" of someone in the congregation, to recite the wedding vows. Frisner carried a small lithograph of Ezil Dantò in her form as the Catholic saint Our Lady of Czestochowa. "That's my wife," he would tell people, enjoying the look of confusion on their faces.[3]

During one ritual prayer and dance, the mistè Ogou appeared and instructed the society to initiate Frisner as an Ountògi, or a *sèvitè* (lit. "servant") of Ountò. Ountò, the "spirit of the drum," does not possess people—or if it does, it enables them to play the rhythms stronger and better. It has its own songs of invocation and blessing, and its own flowery invocation designs called vèvès. It is saluted in the ritual règleman (ritual order, protocol) that includes the Papa Legba in the doorway, the many spirits at the poto-mitan (center post), and Ountò at the drums. The spirit Ountò speaks to the other spirits through the drums, and with the help of Papa Legba, these divinities manifest in people by "dancing in their head." Ountò's energy is placed into drums in a complex and lengthy consecration ritual called *kouche tanbou* (lit. "lay down the drum") in which the drums are washed and fed prayers and a ritual meal and are thereby brought into being with a personhood of their own.

Frisner was dedicated to Ountò in a separate initiation. Frisner took this initiation at Kay Djòn, during which he lay dressed in white on the floor of Papa Djòn's secluded, sacred djèvo (sanctuary) for seven days with a set of drums lying next to him as his siblings. The costs were born by the entire congregation in the tradition of *la men fò* (lit. "the strong hand"), where everybody pitches in and donates what they have to perform the ritual work.

Figure 12.2. Frisner Augustin plays the Maman Petwo drum. Brooklyn, New York. Photograph by Chantal Regnault, 1984.

All such initiations, called *kouche kanzo*, are classic rituals of death and rebirth, and here we can see how one moment in the cycle leads to the other. Just before the kouche, the initiates are tearfully embraced by members of the congregation, who say good-bye as if they will never meet them again. Once they enter the chamber, their ritual elders transform them into liminal, socially dead figures all bearing a single, common name. They are laid down on the floor, symbolically spooned together in an echo of the coffle inside a ship's hold, and carefully rebirthed in a complicated spiritual process of stripping down and building back (Dunham 1969, 60). The primary divinity that governs one's head is discerned (called the *mèt tèt*), and one's ancestral spirits are "lined up" in one's head to bring calmness and strength, healing any maladies (Métraux 1956).

At some point during the seven days, the initiates travel mystically anba dlo (under the waters) that separate the land of the living and the dead. In dreams and visions, these liminal figures, stripped down and ritually dead, visit Ginen, the mythic realm of the ancestors from whence people begin their lives and to which they return after death. Making the trip "back" to symbolic Africa and returning, the Middle Passage is remembered, memorialized, and, just as importantly, drawn upon as a source of konesans and *fòs* (knowledge and strength) (Schuler 2005). The divinity who keeps the secrets of initiation is Ayizan, known as a female mother figure who lives in palm trees and who purifies during rituals of transformation. Maya Deren (1953, 220) calls her "the loa [lwa] of the psychic womb entrance to the world; she is the spiritual mother principle." At the hands of Haitian ritual experts, the result of initiation is to be augmented, strengthened, enlarged, and empowered. It is to belong inside a web of spirit forces and ancestors. It is thought to bring enormous good luck (fig. 12.3).

Rising up with a new ritual name and consecrated and dedicated to Ountò, Frisner only became stronger and more passionate. He began playing for the folkloric dance troupes that, under the Duvalier regime, were gaining funding and attention in the pro-Black atmosphere of *négritude* that animated intellectuals and artists at the time (Richman 2007). He played in the folklore troupes of such great artists as Viviane Gauthier, Lavinia Williams, and Lina Mathon-Blanchet. Invited to play with the famous orchestra Jazz des Jeunes for a tour in New York in 1972, at twenty-four years of age Frisner decided to enter the diaspora and to stay (Wilcken 2012, 7).

When members of the folklore group La Troupe Makandal left Haiti to play New York City in 1981, Frisner became their musical director and host as they too declined to return home. For the next thirty years, in partnership

Figure 12.3. Frisner Augustin at his *kouche kanzo* initiation at Sosyète La Fleur d'Or, Bronx, New York. Photograph by Chantal Regnault, 1984.

with the ethnomusicologist Lois Wilcken, Frisner built Troupe Makandal into a front-facing performance ensemble. They specialized in presenting Vodou rituals as authentically as possible in front of mixed American audiences, often at colleges and universities where students studying anthropology, religion, and ethnomusicology embraced the chance to see "a real Vodou ceremony." Frisner drew criticism from Haitian community members who objected on the grounds of respectability politics—that Vodou is too raw and spirit possession too foreign for Americans to accept. He also drew criticism from cultural purists who objected to the troupe presenting religious ceremonies as a form of performative spectacle. When Frisner began to teach a cadre of white American men and some women (including myself), he was roundly castigated by some Black producers for giving away the tradition too freely to whites and by some white producers for inauthenticity. All this controversy Frisner found hilariously funny, and he enjoyed forging ahead according to his own sense of who belonged in the troupe and what the troupe would present. He had a talent for turning a critique into a joke, and when one producer told him he had "too many whites" in his ensemble, he would yell to his drummers, "Hey! Too many whites! Come play, time to rehearse," with extravagant and contagious laughter. He was uncompromisingly Haitian and unwavering in his passionate outspokenness on behalf of Vodou as a valuable, worthy, and precious religious tradition.

One learned the rhythmic patterns from Frisner via a steady process he developed into a masterful pedagogy. After passing a few preliminary sessions playing a steady beat on the *bas* (bass) drum, our foundation was built on the bell, the *ogan*, on which we learned to play the sonic marker of the 6/8 pattern that holds down most of the Rada rhythms (from Bight of Benin in western Africa). Once Frisner was satisfied that we could keep the bell part going without dragging the beat, we were ready to learn the very specific and beautiful rhythms of the *segon* (the second drum). Lois Wilcken (2012, 9) writes, "I understood that making divine music entailed locating the groove, the place where the physical and the spiritual meet, and unwinding into it." Frisner doled out the rhythms in small chunks, building a foundation, one leading into the next, and he taught them so well that my *frè kanzo* (godbrothers) and friends became excellent drummers themselves, going on to play at ceremonies and onstage.

In 1984, Frisner brought the reconstituted Troupe Makandal back to Haiti for a series of shows (most of which never came to pass for what I'll politely call a lack of commitment on the part of the producer). Two of his drumming students were named Steve, so we all became known as "the Steves," and Frisner did his best to arrange romantic relationships between the American band members and his Haitian family and friends still living behind the Port-au-Prince cemetery. This would prove to create a stream of remittances back to Haiti when the Steves returned home. He often arranged for his mother, Ti-Nini, to cook for us, and we would sit in her modest one-room home to enjoy her delicious and elegantly served midday meal. In this way we could avoid the higher-priced restaurant food, and Ti-Nini could earn a small income while eating well for the day.[4]

An anthropology major in college, I became interested in the adjacent cemetery, which by now was surrounded by high white walls and featured tombs painted pastel blue and green sitting upright like thrones. This necropolis was a bustling social space with an order and hierarchy all its own. Although there are a few small cemeteries scattered throughout the city, the Grand Cimetière is one of the only public institutions that almost everybody in downtown Port-au-Prince—rich or poor, Catholic or Vodouist—still has to use. Following French tradition, the dead in Haiti are buried in high tombs painted in the bright colors of Caribbean houses. A little way into the graveyard, the tombs abandoned their neat rows and arranged themselves into a labyrinth of tall square boxes, each holding about six coffins like a big file cabinet. Some had concrete crosses decorating the tops like crowns. Some tombs were miniature replicas of middle-class homes, complete with curving steps leading into second floors with little balconies. Eternal flames and photographs beamed from inside wrought-iron gates. (The tomb of Francois Duvalier, the dictator "Papa Doc," featured such an eternal flame and was guarded by soldiers at the time.) These fancier ones looked almost comfortable, as though they were little dwellings for the dead. Frisner would install the coffin of his grandmother, Rose, when she died, in a beautiful blue tomb and directed workers to build enough spaces for his mother and himself.

Since Frisner had grown up in this neighborhood, often called *dèyè simityè* (behind the cemetery), he became one of its army of workers as a youth, making coffins, repairing and painting tombs. The quartier was—and still is—home to funerary enterprises of all sorts, from making tin flower wreaths to providing ritual singers for the *libera*, the funerary rite chanted in Latin by Catholics and Vodouists alike. Frisner was friendly with various spiritual entrepreneurs, known as malfektè, who specialized in deploying spirits of the dead to seek justice for clients for a fee. They had *biwo* (offices) in abandoned tombs and built altars there for their mystical works (Smith 2010).

We made one trip to the cemetery in 1989 as mourners, in the slow, sad funeral procession for Tony Love, a cousin of Frisner's who lived his life in the quartier next to the graveyard. Tony Love was a low man on the ladder of a new and deadly crack trade in the slums in the 1980s, an offshoot of the hemispheric narcotrafficking beginning to involve Haiti, whose ugly story journalists were just beginning to piece together. Tony Love had made a wrong move and had been arrested and beaten badly by the police. Soon afterward, he began to waste away. His family blamed it on internal bleeding from the blows, but a neighbor claimed that a sorcerer had given Tony Love a poison that produces in its victims the symptoms of AIDS. In any case, Tony Love did not have the money for a doctor and a diagnosis.

For the funeral, the family overdressed me in a tight black linen suit with puffy sleeves after the fashion of the bourgeoise women uptown. Breathing carbon monoxide, we followed the rickety station-wagon hearse from the nearby church down the grim street to the cemetery. Two women held each of the widow's arms and propped her up while she screamed and writhed in grief. Driving into the cemetery, the station wagon was sixth in line behind the other four-o'clock funerals that day. Once we got through the gates, the car stopped, and the pallbearers dragged the slim, wooden coffin out of the car and headed inside toward the tombs for the poor.

We stumbled along the winding paths through the graves to Tony Love's tomb, which was in the section of the cemetery called "Site Solèy," named after one of Haiti's worst slums farther down the bay. Each little area of the jumbled maze of the graveyard is mapped out in a mirror of greater Port-au-Prince: Petionville and Pacot for the rich and Belair and Site Katon for the poor. Like the house where he had lived his life just a stone's throw away, Tony's tomb was made of unpainted concrete blocks with no decoration. His family had no tomb, so his wife had rented one from a graveyard real-estate agent.

In death as in life, people must pay rent. Tombs are leased for twenty to thirty years to the well-to-do and six months to the poor. Because the bodies are entombed in concrete, aboveground spaces, soil, and rainwater never mingle with the flesh. A thin person, Frisner explained, will decompose in one year. If the family can't pay again at the end of the lease, out they go. One of the workers breaks open the specified slot in the tomb, draws out the coffin, and the bones are moved to the middle of the graveyard and inserted into a large, square concrete ossuary called the Tombe Universelle. The tomb goes on the market again for the next tenant. This is how this same square city block could continue to house so many dead, year after year since the first men were buried here in 1789 when Haiti was still a French colony. An irony of history is that the first men buried here were British soldiers who died of yellow fever, having come to occupy the island in 1785 (Corvington 2007).

The pink sun was falling into the Port-au-Prince bay as we veered away from the mourners so Frisner could show us students to a large cross made of cement. Candles burned on each arm, and smoked fish and hot peppers dotted its base. This was the cross set aside for Bawon Samdi. He inhabits the grave of the first man buried in any cemetery, while his wife, Grann Brijit, dwells behind the first woman's grave. Together they are the keepers of the cemetery and the dead, which makes them extremely powerful, as we see in the next section. No spirit work can be done here without their permission.

Most people in Port-au-Prince, unless they die abroad or in the provinces, are buried in this cemetery under the auspices of this Bawon and Brijit but ultimately end up in the Tombe Universelle. The rich, of course, stand a better chance that they will never leave their original tombs. They buy them outright from the beginning and then send guards to patrol them from time to time, to make sure that nothing disturbs their sacred rest. Frisner, in working in the diaspora to pay for a family tomb that would be theirs for decades, would achieve this status and its enormous privilege when he died tragically and suddenly in 2012.

DEATH OF A DRUMMER: SAILING TO GINEN ON THE WIND OF FORTY-EIGHT WESTERN UNION MONEY TRANSFERS

In the Port-au-Prince Vodou rites that Frisner followed, mortuary rituals are complex and must be accomplished by a group of experienced priests and priestesses. They *should* be done by the one who gives the initiation, the first one to touch the head. This ideal presents a difficulty, because it goes against another ideal: that the priest who initiates others, and is naturally older, dies before them. Papa Djòn and Papa Mano, our mutual *papa* (initiating priest), had gone on ahead to Ginen. So Frisner's ceremonies would be done by Manbo Marie, head of the sosyete (congregation) in his old quartier near the cemetery.

An ordinary person, when they die, dissipates into the cosmos. But, to use the military analogy in which Manbo Marie explained it to me, to have made the kouche kanzo is to achieve a *grad* (a rank in French). The rank confers konesans (spiritual knowledge). The kanzo is not an ordinary soldier but rather an officer, with knowledge, abilities, and obligations. This konesans cannot remain with the person after they breathe their last breath. For one thing, someone might steal it mystically. For another, the knowledge would be a burden and would drag them down. Rather, the person must return to the earth for burial in the same condition in which they came. If this ritual unburdening were not done, the dead might even agitate against their living descendants out of a need to be unburdened. So the deceased person with a grad must be stripped of all the knowledge they were given, and the mèt tèt (guiding the spirit in their head) and other lwa (spirits) they may have served must be separated. The ritual called *desouni* (or *desounen*) achieves this separation and is effectively the first step in undoing the work of the kouche kanzo. It is literally, in the French, *déssonner*, or *dégradation*. Said Manbo Marie, "The knowledge we gave him we have to take back."

The desounen has been written about by others, and as with all aspects of Afro-Haitian tradition, there is variation by region and by congregation. It used to be taken care of in the house, either right before or directly after the person took their last breath. In earlier times the deceased was then washed with an herbal bath and laid out on a table for the day before burial. Alfred Métraux (2016, 188) writes of the desounen that it used to be that when the priest whispered into the ear of the deceased, the corpse would be made to sit upright one final time, often emitting a vocalization, a last breath. At this juncture, the dead could be entreated to name anyone who might have had a hand in killing them through sorcery. This moment is a charged one, since the nanm (soul) of the person might seek cool spaces and jump into nearby pools of water or even propel itself toward a mirror, thinking it to be water (Daniels 2017). Several ethnographers write in the 1950s of a ritual treatment performed on the crown of the head, wherein the oungan or manbo would sit the corpse in a chair with a candle in its hands and draw a vèvè on their head, topping it with an egg nestled in flour or cornmeal. While singing their way through the prayer-songs for their lwa, the corpse's head will shake, and the egg will fall to the floor and shatter. This mystical process will liberate the spirits that used to "dance in the head" of the person (Comhaire-Sylvain 1959, 216). Initiates reading this will understand that this ritual reverses a process performed carefully during the kanzo initiation inside the djèvo. Now, in the days of funeral parlors, embalming, and other contemporary funeral practices, it can be a tricky affair to perform the desounen. It is possible to perform the ritual *sou kwa* (at the cross of Bawon) if the body is not accessible. But Manbo Marie is a professional, and she knew how to take care of business. "We did it in the funeral parlor," she said, just like that. Funeral parlors in Port-au-Prince understand that spirit workers may need to come and attend to the bodies there, to address the dead, remove mystical knowledge, or even to *ranje* (mystically arrange) the body against malevolent magic.

The next step was the night before the funeral mass that would be chanted at the cathedral. The menfolk enjoyed themselves at a modest *vèy* (wake) in the koridò by drinking, playing dominoes, and roasting Frisner with jokes. The wake is important in Sharpe's sense of "keeping watch with the dead"; since their nanm is still present, it is the last time the person will feast with their community. But the body was in the morgue, costing a great deal of money each day in keeping cold, money that would be paid through the forty-eight separate wire transfers that Frisner's friends and students had sent from the US through Western Union to support the funeral expenses.

So it was also time for the sosyete to assemble for the next phase of spiritual wake work for Frisner. This consisted of several rituals, condensed into one long night: the Priye Djò (Djò prayer), the *bohoun* (a funerary chant), the *kase kanari* (lit. "breaking a clay pot"), and *voye mò anba dlo* (lit. "send the dead under the water"). To prepare, the ounsis (initiates) had all gone to the neighborhood of Carrefour to have new white dresses tailored. They were cut from the whitest white cloth, each in a different style and different material, and most with a tight waist and generous flounced skirts reminiscent of the famous "Creole" style of the colonial era. Each ounsi wrapped her head in a white cloth, tied in the style that best suited her (Nwokocha 2019). We began singing the Priye Djò, a long litany of prayer songs naming scores of lwa, in their proper order. This prayer is an important foundation for all Rada rites and, in some houses, is taken care of by the core members of the congregation before the more public services will bring guests and visitors. The bohoun has become a specialized liturgy, and knowing its prayers, music, and protocols is a prized form of knowledge.

The bohoun ritual of prayer songs has been called a Vodou funeral chant (Bien-Aimé 2014, 133) and as with other rites in the Rada branch of the tradition, it likely preserves some of the highest concentration of elements from the Dahomean kingdom from which so many African people were kidnapped and shipped to the colony (Beauvoir 2008). We all cried out the sound "woukoukou," as we tapped our fingers to our lips, which seems somehow to echo as a sound of pure grief, a sound surely stemming from the Fon word for death, *ku*, and Yoruba word for death, *iku*.

As we sat dressed in white in our small chairs in Manbo Marie's temple, I listened to the prayer songs and realized that this little group of initiated brothers and sisters were singing the philosophy of death for each other and for Frisner. He would have appreciated that Manbo Marie had organized the appropriate instruments for the occasion—and the drummers to play them—including two of Frisner's American students besides myself. The resonant *gamel* is a hollowed log with calabashes floating in it in a watery herbal bath and played with two sticks as they roll in the water. The tone of the calabashes is tempered according to the depth of water they float in. Its haunting tones are answered by someone playing kanari, a large clay pot whose tone is achieved by slapping down a lid on the opening of the pot, producing a deep, echoing timbre. In some regions, the music is played until the pot breaks, hence the name *kase* (break) *kanari*.[5] We played and sang with these instruments and rhythmic accompaniment of *bat men* (clapping hands). The prayer songs presented a philosophical and theological account of what death is and where it leads.

Brother Jean, the priest is not God, and one day he will die.

Frè ti-Jean, oungan pa Bondieu, on jou lap mouri.

Other songs wailed, "My drummer, my drummer is gone," and "Frisner tonbe, Frisner has fallen." "Today we won't see him again; one day we will meet again."

Some songs reminded the congregation of the inevitability of death and of the congregation's duty and pledge to bury one another:

> Nobody dies who is not buried
>   Brother Frisner this makes me sad
>   Whether money borrowed or money saved
>   You'll be buried for sure.

Nan pwen moun ki mouri ki pa antere
   Frè Frisner sa fèm lapenn
   Lajan prete oubyen lajan sere
   Wap antere kan mem.

The lyrics slowly switched into the voice of the deceased:

I'm going to Sobo, I'm going to Badè
   I'm going to the house of Agwe
   I'm leaving the world for Segwelo [i.e., mere humans].

M prale Sobo, M prale Badè
   M pral kay Agwe
   Map kite won-an nan men Segwelo.

This song presents the image of the soul going to the realm of Sobo and Badè, known as brothers and spirit forces of thunder and wind. The dead person announces that they will depart with them to the house of Agwe, the ruler of the ocean, and leave the world behind in the hands of mere humans.

One particular song moved me to tears in its beautiful sense of finality and acceptance:

Wherever death takes me, bury me there, don't you know that all the earth is blessed.

Kote la mò pran mwen, antere mwen la, ou pa tande tou latè beni O.

Gradually the songs assumed the voice of Gede, the spirits of the ancestral dead who rank under Bawon Samdi and Grann Brijit. The Gede brought their classic comedy and irreverence by making fun of the dead Frisner:

Spirit, wake up!
   Look at the moron with the spittle mouth.
   Can't you see your body has become a lifeless thing?

Lwa, reveillez-Vous
   Gade mandan dondon djol boukye [spittle mouth]
   Ko'w tounc matye.

Next, the songs shifted to address Bawon, plaintively questioning this authority figure on all matters of justice and of death:

Who will the children be left with, Bawon?

Bawon ale, nan men ki moun wa kite zanfan la yo, Bawon ale.

I had not assisted at a bohoun before, and by the end, I was moved to tears. I did not expect such a poignant and emotional ceremony, such a lyrical rendering of the heartbreak of death. But there was not much time to cry, because soon Manbo Marie disappeared behind a white curtain erected in the corner. It was time to do the ritual work that would prepare the part of Frisner's soul that had been separated from him in the desounen for its next move. After a series of prayers, her Haitian Creole speech intertwined itself with *langaj* (lit. "language"), a mystical language intelligible to the spirit world (and composed of various words and syllables from West African languages, such as Fon and Yoruba). "Wekenn do kwa la mityò," she announced, shaking the sacred rattle (ason) and ringing its high bell as she spoke. "Listen, Ti-kèlèp," she said. "You have to understand your situation right now and start moving on. We did what we had to for you. Now you've got to go." She bore down on Frisner's *bon-anj* and his lwa in the mystical realm, speaking to them in the govi (clay pot) where they had been placed. As I learned later in conversations with other priests, this is a moment when the priest has to be firm with the dead. It's a violent moment, when the dead is told in no uncertain terms that they are *degrade*, literally degraded, a *sinp solda*, a simple soldier and no longer an officer. Moreover, the time for amicable relationships was up.

At about two a.m., the ounsis were lining up. The important moment had come to take the stripped-down spirit of Frisner to the crossroads. Manbo Marie sang loudly: "Reveille-toi, lè a deja rive, kote Mesye Lakwa yo vin akonpanye Ti-kèlèp." "Wake up and get up; it's time when the Gede will take away Ti-kèlèp."

The ounsis processed with the clay jars containing Frisner's guardian spirits on their heads as we all sang. We walked slowly out of the temple and through the corridor into the street. It was time to send Frisner's spirit on its way, to take the first step to voye mò nan dlo (send the dead under the water).

Manbo Marie stopped our little parade in the middle of an intersection, where surely, if there had been cars trying to pass, they would have seen the business at hand and turned around. Balancing the govi (clay pot) containing the spirits on her head, Manbo Marie spoke firmly to the entities populating the unseen world.

"All that is mine stays with me. All that is yours is returning to you. If anything has harmed you, it will come back on them, and you can avenge them." This statement was a classic and necessary pronouncement that signaled both that Frisner's soul was purified and light and unburdened with any leftover mystical knowledge. It also sent the important message that if Frisner had died because anyone had meant to harm him, that justice would ensure that the culprit was routed out, exposed, and punished.

Manbo Marie smashed the govi to the ground from the top of her head and then spun on her heels and ordered the assembly to return to the temple. "Don't look back," she said. "Let the dead go." Now the dead would begin his journey under the water.

However, the nanm (soul) does not go alone; nor is the soul free. "Li pa gen libete l" (He does not have his freedom), explained Manbo Marie later. The soul is released to the auspices of Bawon Samdi and Grann Brijit, the keepers of the cemetery and the spirits said to govern all the dealings with the dead. Vodouists see the cemetery not as an end point but as an active spot where the person's spirit uncoils. Frisner's spirit would briefly be a captive of Bawon, who would turn him over to Mèt Agwe, the owner of the oceans. Mèt Agwe is the captain of the boat that would carry the soul. The crew of this mythic ship would include the other spirits Grann Adja, Grann Alouba, Ezili Freda and Ezili Dantò, Ogoun Balendjo, Lasiren and Labalen, Papa Zoklimo, and Papa Fatada. This crew would lead the soul to the Fòs Abizmal, the spot where the sea is deepest. The spirits take there you to do the ceremonies where they remove the knowledge in your head, said the renowned spiritual leader Ati Max Beauvoir in a later conversation. "In this sense, the life of the person and the life of the lwa and the dead are as one." Papa Max said there is some suffering involved in remaining captive. "You know this; you have taken up this commitment, so you pass some time in captivity. After that you are free." After Frisner was given to Bawon for his period of captivity, we made our way back to the temple for a short sleep.

The next day was to shift registers entirely, to exchange our white clothing for mourner's black. As a spirit priest, Frisner would have a Catholic funeral Mass. Two years after the earthquake in overpopulated Port-au-Prince, he would share the rite with six others and their families in a partially collapsed and overflowing church. The great artists Viviane Gauthier, Tido Lavaud, and Sò Ann (Annette August) were there to pay their respects. To honor Frisner with musical accompaniment at every step, a traditional brass band played dirges for the casket during the procession to the cemetery. But my favorite moment came at the cemetery gates themselves. When the funeral procession reached the cemetery, the brass band stopped playing, and suddenly a battalion of Rara players emerged from behind the gates and struck up the piercing and raw sounds of Rara's parade music (see McAlister 2002). Blowing bamboo horns cut at different lengths to achieve singular tones, they played the casket and mourners forward as we scrambled toward the tomb. The musicians had assembled to play not for a fee but out of love and respect. When the casket arrived at the tomb, Manbo Marie and the Vodou drummers took over for the burial. Beautifully, organically, one *corps de musique* handed Frisner's coffin off to the next.[6]

WATERY PASSAGES AND DIASPORIC NECROSCAPES

According to the ideal, the soul of a Vodou initiate spends one year and one day anba dlo, under the waters, being washed and purified and cooled by the ship's crew of the lwa Agwe. The bon anj is said to be anxious to leave the waters, since it is cool and isolated there, and people and spirits tend to prefer warmth. After this period, it is possible to call them up out of the water and hear them speak in the *wete mò nan dlo* (bring the dead from the waters) ritual. This, as everything, costs money. The priest must be compensated, but so must the other members of the congregation, and there is ritual food, drink, and clothing to organize. Materials must be purchased. Drummers must be paid. After already bearing costly funerals, many families simply cannot afford to quickly bring their recently dead out of the water.

Frisner's life partner, Lois, had returned to New York, and her status as a professional in the United States allowed her to save money and raise funds. She wasted no time in organizing the retrieval ceremony so that it could be performed at the earliest possible time. Because of a suspicion on the part of some of Frisner's family—although not Lois—that he had been killed through sorcery, Lois retreated to a temple near Jacmel to perform this important spiritual work. Frisner's grandmother had been from Jacmel, and so calling him back to that location was proper. One of Frisner's drumming students and I joined this small party, as did the renowned sociologist Laennec Hurbon, who is based in the diaspora—in Switzerland—but happened to be in town. The ritual was successful, and Frisner's purified and cooled spirit was placed into a govi, which lives at the present writing in his Brooklyn apartment under Lois Wilcken's care. After some months, Lois expanded this necroscape and consecrated for Frisner's spirit a *tonbo*, a small repository under a tree near Jacmel, from which it would be possible to consult with Frisner as an ancestor. Eventually, in time, it would be possible for Frisner's own spirit to uncoil toward a rebirth as another person entirely.[7]

Frisner's sacred biography—which included a spirit marriage, a ritual making and unmaking as a drummer-priest, being sent to Ginen, and being called back—took place in two countries and involved numerous water crossings, both cosmological and material. The precarity of contemporary transnational and diasporic life for Haitian people renders the philosophies and histories encoded in ritual all the more precious. I want to emphasize, as one scholar who was a fan of Frisner's put it, Afro-Atlantic funerary art as "a heroic form of cultural memory, encoding philosophic issues of life and death in terms of some of the most elegant elaborations of the land" (Thompson 1981, 31). However, the expense is prohibitive. Some families take on enormous debt shipping bodies for a home burial, and the expense of traditional rituals can add a layer of expense that can produce great anxiety. For if the sèvitè is not sent under the waters (or, later on, brought back up), the person is not resting properly. It is for this reason that mass funerary rites were held for the dead after the 2010 earthquake.

Funerals are occasions for families to ensure that their deceased make a proper transition to the afterworld that awaits them. Likewise, the family members must also reconcile themselves to the loss and transformation of roles they inevitably face. Richman (2018) writes helpfully about the agency of the dead in Haitian Vodou, where they are given the chance to communicate at the desounen and the wete mò nan dlo. Meanwhile, the relatively new funeral industry takes control over the embalming and entombment of the corpse in a modernizing of the necroscape that diaspora creates. The funeral becomes an important social ritual of return for family in diaspora, who must save, borrow, and spend enormous sums of money. However, the fact that so many families are stretched between Haiti and spots in the diaspora makes a full mortuary treatment all the harder. Often spirit work for several ancestors is performed at once, which means waiting for long periods until things can be organized.

Still, the new possibilities of shipping refrigerated corpses home from the diaspora, for those who can afford it, can mean a reunification of a scattered family and the chance for the dead to be properly ritually prepared for ongoing spiritual communication. And the rise of social media has meant that ceremonies can be announced and invitations can be made instantly across the diasporic necroscape. One beautiful 2019 invitation to the rituals for a well-known international manbo, for example, featured bohoun rituals in both Montreal and Port-au-Prince, culminating in a burial in the southern coastal town of Côte de Fer, Haiti. The necroscape of traditional funerary rites has expanded in this age of globalization, from the uncoiling and watery sojourn of the spirit to the return of transnational family, to include also social mediascapes depicting multisited funeral rites and international audiences. The forms of wake work that Haitian people initiate toward restoring the ruptures of death in the digital age superimpose themselves onto the traditional, generations-old work of watching, remembering, ritualizing, and coming full circle.

Technology allows for those in diaspora to view ceremonies in Haiti they may not be able to attend, as bohoun, funeral masses, and burials are posted to

YouTube and Facebook. In the increasingly contested religious landscape of Haiti, where Evangelical Protestants are increasing attacks on Vodou, funerals are a public statement of identity and are therefore political. All of these topics bear future research.

Frisner's funeral cannot be told as one about a drummer in the lower city, since Frisner had lived in the US for thirty years and counted as a diaspora. But he had really not taken on the style, language, affect, or sense of himself as a diaspora. He was a transplanted Vodou drummer who remained very much a person from his old neighborhood. When he brought his students back to Haiti—which he did many times—we usually stayed in the koridò with people he knew. No, Frisner lived in the crossroads of the mystical realm of Vodou and the transnational reality of the Haitian diaspora. But he knew what he was doing when he died in Haiti, however unexpectedly. Ti-kèlèp had crossed the water to live most of his life in Brooklyn. In March 2012, he went back to Haiti to go back anba dlo to Ginen. He crossed two waters and went back home.

This chapter is dedicated with respect to three late leaders who lived lives of integrity in an uncommon public pride in Afro-Haitian religion: Ountògi Frisner Augustin, Ati Papa Max Beauvoir, and Manbo Professor Rachel Beauvoir-Dominique. For help understanding these beautiful rites and their songs, the author is immeasurably grateful to Oungan Erol Josue, director of the Bureau of Ethnologie in Port-au-Prince, Anpere Jean-Daniel Lafontant of Nah-Rih-Véh Temple, Ronite Louima, Dr. Lois Wilcken, and Paul Uhry Newman for his account of rituals he attended for Frisner Augustin.

NOTES

1. See Giafferi-Dombre, this volume, for discussion of the dynamics of the transnational Haitian art world.
2. See "Family Visit to the Grand Cemetery in Port-au-Prince 7 January 1994," posted by the Frisner Augustine Memorial Archive on February 19, 2019, YouTube video, 01:02:44, https://www.youtube.com/watch?v=p5Z6KGgQbIY&feature=youtu.be, for footage of Frisner's visit to his family's tomb in 1994. A rich archive of videos of his performances is at the Frisner Augustin Memorial Archive YouTube channel: https://www.youtube.com/channel/UCWxkf4-nBCIHDUCGm-AoqCA.
3. See a 1982 interview between Lois Wilcken and Frisner Augustin at https://frisneraugustinarchive.org/repository/text-documents/.
4. Frisner's mother was named Andrea Laguerre, née either Altine or Justin (personal communication, Lois Wilcken, July 2019).

5. These instruments are featured on the track "Azouke Legba" on the Smithsonian Folkways album *Rhythms of Rapture*. Ideally there are many ounsis playing kanaris.
6. The drummers playing for the entombment can be viewed online: "Frisner Augustin's Funeral," posted by Troupe Makandal on March 4, 2012, YouTube video, 01:17, https://www.youtube.com/watch?v=cPJhitUdrqs.
7. The technologies and sciences of much of Vodou bear taking seriously as ontologies worthy of elaboration. See Adjibodou, this volume.

REFERENCES

Angels in the Mirror: Vodou Music of Haiti. 1997. Roslyn, NY: Ellipsis Arts.
Beauvoir, Max G. 2008a. *Lapriyè Ginen*. Port-au-Prince: Edisyon Près Nasyonal d'Ayiti.
———. 2008b. *Le Grand Recueil Sacré: ou Répertoire des Chansons du Vodou Haïtien*. Port-au-Prince: Edisyon Près Nasyonal d'Ayiti.
Bien-Aimé, Kesler. 2014. "Chant de Deuil Traditionnel Haïtien: Enjeux de Patrimonialisation." *Bulletin du Bureau National D'Ethnologie* 48 (1): 131–146.
Brown, Vincent. 2008. *The Reaper's Garden: Death and Power in the World of Atlantic Slavery*. Cambridge, MA: Harvard University Press.
Comhaire-Sylvain, Suzanne. 1959. "Mort et funérailles dans la région de Kenscoff (Haïti)." *Revue de l'Institute de Sociologie* 32 (2): 197–232.
Corvington, Georges. 2007. *Port-au-Prince: Au Cours des Ans, Tome I, 1743–1804*. Montreal: Les Editions du CIDIHCA.
Danticat, Edwidge. 2010. *Create Dangerously: The Immigrant Artist at Work*. Princeton, NJ: Princeton University Press.
Daniels, Kyrah Malika. 2017. "Mirror Mausoleums, Mortuary Arts, and Haitian Religious Unexceptionalism." *Journal of the American Academy of Religion* 85 (4): 957–984.
Deren, Maya. 1953. *Divine Horsemen: The Living Gods of Haiti*. New York: McPherson.
Dunham, Katherine. 1969. *Island Possessed*. Garden City, NY: Doubleday.
Forde, Maarit. 2018. "Introduction." In *Passages and Afterworlds: Anthropological Perspectives on Death in the Caribbean*, edited by Maarit Forde and Yanique Hume, 1–27. Durham, NC: Duke University Press.
Forde, Maarit, and Yanique Hume, eds. 2018. *Passages and Afterworlds: Anthropological Perspectives on Death in the Caribbean*. Durham, NC: Duke University Press.
McAlister, Elizabeth. 1993. "Sacred Stories from the Haitian Diaspora: A Collective Biography of Seven Vodou Priestesses." *Journal of Caribbean Studies* 9 (1): 10–27.
———. 2002. *Rara! Vodou, Power and Performance in Haiti and its Diaspora*. Berkeley: University of California Press.

---. 2005. "Globalization and the Religious Production of Space." *Journal for the Scientific Study of Religion* 44 (3): 249–255.
McFadden, David. 2017. "Grieving Haitians Go into a Lifetime of Debt to Fund Funerals." *New Haven Register*, May 13, 2017. https://www.nhregister.com/business/article/Grieving-Haitians-go-into-lifetime-of-debt-to-11313958.php.
Métraux, Alfred. 1946. "The Concept of Soul in Haitian Vodu." *Southwestern Journal of Anthropology* 2 (1): 84–92.
Métraux, Alfred. 2016. *Voodoo in Haiti*. Auckland, New Zealand: Pickle Partners Publishing.
---. 1956. "Les Rites d'Initiation dans le Vodou Haitien." *Tribus* (4–5): 177–198.
Michel, Claudine. 1996. "Of Worlds Seen and Unseen: The Educational Character of Haitian Vodou." *Comparative Education Review* 30 (3): 280–294.
Nwokocha, Eziaku. 2019. "Vodou en Vogue: Fashion, Ritual and Spiritual Innovation in Haitian Vodou." PhD diss., University of Pennsylvania. https://repository.upenn.edu/edissertations/3335.
Potter, Parker B., Jr. 1991. "What Is the Use of Plantation Archaeology?" *Historical Archaeology* 25 (3): 94–107.
Richman, Karen. 2007. "Peasants, Migrants and the Discovery of the Authentic Africa." *Journal of Religion in Africa* 37 (3): 1–27.
---. 2018. "Mortuary Rites and Social Dramas in Léogâne, Haiti." In *Passages and Afterworlds: Anthropological Perspectives on Death in the Caribbean*, edited by Maarit Forde and Yanique Hume, 139–156. Durham, NC: Duke University Press.
Rhythms of Rapture: Sacred Musics of Haitian Vodou. 1995. CD Smithsonian Folkways.
Schuler, Monica. 2005. "Enslavement, the Slave Voyage, and Astral and Aquatic Journeys in African Diaspora Discourse." In *Africa and the Americas: Interconnections during the Slave Trade*, 185–213. Trenton, NJ: Africa World.
Sharpe, Christina. 2016. *In the Wake: On Blackness and Being*. Durham, NC: Duke University Press.
Smith, Katherine. 2010. "Dialoging with the Urban Dead in Haiti." *Southern Quarterly* 47 (4): 61–90.
Thompson, Robert Farris. 1981. *Four Moments of the Sun: Kongo Art in Two Worlds*. Washington, DC: National Gallery of Art.
Wilcken, Lois. 2012. "Drummer, Give Me My Sound: Reflections on the Life and Legacy of Frisner Augustin." *Voices: The Journal of New York Folklore* 38 (3–4): 3–11.

ELIZABETH MCALISTER is Professor of Religion at Wesleyan University. She is author of *Rara! Vodou, Power, and Performance in Haiti and Its Diaspora* and coeditor of *Race, Nation, and Religion in the Americas*.

CONCLUSION

Global Vodún and Vodou—Encounter
and Engagement

Eric J. Montgomery and Timothy R. Landry

IMPENDING TRENDS IN VODÚN AND VODOU

Throughout this volume, we have discussed a wide array of themes focusing on the past, present, and future of Vodún and Vodou. Its future, although unknown, tends toward growth and mainstream acceptance as both popular and scholarly interest grows. The encounters, entanglements, and engagements, documented in this volume, highlight Vodún and Vodou's remarkable ability to adapt quickly to changing social and economic conditions. This equips scholars to grapple with emerging questions tethered to modernity and globalization, growing economic inequalities, environmental entanglements, and developing issues of gender and racial equity. Additionally, there is a mounting trend to merge science, religion, witchcraft, sorcery, and other manifestations of the occult (Falen 2018; see Abidijou chap. 7 in this volume.). In light of prevalent—and often racist—misunderstandings, the contributors of this volume have all endeavored to tackle the seemingly incessant attacks that have been levied against Vodún and Vodou. Every encounter between Europeans and Africans involved engagements that were marked by asymmetrical power dynamics. Blacks were subjected to domination and slavery in a global capitalist system, while African religious systems, such as Vodún, were imperiled by the spread of Christianity and Islam. As such, a double dehumanization took place on both sides of the Atlantic—one upon the body and the other upon the soul. The demonization of one of the world's most dynamic and misunderstood religious systems inspired this volume. Collectively, the authors here have attempted to unhinge the reality of Vodún and Vodou from the racist Western imaginings that seek to frame the religions as "irrational" and "superstitious" beliefs from the so-called Dark Continent.

This book is a corrective endeavor aimed at eradicating the position of illegitimacy while validating these systems with historical, ethnographic, and empathetic analysis that seeks to speak truth to power. Signs of Vodún and Vodou's growth, coupled with the realization that variously identified religious agents still participate actively in Vodún and Vodou, are promising trends for the future of these religious systems. Vodún has long been dubbed a "Black religion" and therefore on the frontlines of symbolic and physical acts of violence and trauma carried out on Black bodies. This book and its contributors stand in solidarity with those fighting anti-Black racism in amplifying and magnifying the voices of the spirits and ancestors in concert with the Black Lives Matter movement.

Stories may not have endings, but they do have beginnings. As ethnographers, practitioners, and historians, we write with a conscious reflexivity and embrace of storytelling, but the measured worth of anthropological and historical narrative stems from how well we unpack the complex social lives of our interlocuters. In a global world that's been compressed temporally and spatially, encounters and engagements intensify exponentially, opening doors for new voices and new ears—perhaps forever eroding the "graven images" of African religions that scholars have helped to uphold (Baum 1990). Practitioners of Vodún and Vodou would most certainly concur that there are no conclusions in Vodou and Vodún. Indeed, these systems are unfinished and forever open-ended (Landry 2018; Rush 2013). Despite an all-encompassing onslaught by outsiders (and some insiders) who seek to demonize and belittle these religious systems, religions like Vodou and Vodún continue to flourish and expand, offering a blueprint for the African and Global South renaissance that is upon us (Comaroff and Comaroff 2012; Evans 1999; Olupona and Rey 2008). Vodún and Vodou can serve as the decolonializing lifeblood of inclusion and empowerment overcoming the overwhelming Christian, Muslim, colonial, and postcolonial mandate to degrade and devalue so-called African religions on a scale with no other comparisons. African organizing principles found in Vodún and Vodou forged the baseline of resistance to colonial hegemonies and will also inform and insist on the collective mobilization and corresponding social movements to countercolonize the neoliberalism and its discontents currently gripping West Africa and the Caribbean (Sylla 2014). Yet, in such places as West Africa, Haiti, and throughout the African diaspora, categorizations such as Muslim and Christian do not override the ontological and philosophical foundations of "African religion" (cf. McIntosh 2009). As Orobator (2018, 171) writes, "Christianity and Islam are fruits produced from those roots that reach down into the soil . . . [and] that soil is African religion." Even those who do not consider themselves to be followers or adepts of Vodún and Vodou are often still moved by its power and underlying tenets, and many so-called nonbelievers regularly embrace it in times of desperation. In such places as Togo, Benin, and Haiti, Vodún and Vodou continue to be one of the most firm and misunderstood threads in the tapestry that is "African religion." However, Vodún's impact stretches beyond these locales. Indeed, Vodún also persists in such places as Brazil, Cuba, France, Canada, the United States, and beyond.

The chapters in this volume demonstrate the enormous impact of encounter and engagement on vast ritual complexes throughout the Black Atlantic world. Historians have demonstrated their impact in the past, from the construction of the early modern Atlantic world (Gomez 2017; Sweet 2011) to the ties between American jazz, blues, and rock 'n' roll, and Haitian migrants and "Voodoo" practitioners in New Orleans at the turn of the twentieth century (Berry 1988; Lomax 2001; Thompson 1983). Although this book has focused on Vodún and Vodou mostly in West Africa, the US, and the Caribbean, related ritual complexes thrive in other places of the diaspora—and the future is trending toward expansion in other nations throughout the globe.

The contributors to this volume have outlined Vodún and Vodou through the lenses of encounter and engagement—and the sections and chapters of this volume encompass the enormous complexity that these ways of life embody. By "encounter" we refer to the unexpected and casual meetings that the authors and their respective research communities have experienced with Vodún or Vodou as ways of being and knowing in the world. Regarding "engagement" we speak about arrangements and commitments that devotees and researchers partake in regarding Vodún and Vodou. Additionally, because so many of our contributors partake, apprentice, and otherwise immerse themselves in the rituals and day-to-day activities of their respective communities, we also attend to the line that fades in and out between researcher and interlocuter.

Engagements and encounters often lead to annihilation, expansion, or various levels of assimilation and syncretism. In the case of Vodún, we have seen recent evidence of growth. Vodún and Vodou are enlarging their impact in Africa, the Caribbean, Latin America, and elsewhere, such as Europe and the United States. As we look to the future regarding Vodún and Vodou, we see the themes of encounter and engagement as useful starting points for contextualizing the unframeable, for these systems are both ephemeral and complex. Although the future of these systems is unknown, we believe encounters and engagements between these systems and the world will expand and grow—and we are hopeful that this can contribute in its own way to the African renaissance that is upon us. People of all cultures are clamoring for ways to enhance and grow their souls, and Vodún and Vodou are destined to be a part of this "archaic revival" of human consciousness, both in the Atlantic world and elsewhere (McKenna 1991).

ENCOUNTERS WITH VODÚN AND VODOU

Spirit Service: Vodún and Vodou in the African Atlantic World examines the contemporary sociocultural order of the world with a focus on a magico-spiritual reply to globalization by adepts and devotees. We attempt to raise the volume on the voice of an often marginalized and maligned religious group. The very mention of the word *voodoo* is powerful, imparting images and dialogues often ensconced in racism and mystification. In the history of the world, perhaps no religion has been more misunderstood and maligned than African and African diasporic religions, and none more so than "Voodoo." This book is the first macroscopic attempt to encompass the multivocality of these belief systems across space and time. With interdisciplinary contributions focusing on encounters and engagements on both sides of the Atlantic, *Global Vodún* provides an ethnographically and historically up-to-date account of the cultural meanings and practices of Vodún and Vodou and potentialities concerning their future.

The first six chapters of the volume encompass West Africa and its transatlantic connections with the African diaspora, which have been characterized by encounters and exchanges of commodities, bodies, and cultural productions since the seventeenth century (Forte 2007). These encounters have created a wide range of cultural productions and identity constructions informed by African beliefs and rituals, which must be considered the results of intense dialogue on both sides of the Atlantic (Gilroy 1993; Matory 2005). Rey focuses on Vodou's genesis as the national religion of Haiti while attending to how Vodou was encountered by various colonial authors. With a careful, fresh, and detailed reading of five of the most important primary source accounts of Africana religious culture in early Saint-Domingue, Rey contextualizes Vodou's birth. In chapter 2, Falen lends credibility to the dynamism of Beninese Vodún by looking at universalism and syncretism while problematizing the Western exotic curiosity about "Voodoo." He references Vodún's relationship to other religions, explaining that Vodún is more than a "parent of New World Voodoo." It is a multidimensional thought system with local, regional, and global spiritual elements, which inclusively interacts and relates with other religious systems. Like Falen, who attends to Vodún's relationship to Christianity, Vannier tackles Vodún's ritual engagements with Islam by examining Muslim prayers, rites, and alms prevalent in Gorovodu/Tron in Togo.

In chapter 3, Montgomery takes a comparative look at how the spirts of Gorovodu/Tron from Ghana and Togo (Kunde and Bangre), Yewe Vodún (Sakpata), and Mami Wata encounter one another and how they have been migrated internationally, stretching throughout the Atlantic world and beyond. For Montgomery, Vodún is an ever-changing complex in which language itself often conflates and distorts its very essence. It is in the crosscurrents of migrating spirits where the African religious imagination is often most vibrant and raw. Vannier's chapter 4 brings in notions of Islam and its relationships with Gorovodu and Tron religious orders in southern Togo; he displays how Gorovodu is defined by exchange, absorption, and adaptation—the very foundations of encounters between cultures and ideas. In chapter 5, we are introduced to global flows and contemporary stories of migration. Karen Richman, following up on other scholars of Haitian Vodou, highlights disturbing trends and ritual transformations indicating a disappearing Vodou in Haiti. Richman explains how, why, and to what extent this is true, while also offering hope for the future of Vodou based on its resiliency and entrenched nature in Haitian society. Chapter 6 is the final chapter of part I, "Encounters" and, while staying in Haiti, delves deeper into the art, power, and aesthetics of Vodou. Natacha Giafferi-Dombre "sails" between the local and global, placing Haitian Vodou arts in the modern and contemporary world. Aesthetic productions of Haitian Vodou art garner enormous foreign desire, as she documents vividly through a look at Vodou art over the past seventy years in the Caribbean and United States. For her, Vodou's power and efficacy lie in its capacity to incorporate the foreign and refurbish it for its own purposes.

ENGAGING VODOU AND VODÚN

The second section, "Engagement," looks at current tropes, theories, and methods in the study of spirit service through participatory, historical, and embedded approaches by the scholars. The core rationale for serving the spirits is personal, social, and moral because the spirits have the power to punish and reward. In many ways, Vodún fits Marwick's (1982) "social strain gauge theory" (although not exclusively), which he applies to African witchcraft writ large by crafting a certain personal and collective morality among the community, a point made by Falen (2018) and Landry (2019) regarding science, witchcraft, and sorcery. Since the spirits have the power to affect the real lives of people, the need for ritual specialists to work with them and the population is mandatory—an engagement that is both ordinary and constant. Through intense participant observation, many scholars in this volume also engage these mediators and even the spirits directly to interpret what is happening through such dialogues. Chapters here explore many of these methodologies, offering new ways of intellectualizing ritual experience through reliance on apprenticeship and attention to the whole life text of spirit service. Gender and sexuality, ecology and environment, race and class, politics, and economics, even reality itself, are cross-examined through the senses to include such aspects as divination, dream interpretation, healing, and more.

Part II, "Engagement," encompasses six chapters interweaving Vodún and Vodou transatlantic religious and social history with historical and present-day ethnography in Haiti, Benin, and the United States. In chapter 7, Anderson explores Mississippi River valley Voodoo and its many cousins—noting that Voodoo in the US south embodies globalism and is perhaps even more malleable than other traditions since the religion dissipated as a full-fledged religion during the 1940s. For Anderson, Voodoo in the US is weakened by scholars arguing for a particular geographical space or lineage and by others using it as a public-relations tool for tourism—so we need move beyond seeing Voodoo religion as belonging to races, classes, genders, or geographies. In chapter 8, Venise Adjibodou engages Beninese Vodún through the auspices of physics and science while exploring two Vodún rituals, one in Benin and the other in Philadelphia. She deploys the example of a fowl sacrifice to demonstrate how two different practitioners in two distinct spaces at different times can produce the same empirical outcome. For Adjibodou, white Christian epistemologies are universalizing and totalizing, unable to engage "African science," making them inadequate in understanding or explaining Vodún. Alissa Jordan's chapter 9, detailing "Vodou skins," is a participatory look into surfaces, bathing, and residues in Haiti. Her deeply symbolic and experiential approach shines light on the many "layers" of meaning intrinsic to bathing as a practical, appealing, and healing-oriented task. Not only is water feminine, beautiful, and utilitarian, but it also affirms connections between humans and spirits in deeply interesting ways.

Nixon Cleophat in chapter 10 takes us back to Haiti, conceptualizing a "queer Vodou ecotheology" of liberation through analyses of the transformative nature of "despised" bodies through spirit possession. Cleophat teases out Vodou's predestined ability to embrace environmental sustainability and gendered inclusion, while pedestaling its many liberating successes in Haiti. The lwa embody natural elements that give meaning to their mysteries while also representing a wholeness of the cosmos and relationships between gods, ancestors, and humans. In chapter 11, Landry focuses on "spirited forests" in Benin and argues for looking at Vodún and its related systems as "complexes" and thus better capturing its essence holistically. His notion of "spirited forests" seizes the immense spiritual power of the forest to inform personhood, heal the mind and body, and speak to Vodún engagements with insiders and outsiders. Elizabeth McAlister's chapter 12 concludes part II, "Engagement," just as many Vodouisants have done—by blurring the boundaries between life and death. Across space and ancestral time, through funerary rites and customs, McAlister amplifies the stories of the deceased in Haitian Vodou. Mortuary rites are indeed extensive, as she details through her case study of an esteemed priest who passed in 2012. The memorable and enigmatic drummer Frisner, upon his death, made an overwater journey between Haiti and the United States, only to make an underwater migration later. This emotional chapter reflects on the elegant and philosophically rich funerary rites of Vodún in the context of a neoliberal modernity and invokes deep empathy and understanding for agents of the Haitian diaspora.

Engagements of devotees with Vodún and Vodou are multidimensional and commence with birth and naming ceremonies, continue throughout life regarding feasts, festivals, healing rites, services, funerals, performances, divination sessions, and the like. The beliefs of Vodún and Vodou and the manner in which people engage the spirits not only differ between Africa and the Caribbean but also from community to community and person to person. The diversity of types of engagement and encounter are too numerous to list—as this volume demonstrates—and while many share similar experiences, each individual is sure to have unique experiences, and the same is true for scholars. The beliefs vary, the amount of so-called syncretism changes with context, and even the gods—their construction, manifestations, and desires—vary from place to place, person to person, for their "mysteries" are ever evolving. One may "engage" or be "engaged" by a spirit or energy. Other times, disengagement can also lead to new epiphanies and ways of being. While the chapters of this section speak to how people come to grips with their past and present—the multitude of encounters and engagements investigate the vitality of Vodún/Vodou going forward.

VODÚN AND VODOU FUTURES

The age, depth of liturgy, and sheer numbers of Vodún and Vodou followers not only merit more respect and attention but also an argument for it to be recognized as a world religion. Olupona and Rey (2008) made the same argument for

Òrìṣà more than a decade ago, and we want to insert Vodún into this incredibly important conversation. Our proposed reimagination has an eye toward growth and expansion, bolstering the notion of encounter and engagement through analyses of spirits' and adepts' mobility and spiritual callings crossing political, cultural, and religious fields and overcoming the dualistic nature of structural opposites, such as black/white, Western/non-Western, art/science, sacred/secular, local/global, and male/female. Migrations and movement between and beyond people of African descent is enormous, and the scale and scope of this is promising for the religions' expansion in the postmodern world. As the movement for Black lives builds across the globe, so too will the hailing of Black spirits and gods. These migrating ideas and spirits are not born of globalization but have been happening throughout the Atlantic world for hundreds of years (Gomez 2017; Manning 2016; Sweet 2011). In contemporary times, local, regional, and international networks of spirits, devotees, ritual specialists, and shrine communities are magnified, as time and space become compressed, and debates rage between Òrìṣà and Vodún practitioners online and in person on both sides of the Atlantic (Clarke 2007).

The impacts of Vodún and Vodou are not limited by region, race, or time but instead acculturate and amalgamate with external religions and peoples, including Christianity and Islam. While Haitian Vodou is perpetually under great attack from governments, missionaries, and other religious practitioners, it has also set down firm roots in such American cities as New York and Miami and even returned reimagined to Haiti with ex-pats with more force than before (Brown 1991; O'Neil and Rey 2012). Many people assume that Vodún is somehow stuck in the "backward" villages of Haiti or Benin. All the chapters here illustrate the expanding and fluid nature of these systems, past, present, and future. A key feature of African Vodún and Haitian Vodou is—and has always been—movement. Beginning with early cultural encounters and engagements in West Africa, through the transatlantic slave trade, and today via intense globalization and neoliberalism, ritual entrepreneurs have carried Vodún and Vodou to new places, complete with fresh ideas and acts. Understanding these contemporary processes induces us to recognize that Vodún and Vodou are, and perhaps always have been, global and postmodern.

"Voodoo" in its multiple manifestations, orders, and systems in Africa and the Caribbean is often conflated with "gothic tropes," including ideas of the macabre (McGee 2012; Montgomery 2019), and this has been the focus of scholarship and popular culture for many years (Landry 2018). While many adepts flock to Christianity (and sometimes Islam) in fear of the spirits, and what many perceive to be exorbitant costs for initiations and sacrifices, these very acts unconsciously legitimize Vodún, for to fear something is to honor its power. Unfortunately, after a virtual revival in studies concerning Vodún twenty years ago, much of the academic work on Vodún is either quite dated, tightly focused geographically or ethnically, or extremely inclusive of many other religions (Bay 2008; Belgarde-Smith 2006; Blier 1995; Desmangles 2000; Michel 2006; Olmos and Paravisini-Gebert 1997). While popular culture throughout the world continues to engage in mystification that can only be deemed as racist and evil, we have pushed back against this by showing the vitality and nuanced beauty that is "Voodoo" spirit-service in modernity. Research in the African diaspora has bestowed primacy to two key African religious currents: (1) Òrìṣà and Lucumí, which thrive in places like Brazil and Cuba, and (2) Ewe and Adja-Fon Vodún and Vodou (Bastide 1972; Law 2005; Matory 2015a). Although we have not focused on Vodún as a "world religion" in the manner that Olupona and Rey (2008) have suggested for Òrìṣà, these two similar strains together encompass tens of millions of followers, and that should not be ignored. There have been other diffusions of African religions in the diaspora as well, including distinct varieties from Central Africa that are typically lumped together. Ethnic names and religious denotations from West Africa have been numerous and ever-changing in the historical record. There exists much confusion for good reasons evidenced by the myriad of spirit cults tied to Vodún and Òrìṣà (e.g., Candomblé, Lucumi, Winti, Obeah, Santeria), crossing numerous languages and ever-changing political-economic situations. This has led to much ambiguity and debate regarding the extents and impacts of Vodún, Òrìṣà, and other African religious systems within the African diaspora as well as arguments concerning their legitimacy and authenticity (Fandrich 2007). In this volume, we have tried to capture the sheer diversity of Vodún and Vodou, but that is an impossible endeavor. Vodou thrives in places like Miami and New York City in the US. It appears to be among the first African religions in South America, serving as one of the founding forces of Brazilian Candomblé and Cuban Santeria (Montgomery and Gonzalez 2021; Pares 2013). Another challenge for elucidating the bigger picture has been the overlapping gods, liturgical elements, and histories between these religions and within Vodún and Vodou themselves, including their associated ethnic groups, before, during, and after the transatlantic slave trade.

Never before has any volume of Vodún and Vodou captured such an enormous assortment of its many manifestations. We hope our volume adds depth to some of the other great edited volumes on African religions (e.g., Johnson 2014; Olupona and Rey 2008; Paton and Forde 2012). And the past few years have seen an uptick in ethnographies on Vodún from the Bight of Benin, many of whose authors participated in this volume (Falen 2018; Landry 2019; Montgomery and Vannier 2017). There has been a virtual treasure trove of brilliantly written texts on this subject, but most of them focused on Vodún and Òrìṣà in specific contexts, while the goal here was more expansive in measure and extent (Barnes 1997; Goldschmidt and McAlister 2004; McCarthy Brown 1991; Murphy and Sanford 2001; Olmos and Paravisini-Gebert 1997; Rosenthal 1998). The extent to how and why African religions changed the Atlantic world will continue to be topics of intense and fruitful debate. This book began as a double panel at the American Anthropological Association annual meetings in Washington, DC, in November 2017 ("Vodun/Vodou Matters"), and then and now, the subject of Vodún and Vodou sparks passionate debates. And although this was an academic debate that commenced at an anthropology conference, these same debates rage among practitioners and increasingly on the internet (see Montgomery and Gonzalez 2021).

There are never really any final conclusions concerning Vodún and Vodou, although its future seems bright with new initiates coming from every corner of the globe. Whereas life is finite, the possibilities surrounding Vodún and Vodou in today's world are infinite. It seems that Vodún will continue to attract new devotees, maintain cultural legacies, and prepare folks for unpredictable futures. This volume has established that Vodún and Vodou are beautiful, useful, and humane. These religious systems are adaptable, mobile, and intoxicatingly stunning to their practitioners and researchers alike. Service involves an opening up and giving up of oneself: physically, emotionally, and psychologically. Vodún is resilient and shows no signs of slowing down anytime soon, at least not in the Atlantic world.

REFERENCES

Barnes, Sandra, ed. 1997. *Africa's Ogun*. Bloomington: Indiana University Press.
Baum, Robert M. 1990. "Graven Images: Scholarly Representations of African Religions." *Religion* 20 (4): 355–360.
Berry, Jason. 1988. "African Cultural Memory in New Orleans Music." *Black Music Research Journal* 8 (1): 3–12.
Blier, Suzanne Preston. 1996. *African Vodún: Art, Psychology, and Power*. Chicago: University of Chicago Press.
Clarke, Kamari. 2004. *Mapping Yorùbá Networks: Power and Agency in the Making of Transnational Communities*. Durham, NC: Duke University Press.
———. 2007. "Transnational Yoruba Revivalism and the Diasporic Politics of Heritage." *American Ethnologist* 34 (4): 721–734.

Comaroff, Jean, and John L. Comaroff. 2012. "Theory from the South: Or, How Euro-America Is Evolving toward Africa." *Anthropological Forum* 22 (2): 113–131.
Evans, Graham. 1999. "South Africa's Foreign Policy after Mandela Mbeki and His Concept of an African Renaissance." *Round Table* 88 (352): 621–628.
Falen, Douglas J. 2018. *African Science: Witchcraft, Vodun, and Healing in Southern Benin*. Madison: University of Wisconsin Press.
Ferguson, James. *Global Shadows: Africa in the Neoliberal World Order*. Durham, NC: Duke University Press, 2006.
Giafferi-Dombre, Natacha. 2019. "American Women Anthropologists of the Twentieth Century on Haitian Vodou: A Brief Review." In *Shackled Sentiments: Slaves, Spirits, and Memories in the African Diaspora*, edited by Eric J. Montgomery, 3–20. Lanham, MD: Lexington Books.
Goldschmidt, Henry, and Elizabeth McAlister, eds. 2004. *Race, Nation, and Religion in the Americas*. New York: Oxford University Press.
Gomez, Pablo. 2017. *The Experiential Caribbean: Creating Knowledge and Healing in the Early Modern Atlantic*. Chapel Hill: University of North Carolina Press.
Johnson, Paul Christopher, ed. 2014. *Spirited Things: The Work of "Possession" in Afro-Atlantic Religions*. Chicago: University of Chicago Press.
Landry, Timothy R. 2018. *Vodún: Secrecy and the Search for Divine Power*. Philadelphia: University of Pennsylvania Press.
Lomax, Alan. 2001. *Mister Jelly Roll: The Fortunes of Jelly Roll Morton, New Orleans Creole and "Inventor of Jazz."* Berkeley: University of California Press.
Manning, Patrick. 2016. *Slave Trades, 1500–1800: Globalization of Forced Labour*. New York: Routledge.
Marwick, Max, ed. 1982. *Witchcraft and Sorcery*. New York: Penguin Books
McCarthy Brown, Karen. 1991. *Mama Lola: A Vodou Priestess in Brooklyn*. Berkeley: University of California Press.
McGee, Adam M. 2012. "Haitian Vodou and Voodoo: Imagined Religion and Popular Culture." *Studies in Religion / Sciences Religieuses* 41 (2): 231–256.
McKenna, Terence. 1991. *The Archaic Revival*. San Francisco: Harper.
Meyer, Birgit. 1999. *Translating the Devil: Religion and Modernity among the Ewe in Ghana*. Edinburgh: Edinburgh University Press.
Montgomery, Eric J. 2019a. "Gothic 'Voodoo' in Africa and Haiti." *eTropic: Electronic Journal of Studies in the Tropics* 18 (1). https://journals.jcu.edu.au/etropic.
———. 2019b. "Slavery, Personhood, and Mimesis in Ewe Gorovodu and Mama Tchamba." In *Shackled Sentiments: Slaves, Spirits, and Memories in the African Diaspora*, edited by Eric J. Montgomery, 59. Lanham, MD: Rowman and Littlefield.
Montgomery, Eric J., and Rene Gonzalez. 2021. "Missing Vodun and Questions of Authenticity: Yoruba Supremacy in the African Diaspora." *Revista Brasileira do Caribe* 20 (39).

Montgomery, Eric J., and Christian Vannier. 2017. *An Ethnography of a Vodu Shrine in Southern Togo: Of Spirit, Slave and Sea*. Leiden, Netherlands: Brill.

Murphy, Joseph M., and Mei-Mei Sanford, eds. 2001. *Osun across the Waters: A Yoruba Goddess in Africa and the Americas*. Bloomington: University of Indiana Press.

Olmos, Margarite Fernández, and Lizabeth Paravisini-Gebert. 1997. *Sacred Possessions: Vodou, Santería, Obeah, and the Caribbean*. New Brunswick, NJ: Rutgers University Press.

Olupona, J. K., and Terry Rey, eds. 2008. *Òrìṣà Devotion as World Religion: The Globalization of Yorùbá Religious Culture*. Madison: University of Wisconsin Press.

Orobator, Agbonkhianmeghe E. 2018. *Religion and Faith in Africa: Confessions of an Animist*. Ossining, NY: Orbis Books.

Parés, Luis Nicolau. 2013. *The Formation of Candomblé: Vodun history and Ritual in Brazil*. Chapel Hill: University of North Carolina Press.

Paton, Diana, and Maarit Forde, eds. 2012. *Obeah and Other Powers: The Politics of Caribbean Religion and Healing*. Durham, NC: Duke University Press.

Rosenthal, Judy. 1998. *Possession, Ecstasy, and Law in Ewe Voodoo*. Charlottesville: University of Virginia Press.

Rush, Dana. 2013. *Vodún in Coastal Bénin: Unfinished, Open-Ended, Global*. Nashville: Vanderbilt University Press.

Sweet, James H. 2011. *Domingo Alvares, African Healing, and the Intellectual History of the Atlantic World*. Chapel Hill: University of North Carolina Press.

Sylla, Ndongo Samba, ed. 2014. *Liberalism and Its Discontents: Social Movements in West Africa*. Dakar, Senegal: Rosa Luxemburg Foundation.

Thompson, Robert Farris. 1983. *Flash of the Spirit: African and Afro-American Arts and Philosophy*. New York: Random House.

ERIC J. MONTGOMERY is Assistant Professor in Anthropology at Michigan State University and faculty as well as Saperstein Senior Science and Peace Fellow in the Center for Peace and Conflict Studies at Wayne State University. He is coauthor of *An Ethnography of a Vodu Shrine in Southern Togo* and editor of *Shackled Sentiments: Slaves, Spirits, and Memories in the African Diaspora*.

TIMOTHY R. LANDRY is Associate Professor of Anthropology and Religious Studies at Trinity College, Hartford, Connecticut. He is the author of *Vodún: Secrecy and the Search for Divine Power*, the winner of the 2019 Clifford Geertz Prize in the Anthropology of Religion.

CONTRIBUTOR BIOGRAPHIES

Eric J. Montgomery is Assistant Professor of Anthropology at Michigan State University and Saperstein Senior Fellow and faculty in the Center for Peace and Conflict Studies at Wayne State University. He is coauthor of *An Ethnography of a Vodu Shrine in Southern Togo* and editor of *Shackled Sentiments: Slaves, Spirits, and Memories in the African Diaspora*.

Timothy R. Landry is Associate Professor of Anthropology and Religious Studies at Trinity College, Hartford, Connecticut. He is the author of *Vodún: Secrecy and the Search for Divine Power*, the winner of the 2019 Clifford Geertz Prize in the Anthropology of Religion.

Christian Vannier is Lecturer in the College of Arts and Sciences at the University of Michigan, Flint. He is coauthor of *An Ethnography of a Vodu Shrine in Southern Togo* and coeditor of *Cultures of Doing Good: Anthropologists and NGOs*.

Venise N. Adjibodou is an independent scholar with a PhD from the University of Pennsylvania. She is a Diversity, Equity, and Inclusion practitioner and a learning and development specialist.

Jeffrey Anderson is Associate Professor of History at the University of Louisiana, Monroe. He is author of *Conjure in African American Society* and editor of *The Voodoo Encyclopedia: Magic, Ritual, and Religion*.

Nixon S. Cleophat is Professor in the Department of Religion at Bloomfield College. He is coeditor of *Vodou in the Haitian Experience: A Black Atlantic Perspective* and *Critical Approaches to Religion: Race, Class, Sexuality, and Gender.*

Douglas J. Falen is Professor of Anthropology at Agnes Scott College. He is author of *Power and Paradox: Authority, Insecurity, and Creativity in Fon Gender Relations* and *African Science: Witchcraft, Vodun, and Healing in Southern Benin.*

Natacha Giafferi-Dombre is an independent researcher and translator, member of PIND (Punk Is Not Dead) research group (Tours University, France), and author of *Une ethnologue à Port-au-Prince: Question de couleur et luttes pour le classement socio-racial dans la capitale haïtienne.*

Alissa Jordan is Associate Director of the Center for Experimental Ethnography at the University of Pennsylvania.

Elizabeth McAlister is Professor of Religion at Wesleyan University. She is author of *Rara! Vodou, Power, and Performance in Haiti and Its Diaspora* and coeditor of *Race, Nation, and Religion in the Americas.*

Terry Rey is Professor of Religion at Temple University. He is author of several books, including *Our Lady of Class Struggle: The Cult of the Virgin Mary in Haiti*; *The Priest and the Prophetess: Abbé Ouvière, Romaine Rivière, and the Revolutionary Atlantic World*; and coeditor of *Orisa Devotion as World Religion: The Globalization of Yoruba Religious Culture.*

Karen Richman is Director for Undergraduate Studies at the Institute for Latino Studies and concurrent faculty in the Departments of Romance Languages and Anthropology at the University of Notre Dame. She is author of *Migration and Vodou.*

INDEX

Note: Italicized page numbers followed by 'f' indicate photographs.

Abidijou, Venise N., 10, 60, 132, 312
Ablewa, 85, 88, 104, 107–8
acɛ: acquisition of, 243; concept of, 197, 203n5; convergence of, 199; gender roles in, 254n11; interactions among, 193, 201; and rituals' power, 195; as social power, 232
Adéléké: activation of, 199–200; agency of, 194, 195, 197; in bloodless chicken ritual, 193–94; creation of acɛ known as, 198; function of calabash for, 196, 201; gender of, 203n4; power dynamics with humans, 199
Adja-Fon people and traditions, 71, 73, 77, 87, 146, 277, 315
affordances, 192, 194–95, 203n2
African religions: bias against, 190, 308, 310; dynamism and influence of, 8; early French Caribbean practices of, 21–22; healers and maintenance of community in, 18; main religious currents in, 315; metaphysical transformation in, 276; scholarship on, 3–5, 315–16; slave trade and spread of, 2, 3; stereotypes in perceptions of, 7–8. *See also* Vodún and Vodou
African science, 202
Afrocentrism, 182
Agaja (ruler), 1–2, 46
agbègbé, 233–34
Aidohouedo, 200–202
albinism, 230, 236, 254n3, 254n8
Alexandre, Camolien, 120–22, 134
Alvarèz, Maria, 223
American Anthropological Association panel discussion, 316
Amilcar, Faustin, 120
amulets and icons, 21, 27, 31–32, 35, 92
ancestor veneration, 21, 22, 35
Anderson, Jeffrey, 3, 10, 312
anthropology: attention to sacred forests in, 232; ethics in, 203n2; and indigenous epistemologies, 191–92; and legitimization of Vodún and Vodou, 70–71; and new perspectives on spirit religions, 308; and power from betweenness, 234; and syncretism in religious practice, 45; understanding

anthropology (*Cont.*)
of spirits, 190; use of methodological agnosticism in, 201. *See also* ethnography
apotheosis of difference, 236
Apter, Andrew, 4, 54
Arabic language, 100–101
Ashforth, Adam, 57
ason (rattle), 120, 121, 247, *248f*, 254n13, 255n15
assemblages: aesthetic of, 146; and agency, 45; Bangre as an assemblage, 89; bodies as, 228; as hallmark of Vodún culture, 113; Islamic, 112, 116n2; objects as, 247; ritual assemblages, 112
Atis Rezistans collective, 147, *153f*, 158–59, *160f*, 161
Auguste, Oldy Joël, 143
Augustin, Frisner: about, 283, 288–89, *290f*; career of, 287–88, 291–92, 293; Catholic mass and entombment for, 301–2; criticism of, 292; family tomb of, 287, *288f*; funerary rituals for, 285, 286, 296–302; initiation ritual for, 289, 291, *292f*; life as a transnational, 304; migrations of, 313; as priest of the drum, 287–88; as promoter of Vodou, 292–93; retrieval ceremony and sacred biography for, 302; and tour of Grand Cimitière, 295; wake work for, 285, 297–99
Aupiais, Francis, 53
authenticity in art, 152–53, 156
Ayida Wèdo, 266, 267, 269
Ayizan, 291
azevodún, 59
azizà (forest spirits), 235–38, 240–41, 252

Bangede (deity), 108–10, *110f*, 111
Bangre (god of war), 72, 85, 86–90, *89f*, 90, 92
Barnes, Sandra, 75

Barra, Pierrot, 148
Bashkow, Ira, 55
Basquiat, Jean-Michel, 161
bathing: adults and, 216, 228n1; description of infant bath, 213–15; importance of, 213; meaning in, 312; older children and, 215–16, 228n2; women and, 217–18
Baudry des Lozières, Louis Narcisse: Kikongo-French dictionary, 28, 29–30; *Second voyage à la Louisiane*, 28
Bawon Samdi, 161, 295, 299, 301
Bay, Edna, 48, 50, 62n9, 62n11
Beauvoir, Ati Max, 301, 304
Beauvoir-Dominique, Rachel, 148, 304
Beinart, Katy, *Decentering the Market and Other Tales of Progress*, 158
Bell, Catherine, 199
Bellegarde-Smith, Patrick, 260, 278
Benedicty-Kokken, Alessandra, *Intellectual History of Vodou Thought*, 150
Benin: bloodless chicken ritual in, 200–201; fences and barriers in, 239; kingdoms of, 61n8; reassertion of Vodún in, 72; spiritual insecurity in, 57; Vodún and Western tourists, 40; Yoruba and Fon spirits in, 251–52. *See also* Dahomey kingdom; Fon speakers; Vodún
Benoît, Catherine, 152–53, 155
bizango statues, 152
Black people: domination of, 302; mortuary freedoms of, 286; and Vodún, 308; wakes for, 285
Blessebois, Pierre-Corneille, *Le zonbi de Grand-Perrou*, 34
Blier, Suzanne Preston, 7, 75, 91, 112, 234, 236, 239
Blouët, J. P. M., 31, 32
bodies and skin: bedding, life, and memory embodied in, 208–9; deformities and anomalies in, 230, 236,

254n3, 254n8; and eating together, 218–23; importance in Vodou, 209; interconnectivity of, 228; lougawou marks, 225–26; observation of illness and wellness in, 211–12; permeability to emotion and relationships, 212; personal care and the community, 217–18; prevention of intrusions into, 212–13; and social development, 209–10; as vessels inhabited by energies, 277, 279. *See also* bathing; infant care
bohoun ritual of prayer songs, 298–300
Bondye (supreme deity), 263, 266, 268
Boon, James, 76
Bosman, Willem, 46, 47
Boss To (Joseph Fortine), 153
boumba, term of, 25–26
Bourriaud, Nicolas, 163n3; "The Radicant," 159
Bout, Ti, 148
Boyer, David, 148
Brazilian Candomblé, 36n1, 54, 252, 315
Brekete. *See* Gorovodu
Brenner, Louis, 101
Breton, André, 155, 156
Brivio, Alessandra, 99
Brown, Karen McCarthy, 91, 161, 222, 242
Burton, Richard, 46
Butler, Jon, 286
Butler, Judith, 279

call-and-response in Haitian vodou, 24
capitalism, 8, 142, 143, 180, 235, 238, 307
Caribbean culture and religions, scholarship on, 3–5
Cassaise, Marie, 148
Castro, Eduardo Viveiros de, 191
Catholicism: Africans' and Creoles' view of, 27; baptism for West African slaves, 36n6; incorporation of local culture into, 53; and Kunde, 84; and lwa rituals, 130; rosaries in African religious practice, 99, 111; in Saint-Domingue (Haiti), 30, 32–33, 35, 130; and Saint Philomena, 271; and social prestige, 51, 54–55; Vodún and Vodou exchanges with, 9
Catholic missions, 50, 62n16
Céleur, Jean Hérard, 157, 161
Célius, Carlo Avierl, 139, 150
Centre d'Art (Haiti), 155
chants in vodou ritual, 24–26, 30. *See also* bohoun ritual of prayer songs
Charlier, Vladimir Cybil, 161–62; *Haiti Meets Harlem*, 161; *Marassa Andy and Basquiat*, 161
chicken ritual, bloodless: in Benin and Philadelphia, 190, 192–94, 200–201; as challenge to Western science, 191, 192, 194–95, 202; concept of, 191–92; and ethics, 203n2; meal after ritual of, 203n6; and merging of agentic matter, 199; sensory perception involving, 193–94; and sociocosmic relationships, 198
Chinese and Asian healing, 41, 56, 58f, 59
Christianity: African religions and, 62n117–18, 307, 312; African roots of, 308–9; in coastal West Africa, 74, 113; comparison of Islam to, 114; context of arrival of, 115; and fear of the spirits, 314–15; as foreign religion, 44; hypocrisy in, 52–53; and malignment of Vodún, 50–51, 52, 236; as protection from evil, 133; and spirit possession, 275; tolerance in, 45; and witchcraft, 59. *See also* Catholicism; Protestantism; syncretism
Cleophat, Nixon, 10, 210, 227, 228, 312

colonialism: and Ablewa, 104; and capitalism, 140; the colonial gaze in art, 153, 163; economies and religious assimilation, 103; and Islam, 97; spirit service as resistance to, 5; Vodún and Vodou's role in decolonialization, 308; and Vodún as religious category, 253
Conway, Fred, 131, 134
Cosentino, Donald, 91, 146–47, 150, 162
Courlander, Harold, 136n1
Croce-Spinelli, Michel, 52
Cuban painters, 155
Cuban Santería (Lucumí), 54, 82, 251, 252, 315
Cult of the Dead, 144
cultural appropriation and exchange: in Haitian street art, 143; between Islam and African religions, 311; and reinvention, 162; through encounter, 9, 311
Cuvelier, Jean, 25

Da (rainbow serpent), 80, 91
Dahomey kingdom: elements preserved in bohoun ritual, 298; Fá's arrival into, 243; growth of Vodún in, 1–2; incorporation of gods into, 46–47, 56; Masonic insignia and, 146; missionary critiques of, 51; Muslim divination practices in, 101; openness to foreign ideas of, 48; and slave trade, 62n12; syncretism in, 62n17
Danbala: about, 262; and Ayida, 269; cult of, 22, 33–34, 35; in kanzo ritual, 123; and origin of life, 266–67; prominence of, 25; and queer persons, 280
Danticat, Edwidge, 286
Dantó, 273–74, 289, 301
Dàn Wèkè (serpent spirit), 239, 240
Dayan, Joan (Colin), 147, 270

death, dying, and rebirth, 18–19
Declaration of the Rights of Man and the Citizen, 30
dehumanization, 5, 279, 307
Delpuech, André, 152–53, 155
démembré (sacred land), 249, 251
Deren, Maya, 267, 272, 291; *Divine Horsemen*, 163n3
desounen, 296–97, 303
Desruisseau, Rose-Marie, *Ceremony for Gede, 149f*
Dessalines, Jean-Jacques, 36
divination: becoming a diviner, 233; cultural exchange and, 9; in early Caribbean practices, 21; Fá divination, 46, 62n9, 243–44, 254n10; and Gbădù, 243; and human destiny, 247; importance of, 6; origin of Ifa divination, 101; West African influence on, 35. *See also* chicken ritual, bloodless
djabs (malevolent spirits), 276
Doctrina Christiana, 45–46, 50, 62n10
Dogon creation story, 267
Dorsainville, Roger, 132, 133
Drewal, Henry John, 56, 75, 80, 81
drumming and dance, 21, 35. *See also* Augustin, Frisner
dualities, overcoming, 314
Dunham, Katherine, 151
Durkheim, Émile, 29
Du Tertre, Jean-Baptiste, 36n6
Dutty, Boukman, 36
Duval-Carrié, Edouard, 147; *Imagined Landscapes*, 162
Duvalier, François, 3, 130, 151, 294
Dzreke, 99

Eckankar, 56, 57, 63n21
ecocide, 261, 269, 276
ecological ethics: bodies as sites of transmission for, 280; as dimension of Vodou, 260; equality in, 271; and

inclusivity, 262; and interconnectivity of life in the universe, 269; liberation of humans and the planet, 270; source of Vodou ethics, 274
economic development: neoliberalism and emigration from Haiti, 125; and Protestantism, 130; and sacred objects as folk art, 151; and spread of Islamic practices, 103–4, 113
encounter: and cultural exchange, 9, 311; of research communities with Vodún and Vodou, 309. *See also* Christianity; Gorovodu (aka Brekete or Tron); Haitian art; Islam; syncretism; Vodou, French colonial accounts of
engagement: and lived experience of Vodún and Vodou, 9–10, 189, 309. *See also* bodies and skin; chicken ritual, bloodless; Mississippi River valley Voodoo; spirited forests; Vodou cosmology; Vodou funerary rites
Estimé, Dumarsais, 144, 151
ethnography: description of research in coastal Togo, 73–74; fieldwork in Benin, 41–42; and Gorovodu, 83, 98; and Mami Wata, 79; participant observation, 4, 10, 312; storytelling in, 308; on Vodún, 315–16. *See also* bathing; Beinart, Katy; Conway, Fred; Haitian funerary practices; initiation rites; Métraux, Alfred; Price-Mars, Jean; salah ceremonies; shrines
Eugène, André, 157, 161
Evans-Pritchard, E. E., 90, 236
Ewe people: adoption of Islamic practices by, 105, 113; and forests, 252; Islamic influence on, 98–99; slave spirits among, 276; and the slave trade, 56, 101–2; use of *fetish*, 93n3; Vodún of, 61n1, 83. *See also* Gorovodu exhibitions, 157

exoticism: in alterity, 42; as characteristic of Vodún, 60; as feature of witchcraft, 59; in foreign desire for Haitian art, 139; and receptivity to foreign religious practices, 56, 59, 60; in tourism and the international art market, 157–58; of Tron, 50
Ezilis: in the arts, 161, 162; cult of, 33–34; Dantò, 134, 273–74, 289, 301; female agency and, 271, 272; Freda, 143, 147, 272–73, 289, 301

Fá, 192, 232, 247
Fá divination: about, 243, 254n10; arrival among the Fon, 46, 62n9; Landry and, 233, 243. *See also* Gbădú
Fá initiation rituals, 244–45
Falen, Douglas J., 116, 132, 202, 310–11
Fandrich, Ina Johanna, 182
feminism, 182, 260–62, 261–62
Festival of Vodún Arts and Cultures, 40, 61n3
fetishes: commodity fetishes, 143; as god-objects, 72, 73; Kunde fetish, 84, 85; in rubbish, 160; Sakpata fetish, 78; sculptures as, 147; in shrines, 108; use of term, 93n3
Filan, Kenaz, *Voodoo Handbook*, 183
Firmin, Anténor, "Of the Equality of Human Races," 156
Fon speakers: places of power and sacredness for, 232; and references to religious practice, 230; and sacredness, 231
food: recipes and concoctions, 59, 60; sharing of, 218–23, 224
forests: Christian *versus* African religions' treatment of, 265–66; importance of, 252; peril and power in, 239. *See also* spirited forests (sacred forests)
Fortilus, Nadine, *drapo* art by, 145f, 150f

Foster, Hal, 158
Freda, 272, 289, 301
freemasonry, 41, 56, 57, 63n22, 145–47, 163n3
French missionaries. *See* Labat, Jean-Baptiste, *Nouveau voyage aux îles françoises d'Amérique*
Friedson, Steven, 81–82, 99
Frisner. *See* Augustin, Frisner

Gaard, Greta, 261
gamel (instrument), 298
gangan ason (priests): critiques of, 120–22, 136n1; displacement of shamans by, 120; in Haiti, 30; and kanzo practice, 121–22, 124; power from kanzo, 135; Protestants' patronizing of, 133–34
Gauthier, Viviane, 291, 301
Gbădù, 238, 241–43, 245, 247, 252, 253, 254n9
Gbedala, Togo: about, 73; arrival of Gorovodu to, 104–5; case study in, 70, 73; Mami Wata shrine in, 80; scale of spirits in, 72; shrines in, 78–79
Gede (lwa), 146, 158, 161, 277–78, 299
Gede Fest, 144
gender equality: in congregational worship, 131; ecological principles and, 260–61; female liberation and empowerment, 271–73; and labor roles of ounsi, 135; in ritual participation, 118, 122, 129–30; Vodún and Vodou and, 261, 262, 271, 307, 312
gender identity: Ezilis and, 272–73; regendering in spirit possession, 277–78, 279; and spirit possession, 10, 279. *See also* hypermasculinity
Geschiere, Peter, 58f
Ghana. *See* Gorovodu (aka Brekete or Tron)

Ghetto Biennial (exhibition), 157–58, 159–60
Giafferi-Dombre, Natacha, 45, 135, 272, 311
Gibson, James J., 192, 194
Ginen as ancestral home, 284
Girouard, Tina, 153, 154
globalization. *See* modernity and globalization
Gobineau, Count de, "Essay on the Inequality of the Human Races," 156
Goody, Jack, 87, 90, 91, 103; "Myth of Bagre," 88
Gordon, Leah, 159
Gorovodu (aka Brekete or Tron): about, 71, 92n1; and cultural assimilation, 103–4, 115; effectiveness against witchcraft, 59; growth of, 72; inclusiveness in, 74; Islamic practices in, 98–100, 112, 113, 115, 116n2, 311; kola nuts in, 49, 62n14; Mami Wata in, 81; material objects in, 107; medicine shrines of, 82–83; spirit healing in, 76–77, 90; spirits of, 49, 56, 71–72, 84, 91; two "sticks" of, 73, 83; as vibrant religious culture, 92. *See also* Bangre; Kunde; salah ceremonies; Yewevodu
Gottlieb, Alma, 209
Grand Cimetière, 293–95
Grann Brijit, 295, 301
Grimes, Ronald, 195
Guadeloupe, 34
Guyodo, 161

Haiti: burial on family land in, 286; colorism and classism in, 273; funeral costs for burial in, 286–87, 302, 303; identity and tensions of adaptation in, 141; importance of Haitian land in initiation rites, 249; labor migration and economic decline in,

124–28; marginalized populations in, 273; occupation and economic crisis in, 135; Protestant missions and conversions in, 130–34; purifying water in, 213; Vodou as national religion in, 310; women in, 271–72; young people in, 128–29. *See also* Saint-Domingue (later, Haiti); Vodou

Haitian art: as adaptation to local and global forces, 139–40; authenticity in, 152–53; desacralization of Vodou in, 140, 151–52, 153–54; foreign desire for, 157–58, 311; freemasonry elements in, *145f*, 146, 163n3; hypermasculinity in, 161; identity and alterity in, 151, 155–57; international recognition of, 155–56; invention and function of, 139; military elements in, 146; mimesis in, 156; painting in, 154–56; para-Vodou art, 148; pop culture and, 142–44; sculpture as fetish in, 147–48; trash artists, 158–59, 160–61, *160f*; vehicle art, 143; Vodou in, 144, 150, 157, 162–63. *See also* sacred flags *(drapo)*

Haitian Embassy, 286

Haitian funerary practices: burial on family land, 286; Catholic funeral masses, 301; costs and difficulties for, 286–87; importance of historical memory in, 284; local funerary workers for, 294; as political, 304; shipping of corpses, 286–87, 303; tombs in, 295; wake work in, 285. *See also* Vodou funerary rites

Haitian Renaissance, 152

Haitian Revolution, 26–27

Haraway, Donna, 232

Harris, Melanie, 261

Hartman, Saidiya, 284

Harvey, Graham, 232

healing and medicine: accounts of healing, 76–77, 78, 220–22; bloodless chicken ritual for, 193, 195; bodily sites given most attention, 216; cults and shrines for, 90; cultural exchange in, 9; forests and, 235, 237; herbalism, 31–32, 59; Labat's observations of practices in, 18, 19, 21; and lougawou attacks, 225; and maintenance of community, 18; Mami Wata and, 80; and nature's power, 60; and the occult, 63n24; as primary function of Vodou, 242; recipes in, 59; ritual medicinal washes, 109–11, *110–11f*; Sakpata and, 77–78, 79; source of medicinal power, 90–91; and terms in Baudry's dictionary, 30; for underserved populations, 189; Vodún and Vodou concepts of, 7; "wake work" in, 285. *See also* spirited forests; spirit possession

Hearn, Lafcadio, 170, 171, 183n1; "The Last of the Voudoos," 169

Hebblethwaite, Benjamin, "Dictionary of Vodou Terms," 25

hegemony and cultural appropriations, 54–56

Henry, Christine, 52

Herskovits, Melville, 70

Heviesso: as forest spirit, 90; and justice, 88; and Kunde, 85, 85; in Yewevodu, 74, 75, 77

Hinduism: in Beninese Vodún, 56; in coastal West Africa, 74; and Mami Wata, 48, 75; in Tron practices, 50; and Vodún in Benin, 41; and witchcraft, 59

Hirsch, Jennifer, 137n4

Hirst, Damian, 157

homophobia. *See* oppression

Hountondji, Paulin, 191

human beings: affirmation of worth through Vodou, 259, 262; dehumanization of, 269, 279; divinity potential of, 276, 277; infants and becoming human, 209; interconnections within, 200; liberation and the planet, 270; multidimensionality of, 267–68; mutual transformations of, 195; place in the universe of, 263–65, 269; twinned nature of, 267

Hurbon, Laennec, 302

Hurston, Zora Neale, 178, 181, 182, 184n6; "Hoodoo in America," 177

Hyacinthe, 26–27

hypermasculinity, 161, 163n9

Hyppolite, Hector, 139, 152, 155, 156, 157

identity construction: in engagement with spirits, 10; globalization and, 141; influence of American culture on, 161–62; selfhood and interconnectedness, 210; spirits and, 5, 275

Indigénisme, 139, 151, 152

indigenous knowledge: acε in, 197; in analysis of rituals, 192; anthropology and, 191, 198; sensory information in, 194

infant care: and becoming human, 209, 210; as community care, 228; daily bathing, 213; as education, 209–10; and exposure to envy, 227; feeding, 219–20; learning what to avoid, 224–25; and lougawou attacks, 225–27, 228n3; protection and survival through, 227; relocations for, 226–27; treating illness, 220–22

initiation rites: Fá initiation rituals, 242, 243, 244–45; in Haiti, 3, 247, 249; and human destiny, 247; human-plant collaboration in, 234; for priest of the drum, 289, 291; researchers' participation in, 10, 243, 247, 249–50; in the United States, 177, 183n2, 249, 252. *See also* Augustin, Frisner; desounen; kanzo

Innocent, Antoine, *Mimola*, 144

Insoll, Timothy, 90

interconnectedness: Danbala and, 266; of humans and the universe, 264; of spirit possession, 270–71; of the universe, 263; Vodou's celebration of, 260

Islam: African roots of, 308–9; influence on Vodún and Vodou, 49–50, 115–16, 189, 311; relationship with African religious culture, 9, 97–98, 307; in West Africa, 74, 100–105, 104, 113–14. *See also* Kunde

James, B. T., 90

Jell-Bahlsen, Sabine, 75

Johnson, Paul Christopher, 231

Jordan, Alissa, 10, 195, 312

Judeo-Christian cosmology: creation stories, 263, 266; views of indigenous religions, 265–66; women in, 271

kanzo (initiation ritual): as competitive events, 124; decline in, 126; as expectation for women, 122–23; gangan's power from, 120–22; as happenings, 118, 144; as healing ritual, 123–24, 136n2; migrants' funding of, 127; promotion of, 119; as reinvented tradition, 135; season for, 134; and upward mobility, 136. *See also* suleliye

Keane, Webb, 203n2

Kohn, Eduardo, 232

kola nut cults, 102, 103

Kunde (father/hunter god): compared to a dog, 114; emergence and migration of, 103–4; and the forest, 90; material culture of, 85–86, 86f; as medicine god, 87, 90; sacred objects of, 92;

in salah ceremony, 107–8, 109–10; shrines to, 72
Kutito society, 41, 42f, 43f, 46, 61n6
Kyung, Chung Hyun, 280

Labat, Jean-Baptiste, 34–35, 36n5; *Nouveau voyage aux iles françoises d'Amérique*, 17–22
Laguerre, Michel, 32, 54–55
Lam, Wilfredo, 155
Landry, Timothy: centrality of the forest in Vodún, 10, 59–60; and plants' divine power, 75, 196, 313; on pluralism of Vodún and Vodou, 132; on shrines, 204n8; *Vodún*, 175; and witchcraft, 311
Lavaud, Tido, 301
Leclerc expedition, 146
Legba (deity), 47, 51, 62n11, 74, 106, 244
Lennon, Caitlin Elizabeth, 159–60
Léogane: economic crisis and out-migration in, 124; Protestants in, 137n5; reputation for authentic Vodou, 122; temple Vodou in, 119–20
Lerebours, Michel Philippe, 151
Levine, Barry, 125
Lévi-Strauss, Claude, *La Pensée Sauvage*, 151
LGBTQ community: Ezilis and, 272, 273–74; survival of, 279; Vodou ecological ethics and, 262. See also madivin (lesbians); masisi (effeminate gay men); queerness; queer Vodou ecotheology
Lhérisson, Dubréus, 148, 152, 157
Liautaud, Georges, 150, 155
liberation: through spirit possession, 278, 279, 280, 312; Vodou as framework for, 260
liminality: of forests, 247–51, 253; power from, 233–38; and understanding Vodún's success, 231

lougawou and attacks by, 225–27, 228n3
Love, Tony, funeral for, 294–95
lwa (Haitian deities): about, 2, 3, 6; anthropomorphism in, 147; Catholicism and, 130; characteristics of, 262, 266–69; connection with the supernatural through, 259; cultural representations of, 143; determination of right and wrong by, 274; doubts about, 129; ecological ethics, liberation, and, 260; forests and, 251; freemasonry symbols in representations of, 145–46; and images of saints, 151; and infant care, 221–22; as manifestations of the natural world, 262, 268, 269–70; Marasas and, 268; and mediation by gangan ason, 120–21, 135, 136n1; protection from discipline by, 132–33; relationship with the cosmos, 266, 312–13; in spirit possession, 270; West African roots of, 22; and women, 122–23. See also Ezilis; spirit possession

madivin (lesbians), 272, 273, 274
Magesa, Laurenti, 263, 274
Maitre Grand Bois (Rockville), 142f
Malenfant, Colonel, *Des colonies et particulièrement de celle de Saint-Domingue*, 26–28
Mama Tchamba, 90, 91–92
Mama Zogbe, 75, 92n2
Mami Wata (spirit of water and beauty): about, 79–82, 84, 92n2; in artwork, 150f; in coastal Vodún, 91; and Gorovodu, 74, 311; healing through, 90; offerings to, 83f; origin of, 75–76, 81; and queerness, 254n3, 254n8; shrines to, 49f, 72, 80, 81–82, 92; syncretism of, 48–49; and witchcraft, 59

manbo, 122, 129–30, 133, 211, 225, 248f, 297. *See also* suleliye
Marasas (twin spirits), 267–68
Marcelin, Frédéric, *La Vengeance de Mama*, 144
marginalized populations: and Ezili lwa, 272–73; and spirit possession, 280
Martinique, 34
Marwick, Max, 311
masisi (effeminate gay men), 272–73
materialism, new, 204n9
materiality: agentic capacity in, 197; of religion, 201; the senses and understanding, 81–82; transcendence of, 279; and understanding Vodún's success, 231; in Vodún, 192, 203
maternal care, 223–24
Mathon-Blanchet, Lina, 291
Matory, J. Lorand, 97, 210
Maupoil, Bernard, 8
Mbiti, John, 264, 265
Mbumba, 25, 36n10
McAlister, Elizabeth, 10, 127, 277–78, 313
McFague, Sallie, 266; *Models of God*, 261
Mennesson-Rigaud, Odette, 120
Metcalf, Jason, 159
metonymic reason, 190–91
Métraux, Alfred, 33, 120, 122, 132, 296; *Le Vaudou Haïtien*, 119
Meyer, Birgit, 62n16
Michel, Claudine, 260, 278
Middle Passage, 2, 291
migrants: and construction boom in Haiti, 127; dying in diaspora, 283, 286; funding of Ti Rivyè by, 125, 126; lwa as, 162; money for rites from, 124, 127, 136, 287, 302, 303; realities of transnationality of, 284; religious adaptability of, 132. *See also* Augustin, Frisner
migration and movement: and assimilation of deities, 1; and the Ghetto Biennale, 159; from Haiti, 125–26, 135; and Haiti's economy, 124–28, 140; of Islamic practices, 100, 101, 113; as key feature of Vodún and Vodou, 2, 8–9, 314; and spread of Vodún, 2
mimesis: in Haitian art, 156; in ritual assemblages, 112. *See also* salah ceremonies
Mintz, Sidney, 3, 141, 144
Misdor, 121, 123
Mississippi River valley Voodoo: about, 312; claims of ownership of, 171, 176–82; globalism in, 10, 171–76, 183; Montanée's role in, 169–70; practitioners of, 182–83; regionality of, 171
Mobley, Christina, 25
modernity and globalization: affective modernity, 128–30, 137n4; and decline in religious practices, 129; effect on funerary rites, 303–4; and identity construction, 141; Mami Wata and, 82; modern art and, 160; and necroscapes, 283; ritual in, 118; and syncretism in Benin, 61; use of Vodou aesthetics to deal with, 160–61; Vodún and Vodou's role in negotiating, 8, 140–41, 163, 307, 310
Montanée, Jean, 169–70, 182
Montgomery, Eric: on healing underserved populations, 189; on pluralism of Vodún and Vodou, 132; *Shackled Sentiments*, 272; on shrines, 204n8; on spirit possession, 275, 276; on spirits in Ghana and Togo, 311; on syncretism, 116n4
morality, comparison of religious practices regarding, 114

INDEX 331

Moreau de Saint-Méry, Médéric Louis Elie: observation of Vaudoux rituals, 35; relationship with Baudry, 28
Moreau de Saint-Méry, Médéric Louis Elie, *Description topographique, physique, civile, politique, et historique de la partie française de l'isle Saint-Domingue*, 22–26
Morris, Randall, 150
Morse, Richard, 144
Murray, Gerald, 120, 223

Naaeke, Anthony, 88
Nana Wango, 82, 83, 107–8
Napoleon Bonaparte, 146
National Heritage Fellowship, 287
natural world: and embodiment in spiritual energy, 261–62; environmental health of, 260, 269; lwa as symbolic representations of, 262, 268, 269–70, 280; role in fight for justice, 265; sacredness of, 268; as source of Vodou ethics, 274; spiritual energies in, 263; Vodou celebration of interconnection in, 260. *See also* ecological ethics; forests; spirited forests
necroscapes: diaspora and modernization of, 303; difficulties of Haitians in, 284–85; use of term, 283. *See also* Haitian funerary practices; Vodou funerary rites
neoliberalism, 284, 308
New Orleans, 170–71, 182–83
Norman, Neil, 46
Nouvelliste on youthful demand for American culture, 143–44

occult, use of term, 63n20. *See also* witchcraft
Olupona, Jacob, 4, 264, 313–14, 315
O'Neil, Deborah, "The Saint and Siren" (with Rey), 271

oppression: as cosmological assault, 269–70, 276; Ezilis and, 273; weblike systems of, 260–61
Òrìṣà, 70, 73, 75, 314, 315, 316. *See also* Sakpata
Orobater, Agbonkhianmeghe, 308–9
Orozco, Manuel, 126
Ortiz, Fernando, 25
oungan (houngan): about, 120, 144; and access to the supernatural, 155–56; etymology of, 254n12; the forest and, 247, 250; in funerary rites, 297; and healing, 225. *See also* suleliye
ounsi: about, 118; disappearance of, 119, 134; and doubts about spiritual affliction, 129; and economic power of gangan, 121–22; as free labor, 124; kanzo ritual for, 122–24; Protestantism's effect on, 130–34
Ountò, 283, 289
Ouvière, Félix Pascalis (aka Dr. Pascalis), 30–34, 36n18; "Anecdote historique," 31

Palmié, Stephan, 4
Papa Loko Atisou, 247, 249, 250, 254n14
Papua New Guinea, syncretism in, 55
Parfaite, 43–44, 59, 61n7
Peabody, Sue, 54
Peters, Dewitt, 155
Pettinger, Alasdair, 25–26
Philadelphia, Vodún rituals in, 192–96, 312
Philomena (Saint), 271–72
Pierre, André, 147, 152
plants, agency of, 234
Polk, Patrick, 146
popular culture: and Haitian Vodou art, 142–44; racism in, 314–15
Port-au-Prince, Haiti, 119
postmodernism, 182, 314

INDEX

power: adoption of Western sources of, 145; divine power of Gbădù, 241; forests as center of occult power, 239; secrecy and, 239, 250
power dynamics: and Christianity, 54; medicines and, 7; of science and àzĕ, 202; in serving the spirits, 5, 6; in Western encounters with African religions, 307. *See also* resistance
Price, Richard, 3
Price-Mars, Jean, 139, 158
The Priest and the Prophetess (Rey), 31
priesthood of the drum, 283, 289
primitivism, 7, 140, 155, 156, 157
Priye Djò (Djò prayer), 297–98
prophecy in early Caribbean practices, 20, 21
Prospect Park, New York City, 251, 252–53
Protestantism: conversions in Haiti, 130–34, 137n5; critiques of Vodou in, 135; and disappearance of ounsi, 130–34; and patronization of gangan, 133–34; views of Vodou, 130, 131

queerness, 254n3, 254n8
queer Vodou ecotheology, 227, 274–78, 312

Raboteau, Albert, 62n18
racism: in accounts of Voodoo participation, 182; anti-Blackness, 284; spirit service as resistance to, 5; in study of Vodún and Vodou, 70, 307–8, 310; and Western science, 189–90, 203
rainmaking, 19–20, 21, 35
RAM (Vodou-rock band), 144
Rastafarian theology, 270, 279
relational aesthetics, 158–61, 163n6
religion, nature of, 204n10

resilience, art and religion as tools of, 147–48
resistance: serving the spirits as, 5; Vodún and Vodou's role in, 3, 308
Rey, Terry, 4, 54, 310, 313–14, 315; "The Saint and Siren" (with O'Neil), 271
Richman, Karen: on agency of the dead, 303; on the commodification of ritual labor, 141; on Danbala, 25; on disappearance of Vodou, 311; on Haitian art, 156; on Haitian funerals, 286; on mimesis and authenticity, 140; on spirit shrines, 144–45
ritual assemblages, 112–13
ritualization, 199
rituals and ritual practices, 245f; and agency of spirits, 195; apprenticeships to understand, 312; as art, 158; chemistry of, 198; coming of age rituals, 242–43; commodification of, 124, 134, 135–36, 140; congregational structures in, 120, 124; in cultural anthropology, 198–99; decrease in lwa ritual participation, 133; dimensions of knowledge and experience in, 200; dying and rebirth in, 291; as embodiment of cosmology, 195–96; importance of, 6; for the lwa, 135; material objects in, 36n4, 107, 108f, 247, 251; Muslims and, 101; observed by Labat, 19–21; observed by Malenfant, 27–28; public folkloric performances of, 292; secrecy in, 239; and the social order, 232, 242; success of, 259; as technologies, 190, 194; transformative power of, 119–24, 195; Vaudoux serpent ceremony, 23–25, 26. *See also* chicken ritual, bloodless; initiation rites; snake veneration
ritual specialists, 2–3, 311–12. *See also* gangan ason (priests); manbo; oungan (houngan)

Romain, Charles-Poisset, 130, 131
Romaine-la-Prophétesse (née Romaine Rivière), 30–33, 35, 36n16, 36n18
Rosenthal, Judy, 71–72, 76, 98, 204n8
Rosicrucianism, 56, 57, 63n22
Ruether, Rosemary, 260
Rush, Dana, 5, 48, 76, 91, 192, 203n1, 254n7

The Sacred Arts of Vodou (exhibition), 157
sacred flags (drapo): about, 153–54; cultural mélanges in, 146; with freemasonry elements, 145f, 146; international markets for, 157; mass produced flags, 148; military references in, 146–47
Sacred Forests (Zogbe), 90
sacrifice, importance of, 6
Saint-Brice, Robert, 139
Saint-Domingue (later, Haiti): accounts of religious culture in, 17, 22, 54; enslaved Africans in, 18–19; "Voodoo" cells in, 32, 36
Sakpata (earth deity): about, 77–79, 87, 92n2; arrival in coastal Togo, 74; in the forest, 239–40; and Gbădù shrine, 241; power of, 90; sacred forest of, 231–32; shrines to, 72, 239; in Yewevodu, 75
salah ceremonies: complexity of, 106–7; description of, 105, 106–11; as part of Gorovodu ritual practices, 99–100; regularity of, 105; as ritual assemblages, 112–13
Salmons, Jill, 75
Sastre, Robert, 74
Savannah Spirits, 102–5
Scheu, Patricia, 249
sensory experience in understanding Vodún, 312
sexism. *See* gender equality; oppression

sexuality: Ezili divinities and, 272–74; Gede and, 278; intersection with gender and ecology, 260–61, 262; and spirit possession, 277, 279; the vodou and, *149f*; and Vodou's openness to all, 271. *See also* LGBTQ community
Sharpe, Christina, *In the Wake*, 285
Sheridan, Michael, 90
shrines: Bangre shrines, 72, 88; chemistry of, 197–98; comparative study of, 90; in the Dahomey kingdom, 1–2; definition of, 90, 204n8; in the forest, 238–39, 240; Gbădù shrines, 241–42, 245, 247, 254n9; Gbedala shrines, 107–8, *109f*; iconography on, 48; materials in, 9, 62n14; medicine shrines, 82–83; as memorials, 162; migration and establishment of, 103; nature of, 204n8; Sakpata shrines, 78; in Savi, 46; as technological devices, 194, 196–98; as works in progress, 91. *See also* Gorovodu (aka Brekete or Tron); Kunde (father/hunter god); Mami Wata (spirit of water and beauty); Sakpata (earth deity)
Sicre, José Gómez, 155, 156
La Sirèn, 272
skin. *See* bodies and skin
skulls as art, 157
"The Slave Route Project," 72
slavery: afterlife of, 284, 285, 286; collective fight for freedom from, 265; and conversions of the enslaved, 53, 62n19; increase in Kongolese slaves, 28, 34; power relationships in, 307; spirit service as resistance to, 5; and struggles against oppression, 36
slave trade: and encounters with Islam, 101; inclusion of Vodún ritual specialists in, 2; intensification of, 35; source countries for, 34, 35; time frame for, 36n3; and wakes, 285

Smet, Peter De, 79
Smith, Katherine, 144; "Genealogies of Gede," 158
snake veneration: changes in rituals surrounding, 35; chant in, 24–26; European observers and, 36n11; Malenfant's account of, 27; and Mami Wata, 81–82; Moreau's observations on, 23–24; rainbow serpent, 91; Vodou and, 27
Sò Ann (Annette August), 301
social strain gauge theory, 311
sociocosmic relationships, 198–200
socioeconomic inequality: art as resilience under, 102, 140; Vodún and Vodou and, 307
sorcery: azizà and, 240; Labat's accounts of, 19–21; protection from, 41, 133; term of, 61n4
Sou Lapwen, Haiti: about, 210; fragility of infant life in, 211–12; relocation of families in, 226–27; sleeping arrangements in, 208–9
Sousa Santos, Bonaventura de, 190–91
space: secrecy, power, and demarcations of, 239; and understanding Vodún's success, 231
spirited forests (sacred forests): agency in, 196, 232, 234, 244; azizà in, 235–38; as center of occult power, 240; centrality to Vodún cosmology, 10, 234–35, 238, 243; entrance into, 238, 246f; experiencing the forest, 233; forest of Fá, 244; in Gorovodu, 102; and human destiny, 247; liminality of, 233–38, 240; nature of, 238; power of, 252, 313; as protectors of social values, 253; religion, magic, and medicine through, 59–60; rituals in urban forests, 251; sacred groves in, 238–39, 240, 243, 244; secrecy of, 250, 254n4; use of *spirited for*, 231

spirit possession: decline in Haiti of, 136n1; effect of gangan ason on, 120, 121; and gender identity, 10, 277–78; guidance through, 277; as horse and rider metaphor, 275–76; importance of, 6; Kunde possession, 85; manifestation of lwa in, 262, 275, 276–78; and marginalized populations, 262; Moreau's account of, 23–24; and narratives about nationhood, 162; Sakpata and Mami Wata possessions, 81, 82; in salah ceremonies, 107, 108–9, 108f, 110f; of spaces and objects, 231; West African influence on, 35; Western interpretations of, 274–75
spirits: agency of, 189–90, 196–97; communicating with, 231; as cosmological foundation in human life, 5–6; in the forest, 238, 240; and the Holy Spirit, 275; leaves as, 235; materiality of, 193; ontological forms for, 196–97; as particle-like waves, 197, 199, 202; and power dynamics with humans, 199
spirit service: assimilation and acculturation in, 4; interactions between humans and spirits in, 6–7; long history of, 314; rationale for, 311; unifying themes in, 5–7; vitality and beauty in, 315. *See also* Vodún and Vodou
Stevens, Alta Mae, 222
Stoller, Paul, 234
suleliye, 247–50
Sweet, James, 36n11, 62nn11–12, 62n17, 63n19
syncretism: in Benin's Vodún, 41–42, 50–53, 60, 310; in descriptions of religious systems, 116n4; diversity in manifestations of, 313; of Haitian Vodou, 28, 54; hegemony and appropriation of the Other in, 53–56, 60;

Vodún's openness to foreign gods, 42–50

Tall, Emmanuelle, 48
temple Vodou, 122, 131, 133, 135
Thornton, John, 50, 62n17, 62n19
Tibout (Ceus St-Louis), 153
Ti Rivyè, Haiti, 118, 120–21, 125–30, 128
Togo, 72, 83–84, 91, 309. *See also* Gorovodu (aka Brekete or Tron); Yewevodu
tourism: and exoticism of Vodou, 157–58; and Haitian art, 151–52, 153, 154, 155, 156, 159; and marketing of Vodún and Vodou, 8; and sacred forests, 254n4; Vodún and Western tourists, 40; Voodoo and, 312
Tron. *See* Gorovodu (aka Brekete or Tron)
Trou Coffy, 31, 32–33
Trouillot, Michel-Rolph, 144
La Troupe Makandal, 291–92, 293
Turner, Edith, 190
Turner, Victor Witter, 90, 123
twins, 254n3, 254n8

Ulysse, Sterlin, 147
UNESCO conferences, 72
United Nations Stabilization Mission, 143
United States: démembré in, 249, 251; immigration policy and Haitian migrants, 127; neoliberal development activities of, 125; occupation of Haiti, 139, 158; and Protestantism in Haiti, 130–31; visas to, 131–32. *See also* Mississippi River valley Voodoo; New Orleans; Philadelphia, Vodún rituals in; Prospect Park, New York City
universalism: in Benin's Vodún, 41, 310; occult universalism, 56–61

Van Gennep, Arnold, 123
Vannier, Christian, 50, 91, 132, 189, 204n8, 311
Vásquez, Manuel A., 201, 204n10
Vaudoux, use of term, 22
visual perception: and affordances, 192; and the affordances of objects, 194–95; and African science, 202
Vodou: aesthetics of, 155, 158, 311; anti-Vodou campaigns, 147, 151, 155; assimilation of the profane in, 142; authenticity of ritual practices in, 119; beyond Haiti, 314; capacity for resilience, 140–41; Catholic saints and, 53–54; Central African influences in, 29; congregational structure in, 120, 144–45; and daily life, 148; definition of, 3; disappearance of, 311; function of symbolism in, 162–63; growth of, 2; Haitian politics and, 2–3; interest in, 8; Kongolese influences on, 28, 33, 35; Métraux's observations on, 119, 120; "mysteries" in, 26; nationalism in, 151, 182; persecution of practitioners of, 36; resilience of, 136; sacralization of detritus in, 160–61; term of, 34, 61n1; as twenty-first century religion, 140; as a way of life, 274. *See also* Christianity; Haitian art; interconnectedness; ounsi; Vodou, French colonial accounts; Vodou cosmology; Vodún and Vodou
Vodou, French colonial accounts of: Baudry des Lozières's account, 28–30; Labat's account, 17–22; Malenfant's account, 26–28; Moreau de Saint-Méry's account, 22–26; Ouvière and Catholic influences, 30–34; overview of, 17, 310; periodization in, 35–36

Vodou cosmology: Bondye and the lwa in, 268–69; cardinal directions in, 259–60; centrality of forest to, 10, 234–35, 238, 243, 251; creation in, 263–64, 266, 267; death in, 267; differences in, 269; equilibrium in, 269; ethical mandates in, 264–65; the feminine and masculine in, 260, 267, 269; God in, 265, 280; liberation from supernatural principles in, 274; lwa and djabs in, 276, 312–13; the soul in, 270; spirit possession in, 279–80; women in, 271, 272

Vodou funerary rites: and crossing borders, 10; desounen ritual, 296–97, 303; expenses for, 286–87, 302, 303; four crossroads in, 284; Labat's observation of, 21; prayers and chants, 297–300; preparation of the separated soul, 300–301; transformation and rebirth, 285, 302; in Vodún, 313; wake work in, 285, 286, 297–99, 303. *See also* Augustin, Frisner; Haitian funerary practices

Vodún: about, 76, 310–11; as a complex of religions, 230–31, 253; criticism of, 43–44; definition and term of, 3, 11n1, 45, 61n1, 230; dynamism of, 41, 48, 310, 311; effectiveness in worldview of, 252; epistemologies of, 189, 190–92, 203n1; funerary rites in, 313; geographical impact of, 309; importance of, 91; inclusiveness in, 74, 116n4; individual agency in, 47–48; influence on Montanée, 170; legitimization of, 315; materiality and spirituality in, 313; priest in, 41, 42f; as science, 190, 194, 200, 203; speech acts in, 201; spirits of, 70; stereotyping of, 40–41, 45; tolerance and pragmatism in, 51–52; and transformation, 83–84, 202; unfinished aesthetic of, 115; use of Yoruba, 46; water in, 76; Yoruba ritual in, 115. *See also* acɛ; Bangre; divination; Gorovodu; Islam; Kunde; Mami Wata; Sakpata; syncretism; witchcraft

vodún (spirits): about, 6–7; in the Dahomey kingdom, 1; definition and use of term, 11n1, 11n2, 45–46

Vodún and Vodou: adaptability of, 70, 140, 231, 307, 314, 316; diversity of, 315; diversity of engagement and encounter in, 313; future of, 313–16; global character of, 8; growth of, 308–10, 309; heterogeneity of, 4–5; importance of forests to, 252–53; interrelated histories of, 3, 4; legitimization of, 70–71; malignment of, 307, 310; open-ended nature of, 308; philosophical foundations of, 5–6; pluralism in, 132; ritual assemblages in, 113; scholarship on, 10–11, 315–16. *See also* ritual; spirit possession; Vodou; Vodún; Voodoo

Voodoo: about, 61n2; interest in, 314–15; magical goods of, *170f*; malignment of, 40, 310; racism around, 70; use of term, 61n1, 93n3; Western curiosity about, 310

Voodoo surrealism, 155–56

Warner-Lewis, Maureen, 4
Watteau, Antoine, *Embarquement pour Cythère*, 147
wellness: Gbădù, Fá, and the forest in, 247; as a mirage, 212; of the planet, 261–62
Wendl, Tobias, 82
West Africa: encounters and exchange with the diaspora, 310; forests as common home for peoples of, 252; indigenous religions' cosmology in,

264, 265; religions of, 4; religious dynamism in, 46
Western science and epistemology: bias in, 189–90; as incomplete, 199, 200; metonymic reason in, 190–91; and Vodún rituals, 195, 198; wave-particle duality in, 197
Western spirituality, 182
Wilcken, Lois, 291–92, 293, 302
Williams, Lavinia, 291
witchcraft (àzĕ): antiwitchcraft movements, 103; collective morality through, 311; and foreign forms of, 57–59, 60–61; Gbădù and, 241, 245; power of, 63n23; science and, 202; social strain gauge theory and, 311; and spiritual power, 52, 57, 60; term of, 61n4; through food, 78; universalism in, 56–61; and Vodún, 41–42

Yai, Olabiyi, 62n10
Yewevodu: about, 71; ancient practice of, 84; continued traditions of, 74; growth of, 72; healing and dispute resolution in, 83; scholars on, 74–77; spirits of, 73, 86, 90, 92, 311. *See also* Gorovodu (aka Brekete or Tron)

Zannou, Afio, et al., 79
zombies, 34, 143

www.ingramcontent.com/pod-product-compliance
Lightning Source LLC
Chambersburg PA
CBHW021818300426
44114CB00009BA/224